ORGANIZATIONAL DEVELOPMENT THROUGH TEAMBUILDING

ORGANIZATIONAL DEVELOPMENT THROUGH TEAMBUILDING

Thomas H. Patten, Jr.

Professor of Organizational Behavior and
Personnel Management
School of Labor and Industrial Relations
Michigan State University

A WILEY-INTERSCIENCE PUBLICATION

JOHN WILEY & SONS   New York · Chichester · Brisbane · Toronto

69947

Library of Congress Cataloging in Publication Data:

Patten, Thomas Henry, 1929–
  Organizational development through teambuilding

  "A Wiley-Interscience publication."
  Bibliography: p.
  Includes index.
    1. Organizational change. 2. Management by
objectives. I. Title. II. Title: Teambuilding.
HD58.8.P37   658.4'02   80-20726
ISBN 0-471-66945-8

Printed in the United States of America

10 9 8 7 6 5 4 3 2 1

To Jenny Lydia Patten,
newest member of my team and future teambuilder

PREFACE

In the past decade there has been a worldwide "management boom," according to Peter F. Drucker. Management as a concept has repeatedly undergone scrutiny; in the eyes of many observers, management has become the most important human activity in the world today. These people perceive management as nothing less than the body of knowledge concerned with theories and practices for securing cooperative human effort in such a way that individuals satisfy their own and their employing organization's objectives.[1]

One of the most exciting innovations in management in the past 10 years has been the emergence of "organizational development" (OD), an eclectic and controversial term signifying the improvement of management by means of applying both behavioral science and traditional technical nonbehavioral knowledge. Everywhere managers have been challenged to examine their views of management, their philosophies of human nature, and the accuracy of their ideas about employee motivation, commitment, and productivity.

In this book I state my approach to organizational development through the use of teambuilding executive seminars and workshops that I have created and conducted for top management. This program—or, better termed, "OD effort"—has been used to build teams among more than 1300 top managers; the basic ideas involved were personally presented to thousands of others when I have addressed management groups throughout the United States, Canada, Australia, New Zealand, and Europe. The ideas were greeted with enthusiasm because they are fresh and have proven workable. Many do not originate with me, having been stated and used before in isolation by many other experts in personnel management and organizational behavior.

I felt a need to write this book during a sabbatical leave taken from Michigan State University from January 1 to June 30, 1974 and spent in Maui, Hawaii. At that time I had a chance to update myself on OD and to conduct some executive seminars and workshops on teambuilding both in Hawaii and back on the mainland. Favorable evaluations of the programs led me to think that the design I evolved could be interesting and helpful to others in their work as organizational change agents. After all, if the ideas were able to be presented in writing and passed on in a communicable fashion, then there was good reason to believe that the managements of many organizations would be able to experience improvements in their team skills. The book is a result of this thinking. It suggests concrete ways to implement teambuilding in OD, including exercises and proposed modules that may be added or removed to meet the specific needs of any organization. It took another sabbatical in Hawaii to complete the book during 1980–81.

In designing the OD teambuilding program about which this book is written I have benefited from the suggestions of many people, particularly the many experts on management by objectives (MBO) I know. I have been quite heavily influenced by recent writers in the behavioral sciences and management in my thinking about OD, MBO, and reward systems. I have tried to indicate where their ideas not only influenced me but also led me to develop them into experiential tools for application by managers in a learning mode.

Lester E. Dorey, Employee Development Specialist of the U.S. Army Communications Command, enabled me to think through the relevant concepts, try them out, and improve them as a result of my offering a series of executive seminars and workshops on organizational development through teambuilding for top civilian and military executives in the Command. Robert G. Wallace and Charles Stowell of Fort Huachuca, Arizona were also extremely helpful in my endeavors.

The book itself reflects my present thinking about the potential of OD for enriching life at work, for creating the new deal of the 1980s in work organizations. I have no doubt that we have the social technology available right now to help good managers become better ones and poor or inexperienced managers become more competent and wiser ones. I hope the book contributes to these ends.

I believe OD efforts should be carried out by facilitators of learning rather than by teachers of the traditional type. Process facilitators in OD may lecture, marshal learning resources, criticize and praise seminar enrollees, select exercises, and state personal and professional opinions. They should be creative, synthetic, and professional. They should value the adult human being and desire to bring out his* potential. They should value feedback for themselves and others. Teachers also share many of these views. However, whereas traditional classroom teachers make great use of formalized curricula, textbooks, and subject-matter examinations, OD process facilitators are likely to make brief theory inputs followed by the use of group discussions and a wide range of experiential learning devices, extensive trainee feedback sessions, and thorough debriefings and critiques of

---

*Contemporary authors try to avoid sexism by using "he or she" rather than "he" whenever possible in order to include both males and females. Four females share my domicile, and I love them. They do not consider me sexist and I hope the reader will not because I use the generic "he" and "his" throughout this book to avoid redundancy and awkwardness.

blocks of time used for the learning. OD program planning is always subject
to on-the-spot appraisal and revision by the learners and the OD staff as the
learning needs of trainees change during the teambuilding program. This
tentativeness creates an aura of enthusiasm and emotionality in OD efforts
that is seldom seen in the traditional classroom.

Many years ago Kurt Lewin described the change process as consisting
of three stages—unfreezing, changing, and refreezing behavior in an improved mode of functioning.[2] In this book I spend much time considering
unfreezing behavior because the first two days of the model teambuilding
program focus on self-awareness, management styles, and group and individual contributions to teambuilding. The remainder of the program is concerned with changing managerial behavior through the acquisition of
sufficient skill to use a simplified version of an MBO planning and control
system and the proper use of managerial time to accomplish chosen goals.
The program also suggests how changing reward systems to reinforce purposive behavior in energetic individuals can be accomplished. However,
caution is needed when mention is made of "refreezing." We behavioral
scientists do not know enough about team behavior to recommend solidify-
ing a presumed desirable mode once and for all.

Certainly, we want to see that teams such as the "best and the brightest"
or Watergate-type scoundrels who may appear to have all the managerial
answers never again assume important decision-making posts in our society;
similarly, we must insure that pride, self-delusion, pusillanimity, closed
mindedness, and chicanery do not act to freeze lower-level managers and
other affected persons into unsuccessful and deceptive ways of coping.[3]
Refreezing suggests a brittleness that could shatter the team facing a crisis
because it finds itself frozen into prescribed ways when innovation rather
than tradition is needed to develop the appropriate response.

This book is unique in the literature of professional management and OD
because it is based on one of the longest (if not *the* most durable) executive teambuilding efforts carried out and reported in the United States.[4] It
represents seven years of involvement with a supersystem, one large-
scale organization that has been unusually progressive and sufficiently
management-improvement minded to support a sustained effort at organizational development. I am grateful for having had a chance to play a role in
this important addition to the annals of management practice. Yet I feel it is
important to note that my views as stated in the book in no way purport to
reflect the positions of the Department of the Army or the Department of
Defense.

OD and teambuilding are needed in America today. Let us turn next to
what can be done to unfreeze and change, formidable tasks themselves!

THOMAS H. PATTEN, JR.

Kaunakakai, Molokai, Hawaii

Notes

1 Peter F. Drucker, *Management: Tasks, Responsibilities, Practices*, Harper and Row, New York, 1974, pp. 11–26.

2 Edgar H. Schein and Warren G. Bennis, *Personal and Organizational Change Through Group Methods: The Laboratory Approach*, Wiley, New York, 1965, pp. 275–276; and Kurt Lewin, *Resolving Social Conflicts*, Harper and Row, New York, 1948, pp. 56–68, 201–216.

3 David Halberstam, *The Best and the Brightest*, Fawcett Crest, Greenwich, 1972, pp. 810–816, and *passim*; and Leon Jaworski, *The Right and the Power*, Pocket Books, New York, pp. 36–264.

4 Parts of this OD effort are described in the following: Thomas H. Patten, Jr., and Lester E. Dorey, "Long Range Results of a Teambuilding Organizational Development Effort," *Personnel Management Review*, Vol. 6, No. 1, January–February 1977, pp. 31–50; Thomas H. Patten, Jr., "Team Building. Part 1. Designing the Intervention," *Personnel*, Vol. 56, No. 1, January–February 1979, pp. 11–21; and *ibid.*, "Team Building. Part 2. Conducting the Intervention," *Personnel*, Vol. 56, No. 2, March–April 1979, pp. 62–68.

ACKNOWLEDGMENTS

In preparing this book I received several research grants from the College of Social Science, Michigan State University.

Dr. Jack Stieber, Director of the School of Labor and Industrial Relations, provided me with a teaching load that allowed me to do the writing and thinking for this book. In addition, the sabbatical leave that was granted me, as mentioned in the Preface, was a key factor in my finding the time to outline the book, complete a vast amount of reading in a quiet environment, and plan for the book's completion.

University Associates, Inc. of San Diego, California, a preeminent publisher of OD structured experiences, instrumentation, lecturettes, theory and practice essays, and resources has generously granted me permission to adapt for this book certain instruments that I created and they previously published.

Similarly, Dr. Gordon L. Lippitt has granted me permission to use in this book certain instruments developed by himself.

I am happy to acknowledge and grateful to University Associates and Dr. Lippitt for their permissions.

Mary Jane Fuller typed the drafts and Lynda Scullion the final copy of the book, indispensable tasks that were well done.

I am grateful to all these persons from MSU, as well as MSU itself, for the support and assistance given to me. Any deficiencies in the work I accept as my responsibility.

T.H.P.

CONTENTS

chapter 1

INTRODUCTION TO TEAMBUILDING: A LIMITED MODEL

In recent years teambuilding has become one of the most popular and widely used interventions for improving the management of industrial and governmental organizations.[1] Most commonly, teambuilding has been used for enabling managers who either work together or are in some way organizationally related to cooperate and share skills and knowledge so that their work is completed more effectively and efficiently. Teambuilding has also been used for a similar purpose for employees at lower organizational levels, as has been dramatically demonstrated at Texas Instruments, the Topeka plant of General Foods, and Volvo in Sweden.[2] In this book I concentrate on executive teambuilding because that is where most attention has been given and where many designs have been applied.

The concern of this book is organizational development through "teambuilding," which by definition suggests that one way management can be improved is by enabling managers to function as a team. Organizational development is carried out so that the total organization becomes healthier and more purposeful in goal attainment. Although today there are numerous techniques for developing organizations, such as laboratory training, management by objectives, role negotiation, Scanlon plans, and the like, teambuilding has been selected as a technique not only because it is useful in itself but also because it can incorporate or be used in conjunction with a wide variety of other techniques.

In this book organization development and organizational development are considered to be the same and are referred to as OD. It is recognized that distinctions between the two can be made, as has been done by Vaill,[3] but these need not concern us here. Also for the sake of simplicity it is assumed that the purpose of OD is to improve organizations, and that this implies certain democratic and humanistic values.

This book has been prepared for practioners of all kinds who seek knowledge about the improvement of management in work organizations. These practioners would include corporate training specialists, personnel directors, manpower and human resource experts, consultants, and governmental administrators and others who have responsibilities in employee relations. Line and staff managers who seek knowledge about planned change and improved management can also benefit from this book.[4]

The book is built around a model for changing organizations that makes use of both cognitive and experiential learning. The cognitive learning draws on contemporary theory and research from the field of applied behavioral science of primarily the past two decades. The experiential learning draws on the same background but represents exercises, instruments, experiences, and other tools that enable teams of managers undergoing an OD effort to learn from one another in a way that is most effective. The cognitive learning provides a road map for organizational development through teambuilding whereas the experiential learning enables the executive undergoing training to experience together and analyze those experiences for their mutual benefit. The interplay between these two types of learning becomes more clear as the model for teambuilding and its actual utilization in live organizations is developed in the course of the book.

Teams at the Top

The 1970s proved much more turbulent than the 1960s as employers strove and struggled to make a profit and/or provide a public service. Inflation, recession, the stress from new Federal legislation, and domestic conditions and uncertainty caused much of this turmoil. Top and middle managers felt the greatest impact from these crosswinds of change. The 1980s will continue to present managerial challenges of the greatest difficulty.

Many leading American firms have in recent years reorganized at the top using the concept of the presidential office.[5] This organizational design permits the restructuring of the chief executive's position so that three, four, or more persons share in the chief executive's responsibilities by directing their attention to the main areas of the business. The concept has been applied to General Electric, Ford, Exxon, and many other firms. It has not always been successful but, as recurring accounts suggest, it appears to have much promise.

The establishment of teams at the top has led many firms to think that building teams from the top to the bottom of the organization would be highly beneficial for increasing goal attainment and motivating employees to utilize their energy and efforts in a concerted direction.[6] Teambuilding thus appears to have potential as a coping strategy in the challenging times in which we live.

There is no certainty in a competitive and uncertain world. However, the latest thinking in applied behavioral science appears to point out new directions for improving management and putting organizations back on a steady course.

In order to build teams it is necessary to have mechanisms for developing team skills, acquiring knowledge about techniques for managing, examining attitudes and changing them, and acquiring experiences that reinforce the learning of skills, knowledge, and attitudes. Carefully designed seminars and workshops aimed specifically at improving the functioning of managerial teams have been used extensively and hold still greater promise.[7] Yet more and varied designs are needed for OD programs and efforts that meet the specific need for top managers down to middle managers. There is probably a greater need for OD efforts for such a high level of managers than for supervisors or second-level managers who may instead require more basic and intermediate management education and training.

To initiate teambuilding we need a seminar/workshop design that steers a course between "canned-programs," which turn off modern executives, and unstructured learning, where there is no agenda except what the seminar participants dream up while at the training site or conference location. Also, there are many occasions when diagnosis suggests we not use educational interventions such as seminars but instead use action research.

Prior to the early 1970s, management in the United States experienced the sensitivity or laboratory training fad, which has now apparently run its course, having proven to be insufficient in itself for teambuilding. (There are times, however, when the T-group can be used to benefit a teambuilding effort.) The recent literature on the sensitivity training movement has documented its shortcomings and contributions.[8] Today we are likely to see some value in the selective use of sensitivity training. In fact, it occasionally is a worthwhile intervention in an organization prior to the inauguration of a teambuilding effort itself.

Many management educators now believe that in order to develop an organization through teambuilding it is necessary to design enough of the program that the intial thrust in teambuilding has an identifiable cognitive structure obvious to the executives undergoing the OD effort thus allowing them to recognize that the concepts, tools, and techniques to which they are exposed apply to their company or agency. In this way, management-by-objectives (MBO), team consensus-achieving techniques, the building of employee commitment, the proper motivational use of financial and nonfinancial rewards, learning about and trying out new managerial styles, the effective use of scarce managerial time, and fine-tuning of one's self-awareness in employee relations can take on practical meaning.

Managers need to learn that running a tight ship in the contemporary 1980s does not mean stern command-obedience relations, the expansion of detailed rules and procedures for operations, and rigid systems of discipline. Instead, improved management means the careful application of sophisti-cated tools in an environment where subordinates are committed to performing high-quality work in a way that meshes with the times. Underlying the application of the tools there needs to be a philosophy that builds human dignity, equity, challenge, and the right kind of employee participation in the conduct of managerial work.

Goals in Teambuilding

In order to build teams in management it is necessary to clarify the main goals that should be accomplished in our efforts at establishing collaborative and helpful relations. Often in teambuilding we are dealing with groups of managers who collectively may have hundreds or even close to one thousand years of prior work experience as managers upon which to draw. Thus any OD design that is oriented toward teambuilding would be inadequate if it did not utilize the range of experiences of the managerial participants. In addition, if the design is to be fruitful it must be selective and cognisant of the fact that OD can be remedial and preventive only in certain domains. OD should not be oversold and uncritically accepted, because it does have many limitations. However, it also appears to have great strengths for helping managers make their personal resources available to one another because it sets up circumstances so that problem-solving and decision-making are carried out in an optimal fashion.

A well-designed OD effort should, first of all, help managers establish mutual trust in their respective organizational components and a sense of teamwork.[9] In this book the importance of trust in OD work is strongly emphasized because without it any changes introduced in a work organization are likely either to fail or be accepted in only a formal way and given lip service.

Second, an OD effort directed toward teambuilding should enable managers to develop skills in the following areas: interpersonal relations with peers, subordinates, organizational counterparts, and superiors; resolving conflicts with persons and groups; communicating openly with others and disclosing honest and authentic motivations in their behavior; and confronting issues. These kinds of needed skills cannot be reduced to the learning of the dos and don'ts of human relations, thereby adopting ideas from the 1940s and 1950s, or by spreading cheery words from behind an insincere facade.[10] If we have learned anything from the sensitivity training movement as it was applied to organizational management in the 1960s, it is that interpersonal skills are difficult to develop and go far beyond the shallow and hollow ukases that we heard so much about in the personnel management literature after World War II.[11] Managers need to know how to resolve conflicts not by sweeping them under the rug but by confronting them while caring about the outcome. To become interpersonally competent the manager must learn new ways of searching, coping, confronting, and deciding while communicating with persons who are involved in the conflict or are otherwise concerned interpersonally.

Third, managers undergoing a teambuilding effort need assistance in understanding how to motivate others and obtain the dedication necessary to completing the work. This understanding must include a grasp of how extrinsic factors at work effect motivation and how the intrinsic nature of the work itself acts or fails to act as an incentive to performance.[12] The current thinking of contemporary applied behavioral scientists needs to be considered by the manager in understanding the motivation of others as well as his own. The manager also needs to be familiar with current ideas about altering the work itself through job enrichment if he is to help subordinates obtain satisfaction from the work and the incentive to perform in a way consistent with management's standards.

Fourth, the manager needs to review and examine basic skills in such areas as work planning, setting managerial objectives, controlling activities so that goals are attained, managing the utilization of his own and others' time, solving problems, and getting employees on the team. These skills, in many respects, are technical and require the mastery of techniques in personnel administration that are constantly being refined. However, the skills cannot be mindlessly applied without regard to human beings and their feelings and aspirations. In many cases, employees want to belong to the team and make inputs into the conduct of work. The manager must know how to solicit employee participation and use it collaboratively while applying the technical skills of the managerial job.

Fifth, and last, managers need to know how to connect ideas about manager and employee behavior and motivation with the administration of salaries, supplemental compensation, and nonfinancial rewards. Managers do not have to be compensation experts. Yet the financial and nonfinancial rewards systems in organizations need to be thoroughly understood by them, supported by them, and used in an equitable way as levers for performance.[13] Personnel managers, training and OD specialists, and human resource experts have the prime responsibility for building and maintaining financial and nonfinancial reward systems that enable line and other staff managers to connect meaningful ideas and techniques about manager and employee behavior and motivation with the administration of rewards.

The accomplishment of all these goals in organizational teambuilding is never simple but there is a model that has been tested and advocated explicitly or implicitly by many management thinkers in the 1970s.[14] The model is OD → MBO → RS or, in other words, in order to improve the functioning and level of results-achievement of managerial teams in an optimum way the company or agency should undertake a threefold effort. First, it should embark initially on an OD effort to create managerial self-awareness and build team problem-solving, decision-making, and consensus-reaching skills in the organizational culture. Second, it should follow this effort by introducing MBO (or strengthening its existing MBO system) and, in the process, apply a simple but meaningful approach to MBO. This would be a notion of MBO that does not require the organization to drop everything it is doing that it considers sound, such as changing its budgeting approach or any other proven systems. Instead the proper approach to MBO emphasizes the overall planning and control of assigned work in an organization and the development of employees at all organizational levels. Third, and finally, the company or agency needs to complete the sequence of change by examining its financial and nonfinancial reward systems (RS) and determine how they can be made more operational and motivational. This consideration may lead to the alteration, installation, or modernization of various types of pay plans and other formal means for recognizing performance and service.[15]

The above model is logical, easily learned, and quickly adapted to management in organizations of all kinds. It can be very helpful to renew and improve previous efforts at MBO installations that may have faltered or otherwise require revitalization. It truly adds strength and flair to personnel or human resource management, suggests new styles of managing for organizational line and staff management, and signals to top management that, if it is willing to spend a reasonable amount of time and energy, it can draw upon useful scientific knowledge about human behavior to improve management, the organization, and the on-the-job performance of its employees. As in all OD efforts, it is up to top management to authorize it, try it, steer and direct it, and set a new course for the future.

Teambuilding Modes

In this book one model is used to explain and analyze organizational development through teambuilding. I recognize that there is an important difference between an executive seminar/workshop on teambuilding and teambuilding itself.[16] These are two identifiably different learning modes. The former is learning about learning; the latter is translating the learning into action. Learning about learning is, in other words, the phenomenon of adults coming to realize that they are responsible for their own growth and can best learn many complex skills by working together on developmental tasks and by organizational problem-solving and decision-making.

It is relatively simple for an author to expatiate on learning about learning and to suggest how that learning can be transformed into action and to predict the direction of changed employee behavior on the job. The task of the practitioner is to make the transformation; and it is hoped that the discussion in the book, suggested instruments, exercises, cases, and other techniques will be helpful in making a proper translation of the ideas for the practicing manager in a particular company or agency.

It should be recognized that in carrying out teambuilding, and in the further diagnosis of managerial teambuilding problems in an organization, that many other issues and concerns are likely to arise. In many respects these issues and concerns can be dealt with in a teambuilding mode even though the specific issues that manifest themselves appear to be different in content. For example, once groups become open, authentic, and problem-solving in their outlook they are likely to find many imperfections in the organizational climate to which they want managerial attention directed. One such issue might be strenghthening equal employment opportunity and affirmative action programs and efforts. A second could be reviewing the status of women in management and planning positive change. A third could be altering employee relations policies, procedures, and processes. Still other issues might be studying the improvement of productivity, installing or revamping career planning and life planning processes, assessing the functioning of the rewards systems, reconsidering the range and operation of training systems, and studying standards and their application in all areas of employee and organizational performance. The possible systemic results are almost endless because to open up an organization through teambuilding is to open Pandora's box and expose numerous issues that must be dealt with.

Conclusion

I have discussed teambuilding as an important intervention in an organization for the sake of management improvement and have discussed in a general way the direction of this book. Subsequent chapters return to and elaborate on some of this groundwork. However, the OD → MBO → RS model serves as a theme for the book and can be clearly connected with the way in which I believe managers learn how to learn and how they can translate that OD learning into action on the job.

The model can be implemented in five phases which from the standpoint of the practitioner can be five days, scheduled either sequentially or intermittently. Figure 1.1 describes how a specific design already used numerous times can implement this model. The first phase focuses on the manager's self-awareness, managerial leadership styles, and relevant behavioral science concepts in employee motivation and direction.[17] This first phase amounts to unfreezing the manager and can be regarded as a mini-sensitivity experience. A manager who may have had a laboratory training experience prior to the first phase will probably find the first phase a logical outgrowth of the laboratory experience. Depending upon the need, the individual responsible for the teambuilding effort might, on the basis of diagnosis, desire to have sensitivity training utilized before the teambuilding effort, although there is no necessary requirement across the board for this.

The second phase emphasizes group behavior and using human resources to solve problems. The effort here is still aimed at unfreezing the manager and encouraging him to consider the value of participative decision-making using groups, particularly groups of managerial peers. The second phase also includes work on consensus-building and how to resolve conflict in management, particularly interpersonal clashes.

The third phase moves the individual manager, who should hopefully by now be somewhat unfrozen, from his usual ways of thinking and behaving by

Figure 1.1 Design of the Teambuilding Seminar/Workshop

	Monday	Tuesday	Wednesday	Thursday	Friday
	Self-awareness as a manager	Group decision-making and consensus building	MBO and problem-solving	MBO, Interpersonal communication issues, and delegation skills	OD, MBO, and reward administration
8:30–12	Theory input on OD	Theory input on team-building	Theory input on MBO	Theory input on rational and emotional issues in MBO problem-solving	Theory input on OD, MBO, and rewards and penalties
	Johari Window	Desert Survival Problem	MBO exercise on regular objectives	MBO exercise on innovative goals	MANDOERS exercise on development and rewards
	FIRO-B exercise; Form teams	Debriefing and relating exercise to job	Debriefing of exercise	Debriefing of exercise	Debriefing of exercise
12–1	Lunch	Lunch	Lunch	Lunch	Lunch
1–3:30	Theory input on behavioral science	Theory input on consensus	Theory input on problem-solving and innovative objectives	Theory input on the management of managerial time	Theory input on the helping relationship in management and feedback
	Managerial style exercise	Interpersonal conflict management exercise	MBO exercise on problem-solving goals	Time management and delegation exercise	Team peer evaluations
	System intervention exercise				
	Debriefing of exercise	Debriefing of exercise	Debriefing of exercise	Debriefing of exercise	Seminar/workshop evaluations
	Unfreezing		Changing		Refreezing

Source: Adapted from Thomas H. Patten, Jr. and Lester E. Dorey, "Long-Range Results of a Team Building OD Effort," *Public Personnel Management*, Vol. 6, No. 1, January–February 1977, p. 35.

exposing him cognitively and experientially to MBO. More specifically, this phase capitalizes upon the fact that the manager is socially and emotionally loosened up and ready for learning about new rational tools. The manager is likely to have a "so-what" attitude after the initial thrust at teambuilding and to be eager for a change of tempo that caters to rational concerns and on-the-job application of the new learning. As a result, the third phase is used to explain and assist managers in applying a simple but adaptable MBO system relevant for setting "regular" (or "routine") and "problem-solving" objectives. It is important at this time to have the participants work on realistic goals in their present work organizations. Thus, the teambuilding seminar shades into being a workshop and becomes a means for getting started directly in an OD effort.

The fourth phase deals with MBO and applies it to the kinds of problems that are most complex and often most innovative. This phase enables managers to see MBO as something more than a tool for setting objectives about work that is well understood or exceptional only within the normal variances of the job itself. Rather, this phase enables managers to use ideas about problem-solving and decision-making when new issues or new developments arise and causes a rethinking of efficient and effective ways of coping. Also in the fourth phase consideration is given to the effective use of managerial time because time management is most meaningfully understood when it is connected with MBO.

During the third and fourth phases managers in the process of acquiring new team skills start to change their thinking and consider changing their behavior.

The fifth phase is intended to continue the refreezing of behavior and provide ideas about sustained change. However, we need to avoid smugness and closed-mindedness when discussing refreezing because no serious student of the subject is likely to suggest that managers never consider a thaw or reconsider their current behavior in the light of new knowledge.

Accordingly, the fifth phase focuses upon an explanation of how unblocking individual managerial energy can result in meaningful work objectives being established and then related to the planning and control of financial and other rewards for employees. In addition to the explanation there are provided various experiences that act as capstones for reviewing sound precepts for organizational effectiveness, the development of subordinates and employees more generally, and the reward of subordinates. This fifth phase discusses what is presently regarded as desirable behavior on the part of managers, but, in the future, as our knowledge of management and applied behavioral science enlarges, we should be open to a reconsideration of what we advocate.

In summary, the five phases represent a careful thinking through of how to implement the model of organizational development by teambuilding. The remainder of this book involves theories that are not very abstract and explanations of how selected exercises and experiences as well as alternative exercises and experiences can be creatively used in the practical team-building situation. Naturally, in a field such as this we all have much more to learn but some breakthroughs exist; it is some of these that are uncovered and fully described in this book.

Notes

1. The literature on the subject has started to emerge. 1977 was apparently a banner year for such publications. See the following: William G. Dyer, *Team Building: Issues and Alternatives*, Addison–Wesley, Reading, MA, 1977; Roger J. Howe and William I. Gordon, *Team Dynamics in Developing Organizations*, Kendall/Hunt, Dubuque, 1977; Uri Merry and Melvin E. Allerhand, *Developing Teams and Organizations, A Practical Handbook for Managers and Consultants*, Addison–Wesley, Reading, MA, 1977; Earl J. Ends and Curtis W. Page, *Organizational Team Building*, Winthrop, Cambridge, 1977. An important early book of influence was Richard Beckhard, *Organization Development: Strategies and Models*, Addison–Wesley, Reading, MA, 1969, especially pp. 26–42. See also Pamela Ramsden, *Top Team Planning*, Wiley, New York, 1973, pp. 183–238.

2. Reviews of these endeavors can be found in the following: David Jenkins, *Job Power: Blue and White Collar Democracy*, Doubleday, Garden City, NY 1973; and Thomas G. Cummings and Edmond S. Malloy, *Improving Productivity and the Quality of Work Life*, Praeger, New York, 1977.

3. Peter B. Vaill, *The Practice of Organization Development*, American Society for Training and Development, 1971, pp. 3–8.

4. An excellent analysis of the role of the line and staff manager in OD can be found in Michael E. McGill, *Organization Development for Operating Managers*, AMACOM, New York, 1977, pp. 62–184.

5. Stanley C. Vance, "Toward A Collegial Office of the President," *California Management Review*, Vol. 15, No. 1, Fall 1972, pp. 106–116.

6. D. Ronald Daniel, "Team at the Top," *Harvard Business Review*, Vol. 43, No. 2, March–April 1965, pp. 74–82. The totally team built organization, top to bottom, with supervisors acting as linking pins is described in Rensis Likert, *New Patterns of Management*, McGraw–Hill, New York, 1961, pp. 105, 113.

7. See, for example, "Aetna: Where Group Management Didn't Work," *Business Week*, No. 2419, February 16, 1976, p. 77; and "GM's Test of Participation," *Business Week*, No. 2420, February 23, 1976, pp. 88–90.

8. Several critiques of this phenomenon are available, including the following: Kurt Back, *Beyond Words: The Story of Sensitivity Training and the Encounter Movement,* Russell Sage Foundation, New York, 1972; and C. L. Cooper and I. L. Mangham, *T-Groups: A Survey of Research,* Wiley, New York, 1971.

9. Trust-building and team-building may be concurrent or the one may be the cause of the other. The OD literature seldom deals with trust at length but the concept is repeatedly mentioned. For example, see Gordon L. Lippitt, *Organization Renewal,* Prentice-Hall, Englewood Cliffs, NJ, 1969, pp. 89–90; Edgar F. Huse, *Organization Development and Change,* West, St. Paul, 1975, pp. 257–258; and Jack R. Gibb, *Trust: A New View of Personal and Organizational Development,* Guild of Tutors Press, Los Angeles, 1978, *passim.*

10. For a discussion of the evolution from human relations to contemporary concepts of human resource management see Raymond E. Miles, "Human Relations or Human Resources?" *Harvard Business Review,* Vol. 43, No. 4, July–August 1965, pp. 148–155, and his *Theories of Management,* McGraw–Hill, New York, 1975, *passim.*

11. For background see Loren Baritz, *The Servants of Power,* Wesleyan University Press, Middletown, 1960, and Henry Landsberger, *Hawthorne Revisited,* Cornell University Press, Ithaca, NY, 1958.

12. On extrinsic motivation see the literature on expectancy theory and particularly the work of Edward E. Lawler III, *Pay and Organizational Effectivness: A Psychological View,* McGraw-Hill, New York, 1971, pp. 100–284; and his *Motivation in Work Organizations,* Brooks-Cole, Monterey, 1973, pp. 47–88. On intrinsic motivation see Edward L. Deci, *Intrinsic Motivation,* Plenum, New York, 1975, pp. 23–125.

13. Lawler, *Pay and Organizational Effectiveness: A Psychological View, op. cit.,* pp. 107–116.

14. I have discussed this model at length elsewhere. See Thomas H. Patten, Jr., *Pay: Employee Compensation and Incentive Plans,* Free Press, New York, 1977, pp. 136–140.

15. Additional material on this subject can be found in Thomas H. Patten, Jr., "Intervening in Organizations Through Reward Systems," in John E. Jones and J. William Pfeiffer, Eds., *The 1977 Annual Handbook for Group Facilitators,* University Associates, LaJolla, CA, 1977, pp. 195–207.

16. Dyer, *op. cit.,* focuses upon the action research model of teambuilding itself. Gordon and Howe, *op. cit.,* and Merry and Allerhand, *op. cit.,* report a series of teambuilding and interpersonal relations exercises that could be used in workshops but do not seem to have an explicit

theory base (such as OD → MBO → RS) or "stance," such as I set forth in this book and have discussed elsewhere (Thomas H. Patten, Jr., "Team Building. Part 2. Conducting the Intervention", *Personnel*, Vol. 56, No. 2, March–April 1979, pp. 63–68).

17. I believe that OD practitioners should be thoroughly acquainted with the intellectual basis of the field and have described this basis elsewhere. See Thomas H. Patten, Jr., "The Behavioral Science Roots of Organizational Development: An Integrated and Overall Perspective," in John E. Jones and J. William Pfeiffer, Eds., *The 1979 Handbook for Group Facilitators*, University Associates, LaJolla, CA, pp. 194–206.

chapter 2

DATA GATHERING AND INSTRUMENTATION IN OD

OD is an emerging field whose boundaries are unclear and changing. Yet if there is one characteristic of OD that seems stable it is the emphasis in OD on the gathering of data in work organizations and the use of the action research model. The respect for data as the basis for action was generated by applied behavioral scientists beginning with Lewin[1] and continuing through Whyte,[2] Beckhard,[3] French,[4] and many successors[5] who have contributed to the development of the field. Data gathering is used in intervening in work organizations and occupies a prominent place in intervention theory, as has been suggested by Argyris[6] and many others.[7] Survey research and the use of attitude polls, such as those made popular by Likert,[8] as well as the array of diagnostic studies reported by Mahler,[9] are available to OD practioners and should be consulted. Lippitt in his concept of organizational renewal also displays a high regard for data-based interventions and the use of instruments in OD.[10]

This chapter focuses on selected methods of data gathering and the application of instruments in OD efforts that are primarily concerned with teambuilding. However, it is desirable to inquire at the outset, data gathering and instrumentation for what? I believe that there is value in informing the group undergoing teambuilding at an early stage in the effort why data are being gathered and certain instruments used. This is done by discussing the difference between a healthy and an unhealthy organization, recognizing that the term "organizational health" is largely a metaphor but nevertheless a useful one for setting the stage and explaining the purpose of a teambuilding OD intervention.

I indicate in this chapter how the concept of organizational health can be used at the outset as a part of the unfreezing process in teambuilding and in laying the groundwork for data gathering, using instruments, and providing experiences in self-awareness and team-awareness.[11] This explanation is important because it informs a group where the facilitator is "coming from" in terms of values, philosophy, and norms. Program participants often feel uneasy if they lack this knowledge, and their anxieties can be easily allayed.

Figure 2.1 Characteristics of Unhealthy and Healthy Organizations

Unhealthy	Healthy
1. Only top management "owns" objectives. Goals are not always clear or strongly supported.	1. Objectives are widely shared with employee energy behind them. Organization is seen as purposeful; managers have personal–organizational goal integration and a sense of movement toward goal attainment.
2. Things are wrong but not dealt with; employees are disgruntled but silent.	2. Employees talk openly about issues and expect them to be dealt with and resolved.
3. Stress on formality in structure and relations. Nonconformity frowned upon.	3. Stress on informality and pragmatic problem-solving. Much nonconformity is tolerated. Form often follows function.
4. Decisions are made and controlled at the top. Management bottlenecks appear and decisions are tardy and irrational.	4. Decisions are delegated to where knowledge and motivation to solve problems are in the organization.
5. Managers are "alone" in getting things done; directives get garbled.	5. Team sharing of responsibility.
6. Judgment of lower-level managers is not respected.	6. Judgment of such employees is respected and used.
7. Personal needs and feelings are side issues.	7. Needs and feelings are regarded as interpersonal "process" items affecting task "content"; hence, they are central issues.
8. Competition and jealousy are common. No help is sought, offered, or accepted. Much "bad-mouthing" exists and is tolerated by management.	8. Collaboration is the mode. Help is freely requested and used. Ways of helping are highly developed. Competition is over shared goals.
9. If there is a crisis, managers withdraw or blame others.	9. If there is a crisis, managers team and collaborate till the crisis departs.
10. Conflict is covert and political; there may be interminable and irreconcilable arguments.	10. Conflict is considered openly and dealt with in a growthful way. Managers talk about it and try to settle it.
11. Learning is difficult because managers have to learn by mistakes. Peers' experiences are either rejected or not shared. Feedback is scarce and not helpful.	11. Managers have learned how to learn. Feedback is requested and used well. People believe they can grow and help one another.
12. Facades and fear contaminate relationships.	12. Honesty and caring are inherent in relationships.
13. Managers are security-conscious and bored. They get most of their kicks off the job.	13. Managers are turned on and highly involved in their work by choice.
14. Repertoire of managerial styles is limited.	14. Styles are flexible and tailored to the situation.

Figure 2.1 (*Continued*)

Unhealthy	Healthy
15. Managers tightly control small expenditures and keep detailed records and justificatory "Pearl Harbor" files on finances and all other matters.	15. There is an atmosphere of trust and freedom. People know what is important to the organization and what is not. Records are ample but not excessive.
16. Risk is avoided. When it is taken, it is ill considered, often destructive, and sometimes wild.	16. Risk is accepted as a constructive condition of growth and change. It is calculated and controlled.
17. Poor performance is glossed over or handled arbitrarily.	17. Poor performance is confronted and a joint resolution sought.
18. Organizational structure, policies, and procedures are used as a refuge for incompetence and game-playing.	18. These items are fashioned to help people get the job done and protect the long-term health of the organization.
19. Employees are forced to play limited roles that correspond with their jobs. They restrict their energy and concerns.	19. Employees are encouraged to use all their resources, be authentic, grow, and stretch themselves.
20. Tradition, the status quo, and the past way of doing things are considered sacrosanct.	20. There is a sense of order and transition from the past. There is a high rate of guided innovation and planned change.

Next follows a more general discussion of instrumentation and a discussion of how to handle the Johari Window and the FIRO-B at an early stage in unfreezing a group and creating a climate in which it is legitimate to examine self-awareness and managerial style and give and receive interpersonal feedback.

Organizational Health

As suggested, it is very useful at an early stage in an organizational development effort for the facilitator to state his values and the way that he approaches work with organizations as an internal or external consultant. Figure 2.1 is a comparison of unhealthy and healthy traits in work organizations, which becomes a useful way of orienting a group of the facilitator's stance on the direction of organizational change.[12] Many individuals who spend sizable portions of their careers as change agents have such characteristic stances, including, for example, the following men: Gordon Lippitt, with his model of the birth and maturation of organizations and other models for visualizing change[13]; Richard Beckhard and his models for dealing with organizational issues and change efforts[14]; and Kepner and Tregoe, who have a distinctive way of servicing client systems in OD efforts that start with workshops on problem-analysis and decision-making.[15]

Figure 2.1 indicates unhealthy traits on the left and healthy traits on the right. The facilitator's normal goal is to assist organizations that are in various states of "disease" (which should be interpreted as dis-ease) move from an unhealthy to a more healthy mode. Probably no organization is totally healthy any more than any individual is totally healthy. However, a comparison of unhealthy and healthy traits can serve a diagnostic purpose in working with a group by helping them focus upon what they may be already feeling about what is "good" or "bad" in their present work units and what causes them to feel uncomfortable and ill at ease.

There are 20 points of comparison between the unhealthy and healthy organization; while they need not be repeated in detail in the text, it is useful to elaborate on each with a sentence or two. To begin, in the unhealthy organization there probably are few objectives except those that are extremely gross; here, only top management "own" the objectives. In a healthy organization objectives are widely shared, the organization is perceived as purposeful, employees and managers have a sense of movement toward goal attainment, and there is some degree of personal–organizational goal integration.

Unhealthy organizations typically have many problems but they are not dealt with, and employees remain disgruntled and silent. Healthy organizations have an ample number of problems but the difference is that employees talk about them and expect the problems to be resolved.

In an unhealthy organization there is an excessive stress on formality in structure and relations whereas in a healthy organization there is sufficient structure and formality to get the work done. However, the difference is that stress is placed on informality and pragmatic problem-solving. Much nonconformity is tolerated because it is recognized that work can be accomplished in alternative ways that are equally effective. Forms for organizational design and structure and procedures for carrying out work are more likely to follow the functions that are to be accomplished rather than be patterned after rigid bureaucratic beliefs.

Unhealthy organizations are characterized by creating environments where managers feel alone in getting the work done and perceive that the directives that they issue become garbled at lower levels of management. In healthy organizations there is a team sharing of responsibilities and greater possibilities for clear communications.

Respect for the judgment of subordinates differs between unhealthy and healthy organizations. There is likely to be more delegation in a healthy organization because the judgment of lower-level managers is respected and used.

Personal needs and feelings are definitely considered side issues in the unhealthy organization. On the other hand, the needs and feelings of employees are regarded as important in healthy organizations and, in fact, become central issues of concern. There is widespread recognition that interpersonal "process" items affect tasks, accomplishment, and the "content" of the work itself. In healthy organizations social and emotional issues are considered legitimate topics for discussion, and there is no absolute ban on becoming emotional in meetings and in dealing with others. It is thought that both the social–emotional and rational sides of the person can be expressed in the work situation.

In unhealthy organizations competition and jealousy are commonly found. Managers do not seek, offer, or accept help because this could be considered a weakness. There is much criticism and belittling of the organization, which, curiously, is tolerated by management. The healthy organization has a mode of collaboration. Help between managers is freely requested and used. In fact, ways of helping are highly developed. The competition that does exist is over shared goals and the determination of the best means for goal attainment. There is none of the sandbagging and mousetrapping that is found in dysfunctional bureaucracies that are shot through with petty politics and internal bickering.

In unhealthy organizations, if there is a crisis, managers either withdraw or seek ways to blame others. Running for cover and blame-fixing behavior are typical. If there is a crisis in a healthy organization, the managers are likely to team together and collaborate until the crisis is dealt with and surmounted.

In the unhealthy organization, conflict is covert, political, and insidious. There may be interminable and irreconcilable arguments that are allowed to go on indefinitely and, sometimes, literally for a matter of years. The conflicts are regarded almost as uncontrollable and expected rather than considered as matters that should be dealt with openly and in a growthful way. In healthy organizations, managers talk about conflict, never sweep it under the rug, and try to settle it in a mutually acceptable way.

The kind of world in which we live today is constantly changing, requiring not only managers but the citizenry in general to learn constantly and keep up-to-date. In the unhealthy organization learning is extremely difficult because managers have to learn by mistakes. This is because peers' experiences are either rejected or not known because they are not shared. Feedback between managers is scarce and, when it does exist, is perceived as not helpful. The opposite situation exists in a healthy organization because here managers have "learned how to learn." As Lewin, Bennis, and Schein[16] have shown, managerial behavior changes in style so that managers are open to new ideas and attack problems by using as many resources as they can marshal and apply. Feedback is requested by teams that are tackling problems, and team members use the solicited feedback effectively. Team members believe that they can grow and help one another, and these beliefs have a dynamic effect on learning and the organizational climate.

In unhealthy organizations, facades and fear contaminate interpersonal relations. People seem to be hiding, posing, and attitudinizing in their work roles. The healthy organization is built upon honesty and caring in interpersonal relationships and minimizes fear and facades.

In the unhealthy organization, managers are excessively concerned with security and are often bored with the work itself. They are likely to get most of their satisfactions in life through off-the-job experiences, hobbies, mobility in fraternal organizations, and the like. For these people, as Dubin has so well put it, work is not a central life interest.[17] Managers in the healthy organization, on the other hand, although not "workaholics," are likely to be highly turned on by the work itself and to perform effectively as a matter of choice and personal pride.

In unhealthy organizations there is a stifling of behavior that limits the repertoire of managerial styles. However, styles in healthy organizations are likely to be varied, flexible, and tailored to the situation or situations as they arise. The level of tolerance for personal idiosyncracies is higher.

Probably one of the most distinctive characteristics of an unhealthy organization is that the manager tightly controls small expenditures and keeps detailed records on what he does. He is likely to have a justificatory "Pearl Harbor" file on finances and all other matters because he fears that on some future occasion (such as on a managerial "judgment day") that he will be called upon the carpet to explain himself and justify his actions. He hopes to be able to defend himself by displaying a record of prudence and extreme documentation that, like Caesar's wife, make the individual above reproach. In the healthy organization there are ample records for tracking the conduct of work but they are not excessive and they are not maintained for defensive purposes. Because there is an atmosphere of trust and freedom rather than fear and impending danger, employees know what is important to the organization and what is not. As a result, they are not excessively concerned with documentation.

Another key characteristic is the way in which risk is handled. In an unhealthy organization risk is avoided because of the fear in the climate. When a risk is taken (on those rare occasions when it is) it is often ill considered, destructive, and sometimes just plain wild. Risk is used as a defensive strategy; because there is little accumulated experience with using it, the result is likely to be dangerous and unwanted, further increasing the tendency for managers to withdraw or fix blame when risks backfire. In the healthy organization, risk is accepted as a constructive condition of growth and change. It is calculated and controlled so that if the risk is seen at an early stage to not have a chance of success, gears in the organization can be reversed to stop losses and minimize any adverse results. Byrd has provided us with probably the most important discussion in the OD literature on creative risk-taking both for individuals and teams, which describes the manner in which healthy and successful risk-taking operates.[18]

Poor performance is almost expected, glossed over, and inadequately handled in an unhealthy organization. There is probably more poor performance than there is successful goal-attaining performance in the unhealthy organization; when "drives" from the outside force managers to deal with poor performers, the process is often, if hurried, handled arbitrarily and, if delayed, so arduous and paperwork-laden that poor performers are not terminated from employment or even moved into positions where they can perhaps perform acceptably. Mediocrity is tolerated and dysfunctionally protected. The greatest fault of the unhealthy organization is the failure to deal with inadequate performers and to allow desirable grievance procedures and termination review procedures to be turned against healthy approaches to managing employees. Poor performance is found in healthy organizations too, but it is confronted and dealt with so that a joint resolution is sought and obtained sufficiently often to prevent the healthy organization from becoming stigmatized as being tolerant of inadequate performance. The approach to managing poor performance is always humane and understanding but standards are applied and judiciously administered.

The organizational structure, policies, and procedures used by unhealthy organizations become a refuge for incompetent employees and for game-playing managers who know how to dodge behind these features of organization for their own protection. Classical management theory gives cognizance to formulating structure, policies, and procedures in a rational way but condemns the dysfunctional use of these for masking incompetent performance and undesired behavior.[19] In the healthy organization these same features are present but they are fashioned to help people attain their work goals and to protect the long-term health of the organization with the minimum formality necessary for adjusting to change and survival.

The unhealthy organization has a constricting effect on employees and requires them to play limited roles that correspond with their jobs. Few institutions are sufficiently loose to allow individuals extremely wide latitude in their performance of job roles, but the unhealthy organization is notable for the way that the energy and concerns of employees are channeled in the narrowest possible way so that they take a limited view of their work and responsibilities. "That's not my responsibility" becomes the alibi for lack of results. Interestingly enough, such dysfunctional organizations are often likely to assert that they want creative employees and to engage in the brainstorming of problems to obtain better solutions; but the *modus operandi* of the organization effectively constricts creativity. In healthy organizations employees are encouraged to use all their resources, be authentic in their relations with others, and to grow and to stretch themselves so that the work role becomes a general jurisdiction for accomplishment rather than a limitation. Yet they do not become imperialistic territorial seizers.

Lastly, in the unhealthy organization tradition, the *status quo,* and the past way of performing work and solving problems are considered sacrosanct. There is great resistance to change and, as Weber pointed out many years ago, constant need to seek coordination of diverse activities.[20] The organization becomes, as President John F. Kennedy stated in relation to the U. S. Department of State, a bowl of jello impervious to being reshaped and capable of absorbing all kinds of saber thrusts and surgery intended to change its basic shape. Many organizations are quite similar to this because they, as the State Department, are able to swallow up all interventions designed to cut into or change the organization itself.[21]

This discussion of unhealthy and healthy organizational characteristics needs to be interpreted so that it does not appear to be naive or utopian to persons undergoing a teambuilding effort. The goal in teambuilding is to shift an organization as far as possible from the unhealthy state to the healthy. Obviously, it is much easier to state this goal than to bring it about, but normative concepts such as these are useful for communicating the kinds of results that we are attempting to attain in teambuilding.

The Johari Window and Feedback

Having set some normative ideas into place, it is useful next for the change agent to continue the unfreezing process and create an interest in moving towards self-awareness goals in the teambuilding effort. One device that is extremely helpful in this regard is the Johari Window and its connection with feedback.

Feedback is essential for individual growth and development and needs to be built into any teambuilding effort so that participants can learn how to learn. In the type of teambuilding effort discussed in this book, great emphasis is placed upon feedback and it is believed that in the final analysis when a teambuilding effort has been completed all of those who have undergone it should get specific feedback from their team members for the entire time encompassed by the teambuilding effort. In the last chapter I suggest a way in which this type of feedback can be obtained at a point in time when the recipient is likely to take it seriously and benefit from it. I also have a recommended format that can be used at that juncture and is constructed to enable individuals to get and receive feedback in terms of the specific goals of the teambuilding effort.

Turning to the Johari Window itself, it should be noted that this notion is not very new and was first developed in 1955 by Joseph Luft and Harry Ingham.[22] The window is an acronym using the first two or three letters (plus an i) from the surnames of the creators of the concept. They were interested in creating a device that would be useful for heightening one's awareness in human behavior, provide for giving and getting feedback, and have a use in achieving individual and group openness.

Feedback is a type of verbal and nonverbal communication that gives a person information on how his behavior presently affects someone else. Feedback also is information that is received from others on how one's behavior is affecting the other's feelings and his perceptions. Feedback is nonevaluative and is in its most useful form simply a matter of telling to a person how he is coming across. The best type of feedback is nonevaluative and given and accepted undefensively.

The Johari Window itself is a device through which an abstract concept like feedback can be made clearer to a group undergoing teambuilding so that they can give and receive information in a way that has meaning for them. The window is particularly valuable because it makes no assumptions about individual needs and drives and is therefore not necessarily connected with any particular kind of psychological theory, although it can be tied in with various bodies of theory, if that is desired. The Johari Window also is useful because its structure joins the known and unknown in behavior. We return to this point subsequently.

The Johari Window itself makes no value judgments and simply acts as a rubric for categorizing information. As one accepts himself and others, the need for giving judgmental feedback decreases and a device such as the Johari Window simply has an organizing and communication function. It is not itself a theory but rather a schematic. Its theoretical underpinning can be traced back at least as far as Cooley's "looking-glass" self and similar early work in social psychology.[23]

Figure 2.2 contains the basic model of the Johari Window. It can be seen to be a paradigm that represents the total person in relation to other persons. The bases for the division of the paradigm into quadrants is awareness of behavior, feelings, and motivation. Thus, we have an area of the self that is known to the self and known to others; this we call the open area or sometimes the arena. Part two of the quadrant is the blind part of the self, which is known to others based upon one's interaction with them but is not known to the self. The third quadrant is the hidden part of the self, which is well known to the person but is not known to the others because it is not re-

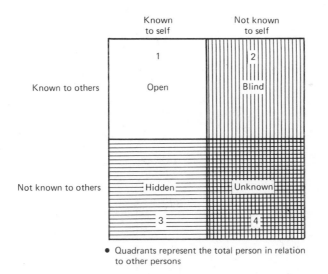

- Quadrants represent the total person in relation to other persons

- Basis for division into quadrants is awareness of behavior, feelings, and motivation

Figure 2.2 Quadrants representing the total person in relation to other persons. Basis for division into quadrants is awareness of behavior, feelings, and motivation. (**Source:** Joseph Luft, *Group Processes, An Introduction to Group Dynamics,* by permission of Mayfield Publishing Company. Copyright © 1963, 1970 by Joseph Luft. See also *Of Human Interaction.*)

vealed in everyday life to them. The fourth quadrant in the self is what we call the unknown, which is known neither to others nor to the self. We do know that in life we experience inclinations and tendencies in behavior that appear to be inexplicable; yet if we knew everything about ourselves, we would probably be able to explain these peculiarities. Thus when we find strange behavior in ourselves, or others observe in us behavioral patterns that are not obvious to us, we have an example of what is subsumed in the fourth quadrant of the self.

Figure 2.3 is useful because it helps us relate the Johari Window to the feedback process that is considered to be so important in personal growth and in organizational development through teambuilding.

The arrows in Figure 2.3 indicate how the self solicits feedback and how the group, when an atmosphere of self disclosure has developed, can be used to give feedback. The two columns represent the self and the two rows represent the group. The arrows indicate that as the individual solicits feedback, he learns more and more about the behavior that is known to himself as well as an increasing amount about the kinds of behavior that he might exhibit but of which he might be unaware.

In building an atmosphere of self-disclosure in which feedback is given, the group can provide an atmosphere where the arena of the self and the facade of the self become topics for discussion. Individuals engaging in these

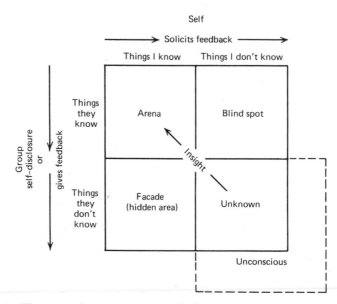

Figure 2.3 The two columns represent the self; the two rows represent the group. (**Source:**   adapted from Phillip C. Hanson, "The Johari Window: A Model for Soliciting and Giving Feedback," in John E. Jones and J. William Pfeiffer, *The 1973 Annual Handbook for Group Facilitators*, University Associates, San Diego, Calif., 1973, p. 113.)

discussions are given feedback that can be helpful both in personal growth and teambuilding.

Although the Johari Window is not intended to be a device for making a theoretical contribution, the last quadrant of the window indicates a connection between the unknown and the known in behavior. In a learning situation it becomes possible through the giving and receiving of feedback for unknown aspects of behavior to be brought more into the open and for individuals to become more aware of their arenas because more recondite types of behavior manifest themselves there when the interpersonal environment becomes permissive. In other words, they are likely to obtain greater information about the unknown parts of themselves, which may be equivalent to the unconscious, as a consequence of feedback.

There are some interesting propositions for teambuilding that are connected with the Johari Window and feedback. For example, as the level of trust increases in a group, the arena exhibited by the various group members also tends to increase. Again, this insight suggests the importance of trust-building in any teambuilding effort.

A second proposition is that the more one participates in a group, the more blind spot data are displayed to others. In this way individuals become off guard and reveal themselves and place themselves in a position for getting feedback about aspects of themselves of which they are not aware.

The more the facade is dropped, the greater the amount of information revealed. Earlier in the chapter we discussed the concept of a healthy and unhealthy organizations, and it was noted that in unhealthy organizations individuals carrying out their customary work behavior roles are hiding behind facades to a very great extent. Although any organizational role requires a certain degree of formal behavior, we find that some individuals are excessively formalistic and use their organizational role for hiding rather than for facilitating the conduct of work. In a feedback situation the facade is penetrated and a greater amount of information about the person becomes available and can be fed back to him.

The unknown quadrant, as previously mentioned, ties together the conscious and unconscious, the known and the unknown, in behavior. It is not recommended that in a teambuilding situation a great deal of effort be exerted towards exploration of the unknown. It is of interest, however, to note that often individuals will behave in a way they cannot explain and that is even surprising to them. This is because the unknown includes a host of past experiences that are likely to result in unpredictable and even embarassing behavior. We might say that the unknown includes childhood memories, intrapersonal dynamics, latent potentialities, and many other kinds of unrecognized sources of feelings and behavior and unidentified resources. The unknown in the individual probably will never be totally known but it is possible to get insight into how these unconscious elements do influence everyday behavior through the use of the Johari Window in teambuilding groups.

As one gets and gives feedback he finds that the boundaries of the self are expandable. For example, the blind spot can be significantly reduced through soliciting or giving feedback. The facade can be reduced through giving feedback and expressing reactions. It becomes possible to move information from the blind spot and facade into the arena, where it is then "available" to everyone. Furthermore, as suggested, it is possible to move newly found information from the unknown into the arena, thereby providing the individual with what is commonly called "insight."

Luft and Ingham have also suggested possible ways in which individuals can be perceived through using the "Window." The ideal Window for a manager, for example, is one where there is a fairly large arena and a fairly small unknown quadrant with the facade and blind spot considerably smaller than the arena but much larger than the unknown. The individual who typically shows bull-in-a-china–shop behavior is likely to have a Johari Window that indicates a very large blind spot in his own behavior. On the other hand, an individual who is turtle-like in his behavior is likely to have a very small arena and a very large unknown quadrant in his self. He is likely to have also a facade and blind spot that are about double or triple the size of the arena.

In addition, there are organizational roles that require individuals to take on a typical pattern in the Johari Window scheme. For example, an individual who is acting as an employment interviewer is likely to have a very large facade and a somewhat smaller arena with a very small blind spot area and not a very large unknown area. The interviewer is someone who because of his occupational role requirement has taken on himself a large facade in order to encourage the interviewee or applicant to be more revealing about himself. It is not important for the interviewer to have a large arena in the work situation because his job is to listen to the interviewee and obtain information. He would probably feel that this can best be done if he stays in role; hence, he is likely to have a very large facade corresponding to his concept of his organizational role.[24]

The Johari Window has been used in many organizational development and personal growth learning situations. It can be used in teambuilding by explaining to a group the idea behind the Window and asking the participants to discuss their concepts of their own Windows with one another. This can be done in small groups and be extended into an hour or more. The exchange of perceptions about Johari Windows can be extremely beneficial because the exchange does foster the giving and the receiving of feedback and aids in the unfreezing process by the surfacing of relevant data.

Data-Gathering Modes in OD

There are a number of other means for gathering data in an OD teambuilding effort or in other kind of OD activity. Very broadly these modes may be classified as polling, instrumentation, and observation. In polling, data can be gathered in a number of ways: attitude surveys, which have been very popular and emphasized by Likert and the Institute for Social Research, University of Michigan[25]; organizational interviewing, which is a method that has been used not only in social psychological but also in anthropological research work, and, coupled with observation, has been given considerable stress by Whyte[26]; and sensing and reporting, which is a method or a combination of methods that enable a group to sense or ask one another about what they perceive as transpiring in a group and then reporting these perceptions, which in turn are processed by the group. Fordyce and Weil have described the sensing and reporting process in some detail.[27]

Instrumentation has become very popular in OD, and many instruments used by psychologists in the past for the purposes of testing have been utilized in a different manner by OD specialists and group facilitators. Tests are now used for generating data that can be analyzed by a group. Similarly, inventories (personality and interest) are being used by OD specialists for new purposes. We return below to a more extended discussion of instrumentation.

The third major type of data-gathering mode in OD is observation, which can be coupled with polling and instrumentation. Diagnostic meetings can be utilized for reporting on observations and for checking perceptions in a group. Exercises can also be used as vicarious learning vehicles and for experiential learning itself. When exercises are completed, the groups that utilized them can then process what took place in the exercises and determine what has been learned.

There are many useful resources concerning data-gathering modes and I do not attempt to cover them all in this book. A number of the attitude survey instruments, including both questionnaires and interview schedules, used by the Institute for Social Research at the University of Michigan have been published. Likewise, the work of Likert is well known and available in several popular management books. Mahler has recently contributed an extremely valuable volume on diagnostic studies that should be consulted by anyone interested in polling and observation techniques.[28] The aim of the remainder of this chapter is to expand the comments made in respect to instrumentation and this subject is considered next.

Instrumentation in OD

Pfeiffer and Heslin have pointed out that the earliest use of instruments in OD was to generate research-oriented data for the purpose of assessing behavioral changes in training groups. However, over the years this practice has evolved into a more common use of instruments to generate data fo processing and consumption of the group undergoing the training or team-building experience. Thus, instrumentation has become an invaluable aid in OD not only for the original purpose of research but also for increasing the participants' self-understanding and helping to identify behaviors that might be perceived as dysfunctional to interpersonal relations or to the accomplishment of group tasks.[29]

In recent years, as OD has reached beyond the realm of the social sciences into nearly every phase of contemporary life, but particularly work organizations, instrumentation has become increasingly popular. Although it is perfectly legitimate for an OD facilitator regardless of his background to use instrumentation, it is likely to be of no use to him or to the participants in his groups if he fails to provide the opportunity for a learning experience. Thus the person who uses an instrument must have an understanding of instrumentation in general and, of course, the particular instrument he plans to use.

Many well-intentioned group facilitators have fallen into the practice of administering an instrument, such as the FIRO-B[30], to a group and then providing little or no interpretation of what the instrument discloses. Such an approach very sharply decreases the potential learning for the person to whom the instrument is given. It is not suggested here that instruments be used in only one way and that the innovative applications be discouraged. However, it is suggested that for the greatest benefits to be derived from these instruments the OD facilitator must provide sufficient information so that the capacities and uses of the instrument are thoroughly understood. The organizational setting should be appropriate for the use of any particular instrument. The discriminating ability of the OD facilitator will be tested in this regard. Also, he must make intelligent decisions regarding those instruments that are appropriate to the needs and goals of a particular clientele with a particular time limitation. In other words, not all instruments are of equal value in an OD effort; hence, a choice must be made as to which instrument should be utilized.

In the teambuilding program that is the concern of this book I make use of the FIRO-B at an early stage of the OD effort because it is the most generally used instrument in training and teambuilding. The contention is that a facilitator[31] can extrapolate similarly useful information from any particular instrument that he wishes to explore. The detailed treatment of the FIRO-B given in this book, as Pfeiffer and Heslin have shown elsewhere,[32] should provide an example of how to use one very popular type of instrument.

I should note that it is sometimes felt that the only legitimate data to use in a laboratory training or teambuilding situation are data internally derived and that the interjection of instrumented data interferes with the natural progression of the learning process. Thus it is important for OD teambuilding facilitators to understand the appropriate uses of instrumentation and for them to consider the issues of feedback sources. It is clear that externally derived data can help promote the individual's growth if the facilitator is aware of the ramifications of using instruments. There are several conditions that must be satisfied. Certainly he must be personally familiar with the specific instrument that he is administering. He must choose the instrument solely on the basis of the needs and goals of the client group. He must also be competent to interpret the data that emerge so that the feedback can be used meaningfully.[33]

It is very likely that more growth can occur for a group participant if he is provided with a method for specifically focusing upon his own behavior. This is in addition to any feedback he receives from fellow group members that can aid growth on a different and equally important level. It is not enough that a person leave a laboratory learning situation or teambuilding effort feeling exhilarated, more open, changed, and so on. He must have been given the opportunity to understand himself and his behaviors in highly specific ways and then be able to make decisions concerning behavior changes based upon this learning if he so desires. Being able to relate to the particular outcomes of instruments he has taken may serve to reinforce new behavior patterns and positive self-concepts when the glow of the group experience has faded with his return to the real world back on the job.

Instrumented feedback can be more useful than the verbal feedback one receives in small groups or teams, although it is not worthwhile to argue this point in too much detail because, obviously, groups can have a beneficial impact. Too often participants give feedback that is absolute whereas well-constructed scales can provide feedback in terms of a behavioral continuum. The instrument can be used to locate the person in reference to degrees of a trait or to a group norm. Yet perhaps the primary value of instrumentation is as a source of personal feedback for individuals. This use involves the straightforward completion, scoring, and interpretations of scales.

Instruments can also be used as vehicles for giving and receiving feedback among individuals. For example, it is commonly found in OD efforts that participants can be asked to predict each other's scores so that individuals become more aware of their facades and of the impact that they have on each other. It is even possible for participants to complete entire instruments for each other for a more in-depth examination of interpersonal perceptions.

A related use of instruments is to help participants to study "here-and-now" processes within a group and to assist the group in diagnosing its own internal methods of functioning. These instrumented data can focus on what is happening in the life of the group and may point the way toward changes that are considered desirable. In this way, the group may be able to more quickly arrive at optimal functioning so that learning can take place. The unique advantage of using instrumented feedback is that the specificity obtained enhances the probability that the group will be able to monitor and manage its own processes effectively.

Participants can also learn more when they are actively involved in the learning process, and instruments create an active role in learning. For example, when participants have invested time and energy in an activity such as completing an inventory related to a model being explored, they have also invested in learning the theory; the entire process becomes more meaningful and easily relatable in terms of the group or teambuilding experience. Also, participants can be encouraged to study the items in detail because the items in the instrument constitute a behavioral definition of the trait being measured. This process can result in the participants' giving consideration to changing specific behaviors.[34]

Despite what has been discussed above, it is important to recognize that there are both advantages and disadvantages to using instrumentation in OD work. These can most appropriately be dealt with by acknowledging their existence and working on ways of minimizing the problems connected with their utilization and maximizing the advantages of using instruments. Let us consider the disadvantages of using instruments first.

One of the main disadvantages of using instruments is that the individual may fear that he has overexposed himself. This fear may be accompanied by resentment, a loss of potential learning, and the tendency to label individuals in the group because of what a score on an instrument revealed. The labeling can, in turn, amount to stereotyping the individual and get in the way of open, honest, authentic communication.

Instruments sometimes promote flight from confrontation and from personal and interpersonal issues that would be better confronted than avoided. The flight can be experienced in several different ways, including excessive and time-consuming nitpicking. Nitpicking, in turn, can lead to defensive behavior and divert the individual's as well as the group's attention from key issues, arousing hostility that must be dealt with before the group or the team can proceed with its business.

On the other hand, the use of an instrument can dissipate the tension of person-to-person encounters, which have potential for personal growth. The instrument may also tend to pull an individual away from the interpersonal process of the group if the data from the instrument have created an emotional overload for him. He may become too preoccupied integrating the data and dealing with it. His behavior may become dysfunctional for the rest of the group. Some of this difficulty can be eased if the OD facilitator takes time to process the data from the instrument to the point where the participant can handle and manage to integrate it without its interfering with the learning situation.

On the other hand, if the feedback overload is not handled well the OD facilitator may create a dependency on him that is unhealthy. It is important for the OD facilitator to shift the responsibility for learning during the feedback-processing stage as early as possible to the participants themselves and thereby aid the transition from a highly structured experience to one where experiential learning at the group level can take place. It should always be borne in mind that the responsibility for learning rests with the participant. The meaning is his as he integrates these data with his understanding of himself.

Another disadvantage of using instruments is that they sometimes provoke subtle anger or undue anxiety on the part of the participants because they trigger unpleasant memories of school grading practices. Thus it is very important for the OD facilitator to avoid using the word "test" and to stress that the use of the instrument is nonevaluative, that is to say, there are no right or wrong answers.

Finally, it is a fact that many instruments are subject to distortion, lying, and answering in a socially desirable way and that virtually all instruments have a great deal of transparency. Participants can confound the results of using the instrument if they desire but, on the other hand, if they are committed to their own learning, the tendency to distort will be greatly lessened. If the participants have volunteered for the teambuilding experience, their level of commitment to their own learning is likely to be high. If the group is an intact, nonvoluntary one, the OD facilitator should attempt to inspire commitment to the learning goals of the experience because this commitment must exist if the experience is to be a productive one.[35]

Turning to the advantages of using instruments, it should be noted that instrumented approaches give a participant early opportunities to understand the theory involved in the dynamics of his own group situation, which could have the effect of increasing his involvement. In many ways instruments provide an opportunity for early and easy theory learning and subsequent high personal involvement. By the careful choice of an appropriate instrument during the early part of a training or teambuilding effort, the OD facilitator can quickly offer the participant a theory about personality style, group development, interpersonal relations, or leadership that he can use throughout the rest of the teambuilding effort if he so desires.[36] This is accomplished by using the FIRO-B at an early stage of the teambuilding effort and by making reference to it repeatedly on subsequent occasions while working experientially and cognitively to build the team.

The main advantage in using instruments is that they give the person a chance to learn some constructs and terminology early in the teambuilding experience that he can use in looking at his and other people's behavior and categorizing and describing what goes on between individuals or within an individual. Another advantage of using instruments is that the participant forms a commitment to the information, constructs, and theory that he has been given. This occurs because his instrumented feedback describes him in terms of these relevant constructs and theory. One way of tying a person's self to some useful theory about groups and interpersonal relations is to give the theory a degree of personal impact, crystallizing the participant's learning in the process.

Through instrumentation a participant can be given feedback about his personal behavior quite early in the teambuilding experience. Unless it is developed rather early we find that a person typically does not obtain feedback from other participants about his managerial style or about the way he relates until the later stages of teambuilding. This is because it often takes that long before the other participants have developed the skills necessary to give effective feedback to someone. It also often takes considerable time before an atmosphere of trust is developed in the group so that members can feel comfortable in giving meaningful feedback to another member.

Regardless of the reasons, the tragedy of tardy feedback is that the person obtains information that he needs to know about himself with no time to work on new behaviors that might modify the aspect of himself that has been described. Instruments administered early in the group experience can help to compensate for the lack of feedback from others. The person can, for example, generate an agenda of behavior modification for himself on the characteristics uncovered by the instrument while he has the remainder of the teambuilding experience to work on it. Alternatively, the person can contract with the group to experiment with new behavior based on the clearer focus that the instrument gives. The instrumented feedback also is likely to increase the chances that the individual will form a commitment to personal change and growth that may not occur with a group member's feedback, which is sometimes easier to discount or simply forget.

Instruments have the advantage of giving feedback to an individual or to an organization in a way that is characterized by relatively low threat. For example, when an individual obtains information from a questionnaire that he has filled out himself, he is more likely to trust that data than data he receives from another individual regarding perceptions of his personal style. At least he does not have the problem of trying to sort out whether the information he is fed back is truly representative of his behavior or whether the feedback is caused by the bias of the other person. He can be fairly certain that the instrument holds no personal malevolence toward him.

An instrument provides for the comparison of the individual with group norms, and it is often an eye-opening experience to find out, for example, that we are stronger in one or more of our characteristics than 99% of the people in a certain teambuilding group. This last piece of information indicating that a person is unusually high on a characteristic may cause him to pause and examine whether this characteristic is actually becoming dysfunctional for him because it is so unusual. It may be getting in the way of his performance on the job or at home.

Another important advantage of instrumentation is that it can promote involvement with data of all kinds. Starting to deal with feedback obtained from instruments can have a very beneficial effect on the individual and afford the teambuilding experience a greater chance to impact the behavior of the participants undergoing it.

Instruments can be extremely useful in providing feedback to group members by use of a uniform measure that allows comparison to norms. Instruments can be used to build base groups for discussions, problem-solving, and exercises. Instruments are extremely useful in cutting through the group climate to get at latent issues that might be difficult and time-consuming to otherwise bring to the surface. For example, it is possible to use a team group so that the prevailing atmosphere is penetrated and issues that are of interest to a group are discussed, but the amount of time and energy that would be required might be inordinate relative to the benefits received. Hence, an instrument that is adaptable and can be used without a great deal of preparation can obtain the same result or even a better result in a lesser time period.

Instruments bring to the surface covert issues that can be dealt with in a group setting. By administering an instrument that uncovered these issues, concerns are made public and become legitimate topics to discuss, deal with, correct, or improve.

From the standpoint of the OD facilitator, instruments allow him to focus the energies and time of the participants on the most appropriate material and also to control, to some extent, the issues that are dealt with in the learning situation. In this way, he is assured that the critical existing issues are worked on rather than the trivial ones that the members may focus upon to avoid grappling with the more uncomfortable ones.

A final advantage is that instruments allow longitudinal assessment of change in individuals and teambuilding groups. This assessment can be very useful in OD for demonstrating that the various interventions in which the organization is involved are compatible with the goals of the OD effort.

To this point we have been considering the advantages and disadvantages of using instruments in teambuilding. By way of summary it may be useful to list how the disadvantages of instruments can be avoided. First, in an OD teambuilding effort, and in laboratory training generally, we should begin by legitimizing with the participants the use of instrumentation. This means that, prior to the beginning of the teambuilding effort, we should be clear in our expectations concerning instruments and their advantages to the group experience. It also means that we should be ready to intervene to refocus the direction in which the teambuilding group is moving if the participants use the instrument as a flight mechanism. It also means minimizing anxieties so that more learning can occur.

Second, we need to make a concerted effort to remove the mysticism surrounding instrumentation. In order to do this we should discuss the margin of error and other factors which contribute to less than absolute results. We should allow and encourage participants to explore the instrument thoroughly so that they understand how it was designed and how the scores were derived. We should also clarify the theoretical basis of the instrument.

Third, we need to insure that sufficient time is made available for processing the data derived from using the instrument. This means giving the participants an opportunity to talk through their scores and to compare them with others. It also means emphasizing and legitimatizing the differing life perspectives and orientations among people. We should generate no more data that we can process.

Fourth, we need to assure the participants that they have control over their own data. This means defining carefully the boundaries within which scores are to be shared or not shared. It certainly means placing security on the reporting of scores so that organizational superiors are not told them and that the participants clearly understand that the scores will not be used against them in any way.

Beyond what has been suggested in this section there are many additional administrative issues in presenting an instrument as well as many technical considerations with which the OD facilitator may wish to become thoroughly familiar before proceeding to use an instrument. Pfeiffer and Heslin have provided excellent discussions of these subjects to which the reader may turn if he wishes to pursue the matter in more detail.[37]

FIRO-B

I have already suggested that the FIRO-B is a prototype of an OD instrument and that it has had great use in both training and teambuilding. More specifically, the FIRO-B is an instrument that is uniquely well suited to providing meaningful feedback data and theory input for groups of all kinds but especially for teambuilding groups. FIRO-B means Fundamental Interpersonal Relations Orientation–Behavior.

The FIRO-B was designed by Dr. William C. Schutz and was copyrighted in 1957. Thus it is a tried and tested instrument that continues to be valuable to this day.

There are varying views on how the FIRO-B should be administered in a group situation. Pfeiffer and Heslin recommend that, although there is a theory base for the FIRO-B, the manner in which it is administered should avoid giving any clues regarding the nature of the traits that are being measured by the instrument itself.[38] On the other hand, I believe that it can be valuable to explain the theory base of the instrument and its objectives when conducting teambuilding sessions. After all, participants are adults and expected to be treated on at least a peer level with the group facilitator if not given special consideration because they are high-level executives and have expectations concerning their status and appropriate treatment. Discussing the instrument before its administration in a group can quite possibly result in some later nitpicking and some earlier mind-setting in the direction of faking one's responses to the items on the instrument. I believe in taking these risks, nevertheless, and providing some explanation before the actual administration of the FIRO-B.

In fact, there is particular value in explaining some of the dimensions of the FIRO-B in advance of its administration because they are especially pertinent to executives in carrying out their work and improving their abilities to be team members.

We begin by explaining the function behind the FIRO-B as, to quote Barbra Streisand, people need people. More specifically, the person, because of his social nature, has certain interpersonal needs that must be satisfied to some degree while avoiding a threat to one's self. Each person has different intensities of need and different mechanisms for handling them.

The theory behind the FIRO-B is that all human interaction can be divided into three catagories: issues surrounding inclusion, those surrounding control, and those surrounding affection. These three types of needs pertain especially to management and executive teambuilding but obviously have universal application in nonwork settings.

Schutz's theory of group development suggests that a group proceeds through inclusion issues into control issues and finally into affection issues. Then it recycles. To illustrate these catagories, the teambuilding facilitator can ask the participants to consider a group of people riding in a boat. The inclusion issue in this case is whether or not individuals have come along for the boat ride. The issue of control is who is running the motor or operating the rudder. The affection issue concerns how closely people are seated together in the boat.[39]

The interpersonal issues in the FIRO-B can be explained in a different way. Figure 2.4 illustrates how the interpersonal issues can be viewed and shows that the inclusion issue (I), the control issue (C), and the affection issue (A) have a clear bearing on some of the common phenomena experienced in group life. In every group there are issues of who is going to be in or out, which can be viewed as a boundary problem. Boundaries delimit any one group from all other groups in the organization. Control issues are important in groups because they have a bearing upon decision-making and power. Affection issues are important because they bear upon the extent to which a team can be integrated and individuals made to feel team members. Thus we experience in many groups an evolution from settling the boundary problem, to resolving the control, decision-making, and power issues, and, finally, movement towards building the solidarity of the group and integrating the team.[40]

When dealing with adults and particularly with executives in large-scale organizations, it is extremely difficult to get them to verbalize on their inclusion, control, and affection needs. If a laboratory approach is utilized, we can expect to spend many hours before a group is ready to discuss these

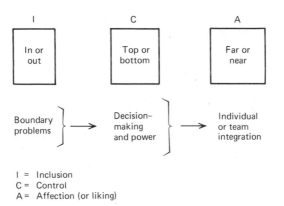

I = Inclusion
C = Control
A = Affection (or liking)

Figure 2.4   Interpersonal issues in the FIRO–B.

issues; even when that point is reached, many participants may still feel uncomfortable about talking and directing their attention to "affection needs." Surmounting this difficult situation through the use of an instrument clearly shows how instruments can be more valuable than discussion in rapidly reaching the point where the teambuilding activity itself becomes meaningful.

Figure 2.5 describes the FIRO-B Scales in a way that is comprehensible to individuals who are asked to complete the instrument. The two dimensions that the figure illustrates are (1) inclusion, control, and affection in terms of what the individual expresses to others and (2) inclusion, control, and affection in terms of what the individual wants from others in their behavior towards him. It is important for participants to understand that the expressed is their own behavior and that the wanted is the behavior they wish others would exhibit toward them. Sample items from the FIRO-B are shown in Figure 2.5.

The FIRO-B produces six scores—three on behavior expressed towards others and three on the behavior wanted from others in the areas of inclusion, control, and affection. It measures the expression of orientations by the degree to which a person joins and includes others, controls and leads others, and is friendly and personal with others. It also measures the desire for such behavior from others by an indication of the extent to which a person wants others to include him and invite him to join them, influence and lead him, and express friendly and affectionate feelings toward him.

The FIRO-B can be administered to a group in 5 to 12 minutes and scored in various ways in 5 to 10 minutes. The instrument itself contains 54 statements, 9 in each of six scales, and can result in scores from 0 to 54.

The primary appeal of the FIRO-B is that it measures three characteristics of interpersonal relations that are normally of concern to a person undergoing a group experience and teambuilding if he is to come to increased self-understanding. A second positive aspect of the instrument is that it makes a distinction between what the individual wants from others and what

Figure 2.5 Description of the FIRO-B scales.

	I Inclusion	C Control	A Affection
E	I join other people, and I include others.	I take charge; I influence people.	I get close to people.
W	I want people to include me.	I want people to lead me.	I want people to get close and personal with me.

E = Expressed (toward others).
W = Wanted (from others).

Source: Adapted from Pfeiffer and Heslin, Ref. 29, p. 140.

he expresses toward others. The relative scores in the six combinations of inclusion–control–affection and want-from, express-toward are very useful for gaining this self-understanding. A third positive feature is that the dimensions are also relevant for understanding some aspects of group process and do tie into Schutz's theory of group development.

There are additional positive features of the FIRO-B that are worth mentioning. For example, the items and scales have no assumed social desirability and can be answered by an executive or manager from the frame of reference of his job-related behavior. Both extremes of the scales represent various styles that people use with relative comfort. Also, the instrument is fairly brief and has highly reliable scales. In addition, the FIRO-B is non-threatening and does not suggest possible interpretations of psychological abnormality in any way. The scores are easy to interpret because all the scales have the same number of items. Lastly, it is possible to look at score combinations for insight into both individual behavior and the relationship between people.

As with all instruments there are some minor negative aspects of the FIRO-B. For example, occasionally some respondents begin to feel that the statements are repetitious; but this is more of a minor annoyance than a major problem. Secondly, because the FIRO-B is a self-report instrument it is open to lying and self-deception biases. However, since the statements and the subscales are relatively free from overtones of psychological abnormality, the individual should feel less need to be defensive.

There is also a problem in response style or the tendency to be cautious and use only moderate response choices on any questionnaire, or the tendency to see all relationships in either a basically negative or positive light. Such response styles will clearly affect a person's scores on all scales. Therefore, an inflation or depression of all scores could be interpreted as a response bias. Of course, the discovery of a response bias gives insight into the personality of the individual and may become material for discussion and interpretation in its own right.[41]

Using the FIRO-B in Teambuilding Workshops

The manner of interpretation of the FIRO-B and its specific use in a teambuilding situation are of great concern, and we turn to them next. The manner of interpretation may vary sharply depending upon the participant group and desires of the OD facilitator who uses the instrument.[42] I feel that it is important to indicate that the FIRO-B scores are useful for obtaining feedback and also for providing a uniform measure that allows comparison to norms. The instrument cuts through the group climate to get at latent issues and has a special value in building base group teams for discussions, problem-solving, and exercises. As a result, we ask the individual to score his own FIRO-B and by the use of templates spend approximately 10 minutes scoring the instrument together. When this is done, we then ask team members to report their scores to the total group by simply calling them out while the group facilitator goes to the chalkboard and writes numbers from 0 to 54. The individual scores are readily tallied against the total score numbers until everyone has reported his score to the group. This reporting becomes an ice-breaking experience and starts to legitimatize the discussion of the meaning of the various items in the FIRO-B. The group facilitator himself should probably reveal his own FIRO-B score so that the group can determine where average scores, individual scores, and the group facilitator's score may be congruent or incongruent.

The interpretation of the scores can proceed along several different lines depending upon the desires of the teambuilding facilitator and the goals of the group at that particular point in time. We usually simply take the FIRO-B scores and, based upon them using a high–low alternation method, assign individuals to teams so that persons with various kinds of FIRO-B scores are in the same group, attempting as far as possible to have a roughly similar average score for the five or six people that are in each individual team. The result of this is probably to mix individuals who have different styles in interpersonal relations in groups and tends to spread around the introverts and extroverts, if we may heuristically resort to those gross personality categories for the purposes of discussion. Also, in building teams by the use of FIRO-B scores the logic for arbitrarily assigning individuals to teams becomes apparent; individuals get a feeling of trust at the beginning of a teambuilding effort concerning the so-called rules of the game. While the assignments are taking place, individuals can ask questions about the FIRO-B scores and the theory base and express any concerns that they may be harboring in respect to the instrument. Thus, there is probably a special way to handle the FIRO-B in cases where the goal is teambuilding.

We sometimes ask individuals who work together in a superior–subordinate relationship to identify themselves so that they need not be put in the same team (which might otherwise be the result of a simple application of FIRO-B scores). We have found that some individuals object to being in the same team with their organizational superior whereas others feel it to be a definite advantage.

The interpretation of the FIRO-B can then proceed along many different lines, and the OD facilitator must decide which way seems to be appropriate for the teams with which he is working. One alternative is to compare the actual score cell by cell in the instrument. Another is to compare the actual scores to norm averages. If this interpretation is pursued, a rough rule of thumb is to consider scores that vary from the norm by 2 or more points to be significant for the purposes of discussion.[43] A third interpretation is to examine the column scores to determine the significance of inclusion, control, and affection scores by their relative importance to each other. For example, if the highest score is on control, control issues are probably most important to that individual. If the second highest is on inclusion, perhaps that is of second importance, and so on. It is also possible, of course, to compare the column scores in relationship to the norm scores and compare the individual scores against the totals for each of the columns. Variances of more than 3 points are deviations worthy of discussion.

Scores can also be examined by row, looking at the expressed and wanted dimensions. The first comparison that could be made is the relative importance of expressed behavior versus wanted behavior in terms of which seems to be a more characteristic or logical pattern for the person. The second comparison is to consider the actual score in relationship to the norm score totals for the two dimensions. This process allows persons to see their scores in relation to other individuals' scores. Here a variance of more than four points is worthy of discussion.

A final way of discussing the FIRO-B is most useful in teambuilding OD. In this case an interpretation is made of the fit between the profiles of two persons. For example, the expressed control of one person is compared to the wanted control of the other and the compatibility of their behavior then can become a subject for discussion. Figure 2.6 indicates some interpersonal compatibility score patterns on the FIRO-B for two managers named Bill and Jack. The individual FIRO-B scores for Bill and Jack are shown and a reciprocal compatibility figure is computed in the manner shown. It can be seen that the reciprocal compatibility of these two managers is 5 in total score but if we look at the I, C, and A scores all of these are less than 5 and indicate generally high compatibility between the two. In this particular example it is interesting to compare the control scores of both Bill and Jack because it appears that Jack's expressed need for control is extemely high

Figure 2.6 Some Interpersonal Compatibility Score Patterns on the FIRO-B

Bill

	I	C	A
E	2	2	2
W	3	4	4

Jack

	I	C	A
E	3	7	4
W	4	1	3

RC (Reciprocal Compatibility)

RC = (BILL's E − JACK'S W) + (JACK'S E − BILL'S W)
RC = (6 − 8) + (14 − 11) = 2 + 3 = 5

I (2 − 4) + (3 − 3) = 2
C (2 − 1) + (7 − 4) = 4
A (2 − 3) + (4 − 4) = 1

[0] 6 or above suggests an area of incompatibility to improve upon.
[0] 4 to 10 indicates range of low compatibility.
[0] 0 to 3 indicates high compatibility.
[0] Bill and Jack are very compatible.

Source: Adapted from Pfeiffer and Heslin, Ref. 29, pp. 148–151.

whereas Bill's is rather low. On the other hand, Bill's desire to be controlled by another is sufficiently high so that he could probably relate rather well to Jack.

It should be obvious that there are many ways in which the FIRO-B can be utilized in a teambuilding situation in order to deal with issues that are common in interpersonal relations in work organizations. The literature on the subject provides many interesting examples of analysis that can be consulted. Articles by Underwood and Krafft, Hill, and Varney and Hunady should be scrutinized for theoretical data on application of the FIRO–B.[44]

The FIRO-B should be used as an exercise as well as a feedback device. We have already seen how the FIRO-Bs can be used for assigning individuals to teams. It is useful to do this and then follow up with an exercise that has the team members exchange their FIRO-B scores with one another and discuss their own opinions of whether their FIRO-B scores fit themselves as they perceive themselves. Such a discussion is useful at a very early stage of a teambuilding effort in obtaining some practice with feedback, especially if a presentation of the Johari Window has preceded the administration of the FIRO-B. Thus the FIRO-B scores can be exchanged with one another and discussed. Then the group can be given the task of deciding what they would do if they were asked to supervise or be supervised by individuals who have highly incompatible FIRO-B scores. The team can be allocated 20 minutes to discuss their own scores and 20 minutes to discuss their response towards the incompatibility issue. They can be directed to reduce their conclusions to newsprint (or large sheets of "butcher paper"). The comments can then be posted on the wall of the training site where the seminar/workshops are taking place and subsequently debriefed. The result of this experience can be to get started on feedback and help individuals become more conscious of their interpersonal and incipient managerial styles. In fact, we advocate an early explanation of the Johari Window, FIRO-B, and the use of the exercises discussed in order to heighten the self-awareness of the individuals undergoing the teambuilding effort and lay a useful groundwork for discussions of managerial styles, the grid, and other instruments that are helpful in the unfreezing process.

Conclusion

In this chapter we have considered selected types of data-gathering and concepts of instrumentation in OD. The intent has been to set forth an approach, the reasoning, and an explanation of certain useful instruments. References were made to alternatives and limitations and advantages to the approach proposed.

The key points are as follows. If the OD team facilitator is working from an OD $\rightarrow$ MBO $\rightarrow$ RS model, he should begin his effort by starting to unblock the individual participants and encouraging the unfreezing of their behavior. A way of doing this is to explain his orientation to management and indicate his own values. The OD facilitator thereby creates a model of openness and value clarification and provides a baseline to which a group undergoing teambuilding can compare themselves. He next offers a useful way of exploring self–other patterns and legitimizing feedback, by utilizing, in particular the Johari Window, although there are perhaps other schematics capable of making the same point. Finally, he introduces notions about instrumentation in OD and starts the feedback and experiential learning process by the administration of FIRO-Bs. These can also be used creatively for assigning groups of individuals to five-person teams if that is desired unless it is decided that other bases are preferable.

By the time a group has experienced these efforts at unblocking, unfreezing, formal teambuilding, and completed some tasks in exercises it is probably prepared for a change of pace and some cognitive inputs from applied behavioral science, to which we turn in the next chapter.

Notes

1. Kurt Lewin, *Resolving Social Conflicts,* Harper and Row, New York, 1948, pp. 56–70, 201–216. See also: Alfred J. Marrow, *The Practical Theorist: The Life and Work of Kurt Lewin,* Columbia University, Teachers College Press, 1969, pp. 168–172 and *passim.*

2. William Foote Whyte and Edith Lentz Hamilton, *Action Research for Management,* Irwin, Homewood, IL, 1974, is an early case study OD report relevant here.

3. Richard Beckhard, *Organization Development: Strategies and Models,* Addison–Wesley, Reading, MA, 1969; Richard Beckhard and Reuben T. Harris, *Organizational Transitions: Managing Complex Change,* Addison–Wesley, Reading, MA, 1977.

4. Wendell French and Cecil H. Bell, Jr., *Organizational Development: Behavioral Science Interventions for Organizational Improvement,* Prentice–Hall, Englewood Cliffs, NJ, 1973.

5. See for example, Raymond E. Miles, "Organization Development," in George Strauss et al., Eds., *Organizational Behavior Research and Issues,* Industrial Relations Research Association, Madison, WI, 1974, pp. 165–191; George Strauss, "Organization Development," in Robert Dubin, Ed., *Handbook of Work, Organization, and Society,* Rand McNally, Chicago, 1976, pp. 617–685; Thomas H. Patten, Jr., and Peter B. Vaill, "Organization Development," in Robert L. Craig, Ed., *Training and Development Handbook,* 2nd ed., McGraw–Hill, New York, 1976, pp. 20-3–20-21; Michael Beer, "The Technology of Organization Development," in Marvin D. Dunnette, Ed., *Handbook of Industrial and Organizational Psychology,* Rand McNally, Chicago, 1976, pp. 937–993.

6. Chris Argyris, *Intervention Theory and Method: A Behavioral Science View*, Addison–Wesley, Reading, MA, 1970, pp. 127–216 and *passim*.

7. David A. Nadler, *Feedback and Organization Development: Using Data-Based Methods*, Addison–Wesley, Reading, MA, 1977; David G. Bowers, *Systems of Organization*, University of Michigan Press, Ann Arbor, 1976.

8. Rensis Likert, *New Patterns of Management*, McGraw–Hill, New York, 1961, pp. 222–248; Rensis Likert, *The Human Organization: Its Management and Value*, McGraw–Hill, New York, 1967, pp. 196–229; more recently Rensis Likert and Jane Gibson Likert, *New Ways of Managing Conflict*, McGraw–Hill, New York, 1976, pp. 82–86.

9. Walter R. Mahler, *Diagnostic Studies*, Addison–Wesley, Reading, MA, 1974, pp. 1–156.

10. Gordon L. Lippitt, *Organization Renewal*, Prentice–Hall, Englewood Cliffs, NJ, 1969, pp. 63–97.

11. The notion of organizational health is an elaboration of material from Beckhard, *Organization Development: Strategies and Models, op. cit.*, pp. 9–19.

12. The notion of stance is explained in more detail in: Thomas H. Patten, Jr., "Team Building. Part 2. Conducting the Intervention," *Personnel*, Vol. 56, No. 2, March–April, 1979, pp. 63–66.

13. Lippitt, *op. cit.*, pp. 63–99. See also for an extended treatment Gordon L. Lippitt, *Visualizing Change: Model Building and the Change Process*, University Associates, LaJolla, CA, *passim*.

14. Beckhard, *Organization Development: Strategies and Models, op. cit.*, pp. 93–115.

15. Charles Kepner and Benjamin Tregoe, *The Rational Manager*, McGraw–Hill, New York, 1965, pp. 7–228.

16. Warren G. Bennis and Edgar H. Schein, *Personal and Organizational Change Through Group Methods: The Laboratory Approach*, Wiley, New York, 1965.

17. Robert Dubin, "Industrial Workers' Worlds: A Study of the 'Central Life Interests' of Industrial Workers," *Social Problems*, Vol. 3, No. 3, January 1956, pp. 131–142.

18. Richard E. Byrd, *A Guide to Personal Risk Taking*, AMACOM, New York, 1974, *passim*.

19. See, for example, Harold Koontz and Cyril O'Donnell, *Principles of Management: An Analysis of Managerial Functions*, McGraw–Hill,

New York, 1972 and/or Ernest Dale, *Management: Theory and Practice,* McGraw–Hill, New York, 1965.

20. Max Weber, *The Theory of Economic and Social Organization* (translated by A. M. Henderson and Talcott Parsons), Oxford University Press, New York, 1947, pp. 324–386. See also Robert K. Merton et al., Eds., *Reader in Bureaucracy,* Free Press, Glencoe, IL, 1952, for a series of articles on the problems of large-scale organizations.

21. The failure of OD in the rigid hidebound confines of the U.S. Department of State is thoroughly explained by William Crockett, "Introducing Change in a Government Agency," in Philip Mirvis and David N. Berg, Eds., *Failures in Organizational Development and Change,* Wiley, New York, 1977, pp. 111–147.

22. Joseph Luft, *Group Processes, An Introduction to Group Dynamics,* 2nd ed., Mayfield, Palo Alto, CA, 1970, pp. 11–20.

23. Richard Dewey, "Charles Horton Cooley: Pioneer in Psychosociology," in Harry Elmer Barnes, Ed., *An Introduction to the History of Sociology,* University of Chicago Press, Chicago, 1948, pp. 833–852.

24. Much of this summary of the Johari Window is based upon Phillip C. Hanson, "The Johari Window: A Model for Soliciting and Giving Feedback," in John E. Jones and J. William Pfeiffer, Eds., *The 1973 Annual Handbook for Group Facilitators,* University Associates, Iowa City, 1973, pp. 114–119.

25. See the works of Likert cited in note 8.

26. William Foote Whyte, "Interviewing for Organizational Research," *Human Organization,* Vol. 12, No. 2, Summer 1953, pp. 15–22.

27. Jack K, Fordyce and Raymond Weil, *Managing With People: A Manager's Handbook of Organization Development Methods,* Addison–Wesley, Reading, MA, 1971.

28. See note 9.

29. J. William Pfeiffer and Richard Heslin, *Instrumentation in Human Relations Training,* University Associates, Iowa City, IA, 1973, p. vii. Much of what follows is based upon pp. vii–ix, 7–17 in this important book.

30. FIRO-B is an instrument that provides a measure of the Fundamental Interpersonal Orientation in terms of one's Behavior, hence the intitials FIRO-B, pronounced Fī - rō - bee.

31. I use the terms facilitator, group or team or OD facilitator, consultant, renewal stimulator, and change agent interchangeably in this book. These are names for individuals who make conscious efforts to alter the

status quo in organizations, that is, change some aspect of a work culture in order to improve it in ways perceived to be consistent with normative ideas derived from applied behavioral science. Those individuals who are employed by a work organization in this role and have employee payroll status are said to be "internal" facilitators whereas persons hired from the outside to consult or provide OD services and do not have employee status are "external" facilitators.

32. Pfeiffer and Heslin, *op. cit.*, pp. 139–151.

33. *Ibid.*, pp. 7–8.

34. *Ibid.*, pp. 8–11.

35. *Ibid.*, pp. 11–13.

36. *Ibid.*, pp. 13–14.

37. *Ibid.*, pp. 14–17.

38. *Ibid.*, p. 19.

39. *Ibid.*, p. 20. For more detail see William C. Schutz, *The Interpersonal Underworld*, Consulting Psychologists Press, Palo Alto, CA, 1966; also see his well-known article, "The Interpersonal Underworld," *Harvard Business Review*, Vol. 36, No. 4, July–August 1958, pp. 123–135.

40. Schutz, *The Interpersonal Underworld, op. cit.*, pp. 132–134.

41. Pfeiffer and Heslin, op. cit., pp. 140–141.

42. See William J. Underwood and Larry J. Krafft, "Interpersonal Compatibility and Managerial Work Effectiveness: A Test of the Fundamental Interpersonal Relations Orientation Theory," *Journal of Applied Psychology*, Vol. 58, No. 1, August 1973, pp. 89–94; Raymond E. Hill, "Interpersonal Compatibility and Workgroup Performance," *Journal of Applied Behavioral Science*. Vol. 11, No. 2, April–May–June 1975, pp. 210–219; Glenn H. Varney and Ronald J. Hunady, "Energizing Commitment to Change in a Team-Building Intervention: A FIRO-B Approach," *Group and Organization Studies*, Vol. 3, No. 4, December 1978, pp. 435–446.

43. Ideas about how to use the FIRO-B in an OD mode can be obtained from perusing: William C. Schutz, *The FIRO Scales Manual*, Consulting Psychologists Press, Palo Alto, CA, 1967; and Leo Robert Ryan, *Clinical Interpretation of the FIRO-B*, 1977 ed., Consulting Psychologists Press, Palo Alto, CA, 1977.

44. See footnote 42.

chapter 3

MANAGEMENT STYLES AND ORGANIZATIONAL TEAMS

We have already seen that there are insights from the behavioral sciences that can be used by the practicing manager to improve his performance both as an individual contributor and team member. The behavioral sciences have evolved rapidly in recent years and presently have many insights to offer both in thinking about and practicing the managerial role.

Persons who are undergoing an OD teambuilding effort need a theory base to understand why they should consider moving from one managerial style to another in order to incorporate the insights of the behavioral sciences for their benefit. Older managers often become comfortable in continuing what they consider to be successful managerial styles of the past by applying them to their present situations. They particularly need to approach teambuilding in a way that enables them to compare what they have experienced with new ways in which they could behave.

It is often useful to present not only older managers but younger ones with a conception of healthy and unhealthy organizations at an early stage of a teambuilding effort, as was pointed out in Chapter 2. They should understand, of course, that the term "health" when applied to an organization is a useful metaphor in planning for change, or, as Argyris would put it, for understanding how to move from xA to yB.[1] Although we probably know more about the health of individuals than the health of organizations, there is value in discussing organizational health because the overwhelming consistency in thinking about the components of a healthful, effective, efficient work culture, despite the variation in terminology among behavioral scientists, is impressive and persuasive.

Specifically, a large number of contemporary thinkers, coming from different backgrounds and points of view, have in their writings arrived at similar conclusions regarding effectiveness in managerial style and the treatment of employees.

In this chapter these similarities in thinking and focus are explored, particularly as they relate to Levinson's conception of man, one that is consonant with much other thinking and yet integrative and original. From this conception I then indicate my own notions of human behavior and suggest exercises that can be utilized in the first phase of a teambuilding effort to give managers additional feedback on themselves, their own styles, and some practice in trying out new styles.

Maslow and The Prepotency of Needs Theory

I begin by mentioning the late Abraham H. Maslow, who was trained in psychology and has probably been one of the most quoted men in the field of psychology. Maslow, beginning in the 1940s and 1950s, formulated the theory of the prepotency of needs in human beings. He pointed out that man is a creature with needs, certain of which remain forever unfulfilled. He also indicated that man works to satisfy his present needs according to their importance in a kind of hierarchical manner, being what he refers to as "lower-order" and "higher-order" needs. The lower order are needs that are essentially physiological or have to do with individual safety or security. The higher order are social needs or deal with the individual's ego needs or with his self-fulfillment (sometimes called his self-actualization).[2]

People are thus initially motivated to think in terms of whether their physiological needs are met or not. If their physiological needs are not met, they are motivated to fulfill them. If their physiological needs are met, they are motivated by their safety needs. If their safety needs are met, they are then motivated by their social needs and so on up the line as shown in Figure 3.1. The needs are prepotent in a hierarchical sense, and the lower-order needs must be met before people are capable of being motivated on a higher level.[3]

In making a very rough cut at considering the need levels of people in the United States, Maslow estimated that approximately 85% of the needs at the physiological level are met but only 10% at the self-fulfillment or self-actualization level are met. Figure 3.1 shows other estimated percentages of need-fulfillment for the various needs but it is doubtful Maslow or anyone could defend the estimates very specifically.

We should take a closer look at the various needs shown in Figure 3.1, although they are almost self-explanatory. The physiological needs pertain to food, clothing, shelter, dress, air, and water. They are all tied into physical survival; if one considers it, most of these needs could be satisfied by money, in the sense that with money, one can buy a certain type of food, a specific type of clothing, a distinctive type of housing, and so on. The second level (or safety needs) are those that provide protection against danger or against threats to one personally such as unemployment, discrimination, and favoritism. These would be needs that also tie into individual security. They would be related to one's reference group, that is, to the group that the person considers himself as belonging to or wanting to belong to.

The third or social need relates to belonging and being trusted, either on

A Hierarchy of Needs
Lower-order and higher-order needs
Lower are prepotent as motivators
Five categories or levels of needs

Basic or physiological	85%	
Safety	70%	% of needs satisfied
Social or belonging	50%	(United States)
Ego or status	40%	
Self-actualization	10%	

Figure 3.1 A heirarchy of needs. Lower–order and higher–order needs. Lower are prepotent as motivators. There are five categories or levels of needs. The percent of needs satisfied in the United States: basic or physiological, 85%; safety, 70%; social or belonging, 50%; ego or status, 40%; self–actualization, 10%. (**Source:**   adapted from Sandra L. Pfeiffer, ''The Maslow Need Hierarchy,'' in J. William Pfeiffer and John E. Jones, eds., *The 1972 Handbook for Group Facilitators*, University Associates, Iowa City, IA, 1972 pp. 125–126. Statistical data source unknown.)

the job or off the job, probably in many cases on the job. Again, many of the social needs could be satisfied by money.

The fourth level are the ego needs; these are the needs for self-respect, achievement of status, personal recognition, and the esteem of others. These refer to the need for the mastery of something, whether that be a hobby, a skill, an occupation, or an occupational role. The ego needs are continuous and probably never cease to motivate an individual. Levinson, another previously mentioned writer in this field, emphasizes this point very strongly in a number of his publications. Pay can be readily related to an individual's sense of self-worth. Managers who have a lot of money still seem to want more, as Drucker has pointed out, in contradiction to much conventional wisdom in the field of compensation.[4] Such individuals certainly do not need the money for subsistence but they seem to regard it as something to keep score by—making more money than their neighbor or friend or some other individual in their reference group.

The last Maslovian need is the need for self-fulfillment or self-actualization. This is the need to reach one's potential and be self-actualized, which is seldom attained.[5] Whether Maslow's 10% figure is right is debatable; even in a case where self-actualization takes place, it is nevertheless possible that money could be a motivator in that it can remove obstacles to self-actualization. Money alone will not make a person self-actualized, but it does allow many individuals the freedom to devote their time to activities that are potentially self-actualizing, something they would be unable to do if they lacked the money. Such individuals probably have come to the realization that time is the most meaningful resource in life—or indeed life itself—and they prize being in total control of it, which the possession of wealth might make possible.

Taking a quick look at Maslow's contributions, we can quickly discern that, regarding motivation, the various needs are interdependent and overlapping. Needs can be categorized, but some appear to fall between the categories. Maslow indicates that most people are partially satisfied and are partially dissatisfied in each area.

The theory is useful because the level of needs of each employee can be viewed individually. There are apt to be employees in an organization who are so concerned with their physiological and their safety needs that all they really want is a secure or steady job, security or seniority rights on the job, and security of tenure in employment. They prize seniority, and they want a mechanism to provide them justice in the workplace through a grievance procedure. That is all they want; they do not want a promotion; they do not actively aspire to rise in the organization.

Knowledge of Maslow's heuristic scheme of certain levels of need satisfaction can be potentially helpful to a foreman, supervisor, or higher executive. This knowledge can assist a manager in understanding employee motivation and enable him to hypothesize as to what need level a specific employee occupies at a particular time. On the other hand, if top management attempts to motivate an executive by constructing a motivational appeal to him at the physiological or safety level and his goal is to be self-fulfilled or he has extreme social needs, top management may be making the wrong kind of appeal. However, an executive can be reduced to concern at the physiological need level if a reduction in force is imminent and he perceives no equal employment alternative for himself. This was dramatically portrayed in the 1974–75 and 1980 economic recessions in the United States.

Thus, the Maslow hierarchy may be viewed as a useful conceptual tool. However, we should also recall that the motivation of need fulfillment can, in theory, be monetized at each level. Money apparently fits into the satisfaction of all those different needs in a certain sense. This is why organizational reward systems are such important parts of teambuilding OD efforts.

The Maslow scheme makes intuitive sense in the overall but it is so general and apparently universally applicable that it is probably too loose and requires further research. The truth of the matter is that his theory has been very widely accepted and has apparently moved beyond theory into a kind of dogma or doctrine in contemporary applied behavioral science.

McGregor and Theory *X* and Theory *Y*

Turning to another important behavioral theory, we next consider Douglas McGregor and his Theory X and Theory Y. McGregor was very interested in trying to set forth two prevalent and opposite beliefs about human nature and certain kinds of resulting managerial behavior. His conceptualization eventually has become common coin in management thinking about employee motivation and it too perhaps has become a doctrine.

In one of his books McGregor calls the theory embodying X and Y concepts a cosmology, or, in other words, a world view or a set of assumptions about people more than a theory.[6] Figure 3.2 summarizes the difference between Theory X and Theory Y. Essentially, McGregor questioned the assumptions managers held about people in which managers believed that employees were essentially lazy and unmotivated; that is, unless something was done to activate them they would tend to perform indifferently on the job. The latter was the traditional assumption which he called Theory X and the assumptions that he thought were better mirrors of the true nature of man he called Theory Y. Teambuilding is very much founded conceptually on Theory Y.

McGregor also built on Maslow's prepotency theory that man continuously works to satisfy his needs in their order of importance to him, that is, the idea discussed earlier that when needs are satisfied at one level a person is capable of having his motivations shift to a higher order. He also pointed

Figure 3.2 Douglas McGregor's Theory X and Theory Y Cosmologies

Theory X assumptions	Theory Y assumptions
People by nature:	People by nature:
1. Lack integrity.	1. Have integrity.
2. Are fundamentally lazy and desire to work as little as possible.	2. Work hard toward objectives to which they are committed.
3. Avoid responsibility.	3. Assume responsibility within these commitments.
4. Are not interested in achievement.	4. Desire to achieve.
5. Are incapable of directing their own behavior.	5. Are capable of directing their own behavior.
6. Are indifferent to organizational needs.	6. Want their organization to succeed.
7. Prefer to be directed by others.	7. Are not passive and submissive.
8. Avoid making decisions whenever possible.	8. Will make decisions within their commitments.
9. Are not very bright.	9. Are not stupid.

Source: M. Scott Myers, *Every Employee A Manager*, McGraw-Hill, New York, 1970, p. 29.

out, as did Maslow, that a satisfied need ceases to motivate a person. Therefore, to motivate someone we must find out his motivational level and make a proper appeal at that level. McGregor thought that in management, at least, we need a new way to appeal to unmet needs, and he urged managers to manage according to Theory Y assumptions.

Put another way, McGregor thought that managers should believe that the expenditure of physical and mental effort at work is as natural as play or rest for a human being. He also believed that external control and the threat of punishment were not the only ways to solicit employee effort, as many managers have traditionally thought.[7] Of course, pioneers in industrial engineering, such as Frederick W. Taylor, built their systems around Theory X assumptions. McGregor also thought that managers should believe that employees are likely to exercise their own self-direction and their own self-control to attain goals to which they are personally committed.

Building upon some earlier ideas of Peter Drucker, McGregor advocated a management-by-objectives approach to performance review that was Theory Y in concept. The Theory Y idea runs through all his thinking.[8] McGregor also stated that commitment to job objectives is related to rewards connected with their achievement.[9] This kind of idea was later extended to models developed by a number of other contemporary psychologists.

McGregor proselytized that the manager should believe that *many* people in work organizations can solve problems, not only the boss but employees at various levels in the work organization. This is the kind of idea that has subsequently become very popular in OD, namely, that problems should be solved by the employees that are close to them in work flow and assignment and have the greatest knowledge of the job. This is also, of course, an idea that Rensis Likert advocates in his writings. The notion of teambuilding is inherent in all this thinking.

McGregor strongly stressed the idea that human potential as we understand it is only partly tapped. There is a great deal more human potential in employees into which managers can tap if they would only change their assumptions about people and the way in which they relate to them. Furthermore, this potential can best be unleashed under Theory Y assumptions about human resource management.

McGregor uses the labels Theory X and Theory Y simply to make his cosmological theory neutral. We can find these same assumptions about humanity way back in the thinking of American political writers and belle-lettrists as has been documented in Parrington's classical work. For example, this kind of speculation is very much like the thinking of Alexander Hamilton (Theory X) and that of Thomas Jefferson (Theory Y). One is the low and the other is the high view of human nature.[10]

In summary, McGregor suggests that it is better managerially to think that employees have integrity than that they lack this trait. It is better to think that people will work hard towards attaining objectives than to assume the opposite, namely, that they are fundamentally lazy and that they want to work as little as possible. It is better to believe that people want to assume responsibility than it is to assume they want to avoid it. It is more satisfactory to think people have a desire to achieve than have no interest in achievement. It is preferable to assume that they are capable of directing their own behavior than it is to assume that they require direction, that they are not passive and submissive but capable of being very active, and that they can make decisions within their own spheres and develop commitment rather than avoid decisions and commitments. It is better to believe that if they are not very bright at least they are not stupid, that human beings are a resource, that they vary, and that there are individual differences. Once these individual differences are recognized, they can be made available for organizational goal attainment. In a way, these beliefs are the cornerstones of the human resource management philosophy that has been spreading throughout the United States in the past decade.

There are many organizations in the United States today that are run by Theory X assumptions. The typical organization that has a very heavy investment in plant and equipment or assembly-line types of operations is very much built upon Theory X. For costs and other reasons it is very difficult to introduce a Theory Y kind of orientation there because Theory X is essentially an industrial engineering concept and has historically fitted the factory world very well. It assumes that employees are likely to be lazy and need a great deal of guidance. It also assumes much planning has to be done by management in the layout of the plant and that virtually everything in production and maintenance has to be anticipated. Implicitly, it assumes that the workers are really employed only because management has not as yet been able to engineer everything perfectly and have all operations mechanized or automated. Put another way, the fallibility and limitations of the machines make employees necessary! This is why many organizations appear to have Theory X built in as a *modus operandi* and are reluctant to move into Theory Y, even though it might be more desirable from a doctrinal or philosophical standpoint or on the basis of behavioral science research. However, it is worth noting that even organizations as apparently committed to Theory X as the U. S. Army and the Federal bureaucracy have mellowed and attempted to move in Theory Y directions through the utilization of organizational development programs.[11]

Herzberg and Two-Factor Theory

Frederick Herzberg, a professor at the University of Utah, has made some very widely acclaimed contributions to behavioral science in the last three decades. He started his intellectual work with a strong interest in job satisfaction[12] and in recent years has moved most of his interest into the area of job enrichment.[13] His early research was concerned essentially with employees in white-collar occupations, such as engineers and accountants, and the research was based upon job satisfaction attitude surveys of these kinds of people. He concluded as a consequence of his early and subsequent job satisfaction surveys that motivation to work was associated with job content; it was intrinsic to the job itself. If this factor were present, people could be satisfied with their work and would be motivated. However, there was another factor that he called "maintenance" or "hygiene" that could result in employee dissatisfaction. The two factors are, of course, the reason Herzberg's theory is known by the name indicated above.

According to Herzberg, the motivational factor that pertains to job content or intrinsic matters encourages an employee to be more creative and more productive. It pertains only to the job itself and appeals to the employee's higher-order need to grow. These are needs located in the upper part of the Maslovian hierarchical scale and include achievement, recognition, the work itself, opportunities for advancement, and responsibility. If these items are *absent* from the job, they prevent an employee from being satisfied, that is, "job-satisfied."

On the other hand, the *presence* of the maintenance factor (or hygiene, environmental factor) can do very little to motivate an employee to be productive or creative at work or to satisfy him. The factor pertains to job context and essentially appeals to the lower-order Maslovian needs—physiological, safety, and the like. The factor includes such variables as company policy and its administration, supervision, the social relations between supervisors, subordinates, and peers, amount of salary, and working conditions. If all these are present and accepted by employees, they prevent dissatisfaction, but if they are *absent,* they cause dissatisfaction and low morale.

Figure 3.3 displays a summary of Herzberg's dissatisfiers or the items that led to dissatisfaction and the satisfiers or items that led to satisfaction based upon a number of studies. The figure elaborates upon the discussion above in the chapter.

There has been much written about Herzberg's work and it is consequently difficult both to evaluate it and other behavioral scientists' views of it. First, the idea of satisfiers and dissatisfiers sounds like double talk and is quite confusing. Second, many serious observers believe Herzberg has not given sufficient attention to the role of salary as a motivating force, particularly when the way salaries are administered rather than the amount of salary itself is considered. Third, some methodologists question how he analyzed and presented his data, denying the plausibility and validity of the two factors *per se*.[14]

It is worth examining in more detail where salaries show up in Herzberg's thinking, particularly because of his belief that there is not much that can be done about changing the work environment in order to motivate an employee. In Chapter 2 it was noted that many employees in America, both managerial and nonmanagerial, obtain their prime satisfaction in off-the-job non-job-related activities. We can see that for employees who occupy jobs

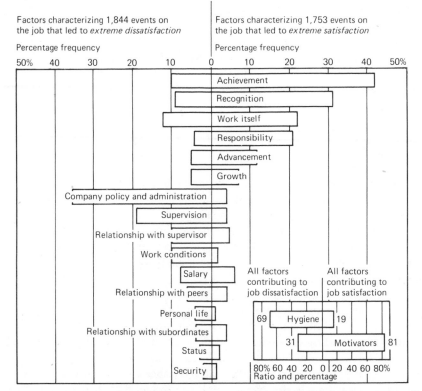

Figure 3.3 Factors characterizing events on the job: 1844 that led to extreme dissatisfaction and 1753 that led to extreme satisfaction. (**Source:** Frederick W. Herzberg, "One More Time: How Do You Motivate Employees?" *Harvard Business Review*, Vol. 46, No. 1, January–February, 1968, p. 57. Reprinted by permission of the *Harvard Business Review*. Copyright © 1968 by the President and Fellows of Harvard College; all rights reserved.)

that demand performance and provide for achievement, growth, and responsibility—with a supervisor who can plan, evaluate, and reward good work (including monetary rewards)—the work itself can be motivational. However, it seems that neither Herzberg nor many other researchers who have tested behavioral science theories about pay have ever compared the actual intrafirm administration of pay as a variable in their studies. For Herzberg, pay may be showing up as a dissatisfier because it was poorly administered in the firms included in the surveys. If it were administered differently and consistently as a reinforcer of performance, it could very well have turned out to be a satisfier. This observation certainly deserves testing and is a fundamental belief of the author of this book.

As far as Herzberg is concerned, motivation to perform is not possible for many low-level jobs in Theory X bureaucratic organizations. This kind of general reasoning has apparently moved Herzberg from the study of job satisfaction into his newly found interest in job enrichment.[15] He now feels that if an employer wants to motivate employees and possesses the kinds of low-level narrow jobs that are endemic in a bureaucracy, that he must reexamine the jobs themselves and enrich them so that the possibilities for motivation can be reinstalled in jobs. The mention of this subject—job enrichment—brings us to the contributions of another contemporary behavioral scientist.

Myers and Job Enrichment

Following from Herzberg and perhaps antedating him in terms of an interest in job enrichment is the work of M. Scott Myers at Texas Instruments. At an early stage of his career Myers' interest in job enrichment was very narrowly limited to enriching jobs by giving employees more of a supervisory say in their work than had previously been the case. As time passed, however, Texas Instruments took the position that if employees were to be motivated, the job enrichment program would have to go beyond merely making jobs richer in content and more challenging by restoring to employees some planning and control functions—they would also have to be given a greater total voice in the management of the organization. This Myers discusses creating a motivational climate in a firm where there is a feeling of achievement and an opportunity for self-actualization, where there is an opportunity to become interpersonally competent and a chance for the individual to work towards attaining goals, for every employee to feel part of the team.

In the days of industrial engineering, particularly among pioneers such as Frederick W. Taylor, there was interest in trying to separate the planning from the operational aspects of the work, and assigning the planning kind of work to the staff and operational kind of work to the line. The industrial engineers carried that distinction to the point where they had a difference amounting to a gulf between planning and doing, with the staffs assigning the planning and controlling work to themselves. Over the years at Texas Instruments, management has been trying to build back into as many jobs as possible the planning and controlling responsibilities. In this way the job becomes enriched and psychologically enlarged, and the employee can feel closer to the company.

Texas Instruments has also taken in a number of other actions in organizational development. Since the late 1960s, it has apparently tried to reorganize the managerial style of the company around problem-solving committees so that individuals can get some feel for what their own unit is doing in terms of financial performance. They also have widespread use of task forces in their problem-solving and goal-setting programs. They have instituted many employee meetings at which suggestions are discussed, plus an extensive kind of committee system that gets employees heavily involved in thinking about problems and proposing solutions.[16]

There is a great deal of theoretical compatibility between Myers and Herzberg on job enrichment. However, job enrichment is not exactly the same thing programmatically to Herzberg and Myers. Myers sees ultimate job enrichment as a total kind of change in management style and organizational development but both are interested in concepts of job enrichment. Myers suggests the teambuilding aspect.

McClelland and Achievement Motivation

Another psychological theorist concerned with motivation and, in part, money as a motivator to perform at work is David C. McClelland of Harvard University who has spent many years investigating what he calls "achievement motivation." He has extensively looked into only one motive in human motivation and that is the individual's need to achieve.

The need for achievement was supposedly found in many people and was something that developed as a consequence of their socialization and rearing. Through their family upbringing, they learned to desire success and accomplishment and to delight in taking circumscribed risks. They were not disposed to unwise wide-open risk-taking but rather to moderate and challenging risks.

He characterized these people as having a need for achievement ("nAch," in his symbolism). McClelland contrasts nAch with the need that other people have for affiliation ("nAff"), which was extensively researched by Stanley Schacter, whom we need not discuss here.[17]

He also makes a distinction between the need for achievement and need for power. The need for achievement hinges on the need that the achiever has to perform effectively in his work, whereas the need for power (nP) is the need to control the behavior of other people at work.

McClelland believes that nAch people require immediate feedback on performance and that they are interested in performing as well as getting feedback. Most managers are high in nAch, and for them monetary rewards have a special significance. Specifically, they believe in greater financial rewards for increasing accomplishments at work.

There have been difficulties in investigating achievement motivation, and McClelland believes that we cannot take at face value what most people say about their motives. However, if we want to test for achievement motivation, the way to do it is to use a certain kind of test, particularly the Thematic Apperception Test, where we can pick out how people interpret achievement and the degree of interest they express in it. This test allows us to obtain a measure of hidden motives. McClelland thinks that the need for achievement can be stimulated in individuals, and he has tried to do this for people through a training program at Harvard University that need not be described here.[18] He also discusses the possibility of generating this type of achievement among minority groups and in underdeveloped and developing countries.[19]

McClelland's early and recent contributions to teambuilding are indirect. He suggests that capable managers are not motivated by a need for personal aggrandizement or by an nAff requirement to get along with subordinates. Rather, they have a need to influence others' behavior for the good of the entire organization. They want power but are not authoritarian in its use.[20] They have sufficient maturity and self-control so that nP, nAch, and nAff flow together in a team-oriented style of managing, as that term (team) is being used in this book.

Likert: Linking Pin and System 4 Theory

Rensis Likert, now retired but for many years Director of the Institute for Social Research at the University of Michigan and a preeminent American industrial and organizational psychologist, has both a normative and descriptive theory in which teambuilding and OD can be fitted. He combines a method for measuring the characteristics of an organization with a prescription for the ideal state of the organization and a formula for moving the organization from its actual state to the ideal state in his theoretical notions, which amounts to a top to bottom team-built organization. Figure 3.4 portrays this conception.

Likert and his colleagues over the years developed a variety of questionnaires—typically ranging from 50 to 100 items that graphically portray what he calls the management system. The questionnaire includes a

Figure 3.4 Characteristic Style Overlays of Four Different Management Systems

	System 1	System 2	System 3	System 4
Leadership				
Motivational forces				
Communication processes	Exploitative and Authoritarian	Benevolent and Authoritarian		
Interaction and influence				Participative Group
Decision-making			Consultative	
Goal-setting and ordering				
Control processes				

Source: Adapted from Rensis Likert, *The Human Organization*, New York, McGraw–Hill, 1967, pp. 4–10.

cluster of factors such as structures, controls, and leadership behavior plus the attitudes, motivations, and perceptions of employees. Everyone in the organization or organizational components being studied completes the questionnaire.[21]

From these data Likert prepared a profile of organizational characteristics that enabled him to identify the organization as being what he called System 1, 2, 3, or 4. System 1 is labeled Exploitative—Authoritarian; System 2, Benevolent—Authoritarian; System 3, Consultative; and System 4, Participative—Group. The ideal state is System 4, and by ideal Likert means organizational performance or effectiveness defined in both humanistic terms—maximum employee satisfaction and morale—and the traditional business criteria of performance: maximum output and earnings. Specifically System 4 appears to be consistently associated—in every type of organization Likert studied—with the most effective performance; and System 1, with the least effective performance. System 2 was more effective than System 1 but less effective than System 3. The four Systems are shown in Figure 3.4.

According to Likert, the System 4 type of management is built principally around a participative-supportive climate in an organization where there is much confidence and trust among employees at all organizational levels. Rewards based on compensation in the organization are determined through participation where employees rate one another, and there is consensus as to who should be compensated for performing at a given level.[22] Rewards are not stressed as motivators, however. Performance results from systematic change.

Likert identifies three sets of variables that move an organization to action. There are causal variables, which are factors controlled by managers, such as organizational structure, controls, policies, and leadership behavior. There are intervening variables, such as the attitudes, motivations, and perceptions of all employees. The end-result variables are considerations such as productivity, costs, and profits. His break with traditional theory came first in his insistence that there is no direct linear relationship between managerial actions and organizational end results; this was followed by his insistence that the only way to affect either employee attitudes or organizational success is to change managerial behavior.

The manipulation of incentives and pay is not seen as vital for managerial performance. It is useless to attack either the intervening or end-result variables directly. This brings us back to managerial behavior and how to move into a System 4 mode whereby employees will be satisfied and perform.

The System 4 organization is held together by people who hold overlapping memberships, who are called "linking pins" between organizational families. Figure 3.5 displays the linking pin notion and other modes of managerial–employee interaction. Linking occurs both vertically and, when necessary, laterally, in order to achieve effective coordination in large complex organizations. In System 4 there is much individual and group com-

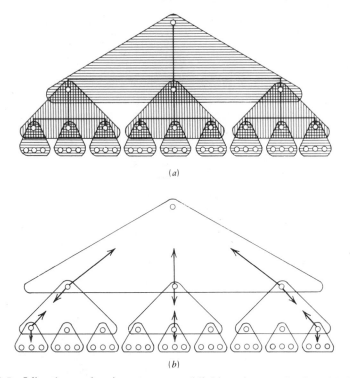

(a)

(b)

Figure 3.5 Likert's overlapping patterns and linking pin organization. (a) Overlapping group form of organization where work teams consist of four people. (b) The arrows indicate the linking pin function. (**Source:** Rensis Likert, *New Patterns of Management*, McGraw–Hill, New York, 1961, pp. 105, 113.)

munication; decision-making is carried on throughout the organization and is well integrated through the linking process among various levels of management in the organization. Goals are set by participation (except in emergencies). There is responsibility among individuals for reviewing and controlling their own work, much as Myers advocated at Texas Instruments. There are supportive relations between superiors and subordinates. In summary, System 4 goes back to reinstalling more of the managerial activities into actual employee job content that are thought to motivate people—participating, making inputs, communicating, setting goals, peoples' committing themselves to their own work goals, and so on. System 4 is compatible with much recent thinking in the behavioral sciences and Theory Y.

For the future, Likert sees a System 5 replacing System 4. The essential difference between them is that System 4 still carries a fair amount of emphasis on the importance of the authority of the superior. For example, if a manager cannot obtain a consensus among his subordinates and there is a need to act, it is up to him to see that action is taken. System 5 will replace hierarchical authority with an authority of relationships. If a group cannot reach a consensus, the next higher group in management through the linking pin will address the problem and make the decision. The manager in the dilemma cited would use the authority of the higher-level group to which he is linked and his responsibility to the total organization rather than his own positional authority to obtain action. The next higher managerial group would also take the responsibility for rebuilding the group as an effective component unit in the organization and thereby reknit the unwoven team-built structure.[23]

Levinson and the Jackass Fallacy

Harry Levinson is an industrial psychiatrist with yet another perspective on motivation and OD. For many years he was the head of the industrial psychiatry program at the Menninger Clinic and conducted a number of the Menninger Clinic training programs on motivation for executives. He left Menninger and spent five years at the Harvard Business School as a Visiting Professor of Business Administration and has completed some influential writing. He now has his own consulting firm and institute in Massachusetts.

He takes the position that much that is being written in psychology and management today amounts to espousal of what he calls the "jackass fallacy" in motivation. In other words, a kind of reward and punishment model has evolved that is so gross that it should be rejected. Levinson believes that behavioral scientists and managers who advocate the jackass fallacy assume employees are like mules and they further assume employees, consequently, have to be manipulated and pulled. Jackasses, like unmotivated employees, are very stubborn, stupid, willful, and unwilling to move unless they are driven. This is another way of trotting out paternalism and some of the old Theory X assumptions because as long as anyone in management operates with narrow reward–punishment assumptions about motivation, he is implicitly assuming that he has (or should have) control over others and that they are in a jackass position with respect to him.

Jackass theory supporters believe that employees act in a way that is consistent with their beliefs because employees are responding only to the "carrot and stick" model. Employees are trying to get more of the carrot and protect themselves against the stick, or, in other words, to obtain more rewards and forestall the punishments. Similar to many writers, Levinson complains that bureaucratic organizations, which are predominant in our society, further compound the motivational problem by stressing the carrot and stick, which, in turn, leads to widespread defensiveness and other kinds of dysfunctional behavior.[24]

As an alternative, Levinson wants managers, following McGregor, to change their assumptions about people and give up both the carrot and stick and paternalism. The managerial assumptions about motivation in a work organization should be based on the idea that an employee ultimately desires

（Management Styles and Organizational Teams）

most of all to fulfill his evolving ego ideal as a total personality. This is similar to one of the higher-order needs in the Maslovian need hierarchy (self-actualization) and is significantly related to the person's emotional health and his motivation to work.

Levinson considers that the ego ideal is developed by the person out of socialization and interaction with others. In other words, the person develops an ideal for himself or a concept of himself from the way that he was reared in his family, community, school, and early life. Once he has an ego concept in mind, and he works toward fulfilling it, he likes himself. When the individual comes close to attaining the ideal, he is, in fact, very satisfied. When he falls short of it, he becomes very angry with himself and restive.

In order for a person to meet his internal demands, to move towards satisfying the ego ideal, Levinson points out that the individual has to master the sex and aggression drives and his various feelings of love, hate, dependency, and mastery of the environment. Levinson also points out that several general kinds of needs have to be met before a person can move towards his ego ideal: his ministration needs must be satisfied, that is, he must receive care and support from others; his needs for growth and development have to be satisfied; and his mastery needs, for control of his fate in life, have to be attained. Levinson acknowledges that there is considerable variation in the definition of these needs among individuals, but insists that these three needs be given due weight in examining human motivation.

Levinson sees various theories of motivation, some focusing outside the person (such as Theory X), inside the person (such as Theory Y), and a combined inside–outside integrated view, which is his own (see Figure 3.6). Industrial engineers look for outside motivation i.: the form of the carrot and the stick. Supporters of the old human relations view of the 1930s and 1940s

Figure 3.6   Levinson's Summary of Motivation Theory

Theory of motivation	Organizational structure	Ethos	Advocates
Outside	Familial, kinship systems	Economic man	Managers, economists, and industrial engineers
	Bureaucratic	Social man	Old human relations school, 1920–1950
Inside	Project, matrix	Self-actualizing man	Recent humanistic psychologists and organizational development specialists, 1950 to present
Inside–outside	Multiform	Psychological man	Psychoanalytically trained psychologists and psychiatrists

Source: Adapted from Harry Levinson, *The Great Jackass Fallacy*, Harvard University, Graduate School of Business Administration, Cambridge, 1973. p. 32.

look for inside motivation. Many contemporary individual and organizational psychologists have a combined inside–outside view. One's view of the ideal work organization is likely to depend upon one's theory of the wellsprings of motivation.[25] An employee is likely to be team-oriented to the extent he feels it is consistent with his ego ideal.

Comparison of Behavioral Scientists

Figure 3.7 is an attempt to compare on an overall but simplified basis the various views of the previously discussed psychologists concerning human effectiveness. The figure may be construed as displaying in one configuration what types of climates and support systems facilitate effective human behavior in work organizations and effective teambuilding.

It can be seen that when we look from the left to the right on the figure and compare the views of behavioral scientists such as McGregor, Maslow, Herzberg, McClelland, Myers, Likert, and Levinson that they seem to be referring to very much the same phenomena although they use different language to express their ideas. Thus, although here is not the place to attempt to reconcile their minor conflicting points of view and varying terms,

Figure 3.7 Comparison of Seven Theories of Human Effectiveness.

Theorist	Ineffectiveness		Effectiveness	
Abraham Maslow	Lower-need fixation Halted growth		Self-actualization Realizing potential	
Douglas McGregor	Theory X Reductive assumptions		Theory Y Developmental assumptions	
Frederick Herzberg	Environmental comfort ← − − Hygiene seeking − −	− − − − − − − − − − − − − − −	Meaningful work − − −Motivation seeking − →	
David McClelland	Low nACH More interested in affiliation, security, money, and possessions		High nACH Achievement its own primary reward, high challenges, moderate risks, independence	
Rensis Likert	System 1 Exploitative and Authoritarian	System 2 Benevolent and Authoritarian	System 3 Consultative	System 4 Participative group
M. Scott Myers	Separation of doing, planning, and controlling work		Meaningful sharing of the doing, planning, and controlling of work	
Harry Levinson	Economic man ethos		Psychologcial man ethos	

Source: Adapted from M. Scott Myers, *Every Employee a Manager*, New York, McGraw–Hill, 1970, p. 2: Harry Levinson, *The Great Jackass Fallacy,* Harvard University, Graduate School of Business Administration, Cambridge, 1973, pp. 29–33.

it is quite clear that these renowned students of management are essentially in agreement concerning the nature of human effectiveness. Moreover, they have similar ideas about the styles, systems, assumptions, and the like management might use to create employee-motivating incentives.

The importance of the body of theory summarized in Figure 3.7, which has been chosen from an extensive literature—including other,unmentioned authors who came to similar conclusions—is that it has helped overturn much of the thinking about human nature that used to be emphasized in the literature of management. These behavioral scientists have caused us to construct new notions that are now widely known in academic circles and even among practicing managers but that have not as yet been installed in many work organizations. These new notions form the theory base of OD through teambuilding. They point to the path from past, outmoded, and intellectually discredited ideas about management.

Applying Behavioral Science

In the world of complex organizations in which all Americans live and experience the resulting impacts, personal managers, training directors, and human resource experts who function as change agents seek strategies, models, and approaches from the behavioral sciences for consciously altering the *status quo* in the direction of greater individual, organizational, and social health. Words such as trust, authenticity, openness, innovativeness, and a problem-solving, confronting attitude are repeatedly mentioned as missing from much of everyday organizational and industrial life. Change agents typically address these deficiencies in their teambuilding and OD efforts.[26]

When the change agent and client agree substantially on their diagnosis of woes, existing dysfunctions, and imperfections in organizational health, they then begin to jointly plan the manner in which remedial action will be implemented so that the effects will be durable. Some change agents have a diagnostic model that they typically use in deciding on how to proceed in OD. Others are less committed to a characteristic pattern and typically begin by asking themselves questions once they have a fix on the ostensible problems. Should the first intervention be an OD teambuilding thrust? or installation of MBO? or alteration of the reward system? or none of these but instead a training package, policy change, reorganization, new hiring program, and so on, *ad infinitum*. As we have seen, at one time the T-group was widely held to be the only proper way to begin, but OD has now matured beyond this narrow view. Yet there are no certainties about how to strategize. If, for example, the renewal stimulator consults the rapidly amassing literature on OD appearing today in behavioral science, personnel, organizational, and management publications, he could easily be stopped in his tracks by such stern and portentous ukases as the following:

"MBO is yet another technique that requires friendly, helpful superiors, honest and mature subordinates, and high mutual trust. *It works best for those individuals who need it least.*

MBO is best suited to those static, mechanistic environments where adequate alternatives already exist. Rapidly changing conditions and low role clarity render it worse than useless. *It works best in those situations where we need it least.*

MBO adds nothing to our ability to reward and control. It correctly emphasizes goal-setting, feedback and interaction, and participation. These strengths should be maintained, but not at the cost of jolting the organization with massive and simultaneous changes."[27]

Furthermore, we are told that we should *not* link MBO to the pay systems in organizations because "such linkage will induce risk-avoidance and goal displacement except when conditions are so predictable that no deceit is possible."[28]

I and others have argued that there can be no successful implementation of MBO without OD and no durable OD without MBO because the same organizational norms and values are required as preconditions for each.[29] I have also urged that OD and MBO should be connected with changes in reward systems, particularly pay plans, and have found through extensive reading that others have come to the same conclusion in relating MBO directly to pay planning and administration, and, sometimes, implicitly, OD. Still others disagree and despair of tying pay plans to MBO.[30] Contacts in consulting confirm the view that pay planning should be meshed with MBO.[31] Where then should we go from here in setting forth an approach to defining and planning strategic OD based upon behavioral science knowledge?

Strategic OD Models

Evidently, there are varying schools of thought on how and where to intervene in work organizations, but few long-range, comprehensive strategic models for OD have been thought out in any detail, except perhaps for Blake and Mouton's longitudinal design for corporate excellence using the managerial grid and other associated tools.[32] However, reward systems have been mentioned over the years (usually obliquely) by many behavioral scientists of the present and past as being worthy of consideration in change efforts.[33]

Unfortunately, little detailed thought has been given to what should be done to make reward systems more functional and, consequently, organizations more healthy. There has, of course, been an extensive technical literature on wage and salary administration, incentive plans, bonuses, and the like, but this literature has been essentially mechanical in nature and conceptually shallow, if not downright empty, from the behavioral science standpoint. Few scholars or practitioners have viewed altering or installing wage and salary administration systems as being more than complex technical chores.[34] Yet these alterations should be considered OD interventions of prime importance if we are to think clearly about the real world of work organizations.

I take a broader and more thorough look at OD, MBO, and reward system integration than has yet been done elsewhere and of which I am aware. This allows me to bridge some of the inconsistencies and gaps separating the above systems so that the OD practitioners can better employ them. Skilled OD practitioners working in organizational change efforts should intervene directly through reward systems, as has been done and described elsewhere, provided they know where they are coming from strategically and have a proper appreciation of an optimum organizational change strategy using a combined intervention involving OD, MBO, and reward systems.[35]

A Notion of Human Nature

The strategic approach to OD advocated in this theory of change starts with an examination of a conception of human nature. This conception is not an idiosyncratic view and has been expressed before[36] using some notions of Schutz as a starting point.[37] After explaining the conception, it is related to OD efforts begun with formal T-groups and formal teambuilding seminars, and eventually connected below to MBO and Skinnerian and other conceptions of rewards.[38] These linkages are needed and helpful for the change agent concerned with OD strategy.

In changing an organization it is necessary to embark on an OD effort intended to build managerial teams at the outset. Therefore, it is important to have a guiding OD philosophy governing program design because the latter is critical to the success of an OD effort, although there can be many efficacious but somewhat different philosophies. I next attempt to point out some core concepts in my OD and change philosophy while recognizing that others may have different core concepts. Any relevant change philosophy must address social–emotional as well as rationalistic variables, and I review my thinking by sharpening some conceptual issues.

Is an effective MBO program actually critical to sustaining an OD effort? Basically, MBO is essential because work organizations are created to attain goals, such as profit in the private sector and the efficient provision of services in the public sector.

Also, OD for the sake of OD is meaningless in the context of a work organization. To be sure, certain facets of OD offered for the individual growth of employees may be regarded as beneficial to the person, but the cost of providing them without some connection to attaining goals at work can hardly ever be justified when examined from the standpoint of a work organization. Having thus raised and answered certain basic questions, let me spell out some ideas of my own.

Specifically, consider that OD and planned change, compensation planning and administration, and management-by-objectives programs are very closely interrelated and are, in a certain sense, on an equal plane of importance in any correct configuration of effective practicing management. OD, compensation, and MBO have very close connections that tie together social–emotional and rational dimensions in human behavior. I elaborate on these points in order to indicate their conceptual integration and design of a suggested pattern of utilization for an optimum strategy of change.

First, let us consider a work organization existing in a steady state or equilibrium. A decision is then made to intervene in that system and bring about change. If change is to be initiated, we must begin with the individual and the way in which he behaves, particularly in carrying out his occupational role.

Much thinking in this field is strongly influenced by the unfreezing, change, and refreezing conception formulated many years ago by Kurt Lewin.[39] Therefore, an effort at organizational change should begin by intervening in the system at the level of the individual and unfreezing him through experimental learning methods, such as those commonly used in laboratory training.

The initial effort would be intended to bring about self-education and a reconsideration of the individual's values. He would consequently be acquainted with openness, honesty, and authenticity in relationships; he would gain some experience in identifying and building up a trust level in his work group and broader place of employment; he would learn about the birth and death of small groups; he would discover relationships between the individual and the group; lastly, he would learn about the connections between the person, the group, the organization, and the organizational culture. Such training immersion should have provided a learning experience that would enable him to relate more effectively to other people and encourage him to enlarge and draw upon a considerable repertoire of behaviors. He should also, as a consequence, be more accepting of others and be an improved communicator. He should perhaps have lost some of his rigidity and instead delight in moving into a freer and more vital stance with his associates at work. In summary, I am suggesting that an initial OD effort intended to bring about planned change rather than unrestrained revolution or slow-paced evolution should begin with the individual and his existing behavior patterns. The emphasis should be upon social–emotional learning, and knowledge of rational and ultrarational tools should be postponed until one's mind clears and energy flows.

A Useful Analogy

Let us approach this subject, the nature of human nature so to speak, a bit differently—perhaps bizarrely—by referring to some analogies from nature that have been suggested over the years. In drawing upon these analogies I will be referring to some concepts in my own OD philosophy, crudely formed as it may be. Again, it should be stressed that an OD intervention must necessarily always come before MBO in my conception of planned change and philosophy of OD, if MBO is to take hold eventually as a worthwhile and disciplined form of behavior.

At the present time we hear much about mercury in negative terms as an element that is despoiling the ecological balance of the natural world by being dumped in rivers and contaminating fish. However, I would like to suggest that instead of talking about mercury we talk about quicksilver, which is another name for mercury, and, analogically has interesting properties that may bear upon human behavior when viewed in a certain way. For example, given controls in temperature and pressure, quicksilver, when rolling across a surface, manages to conform to that surface and fit it perfectly without giving up its own integrity in surrendering to the surface either by destroying it or being itself destroyed. Thus, at the interface of the quicksilver and surface on which it rests, there is close compatibility and a protection of the integrity of the two surfaces in contact. There is a unity without a disappearance of the components. When it is time for the quicksilver to move on, it does so, leaving behind nothing visible and rolls forward to encounter resiliently whatever it meets next where, again, when it stops, there will be perfection at the interface. There is no absorption, welding, melding, or commingling but instead close contact accompanied by integrity. People need to be like this—independent and autonomous yet interfacing effectively without loss of integrity. Adequate teambuilding involves such individualism and in no sense implies group-think collectivism.

Another analogy has to do with the chameleon. As everyone knows, the chameleon is a lizard that can change the color of its skin when placed in an environment of a characteristic color or pattern of colors. The chameleon adapts and moves on, taking his coloration from whatever environment in which he finds himself and, thereby, survives. People need this same attribute, especially industrial managers who must adapt, blend in, yet remain vital movers with survival power. Otherwise, the changing scene could become not only over-powering but itself, immolative.

My point in drawing these analogies is simply to establish that there may be some lessons from the behavior of quicksilver and chameleons, that, although not comprising a model for man, except crudely, are nevertheless suggestive. From the standpoint of teambuilding efforts, we are often trying to achieve the expression of human potential and preservation of individual dignity and integrity while the person attempts to contribute and meld well into the organizational context by opening up in his relations with others. He strives to be pliant without being totally compliant and to take upon coloration without being totally defensive and brittle. He strives to be all there, in the here-and-now, and for real, as opposed to being partly there, distractible, and posing opportunistically. As Byrd would put it, he needs to be a creative risk-taker.[40] I should simply add that he needs as well, to survive with integrity.

The behavior of quicksilver suggests a high degree of suppleness without a breakdown of the parts or a blending that would serve to eliminate the integrity of the parts. As for the chameleon, the suggestion made here is that individual behavior can become sensitized so that the person realizes he has a repertoire of behaviors and can call upon them by drawing upon those aspects of his behavior that are relevant for successful action in an organizational context.

I am not suggesting a Machiavellian concept of outright expediency or duplicity but, rather, the conscious adaptation of behavior by the person who simultaneously takes into account the behavior of others and works towards problem identification and solution in work organizations. However, let us not push these analogies any further because they are merely illustrative and suggestive but hardly definitive and perhaps not even worthy of additional serious concern. The analogies suggest what we strive for in changing organizational behavior through OD efforts that begin by freeing the individual and encouraging him to think more adaptively as a team member.

The Theory of Open Encounter

One important way of changing the individual behavior of employees in work organizations is explained by behavioral science theory. For example, the theory of open encounter as it exists in sensitivity training and T-groups is based upon the belief that man is a unified being and functions on many levels at once—physical, emotional, intellectual, interpersonal, social, and spiritual. These levels are considered to be intimately interrelated; actions on any one level are accompanied by actions on all others. The theory assumes that there is a life flow in man on all these levels, an energy that flows through cycles of motivation, preparation, performance, and consummation. When these energy cycles are interrupted, a number of blocks can be identified.

There can be physical blocks that lead to physical illness, emotional blocks, to underachievement, social blocks, to incompatibility, and spiritual blocks, to postponement of the realization of the total person. Removal of the blocks is a therapeutic task, but development of the energy cycles is the task of education and fully living. OD can provide this education and a new way of fully living as a turned-on manager or employee when the OD effort results in favorable culture change in a work organization. Therapy can be sought from the relevant professional resources, as needed.

The life flow of man functions best in the presence of openness, which in turn depends upon trust. Blocks can be removed when a person is open to himself and others. Achieving self-awareness and being open and honest with others allows one's energy to flow freely and permits one to become more effective in problem-solving and decision-making, not only in managerial work but also in everyday life. Self-deception and dishonesty block energy and take it out of the life flow potentially available to the person. In a word, the open encounter in everyday life in a work organization unblocks the individual and allows human energy to be used for more productive purposes. Unblocking is thus the first step in strategic OD, unless the change agent determines that it already exists on a widespread basis among team members.

The human being's self-concept is enhanced when he takes responsibility for himself in everyday life, at work, or elsewhere. If he feels that he is responsible, competent, important, and likeable, he will be more likely to express those parts of himself. If he has a weak and restricted self-concept, he will not live up to his full capacity. To the extent that his self-concept is expanded and enhanced, more of the person will be made available and utilized, and his life flow will be invigorated.[41] Thus, successful OD team-building efforts that expand self-awareness, improve one's self-concept, elevate the trust level in an organization, diffuse openness, and enable managers and employees who interface to be more effective in problem-solving and decision-making in a group situation are fundamental to starting strategic OD, launching a MBO effort, or enabling the rewards system in an organization to act as an incentive for performance.

We are likely to find few work organizations today capable of demonstrating to the diagnostic scrutiny of the change agent that they have linked these matters together, even though they might claim to be "doing" OD. In other words, few organizations have, in effect, identified a clearcut ideal model of organizational culture and human nature toward which they are moving by planned stages. Instead, organizations have tended to treat OD teambuilding, MBO, or reward systems on a piecemeal and unconnected basis. Yet each of the aforementioned is an intervention or technique for change that is derived directly from what has just been said about the processes and importance of helping people become unblocked. It now remains for organizations to develop change strategies that link these techniques into an effort that will have more impact and provide managers with information on their current style.

The Idea of Management Style

Style is the distinctive or characteristic mode of presentation, construction, or execution in any art, product, or human endeavor or employment. Style is a manner.

Management style refers to identifiable and consistent manners of executing work designed to influence the activities of employees who are peers, subordinates, or organizational superiors. Such styles may be represented on a griddle configuration, such as a gridiron, which has a network of positions of potential use for managers who are engaged in analytical discussions oriented toward understanding the components of style.

Managers who are undergoing a teambuilding effort can benefit from examining their present managerial style and determining how close it comes to a desirable style. In this way they can obtain some additional initial insight into themselves and feedback from others that should enable them to find a way to improve as team members and team-oriented managers.

A tool that has been extensively used to assist in efforts at changing managerial style is the managerial grid (which is a copyrighted name owned by Blake and Mouton). One type of grid is the two-dimensional grid developed by Blake and Mouton[42] and another is the three-dimensional grid developed by Reddin.[43] Still another instrument that is becoming very popular is the LEAD (Leader Effectiveness and Adaptability Description) developed by Hersey and Blanchard.[44] I next turn to the Blake–Mouton grid and Hersey–Blanchard LEAD instrument and indicate subsequently how they fit into organizational development through teambuilding.

The Managerial Grid

The managerial grid developed by Robert R. Blake and Jane S. Mouton has become a very well-known tool for diagnosing a manager's style. A recent article has indicated that 20,000 managers have participated in managerial grid programs offered by Scientific Methods Inc., the Blake–Mouton Organization; an additional 200,000 managers have been through grid programs conducted by people licensed to provide this instruction by Blake and Mouton.[45]

The managerial grid was created by Blake and Mouton and based upon some research done in the 1950s in which it was found that managers were typically concerned in their interpersonal relations style either with "efficiency" or "security." The degree of their concern varied from manager to manager and scales were developed to measure these varying concerns for efficiency (later called production) and employee security (later called, in short-hand, people). The final scale developed by Blake and Mouton was a concern for people on the vertical axis and a concern for production on the horizontal axis. The two axes were arranged to reflect two respective nine-point scales, resulting in a gridiron effect that has been called the managerial grid.[46]

The two concerns (for production and for people) intersect at a particular point in the grid, and the manager can locate his unique position on the grid when his scores are made known to him. There are 81 positions available on the grid but Blake and Mouton feel that focusing upon 5 main or pure style positions on the grid rather than all 81 contributes sufficiently for using the grid as a tool in OD and teambuilding. The ones focussed on are the following: 9,1; 1,9; 1,1; 5,5; and 9,9.

The position 9,1 on the grid is one of anti-organizational creativity where there is an excessive push for production. It represents a hard-nosed forcing style typified by the bull-of-the-woods supervisor.[47]

The position 1,9 is called the "country club" style position where the work organization is viewed as a club having harmony and happiness as goals. This style produces interpersonal warmth and perhaps a certain kind of happiness but not strength.[48]

The 1,1 position takes great evasive talent on the part of the manager and amounts to being visible without being seen in the organization. It is a position of withdrawal that is considered impoverished from the managerial standpoint.[49] The objective of the manager in behaving in a 1,1 style is apparently RIP (or retirement in place) or OJR (on-the-job retirement).

A 5,5 style is a middle-of-the-road style. In the grid itself 5,5 is seen halfway up the grid and is found in dead center. But a 5,5 style is not ½ of 9,1 and ½ of 1,9. The person having this style has an "organizational man" mentality according to Blake and Mouton and fulfills a very safe style. He never does anything wrong but he never does anything dramatically right either. Status and prestige motivate him. The result of a 5,5 style is to make small steady steps toward progress without rocking the boat.[50]

The style of 9,9 is the one that was thought to be most effective based upon the aforementioned research conducted by Blake and Mouton. It is a style called team management. It involves getting participation from employees in management, and it involves controversy, commitment, creativity, and confrontation.[51]

The five managerial styles have their counterpart in employee reactions to these styles. For example, paternalism may be viewed as a switching between 9,1 and 1,9, where employees are frustrated because of the drive for production and dependent because of the alternating drive for good feelings.[52] This is the wide-arc pendulum.

Most managers tend to see themselves as 9,9; however, when they are given a chance to reflect seriously on their styles they tend to change their evaluation of their styles to lower numbers.[53]

Blake and Mouton believe that 9,9 styles are found most commonly in top management in organizations whereas 5,5 is found predominantly at the middle of the structure. At the bottom of the structure all kinds of styles are found.

They believe that if we were to examine high- and low-producing units and moved a supervisor with a 1,9 orientation to a high-producing unit the unit would become low-producing. Similarly a low-producing unit to which a new 9,1 supervisor was assigned would probably remain low in production.

Improvements in production and in the interpersonal environment would be expected from a newly assigned 9,9 supervisor (who would also bring, interestingly enough, more conflict, more disagreement, and yet more solutions to problems).

Blake and Mouton believe that people have both dominant and backup styles. Any combination of styles is possible. Some people hopscotch around in style and are inconsistent. Others have a basic style and apply it situationally, dependent on the person to whom they are attempting to relate. Still other managers stay essentially in one style and switch only on occasion.[54]

Blake and Mouton advocate teamwork in management and offer the grid as a tool to enable managers to change from their present style to one that makes greater use of human resources in management. According to them a person can change by any of the following:

- Theory—that is to say, he can make use of the grid and learn the meaning of the main positions in it.
- Feedback—by clearing away self-deception and getting a better understanding of his true style through feedback from his peers.
- Motivation—by learning that there is a discrepancy or tension between what a person is and what he wants to be.
- Team support—by relating to people on the team who, in turn, remind him how to confront openly his behavior, desires, and discrepancies.[55]

The Grid in Teambuilding

The managerial grid can also be used in a team exercise and to assist in building teamwork. According to Blake and Mouton the following factors are necessary for teambuilding:

- The existence of challenging and clear goals which stimulate effort.
- Direction by management or the pointing of the way based upon goals.
- Decision making, where the team decides which way to move and pools its human resources for moving in a direction decided upon.
- Communication among team members—with candor.
- Critique of the team or stepping back to examine processes when the team is working on problems or issues. (This is sometimes known as learning how to learn from the managerial standpoint.)
- Climate for commitment so that there is a guarantee that work will get done based upon shared agreements and understandings.[56]

The managerial grid is also thought to be a useful tool in conflict resolution or, in other words, the management of interpersonal conflict at work. For example a manager can circumvent conflict by dealing with his subordinate managers one to one rather than as a team. This leads to compromise (5,5) as a style of managing and reduces synergy.

It is preferable to bring conflicts into the open where they can be understood and dealt with by discussion, dissection, and analysis. The grid can be used to deal with such conflicts, to discuss leadership behavior in conflict situations, and to serve as a basis for team members to criticize one another.

Such a discussion can lead to a revelation of teamwork problems and ultimately may lead to the successful management of conflict rather than a suboptimum splitting of differences.

As another example, a 9,1 boss may have a 1,9 subordinate in which the latter feels suppressed on the job and avoids getting involved in win/lose fights. In effect, he shuts himself in and avoids the boss. The boss may like to fight and have the attitude of: "I may be wrong but I am never in doubt"; the withdrawn subordinate further retreats in a defensive posture. Obviously, there is no teamwork in this situation.

On the other hand, a boss may be 1,9 and consistently avoid fighting by smoothing things over. This behavior does not solve problems but eases them and smooths the sparks of conflict. Smoothed-over problems have a way of accumulating and later erupting with surprising effect.

A boss with a 1,1 style in respect to conflict resolution follows the maxims of "see no evil, hear no evil, and speak no evil." If a manager totally withdraws or stays out of interpersonal relations, he can avoid conflict. In time, with a repeated pattern of withdrawal, he becomes content to stay out and does not expect to be asked for his input. If asked to contribute, he is likely to respond defensively by saying, "it's a very complex problem; let's get more data." He gets into the habit of staying in the corner and is often pushed there sufficiently often by 9,1 and 1,9 colleagues so that the corner is the only place comfortable for him.

As a result of all these dysfunctional styles, the 5,5 style becomes very popular in interpersonal conflict resolution. This is a no-lose approach and amounts to solving problems half-way but not really winning. The 5,5 manager is happy to compromise and is consistently testing the wind to avoid conflict. His behavior frequently leads to premature problem-solving in order to get his colleagues off his back rather than to work through their differences and achieve richness in problem-analysis and decision-making. It is a workable strategy but does not provide very creative solutions. The job gets done but not in an excellent manner.

A 9,9 strategy to conflict resolution leads to an interchange of views and a clearer grasp of why people misunderstand one another and have conflict. It can lead to win/win behavior. The goal is to get more valid data and the soundest possible solutions. The best solution causes everyone to win. We avoid the porcupine theory of keeping away from one another's quills. We enter the fray in an open, problem-solving way and try to identify the real problems that need solutions.

A 1,9 win or leave strategy is undesirable. We often find a 9,1 manager adopting a 1,9 style when there is conflict. In 1,9 situations performance is judged against the past rather than against opportunity.

Blake and Mouton predict that the management of conflict in organizations must improve or lower profit margins and shortfalls on goal attainment can be expected. In order to improve the management of conflict they suggest that managers do the following:

- Enter a managerial grid training effort and learn more about themselves as individual managers and team members.
- Actually do some teambuilding in the organization.

Managers must learn that teambuilding requires the members of the team to extend themselves to one another and take an attitude towards their jobs that is not narrow and ultraspecialized. Managers should look upon conflict as constructive and use it to strike the sparks of creativity rather than to be destructive. Managers should learn more about 9,9, and build 9,9 styles into the organizational climate.[57]

In summary, the popularity of the management grid is well known; the conceptual base for the grid has been found to be useful in many organizations when managerial style is being considered.

Grid Exercises

There are several ways of measuring one's style and for placing one's self on the grid as a manager. A convenient and simple one is to respond to a set of questions related, respectively, to attitudes toward production (or task) and attitudes toward subordinate people. A short list of items that enables a manager to score himself quickly on the grid is available and can be used.[58] However, the managerial grid apparently has led to the creation of many "homemade" versions that have been devised by well-intentioned people but are not the same as the genuine copyrighted Blake–Mouton instrument. Other sources for management-style gridirons are available, such as Reddin and Hersey and Blanchard, as mentioned above in the chapter. We discuss the Blake–Mouton type grid briefly and then the Hersey–Blanchard grid.

Figure 3.8 consists of a grid format that can be used to score oneself in terms of concern for people (P) and concern for production [or task (T)]. Figure 3.8 also displays five types of styles for dealing with interpersonal conflict resolution. These generally accord with those suggested by Blake and Mouton. I do not provide in the book the grid instrument consisting of the items that could be scored for determining one's position on the grid, but these can be obtained from the copyright holder and commercial sources.

I find the grid useful as a feedback instrument in a teambuilding program. Once I have formally built teams in seminar/workshops, I ask individuals to complete two tasks while sitting with their teams. First, they are asked to score their own instruments and decide whether or not they agree with their grid scores. Second, they are asked to share their grid scores with one another and determine if other team members can correctly predict each individual's grid score. After these two tasks are completed, I ask if anyone present has previously taken a grid and if their current score has changed from previous ones. I then debrief the exercise by asking the teams to report how much agreement there is between scores and perceived actual styles, predicted grid scores, and previous scores, if any.

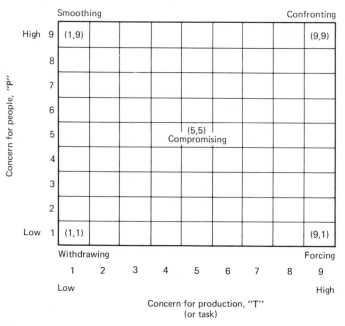

Figure 3.8

They can be asked to discuss what grid scores managers who work together (as peers, superiors and subordinates, and as staff to staff or staff/line counterparts) should have in order to accomplish tasks capably while maximizing smooth interface relations. Following this assignment they can be asked to specify what actions the managers present can take to use grid information for improving their team skills. These exercises encourage managers to articulate their philosophy of management and to start crystallizing views on what personal actions they can take back on the job to perform in a team mode.

Turning to the LEAD instruments of Hersey and Blanchard, it should be noted that they too have made use of gridiron concepts in preparing measures of managerial style or leadership. For some time, especially prior to the work of Blake and Mouton, it was believed that task and interpersonal relationships were "either/or" styles of leadership behavior and, therefore, could be depicted on a continuum ranging from very authoritarian (task-oriented) leadership at one end to very democratic (relationship-oriented) leadership behavior at the other.

In the last two decades the notion that task and relationship were "either/or" styles has been dispelled. Instead it has been found that successful leadership styles tend to vary considerably among managers; and versatility has become the prime concern. There are many styles that are successful depending upon the organizational level of the manager, the situation, and the maturity of the manager as well as the maturity of the manager's subordinates. The Hersey–Blanchard LEAD instruments provide useful data for teambuilding and OD based upon versatility and contingency notions. The instruments are difficult to complete by "faking," that is, guessing at what the correct answer is supposed to be in evaluating styles adaptable to dealing with ten specific situations included in the basic LEAD "test" instrument. Therefore, the instruments appear to work well in teambuilding seminar/workshops and generate useful data that can be dissected by managers who are interested in improving their ability to cooperate in task accomplishment and building better interpersonal relationships.[59]

The LEAD instruments can apparently be used the same way as the grid in teambuilding (as described above) to encourage managers in articulating their managerial philosophies and in crystallizing their views on how to perform in a team modality with peers, subordinates, counterparts, and others.

Insofar as I use grids after FIRO-Bs, questions sometimes arise as to how the I, C, and A items in the FIRO-B are related to grid scores. The consistency between scores on the managerial grid and on the FIRO-B has apparently not been studied, and I have seen varying FIRO-B scores result in quite similar managerial grid scores. However, grid scores are extremely useful in and of themselves in teambuilding and perhaps have their greatest value when discussed among team members in an OD effort that is intended to assist in dissecting the importance of individualism, individual differences, and teambuilding.

Exercise on Intervention in a System: The Nickel Auction

At this point in initial teambuilding the participants have probably experienced considerable unfreezing and obtained affirmative and disconfirmative feedback as well as a heavy dose of behavioral science theory. I consider it a proper time to change the pace and provide a hands-on experience in system intervention. The nickel auction with a change agent is a useful design for this purpose and also for completing the first phase of the OD-teambuilding effort. It seldom takes more than half an hour, although for teambuilding among managers severely in conflict, the exercise can run up to almost two hours including the debriefing.

The nickel or money auction is a well-known design in OD programs.[60] It can be used to

- Understand the impact of power and affiliation motivation on the behavior of people in organizations, that is, McClelland's nP and nACH.
- Explore ways in which cooperative behavior can obtain better results than competition (a "zero sum" game situation).
- Provide practice in intervening in a live system and influencing the behavior of others.

The nickel auction involves the OD facilitator and the program participants and requires that the latter pay close attention to the auction. The OD facilitator begins the exercise by selecting three bidders who take places in chairs in front of the group. Three bidders are ideal but up to five can be accommodated. An empty chair is placed beside the chairs of the bidders and is used by anyone who desires to attempt to influence the behavior of the bidders, whom we call a change agent. Thus, during the auction the group observes not only the exercise but the behavior of bidders and change agents.

When an empty chair is added to the chairs set aside for the bidders, it is possible to use the empty chair to give OD teambuilding program participants a chance to obtain some insight into their skills in intervention and to try out new or seldom-used behavior. It is a good time to determine how much unfreezing has taken place.

The nickel auction is begun when the OD facilitator selects the bidders and commences the auction. The facilitator bids the nickels one at a time and allows the bidders to offer money for each nickel. He role-models an honest auctioneer strictly concerned with process issues. It is assumed that the OD facilitator in the role of auctioneer has an infinite number of nickels that are to be auctioned at any price to the bidders. If no bid is made on a nickel, that round can be declared as passed, much like the case in a real auction where there may be no bids offered on a particular item. No actual money needs to change hands. Score is kept by the OD facilitator using the format shown in Figure 3.9. For each nickel auctioned, the bid price is entered under the appropriate bidder shown as 1 (Smith), 2 (Jones), and 3 (Johnson).

During the bidding, individuals who watch the auction can, on their own initiative, occupy the seat that is vacant. While in the seat, the change agent, in effect, intervenes in the auction and tries out his change agentry, which could be viewed as a proxy for management style. This experience can be full of learning for him. He not only has a chance to practice the art of interpersonal influence in any way he desires but also he displays behavior that can later be discussed when the exercise is debriefed. It is thus possible during the auction to have many change agents with varying styles attempt to influence the bidders. Interventions may emphasize logic, emotional appeals, hidden agenda, naive beliefs, forcing, persuading, and the like. In this way the behavior patterns displayed and results of the auction can be examined by a large number of observers. All the intervenors, bidders, and observers can learn.

The task of the OD facilitator who acts as auctioneer is simply to keep the exercise going and handle questions from the bidders as they come up. He must be able to keep interest in the exercise alive and should be sensitive to knowing when interest in the exercise starts to lag. This will happen when the bidding becomes regularized and the bidders find they can obtain all the nickels they want at a low price. Regularization will probably take place at about the 15th–20th round in the auction. At that point, the facilitator should

Figure 3.9 Nickel Auction Record

Nickel Number	Bidders 1. Smith	2. Jones	3. Johnson
1.			
2.			
3.			
4.			
5.			
6.			
7.			
8.			
9.			
10.			
11.			
12.			
13.			
14.			
15.			
16.			
17.			
18.			
19.			
20.			
21.			
22.			
23.			
24.			

halt the exercise and invite bidders, change agents, and observers to debrief the entire experience.

It is possible to change bidders and resume the auction. However, it may be impossible to recreate the high degree of interest in second and subsequent rounds of bidding once the exercise has been thoroughly debriefed. Additional rounds of bidding become more feasible if the debriefing after the first round is not too detailed. However, once the win/win strategy has been revealed it is virtually impossible (and even undesirable) to resume the auction.

OD facilitators who have never conducted the nickel auction may wonder how it is possible to get bidders to offer more than 5¢ for a nickel although they probably think that bids under 5¢ are likely. In conducting the exercise, the behavior of the bidders becomes very interesting because the needs of some bidders for power and obtaining the nickels no matter what they have to pay become supervening. Also, the ability or lack of ability of bidders to undercut or monopolize the nickels becomes interesting behavior to observe and fruitful material for debriefing.

The use of the nickel auction with a change agent enhances the value of the exercise. The latter becomes an easily designed and easily conducted experience that participants enjoy and benefit from in a limited time period.

The exercise can also be recommended for an initial attempt to train change agents in an organizational development program or as a warmup for subsequent movement into other exercises that provide team experiences.

It is extremely important that the facilitator conducting the exercise avoid having the nickel auction interpreted as "fun and games" unrelated to management style. Although the fun element is appreciated by groups, the actual intervention styles of the managers who attempt to influence the course of the auction and the behavior of the bidders is the proper grist for the debriefing that follows the exercise. The group dynamics unfolded before everyone can be analyzed from the standpoint of everyone who participates. People become disarmed and reveal themselves from a managerial style standpoint. Everyone who participates has a chance to ask himself why he succeeded or failed in the nickel auction and whether that successful or inadequate behavior is carried out back on the job. Thus the nickel auction can easily become a potent vicarious learning vehicle that carries low threat and can be quickly enacted. In many respects, it is the ideal way to complete the first full day of a teambuilding OD workshop that is oriented toward unfreezing participants and getting them acquainted with theories about healthy and unhealthy organizations, OD instrumentation, the Johari Window, the FIRO-B, behavioral science thinking on how best to manage, and gridiron concepts and tools that help in dissecting managerial style.

Conclusion

The review of behavioral science theory and research covered in this chapter is useful in teambuilding because it takes the subject out of thin air and puts it in a context. Many younger managers do not require a thorough review of this material because graduates of business schools since 1960 have usually had considerable exposure to behavioral science. Some, nevertheless, welcome the review and synthesis. However, older managers often are steeped in classical ideas about organization, management, and motivation. They are likely to dispute the material and feel out of step with some of it. All can benefit from an exercise involving their own managerial style and a chance to obtain some practice in trying to influence others in perhaps a new way. The review, exercises, and initial work now done in teambuilding sets the scene for moving from interventions intended to heighten self-awareness to interventions intended to heighten team-awareness, particularly the value of group decisions. We turn to these next.

Notes

1. Chris Argyris, *Management and Organizational Development: The Path from XA to YB*, McGraw–Hill, New York, 1971, pp. 1–26.

2. Parts of this chapter are from Thomas H. Patten, Jr., *Pay: Employee Compensation and Incentive Plans*, Free Press, New York, 1977, pp. 117–133.

3. Abraham H. Maslow, *Motivation and Personality*, Harper and Row, New York, 1954, pp. 83–165.

4. Peter F. Drucker, *Management: Tasks, Responsibilities, Practices*, Harper and Row, New York, 1974, pp. 237–241.

5. Maslow, *Motivation and Personality, op. cit.*, pp. 91–92. For more information on the motivations and gratifications of self-actualizing people see Maslow's *The Further Reaches of Human Nature*, Viking, New York, 1971, pp. 308–310. For a short summary of Maslow's contributions in the OD literature see Sandra L. Pfeiffer, "The Maslow Need Hierarchy," in J. William Pfeiffer and John E. Jones, Eds., *The 1972 Annual Handbook for Group Facilitators*, University Associates, Iowa City, IA, 1972, pp. 125–126.

6. Douglas McGregor, *The Professional Manager*, McGraw–Hill, New York, 1967, pp. 3–5. For a short summary of McGregor's contributions in the OD literature see Albert J. Robinson, "McGregor's Theory X–Theory Y Model," in Pfeiffer and Jones, *op. cit.*, pp. 121–123.

7. Douglas McGregor, *The Human Side of Enterprise*, McGraw–Hill, New York, 1960, pp. 3–57.

8. Douglas McGregor, *Leadership and Motivation*, MIT Press, Cambridge, MA, 1966, pp. 14–17, 184–197. See also his "An Uneasy Look at Perfornabce Appraisal," *Harvard Business Review*, Vol. 35, No. 3, May–June 1957, pp. 89–94.

9. McGregor, *The Human Side of Enterprise, op. cit.*, pp. 54–57.

10. See, for example, Vernon L. Parrington, *Main Currents in American Thought*, Harcourt Brace, New York, 1930, Vol. I, pp. 292–307, Vol. II, pp. 10–14, and Vol. III, pp. xxiii–xxix.

11. See, for example, Thomas H. Patten, Jr. and Lester E. Dorey, "Long Range Results of a Teambuilding Organizational Development Effort," *Personnel Management Review*, Vol. 6, No. 1, January–February 1977, pp. 31–50.

12. Frederick Herzberg, *Work and the Nature of Man*, World, Cleveland, 1966, pp. 70–167 and his classic "One More Time: How Do You Motivate Employees?" *Harvard Business Review*, Vol. 46, No. 1, January–February 1968, pp. 53–62.

13. Frederick Herzberg et al., "Job Enrichment Pays Off," *Harvard Business Review*, Vol. 47, No. 2, March–April 1969, pp. 61–67; Fred-

erick Herzberg, "The Wise Old Turk," *Harvard Business Review*, Vol. 52, No. 5, September–October 1974, pp. 70–80; and Frederick Herzberg and Edmund A. Rafalko, "Efficiency in the Military: Cutting Costs with Orthodox Job Enrichment," *Personnel*, Vol. 52, No. 6, November–December 1975, pp. 38–48.

14. Edward E. Lawler III, *Pay and Organizational Effectiveness: A Psychological View*, McGraw–Hill, New York, 1971, pp. 97–99.

15. For a short summary of Herzberg's place in the job enrichment and OD literature see Francis V. Jessey, "Job Enrichment" in Pfeiffer and Jones, *op cit.,* pp. 127–129.

16. M. Scott Myers, *Every Employee A Manager*, McGraw–Hill, New York, 1970, pp. 16–18, 55–117.

17. David C. McClelland, *The Achieving Society*, Van Nostrand, Princeton, 1961. For a useful summary of McClelland's and Schachter's contributions in perspective see Saul W. Gellerman, *Motivation and Productivity*, American Management Association, New York 1963, pp. 115–141.

18. For more information see David C. McClelland, "Achievement Motivation Can Be Developed," *Harvard Business Review*, Vol. 43, No. 6, November–December 1965, pp. 6–24, 178.

19. David C. McClelland, "Business Drive and National Achievement," *Harvard Business Review*, Vol. 40, No. 4, July–August 1962, pp. 99–112.

20. David C. McClelland and David H. Burnham, "Power is the Great Motivator," *Harvard Business Review*, Vol. 54, No. 2, March–April 1976, pp. 100–110.

21. Rensis Likert, *The Human Organization*, McGraw–Hill, New York, 1967, pp. 1–67.

22. Rensis Likert, *New Patterns of Management*, McGraw–Hill, New York, 1961, p. 240.

23. William F. Dowling, "Conversation: An Interview with Rensis Likert," *Organizational Dynamics*, Vol. 2, No. 1, Summer 1973, pp. 32–49.

24. Harry Levinson, *The Great Jackass Fallacy*, Harvard University Graduate School of Business Administration, Boston, 1973, pp. 10–14.

25. *Ibid.*, pp. 28–33.

26. Part of the remainder of this chapter is taken from Thomas H. Patten, Jr., "Intervening in Organizations Through Reward Systems" in John

E. Jones and William Pfeiffer, Eds., *The 1977 Annual Handbook for Group Facilitators*, University Associates, LaJolla, CA, 1977, pp. 197–207.

27. Steven Kerr, "Some Modifications in MBO as an OD Strategy," in Vance F. Mitchell et al., Eds., *Proceedings of the 32 Annual Meeting of the Academy of Management*, Academy of Management, N.P., 1972, p. 42.

28. *Idem.*

29. See the following: Patten, *Pay: Employee Compensation and Incentive Plans, op. cit.,* pp. 563–568, Arthur C. Beck, Jr. and Ellis D. Hillmar, "OD to MBO or MBO to OD: Does It Make A Difference?" *Personnel Journal*, Vol. 51, No. 11, November 1972, pp. 827–834; and Ronald J. Hunady and Glenn H. Varney, "Salary Administration: A Reason for MBO!" *Training and Development Journal*, Vol. 28, No. 9, September 1974, pp. 24–28.

30. Donald L. Kirkpatrick, "MBO and Salary Administration," *Training and Development Journal,* Vol. 27, No. 9, September 1973, pp. 3–5.

31. Dale D. McConkey, "The 'Jackass Effect' in Management Compensation," *Business Horizons*, Vol. 17, No. 3, June 1974, pp. 81–91.

32. Robert R. Blake and Jane S. Mouton, "Is the Training-Group Consultant Approach a Method of Organization Development?" in William G. Dyer, Ed., *Modern Theory and Method in Group Training*, Van Nostrand, New York, 1972, pp. 201–204; and Robert R. Blake and Jane S. Mouton, *Building A Dynamic Corporation Through Grid Organization Development*, Addison–Wesley, Reading, MA, 1969.

33. A few examples follow: Argyris, *Management and Organization Development: The Path from XA to YB, op, cit.,* pp. 17, 105, 137, 140, 157, 183–184, 195; Richard Beckhard, *Organization Development: Strategies and Models*, Addison–Wesley, Reading, MA, 1969, pp. 96–97; Robert N. Ford, *Motivation Through the Work Itself*, American Management Association, New York, 1969, pp. 91–111; Herzberg, *Work and the Nature of Man, op. cit.,* pp. 71–91; Arthur H. Kuriloff, *Organizational Development for Survival*, American Management Association, New York, 1972, pp. 175, 188, 227–228, 255–257, 265; Edward E. Lawler III, *Pay and Organizational Effectiveness: A Psychological View, op. cit.,* pp. 205–263; Levinson, *The Great Jackass Fallacy, op. cit.,* pp. 87–107; Gordon L. Lippitt, *Organizational Renewal*, Prentice–Hall, Englewood Cliffs, NJ, 1969, p. 212; Alfred J. Marrow, Ed., *The Failure of Success*, AMACOM, New York, 1973, pp. 129–130, 290–291; W. M. McFeely, *Organization Change, Perceptions and Realities*, Conference Board, New York, 1972, pp. 8–12; McGregor,

The Human Side of Enterprise, *op. cit.*, pp. 34, 39–42, 50, 77, 90–109, 163, 189, 191, 199, 208; Anthony P. Raia, *Managing By Objectives*, Scott Foresman, Glenview, IL, 1974, pp. 94–97, 136–144; and Edgar H. Schein, *Organizational Psychology*, 2nd ed., Prentice–Hall, Englewood Cliffs, NJ, 1970, pp. 2, 70, 77.

34. David W. Belcher, *Compensation Administration*, Prentice–Hall, Englewood Cliffs, NJ, 1974, pp. 3–16, 50–84; Robert L. Sibson, *Compensation*, AMACOM, New York, 1974, pp. 5–6, 35, 87, 98, 135–136, 152, 171; and Robert L. Sibson, "New Practices and Ideas in Compensation Administration," *Compensation Review*, Vol. 6, No. 3, Third Quarter, 1974, pp. 40–50.

35. Thomas H. Patten, Jr. and Karen L. Fraser, "Using the Organizational Rewards System as an OD Lever: A Case Study of a Data-Based Intervention," *Journal of Applied Behavioral Science*, Vol. 11, No. 4, November–December 1975, pp. 457–474.

36. Thomas H. Patten, Jr., and Peter B. Vaill, "Organization Development," in Robert L. Craig, Ed., *Training and Development Handbook*, 2nd ed., McGraw–Hill, New York, 1976, pp. 20-3–20-21.

37. William B. Schutz, *Here Comes Everybody*, Harper and Row, New York, 1972, pp. xviii–xix, 116–117, 181–191.

38. James A. Poteet, *Behavior Modification*, Burgess, Minneapolis, 1973, pp. 39–42.

39. Edgar H. Schein and Warren G. Bennis, *Personal and Organizational Change Through Group Methods: The Laboratory Method*, Wiley, New York, 1965, pp. 275–276.

40. Richard E. Byrd, *A Guide to Personal Risk Taking*, AMACOM, New York, 1974, pp. 59–122.

41. See Schutz, *op. cit.*, pp. 181–191.

42. Robert R. Blake and Jane S. Mouton, *The Managerial Grid*, Gulf, Houston, 1964. This has now been updated and given more of a team-building emphasis in *The New Managerial Grid*, Gulf, Houston, 1978. The first book sold more than one million copies and is a major landmark in the OD field.

43. W. J. Reddin, "The Tri-Dimensional Grid," *Training and Development Journal*, Vol. 18, No. 7, July 1964, pp. 9–18; also see his books *Effective Management by Objectives: The 3-D Method of MBO*, McGraw–Hill, New York, 1971, and *Managerial Effectiveness*, McGraw–Hill, New York, 1970.

44. Paul Hersey and Kenneth H. Blanchard, *Management of Organiza-*

tional Behavior: Utilizing Human Resources, 3rd ed., Prentice–Hall, Englewood Cliffs, NJ, 1977, pp. 83–324.

45. Blake and Mouton, *The New Managerial Grid*, *op. cit.*, pp. 306–307 contains a list of studies in which Phase I of Grid training is evaluated.

46. *Ibid.*, pp. 9–15.

47. *Ibid.*, pp. 16–40.

48. *Ibid.*, pp. 41–57.

49. *Ibid.*, pp. 58–74.

50. *Ibid.*, pp. 75–94.

51. *Ibid.*, pp. 95–120.

52. *Ibid.*, pp. 121–127.

53. *Ibid.*, pp. 197–208.

54. *Ibid.*, pp. 128–139 and *passim*.

55. *Ibid.*, pp. 140–169.

56. *Ibid.*, pp. 170–176.

57. *Ibid.*, pp. 177–208 and *passim*.

58. J. William Pfeiffer and John E. Jones, Eds., *A Handbook of Structural Experiences for Human Relations Training*, University Associates, Iowa City, IA, 1969, Vol. 1, pp. 7–12.

59. Hersey and Blanchard, *op. cit.*, pp. 83–324.

60. One source of it is David A. Kolb et al, *Organizational Psychology: An Experimental Approach*, Prentice–Hall, Englewood Cliffs, NJ, 1979, pp. 77–84.

chapter 4

GROUP DECISIONS AND THE QUALITY OF TEAMWORK

Many behavioral scientists and specialists in human resource development contend that teambuilding activities represent the most important single class of OD interventions. Teambuilding is an activity that particularly appeals to many persons who have had experience as group facilitators because of their intensive growth-group background and also because teambuilding generates considerable excitement among team members.

As Reilly and Jones have suggested, there are many kinds of teams and the term refers to various kinds of groups tnat work together.[1] Most typically the term refers to intact, relatively permanent work groups, comprised of organizational peers and their immediate supervisor.[2] However, there are many other kinds of teams, which may be more temporary in nature, whose purpose is to come together for the accomplishment of a specific task. Hence, *ad hoc* committees, task forces, and start-up groups of various kinds can be types of teams.

For a group to function effectively as a team, I believe that several elements should be present. First, the group must have a "charter" or reason for working together. Second, the members of the group must be interdependent. That is, the members must need each other's experience, abilities, and commitment in order to arrive at mutual goals. Third, the members of the team must be committed to the idea of working together as a group because they believe that this type of cooperative teamwork leads to more effective decisions than working in isolation. Fourth, the group must be accountable as an identifiable and functioning unit within a larger organizational context.[3]

In recent years there has been a great deal of criticism of T-group training, which probably has been justified, especially when the T-group was uncritically utilized in an organizational setting where a teambuilding intervention would have been preferable.[4] As Alban and Pollitt have indicated, many trainers and human resource development specialists, impressed by the values, insights, and personal growth that can be achieved in the human relations group of strangers, have often applied the T-group design for the purpose of improving the functioning of work groups (that is, non-stranger groups working together on tasks), confusing this method with teambuilding. Teambuilding should be regarded as a method of improving the work relationships among employees that has a positive contributing effect on accomplishment of tasks and should not be confused with "T-grouping."[5]

Several major concerns are often expressed in distinguishing between T-group training and teambuilding. For example, the following questions often arise: What is teambuilding? How is it different from T-grouping? With whom, and how does one do it, that is, build teams?

A related issue is, What kinds of exercises can be used for teambuilding? Still another is, What is an example of a useful design for the conduct of teambuilding? Beckard has suggested some designs that are reviewed in the end of this chapter.[6] Dyer has provided the most well-articulated statement to date on teambuilding based upon the OD action research model.[7] Others have listed and explained dozens of mini-designs for teambuilding that are essentially adaptations of materials spawned in the past twenty years from the field of experiential learning.[8]

T-Groups Versus Teambuilding Groups

We need to clarify the organizational concept of teambuilding or team development and then suggest guidelines that can be used by internal or external consultants and change agents who design teambuilding efforts.

The completely open, confronting environment of the usual stranger T-group can result in damage to organizational relationships and harm in one's career planning. This assertion is not to disparage the proper use of T-groups. Indeed, many of us have found the T-group experience helpful, if not indispensible, in developing awareness of ourselves and other people with whom we live and work. The main problem is that relationships are fundamentally different when bosses and subordinates meet together in (1) a training and (2) OD mode.[9] Specifically, in OD teambuilding the power is unequal, and that fact changes everything.

There are other basic differences that result from teambuilding that are caused by the fact that teambuilding is oriented toward task accomplishment within a work organization. In Figure 4.1 we contrast T-groups and teambuilding groups. It can be seen that the T-group is basically a group of strangers whereas the teambuilding group in a work organization consists of managers and employees who have a life together and in all likelihood a past history. The T-group focuses upon here-and-now data whereas the teambuilding group uses not only here-and-now data but also there-and-then data because both the past and the future must be dealt with by managers who have a life together in a live work organization.[10]

In the T-group accountability is low and internal, with the members being

Figure 4.1 Contrasting Groups

T-group	Teambuilding group
1. Strangers.	1. Managers who have a life together and a history.
2. Here-and-now data.	2. There-and-then plus here-and-now data.
3. Accountability is low and internal.	3. Accountability is high and to a larger external system.
4. Group is based on training.	4. Group has many bases.
5. Statuses are equal (or unknown).	5. Status differs due to real-life organizational rank of members.
6. Group can reward and punish.	6. Power to reward or punish is unequally distributed and externally linked.
7. Agenda is intra- and interpersonally oriented.	7. Agenda can be task-oriented (interpersonal issues can be dealt with as they affect task).
8. "Cultural island" or "mini society"	8. Awareness exists of the larger employing system.
9. Most action takes place in group.	9. Subgroups form and much action outside the group.
10. Reality is measured against feelings in the group.	10. Reality is measured against the larger system *and* by feelings in the group.
11. Voluntary groups with no future.	11. Compulsory (few opt out) with possibly a future.

Source: adapted from Billie T. Alban and L. Irving Pollitt, "Team Building" in Thomas H. Patten, Jr., Ed., *OD-Emerging Dimensions and Concepts*. Copyright 1973 by the American Society for Training and Development, Inc. Madison, WI, 1973, p. 34. Reproduced by special permission.

only mildly accountable to each other as participants. However, in a teambuilding group accountability is very high and is not only to the small group but, in addition, to the larger external employing system.

The T-group is formed for the purpose of the training event whereas the teambuilding group has many reasons other than training to meet together.

In a T-group the statuses of the participants are either equal or possibly unknown, whereas in a teambuilding group the members have important status differences due to the real organizational rank of the members.

The T-group can reward and punish but in the teambuilding group this power is unequally distributed and controls over it are often external to the group and linked to the employing organization.

The agenda for a T-group is intra- and interpersonally oriented. However, in the teambuilding group the agenda can be work- or task-centered issues. Interpersonal or intrapersonal issues can be dealt with to the extent they affect task accomplishment.

The T-group develops as a self-contained minisociety and often exists at a cultural island such as a resort, camp, or other rural setting away from the workplace and the main population centers in society. In teambuilding use may be made of a remote location simply to take the managers undergoing the teambuilding effort away from their immediate work environment and its distractions. Yet there is a keen awareness of the larger employing system of which the group is merely a part.

In a T-group all action takes place in the group. In teambuilding, subgroups may form and constant activity seems to be occurring outside the group as well.

In a T-group, reality is measured against the feeling of the members within the group at that point in time. In teambuilding, reality is measured against the larger system, and feelings in the group are only part of the data.

Lastly, T-groups have traditionally been voluntary and devoid of a future. A teambuilding group is compulsory in the sense that those asked to attend seldom refuse. It is questionable whether any organizationally sponsored activity focused on task effectiveness can be viewed as voluntary even when it is so intended.[11] Teambuilding groups by their very nature often have a future.

Determining the Need for a Team

Even if it is believed that teambuilding would be appropriate in an organization, top management must carefully analyze the needs of the organization and then decide whether the effort is worthwhile. A manager needs to ask himself if he really wants a team. He needs to consider the ways in which his subordinates are functioning together well and the ways in which they are not. He should also consider his own leadership style. If he is the kind of manager who makes all the important decisions himself and has Theory X assumptions about people, he may have to consider seriously if that style can be continued or whether he wants to modify it especially if he is facing increasingly complex tasks and problems.

In most work organizations the main reason at the present time for building a strong team is the recognition of the need for interdependence. In our technological society most jobs require bringing together the talents of many departments, specialists, or other resources in a collaborative effort where reliable products and services can be made or delivered. If the manager is clear about the need for interdependence, then the next step is to recognize those behaviors or issues that interfere with securing team cooperation. For example, collaborative behavior is often obstructed by the following: dependent or rebellious attitudes towards authority; different feelings of equality of membership or influence in the team; feeling in or out of the group; perceptions that the financial and other rewards are inequitably administered; varied perceptions of the tasks to be performed; difficulties in interpersonal relationships; lack of clarity about work roles; lack of effective means of planning, problem-solving, and decision-making; and inability to manage conflicts between groups.[12]

It is important to recognize that the concept of employees' working together interdependently is a relatively new idea for many work organizations and people. Most Americans have not been socialized in a way that emphasizes the value of collaboration and interdependence. Rather, in our schools and universities competitive, noncollaborative behaviors have been emphasized as the means of accomplishing tasks. Problem-solving is often carried out by the person alone. Rewards are given for individual rather than group work. Students are trained not to share or ask for help especially from one another but instead to strive on their own. Goals are set by others, and most decisions for the group are made by others. The result is that collaborative behaviors are less well known than might be suspected at first blush.

The importance of teambuilding is to develop those skills and behaviors that will foster team functioning. When and how does teambuilding start? Usually the initiative comes from the manager or the work group but sometimes the initiative comes from external forces completely outside the group. Those undergoing the teambuilding or change effort need to be aware of the factors, internal or external, that may be responsible for initiating the movement towards teambuilding. Part of the process of teambuilding OD is the continual assessing of the readiness for change in the system. Thus teambuilding can be viewed as an optimistic, forward-looking process.[13]

Teambuilding should not be attempted unless the group really has the opportunity to influence its own future. It should not be tried if other parts of the organization are likely to undo, or prevent, the changes the group determines to be desirable. If there is no chance for the negotiation of changed or improved relationships with the rest of the organization, then teambuilding can generate aspirations and enthusiasm that will only lead to increased disappointment.

If decisions have been made to phase out the work of a group, it is not likely to be helped by teambuilding. Either the problems are so deeply embedded that they require different solutions or external forces have already precluded survival. Yet OD techniques can be used and have been successfully applied to corporate layoffs, turning an essentially negative human resource decision into one that has potential for growth.[14]

If the manager is planning to terminate a number of employees, or if he sees the teambuilding activity as a therapy group for subordinates whom he cannot manage or motivate, then he probably should not start teambuilding. There should also be a belief that a teambuilding group has the resources to manage its destiny. If the manager does not believe that the group has sufficient confidence to grow and change, then he should not start a teambuilding effort.[15]

There is always the question about who should be included in a teambuilding effort. It is exceedingly unwise to conduct teambuilding with more than two levels of organizational management present at the same time in a workshop environment. There are sufficient problems to work on within a group, including simply the boss and his immediate subordinates, than to attempt working with groups that contain too many levels of management. Of course, in time the teambuilding effort can be extended to cover an entire set of organizational families, as the Likert-type network described in the last chapter suggested.

However, it is appropriate to move further in the teambuilding effort when certain circumstances prevail (such as when trust has become a usual rather than an unusual condition). Another favorable circumstance is when issues about roles, responsibilities, rewards, data flow, and delegation are on their way to being solved. Still another favorable circumstance is when the group has developed effective planning and problem-solving capabilities.

Thus no more than two organizational layers should be involved in the start of teambuilding, even though it is clear that there are issues that need to be resolved vertically or horizontally. Thus, organizational interfaces are important and must eventually be confronted.[16] However, if more than two levels are involved at the same time, the dynamics become very complex and several phenomena may hamper the process. For example, the middle person, or group, may feel squeezed between the top and the bottom, or may even feel bypassed and thwarted. Communication is often careful and guarded, not only because the threat is increased by layers and numbers but also because social norms may dictate that problems should not be opened up with the boss's boss present or in front of another group, no matter how serious the issue.

In discussing who should be involved in the initial teambuilding effort, we need to consider the debate about the level on which the effort should begin—at the top of the organization or elsewhere. There is no doubt that norms and values in an organization are influenced by the need identified from the top. Thus I believe teambuilding and all OD efforts are best begun at that level. This suggestion is a controversial point, and some experts believe successful OD interventions can take place at lower organizational levels.[17] However, it is also possible that starting elsewhere in the organization will before long require approvals that necessarily involve top management. Yet there is some evidence that a number of successful teambuilding efforts have been started in the upper middle levels of an organization and then so influenced the rest of the organization that others became interested and subsequently involved.

There is always the question about what is the organization or entity to be changed or improved? When an answer is given, the issue of whether there should be top management or a lower level intervention can often be solved. As a rule of thumb, I believe that the organizational entity to be changed must have sufficient personnel, policy, and budgetary autonomy so that it has its own integrity and can take certain actions without securing clearances from higher echelons in the organization. This would mean that a plant in a corporation, a division in a corporation, possibly a very large department in a large plant, a major segment of a Federal government agency or agency itself, one campus in a state-wide university educational system, or some other autonomous entity is the appropriate unit for work in teambuilding. In other words, the teambuilding effort should be begun with top management in an organization meeting the criteria of integrity previously specified. When this has been done, we have, in effect, defined "the" organization that can be worked upon through teambuilding OD.

The questions of where and with whom to intervene are also answered when we consider the concept of a psychological contract, to which we turn next.

Teambuilding and the Psychological Contract

The psychological contract is constructed out of reciprocal expectations, shared norms and standards, and mutual commitments. Managers enforce it through their power and authority in the organization. Employees enforce it by influencing the organization or withdrawing all or part of their participation and involvement.[18] In some ways the psychological contract resembles a collectively bargained contract but it is not written and exists in the minds of the participants because it has been negotiated in a teambuilding atmosphere.

In building a team with such a contract, goals are understood and supported; the sense of belonging to a group is strong. Trust and openness are present in communications and in relationships. The resources of the team members are tapped and used well. Leadership is shared. Procedures are developed to cope with problems and solve them. Sensitivity, flexibility, and creativity are present in group process work; and the group can steadily improve its processes.

To review, Figure 4.2 illustrates a teambuilding model that displays how a psychological contract can be expanded to include top management, an internal consultant or change agent, and an external consultant or change agent.[19] Usually in an organizational change effort in which teambuilding is the goal the top management group is interested in becoming a "team at the top."

Then once a teambuilding effort has enabled top management to function more effectively, it becomes interested in cascading the teambuilding effort to lower levels of management and requires some person inside the organization to direct the change effort. To do this it either hires someone from outside the organization or locates someone from within to act as an internal consultant whose mission is to make a conscious alteration of the status quo through an expansion of the initial teambuilding effort. This person becomes an inside resource and may be drawn from either the staff or the line organization. He has a continuous relationship with top management and brings to his job organizational knowledge that is vital for teambuilding.

Usually an internal change agent will need some access to outsiders in order to plan and implement interventions. Thus he attempts to find an

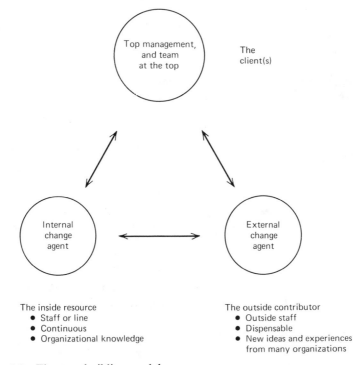

Figure 4.2   The teambuilding model.

external change agent who acts as an outside contributor or staff person to assist in the change effort. He is in a position to help the organization because he has had exposures to many other organizations and can bring this knowledge to bear upon whatever client or client system retains him. His job is to act as an outside resource and eventually to work himself out of a job, as he becomes truly dispensable. Occasionally, some outside consultants attempt to make themselves indispensable and to make the internal change agent or the client dependent upon him for continued contributions. This is very undesirable and ethical external change agents seek only to make their contributions and, having made them, to move on to other organizations.[20]

Figure 4.2 indicates arrows flowing in both directions for the three principals in the change effort. The arrows indicate that the internal change agent should be acceptable to top management and be able to relate to the external change agent. He should be able to initiate the amount and depth of contact with top management he deems necessary. The external change agent, likewise, should be acceptable to top management and be able to communicate with them as needed. In fact, one of the important contributions of an outsider is that often he can be very objective and say things to top management that an insider might fear to mention. He is not an employee of the client and usually only a small part of his livelihood depends on any one client.

In the psychological contract that prevails the three entitites in the change effort should be able to trust one another and communicate with one another in an open, authentic, confronting, and caring way.

As previously suggested in reference to the Likert top-to-bottom linking-pin model, it is often easy to move down and across in most organizations in a teambuilding effort once top management has built its own team. Employees are likely to become so enthused when their own peer group begins to function better with their boss that they use the model with their own subordinates or they bridge into their committee and task force assignments and interfacing departments by using the new behavior.[21]

Occasionally some work organizations get group development activities started with customers, suppliers, and other types of outsiders who interface with the organization. We find that better problem-solving makes work more enjoyable. Part of the reason is that a great deal of relationship-building occurs as roles and resources become clearer. Also, when we learn how to stop playing games, we save most of the energy normally used for fighting and conniving and apply it instead to getting the work done.[22]

Starting a Teambuilding Effort

Ideally, teambuilding is used to start or further many OD efforts. Often it begins with the external consultant's observing and facilitating the work of an intact team in their regular staff meetings. Sometimes there is a growing awareness that the group needs to devote more time to improvement in their problem-solving and decision-making. This can be done through workshops that are scheduled off-site. There are many designs that can be used diagnostically for this first off-site workshop, as has been well described by Beckhard in his confrontation meeting design[23] and in the large number of designs discussed by Fordyce and Weil.[24]

If the external consultant has been working with the team for awhile, he normally has a great deal of data based upon his observations and informal conversations. He knows where the problems are and has some ideas about what can be done to help. On the other hand, if he is new to the group, he needs a way to acquire information prior to the workshop. A common way to obtain data is for the external consultant to spend several days interviewing the group members and a few other managers above, below, and beside them, and then use that information as the foundation or beginning point when the group comes together off the work site.

Having interviewed others, the consultant may end the series of interviews with a discussion with the boss so that he has an opportunity to do some coaching or process consultation with him.[25] This meeting with the boss is never intended to be a punishing or trapping experience, however. Rather it is to use some of the interview information to help prepare him for the forthcoming meeting, to give him a chance to vent some of his feelings, and to explore alternative behaviors for handling difficult situations. In order to have this type of meeting with a boss, it is important, of course, that the external change agent have a psychological contract or understanding with everyone that he will be free to use any information that he is not expressly requested to hold confidential.[26]

Many consultants, particularly those associated over the years with Rensis Likert at the University of Michigan, have gathered information with survey instruments and questionnaires.[27] Data gathered in this way have the advantage of being objective and they provide a foundation for the measurement of team and organizational change. The disadvantage is that the data impose upon the external change agent a real obligation to feed back what he has gathered; this may not be approved by the client system. Surveys often produce much more information than can be handled well. They often cry out for interpretation and have no clear meaning on the surface. Moreover, there is seldom much value in dumping into a discussion more data than can be processed during the time available to work it through to at least a tentative conclusion.

Perhaps the most important part of the data-gathering process is the method of feedback. One style is to display all the data at the beginning of the off-site workshop and then help the group to work through it, providing some guidance and other help as needed. Often the way the team solves the problem of how to handle the data provides an early, real-life, here-and-now model of its working behavior that is useful for examination and discussion. Experiential learning can thus be used in a most practical way when a team has the task of strategizing how to process data.

Another style is to use the survey data generated throughout the duration of the workshop as the team moves from one type of issue to another, thus feeding in the role problem data while working on role clarification,[28] the reward systems problems[29] while discussing accountability and rewards, and so on. In these instances, the external change agent's goal in data feedback is to have the team acknowledge its problems. It is imperative that the team ''own'' the data and step up to its implications rather than have the consultant defend his personal interpretation of the data and the team's behavior.[30]

Exercises and Simulations in Teambuilding

Often internal and external consultants first use skill exercises and non-job-related simulations to create opportunities for learning in a low-threat situation with the safety of objectivity and then help the group to translate what they have learned so that it can be applied to their real-life situation. Unfortunately, some OD specialists have excellent skills in conducting such exercises but fall down badly in helping a group to learn vicariously from the learning experience. Most teambuilding experts believe that the preferred way to use exercises and simulations is in response to the group's own agenda and in relation to what is really happening. We have seen on many occasions that when a team becomes bogged down, an exercise can be very useful. In these cases, the translations of the learning from the exercise to the real-life situation are self-evident.

In the past decade a number of exercise interventions have been found useful and have in fact been widely used. A few of these are discussed next. One is the well-known NASA Exercise, which is used for seeking a consensus decision concerning the ranking of a number of items that would be useful to an individual who happened to land on the moon.[31] Tens of thousands of managers and others have been through the NASA exercise, and we might now regard it as "old hat." Yet the NASA exercise has spawned a large number of similar exercises that require ranking and struggling with interpersonal skill issues. Each of these exercises provides experience in working toward the building of consensus in groups. The Desert Survival Situation (now available in two versions), Subartic Survival Situation, and Project Planning Situation developed by Experiential Learning Methods in Plymouth, Michigan, provide meaningful teambuilding experiences.[32] All these exercises require teams to rank items individually and then to attempt to rank the items by means of a group consensus.[33] The consensus can then be compared to the proper ranking as determined by an expert who designed the respective problems, and scores can be obtained, indicating the relative performance of the teams in the exercise. More recently other variants on this type of exercise have been developed in the Lost at Sea[34] and Wilderness Survival problems.[35]

Desert Survival Problem

Exercises on consensus-building are generally well received by persons who participate in them, but occasionally a question arises about the connection between the exercise and the conduct of managerial work in an organization.

I have found that the use of the Desert Survival Problem is enhanced and the aforementioned problem of job relevancy averted when the exercise is conducted in the following manner.

(1) Participants are given Form A of "How Do You Feel About Teambuilding?" before the conduct of the exercise[36] (Figure 4.3). The questions asked stimulate participants to think about group versus individual

---

Figure 4.3 How Do You Feel about Teambuilding?
(Form A)

The ten questions below are designed to assess your attitudes toward various aspects of teambuilding and to stimulate your thinking and group discussion about them. There obviously are no "right" or "wrong" answers to the questions below. Therefore, please check each item as you see it. You can add your points and attain a score.

Figure 4.3 (*Continued*)

For each item below, circle the *one* number which best expresses how you feel about it.

	Strongly Opposed	Disagree	Undecided	Agree	Strongly Agree
1. Group work proceeds best when all group members speak freely or level with each other, as opposed to sparring or hiding opinions or feelings	1	2	3	4	5
2. An effective group faces up to and encourages disagreement as opposed to smothering differences	1	2	3	4	5
3. Strong feelings, including anger, if expressed will aid group work in the long run	1	2	3	4	5
4. It is important that decisions be made by talking things through—achieving consensus—rather than voting or merely relying on a decision by the boss	1	2	3	4	5
5. An effective group gives support, recognition, encouragement, and earned praise to group members easily and freely	1	2	3	4	5
6. Silent members should be drawn into discussions so that everyone's ideas are secured and no one feels left out	1	2	3	4	5
7. It is important that group work contribute to all members' feeling good about themselves and one another	1	2	3	4	5
8. Leadership roles (e.g., initiating, clarifying, summarizing) should be shared among the group so that all grow from the group experience	1	2	3	4	5
9. "Feedback" to group members should be given freely so people will know when they are helping or hurting the group's progress	1	2	3	4	5
10. An effective group should stop the action now and then and evaluate its own functioning	1	2	3	4	5

Source: Unknown.

Circle your response. Use an *X*
for team average.

	Very little	Little	Some	Quite a bit	Very much

1. To what extent did others pay attention to your specific ideas?   1   2   3   4   5

2. How frustrated did you become while reaching team decisions?   1   2   3   4   5

3. How responsible and committed do you feel for the decisions that were made?   1   2   3   4   5

4. To what extent did you actively seek contributions from others on your team?   1   2   3   4   5

5. How good do you think the team's decisions are?   1   2   3   4   5

6. What percent of the time did you lead the group by

    0%   20%   40%   60%   80%   100%

  a. contributing information?

    0%   20%   40%   60%   80%   100%

  b. helping the group work together?

Figure 4.4 Teambuilding member's perceptions. Complete and give to your team observer. (**Source:** Adapted from Gordon L. Lippitt, "Teamwork Analysis Form." Copyright © 1973 by Organization Renewal Inc.)

problem-analysis and decision-making. The form can be scored although the score is not particularly meaningful.

(2) I then distribute some special instructions for handling the Desert Survival Problem which clarify some questions about the exercise. It should be noted, however, that the creators of the exercise do not believe the clarifications that I use should be discussed in the way I do. They believe that leaving these ambiguities in the exercise increases learning because the participants must deal with them.

(3) I ask that each team be observed and provide a short explanation in "Task of Observers in the Teamwork Exercise" (Exercise in Teambuilding). The observer does not participate in the ranking of the 15 items. The observer role has proven to be a worthwhile learning experience as reported by those who have held it. (I provide a short handout explaining group observation for the person who is nominated to be an observer during the exercise.)

(4) I use the "Teambuilding Member's Perceptions" (Figure 4.4) to give the team members a chance to feed back to the observer how they personally perceived the team's functioning and their own role in it. The observer does

not receive these until after he reports on his observations. He then has a perception check on his observation skills.

(5) I use Form B of "How Do You Feel About Teambuilding?" (Figure 4.5) after the exercise is totally debriefed. Participants can score B and compare the results to A. Usually there is a point difference in a positive direction. Forms A and B are based upon items initially suggested by Douglas McGregor and since used by other prominent applied behavioral scientists.

Exercise in Teambuilding: Role of the Observer

One set of important managerial skills that is seldom discussed in executive seminars is the ability to observe individuals and groups in order to interpret their activities and to be able to communicate back to those what was actually seen behaviorally. These are executive skills that can be learned or sharpened.

In the behavioral sciences a number of studies of groups have been made in which the behavior of group members or participants has been recorded. The means of recording observations vary from reducing information to rather rigid formats to the gross itemization and counting of actions by people in groups who start a conversation, terminate a conversation, dominate an activity, withdraw from group participation, make remarks concerned with task accomplishment, make remarks concerned with interpersonal relations and processes in the group, and so on.

There is clearly much to be learned from the orderly and methodical study of the behavior of people in groups. Insights into the diagnosis of groups can help an executive subsequently in dealing with groups back on the job and in presenting his ideas to them influentially and persuasively. Executives who lack skill and sensitivity in group situations find that when they acquire these skills and sensitivities they also become more effective in diagnosing problems, proposing solutions, and choosing among alternative courses of action.

In Figure 4.6 there are listed a number of items that pertain to achieving group teamwork. Your task for this exercise is to observe the group to which you are assigned on each of the eight items (A–H) by circling the appropriate number. However, you may find the attached observation sheet insufficient for your purposes and desire to take additional notes so that you can report back in more detail and more richly on the performance of individuals and the group in attempting to accomplish its task in the exercise.

Your task as an observer is not to be simply a reporter of chronology but rather to be an analyst of the dynamics taking place in the group. As a consequence, you may now desire a quick overview of ways to observe. Figure 4.7 is an illustration of a way in which an analytical approach can be taken to determine what is taking place in the group. Still another way of examining what takes place in a group can be ascertained by quickly reviewing the categories shown in Figure 4.8.

Regardless of which way you wish to become prepared for this exercise, it is important that you consider how to improve your observation skills and make the necessary effort to observe task-accomplishment and group teamwork processes in the exercise. You will be asked to report back on these and a debriefing will take place on all the observers' observations.

These features extend the time required to carry out the exercise but overcome some of the minor objections mentioned above. The simulative aspect of the Desert Survival Problem is thus very beneficial and a favorably considered diversion. In fact, the relevancy and learning value of the exer-

Figure 4.5 How Do You Feel about Teambuilding?
(Form B)

The ten questions below are designed to review your attitude toward various aspects of team-building. They should help to stimulate your thinking and group discussion about teambuilding. As in the prior "quiz," there are no right or wrong answers to the questions. Simply mark each item with *one* circle to indicate how you feel about it. You can add your points and attain a score that can be compared with your score on Form A.

	Strongly Disagree	Disagree	Undecided	Agree	Strongly Agree
1. Group work is accomplished best when everyone is open and candid	1	2	3	4	5
2. Disagreement and differences are actively brought to the surface in an effective group	1	2	3	4	5
3. The expression of strong feelings will help progress over time	1	2	3	4	5
4. Consensus via free discussion, rather than voting or one-man decision-making, is the best way to make decisions	1	2	3	4	5
5. The ability to provide honest praise, support and encouragement are significant traits of an effective group	1	2	3	4	5
6. Maximizing the use of group resources and team feeling requires bringing "the quiet person" into the discussions	1	2	3	4	5
7. Feeling good about oneself and the others in the group helps to achieve good group work	1	2	3	4	5
8. Sharing or rotating leadership roles (initiating, clarifying, summarizing) aids in group members' growth	1	2	3	4	5
9. Providing data (feedback) to group members about their effectiveness in the group and how they are helping group progress is a must	1	2	3	4	5
10. Groups should take time out to examine their own functioning for greater effectiveness	1	2	3	4	5

Source: Unknown.

cise is noticeably enhanced. I seldom hear anyone complain, "Why don't you use an exercise built around problems in the office where we work? We'd get more out of it that way."

I believe that many consensus-building exercises could be improved if OD facilitators used instruments that gave team participants a chance to involve themselves more in the exercise and relate the experience more directly to back-home job application and managerial skill development.

Very recently, criticisms have been made of the scoring algorithms used in such consensus exercises as NASA and Desert Survival. It was argued that the scores generated cannot be used to prove the superiority of group-consensus decision-making.[37] The creator of the NASA exercise has, on the other hand, countered that the group-decision-making effects in NASA are a combination of a statistical cancellation of individual errors coupled with purely social psychological phenomena set in motion and determined by the nature of the group's interaction. The NASA task when used correctly provides a summary experience regarding those effects that a good deal of research has shown to be characteristic of group effort, particularly under conditions of consensus.[38]

Structured Experiences and Other Exercises

The large number of structured experiences that are now available in pub-lished form often contain exercises related to teambuilding. For example, the tower building[39] and cooperation squares[40] exercises and their various alterations are easily acquired, learned, and utilized. OD specialists in work organizations can examine these exercises and improvise some of their own following a similar pattern if desired. The content may differ but the form is the same.

Unfortunately, exercises are used to the exclusion of dealing with real-world problems too often; they become a crutch for the OD specialist and the team undergoing teambuilding. The purpose of teambuilding, it should be recalled, is to improve work effectiveness. The purpose of exercises is to help accomplish that. If an exercise does not lead back quickly to the real problems of the group at work, then it probably was not a meaningful inter-vention even though it might have been good fun. In other words, exercises should not be used unless the problem in the team can, at a given point in time, best be aided by an exercise or, alternatively, a conscious decision has been made to divert from task-oriented problem-solving within the team to a training mode for specific skill development activities. We want to stay unremittingly with an intention to help managers to learn how to learn, and as long as that experiential goal is attained, we should feel free to use either a live or vicarious learning vehicle.

The second point on diversion deserves some elaboration. To be sure, training is very useful as a part of teambuilding. Many teams, after diagnosis and analysis of their problems in functioning, gradually realize that they

Figure 4.6 Teamwork Observation Format

Observe your group on each of the items A–H below by circling the appropriate number. Record any additional notes that you desire.

A. How clear are the group goals?

1.	2.	3.	4.	5.
No apparent goals	Goal confusion, uncertainty or conflict	Average goal clarity	Goals mostly clear	Goals very clear

B. How much trust and openness in the group?

1.	2.	3.	4.	5.
Distrust and no openness	Little trust, some openness	Average trust and openness	Considerable trust and openness	Remarkable trust and openness

C. How empathetic are group members to each other?

1.	2.	3.	4.	5.
No empathy	Little empathy	Average empathy	Considerable empathy	Remarkable empathy

D. How much attention is paid to process and content (the way the group is working vs the task on which it is working)?

1.	2.	3.	4.	5.
No attention to process or content	Little attention to process and content	Some concern with group	A fair balance between content and process	Very concerned with process and content

E. How are group leadership needs met?

1.	2.	3.	4.	5.
Not met, drifting	Leadership concentrated in one person	Some leadership sharing	Leadership functions distributed	Leadership needs met creatively

F. How are group decisions made?

1.	2.	3.	4.	5.
Unable to reach decisions	Made by a few—or by one person	By majority vote	Attempts at integrating minority vote	Full participation and tested consensus

G. How well are group resources utilized?

1.	2.	3.	4.	5.
One or two contributed	Several tried to contribute but were discouraged	Average use of group resources	Group resources well used and encouraged	Group resources fully and effectively used

H. How much do members feel they belong to the group?

1.	2.	3.	4.	5.
Members have no sense of belonging	Members not close but some friendly relations	About average sense of belonging	Warm sense of belonging	Strong sense of belonging among members

Source: Gordon L. Lippitt, *Teamwork Analysis Form*, Copyright by Organizational Renewal Inc., 1973, 5605 Lamar Road, Washington D.C. 20016.

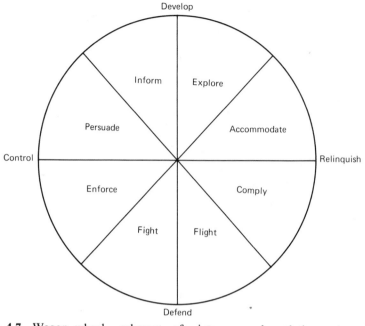

Figure 4.7 Wagon–wheel scheme of interpersonal relations in teams. (**Source:** Unknown.)

need to do special work aimed at increasing their specific skills, for example, in one-to-one communication, goal-setting, the diagnosis of group processes, decision-making, and the like. Then, it is appropriate to revise a psychological contract on the goals of the teambuilding effort and spend some time sharpening skills. When training results from self-diagnosis, it can become very valuable to the individuals in the team. However, when training is imposed on groups it is not likely to be as effective.[41]

In addition to exercises or training activities, a highly relevant and brief theory input by the OD teambuilding facilitator can often help the group by providing a conceptual framework for understanding its activities. Since 1972, University Associates has been providing an annual handbook for group facilitators; each edition contains an extensive repertoire of short theory inputs that can be used in teambuilding programs. The subject matter is very comprehensive, and the annual handbooks should be consulted for ideas and suggestions. In addition, there are some theory inputs that have been used repeatedly by OD specialists to the point that they have passed into common coin of the realm. For example, the Johari Window created by Luft and Ingham, mentioned earlier in the book, has been extensively used to help individuals understand self and other concepts and rudimentary ideas about the nature of human personality. The managerial grid of Blake and Mouton, as we have also seen elsewhere in the book, has been extensively

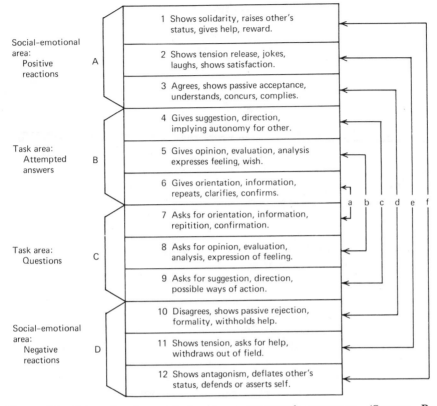

Figure 4.8 Categories for analyzing group teamwork processes. (**Source:** Reprinted from *Interaction Process Analysis* by Robert Bales by permission of the University of Chicago Press.)

used in teambuilding. The models for helping people analyze leadership styles developed by Tannenbaum and Schmidt[42] have also proven useful. In addition, the Transactional Analysis Theory as developed by Berne,[43] Harris,[44] and Jongeward[45] has been used by tens of thousands of persons undergoing OD efforts who were interested in learning how to explain certain types of interpersonal behavior using a simple language for the discussion of complex problems. Finally, the many resources of the NTL-Institute of Applied Behavioral Science should also be consulted in locating theory inputs and other learning resources for teambuilding.

Apart from the special event that culminates in an off-site workshop, the bread-and-butter work of teambuilding is best done over a period of time, paced to accord with the learning ability of the group undergoing the teambuilding effort. We would be very naive to think that the problems of teams can be solved in a two-day or five-day off-site workshop even though a good start can be made in such a short-term situation. Whenever possible, it is desirable that a longer-term relationship be established, free from an atmosphere of rush and rapidity.

Third-Party Interventions and Meetings

An external change agent who is separate from ownership of the problems can provide the greatest ongoing benefits to the work group or team as a third party in several different ways. He can counsel and coach individuals. He can help two people to resolve problems with one another and act as a third-party interpersonal peacemaker. He can facilitate staff meetings so they become more joint problem-solving sessions and less one-way information-providing meetings. In this context, he can also act as a process consultant asking the group working on tasks to stop occasionally and examine the very processes that are taking place in the group while it is working on tasks. Lastly, he can help all other task-centered meetings in the organization to become more effective.[46] This can be the critical first step in moving toward the building of teams.

It is well known that one of the most frequently identified and serious problems in work organizations is the time spent in meetings. The resulting frustration from the sense of not being engaged in the discussion, being personally needed, or used as a human resource in the meeting can turn off a manager very quickly. The tragedy is that usually the individual who called the meeting was really trying to improve organizational communications, use everyone's resources, and get everyone more committed to shared problem-solving. However, most managers do not know how to manage meetings; they can become great time consumers and are resented. Investment in the improvement of managerial behavior in meetings can greatly reduce the time spent there while increasing the level of satisfaction with attending meetings. Soon after the quality of meetings is improved the overall teambuilding effort can begin to address role and sanction problems so that fewer meetings are needed.[47] We come back to additional issues of time management in meetings in Chapter 7 because the subject deserves more detailed treatment than is given it here.

Internal Consultation

Two of the basic tasks of the external consultant are to help an organization to become open and to legitimatize the work of internal change agents. For larger organizations that role usually means development of an internal consulting structure. Experience has shown that a well-functioning personnel or training department within an organization that already has credibility and competence and is well respected can expand into a broader helping role by functioning as internal consultants. On the other hand, if personnel or training specialists cannot be used, then a separate consulting group may have to be formed. However, there is substantial evidence that far more effort should be made to build on existing skills and relationships among persons already in the organization having personnel and training responsibilities than it is to begin *de novo*. Personnel and training specialists often can provide many services, have entree with middle managers, and have a greater capacity to survive thin budget years than newly created staff groups designated as internal consultants. They are also in a good position to help change processes and procedures of a technical nature that have important employee behavioral implications such as pay systems, personnel policies, job design, intergroup relationships, and the like.[48]

Because the external change agent is an outsider and has only a temporary relationship to the organization, he has special freedom and objectivity that allows him to confront major problems in the team. Typically there are three broad areas in human behavior often not dealt with adequately until highlighted by the external change agent. For example, many organizations because they are unhealthy (as that term was defined in Chapter 2) cannot recognize or utilize the resources of their own members. There is an extraordinary reliance on the wisdom of outsiders when in fact there are often unused skills and knowledge within the organization itself. Once dramatized by the external change agent, the management group often becomes able to use its own human resources more effectively.

Another common problem is avoidance, which is shown in the reluctance of managers and members of many organizations to avoid, out of politeness, discussing internal conflict. By covering up conflict, many other important problems are also smothered.

The third area that is often an organizational problem that team members do not want to discuss is the failure to accept accountability. In many organizations considerable time and effort are expended in forming committees and delegating responsibility; yet no one seems to be accountable for completing work, and no one seems to accept responsibility for the failure to bring matters to completion or attain goals. Until managers can trust one another sufficiently to strive for accountability together with freedom and responsibility, the organization will have difficulty functioning effectively.[49] An outside consultant can stimulate an interest in MBO and goal-setting techniques. The inside consultant can follow up and keep alive this type of change effort.

As Alban and Pollitt have put it, most successful teambuilding efforts in organizations require orientation to the task as well as awareness of the realities of unequal power, accountability, and the surrounding larger system. This is why in teambuilding four interventions are normally found quite useful: data gathering; off-site meetings; third-party assistance on a long-term basis; and, lastly, setting up an internal consulting network inside the organization itself, which may be located in the personnel or training function.[50]

Teambuilding Dynamics

According to Huse teams can be categorized as follows: groups reporting to the same higher hierarchical supervisor; groups involving employees with common organizational aims; temporary groups formed to do a specific but temporary task; groups consisting of people whose work roles are interdependent; and, lastly, groups whose members have no formal links in the organization but whose collective purpose is to achieve tasks they cannot accomplish as individuals. To the same extent that there are various types of teams, there also are a number of factors affecting the outcomes of teambuilding, such as the length of time allocated to it, the team's willingness to examine itself and how it operates, the period of time the team has been working together, and the permanence of the team. Consequently, the results of teambuilding activities can range from modest changes in the team's operating mechanism to much deeper changes.[51]

In general, the results of teambuilding can be classified in three main areas: results specific to one or more individuals; results specific to the group's operation and behavior; and results affecting the group's relationship with the remainder of the organization. Usually, results of any particular teambuilding effort will overlap the three classifications. It is even possible for a positive result in any one area to have negative results in another area, as when a very cohesive team may increase its isolation from other groups, thereby leading to intergroup conflict or other results.[52]

In examining the results specific to one or more individuals, we often find that teambuilding efforts help persons obtain a better understanding of the way authority, control, and power affect problem-solving, decision-making, and data-gathering. Individuals on the team can then begin to experiment with different alternatives. Sometimes the results of the teambuilding process generate pressures on individual team members such as requests for greater role clarification, further delegation, and alterations in reporting relationships.[53]

Regarding results that are specific to the group's operation and behavior, we should note that teambuilding efforts are often preceded by clarifying the purpose of the team and establishing a basic framework within which further work can get done. Thus structure and process are both likely to be examined at a fairly early stage of teambuilding. Another issue that is commonly examined is the effective use of time by the team, as we have seen. Also, frequently teams examine and diagnose the nature of their problem-solving techniques. Thus in the early stages of teambuilding the diagnosis is usually applied to specific items that come up. However, as teams become more mature, they tend to broaden the scope of these diagnostic efforts to include areas that are more directly related to interpersonal styles and their impact on other team members. Throughout this process, the norms of the team become clearer, and the team can provide more opportunity for members to satisfy their individual needs within the group. As a result, the team becomes much more willing to take risks, both within the team and the larger organization. Team members become better able to face up to difficulties and they expand this capability by facing up to their relationships with the larger organization. A spirit of trust, openness, and risk-taking often develops.[54]

Turning to the results affecting the group's relationship with the rest of the organization, the team gains a better understanding of itself and becomes more capable in diagnosis and problem-solving, which, in turn, helps it to focus on its role within the larger organization. This realization causes teams to question and clarify their organizational role and explore ways in which the role can be improved or modified. Sometimes, a team may recognize the need for greater collaboration with other parts of the organization and try to establish task forces or project teams that cut across the boundaries of existing teams.

As a team becomes more cohesive, it usually attempts to exert a stronger influence on the other parts of the organization, which can conceivably cause conflict. The internal or external change agent can help a team understand its role within an organization and develop its own diagnostic skills so that intergroup tensions and conflict do not expand.[55]

The Success of Teambuilding

Teambuilding efforts are improved by a number of factors, including the people involved, the perceived relevance of the teambuilding for solving personal and organizational problems, the timing of the effort, and the degree of freedom that the team has to make necessary changes. We have already considered the importance of having top management support. Not only must there be this linkage but the individual team members must want to be involved.

Timing is another critical factor. For example, teambuilding activities are more likely to be successful when an outside event or internal crisis has helped with the "unfreezing" stage. In addition, sufficient time should be allocated so that data gathering can take place and the resulting information presented to the team. As previously mentioned, the teambuilding effort if rushed may not be effective. Yet if it is stretched out too long, personnel turnover, retirement, and deaths as well as such organizational dynamics as reorganization may seriously impede (even cancel) the effort.[56]

The chances for a successful teambuilding effort are increased when the team members are free to discuss the possibilities for change and have had an opportunity to identify and become aware of the constraints within which the team must work.[57]

Teambuilding efforts are not always successful, and the chances of success are reduced under certain conditions. The possibility of failure increases if a manager has not heard about teambuilding and does not fully understand it. In this situation he may not be willing to spend the time to conduct a proper diagnosis or be willing to work to establish mutual planning of the teambuilding effort. Another failure is caused by the manager of a group who uses teambuilding for accomplishing his own purposes rather than for organizational and management improvement.

Failures also stem from situations where team members are highly insecure, either as individuals or as members of the organization, because factors external to the team are perceived as threatening. Under these circumstances the team may be unwilling or unable to work on internal problems.

Teambuilding can be dysfunctional if the process is used as a substitute for management action by allowing managers to avoid an uncomfortable decision or situation while lapsing into a training mode. This may be termed "OD-ing," that is, only going through the motions of OD, learning all the words but never the music. Teambuilding is never a substitute for adequate management although it can help managers to become better interdependent administrators. Finally, teambuilding efforts may fail if the norms and goals of the OD specialist who is handling the teambuilding effort are too far removed from those of the team and he tries to impose his beliefs on the team.

All these factors indicate that proper teambuilding efforts must be based on previously acquired valid information about the present status of the team and its objectives. Diagnostic studies come first, and the OD specialist's intervention must begin at the group's current level, not at the level at which he thinks they should be.[58]

Client Allegiance

The change agent working with a group in a teambuilding effort has a key task, namely, responding to the group and intervening in the group's life in such a way as to facilitate its problem-solving capability. Reilly and Jones have pointed out that the change agent's allegiance is to the entire group, not to the boss or to a particular subgroup within the team.[59] This understanding should be made clear before the teambuilding venture begins. This does not mean that the consultant can ignore the highest level or highest ranking manager who authorized (from a budgetary standpoint) the launching of a teambuilding effort. Indeed, the change agent may need to allocate time outside the formal teambuilding sessions to provide special counsel to the manager, as previously discussed. However, to be most effective, the change agent must be his own person, free to respond equally to each team member.

The essential role of the change agent in teambuilding is as a "process" consultant rather than a "content" expert. His prime responsibility is to create the process awareness by which the team can take a meaningful look at itself, its functions, its methods, of working together, and its objectives for change.

The change agent should help the group solve its own problems by making it aware of its own processes and the way those processes affect the quality of the team's work. When using this approach the strength of the change agent in teambuilding is not obvious either to himself or to members of the team. Yet we find that the change agent's skills and values generally carry considerable weight in the eyes of the team members—and it is incumbent on him to be aware of his own impact on the group.[60]

An Example of Teambuilding—Action Research Mode

Although there is no one definitive example of teambuilding, and indeed the design of a teambuilding effort depends upon specific organizational diagnosis, it may be useful to furnish an illustration of how a one-week off-site teambuilding effort could be designed, following some of the thinking of Beckhard.[61] In the example the action research mode rather than the structured or semistructured seminar/workshop mode is highlighted.

The teambuilding effort could be conducted in a resort or other location off the job and have as its primary task the construction of a statement arising from the discussion and clarification of the goals of a group. The purpose would be to ultimately set forth specific objectives, activities, and timetables.

At an early stage of the teambuilding effort, there would be a discussion of the concerns and hopes of the group members for the joint effort in coming up with the kind of statement that they could all own and enthusiastically support. This discussion might include an analysis of roles, leadership/followership patterns, the use of rewards, and an assessment of whether new types of organizational designs might be warranted. These could be presented as theory inputs.

Hopefully from this discussion there could be a presentation of top management's plans, desires for specific types of organizational structure, aspirations in terms of organizational relationships, and statements concerning policy. This input would be very important for goal accomplishment because top management would presumably have the best understanding of the broad parameters within which goals need to be set, including market, financial, technological, economic, and other data that must be considered.

This discussion and work should result in the desired product of the teambuilding activity and the next stage would be to induct lower levels of management into the team. This would be, in effect, microteambuilding in the manager's own work area and resemble a filtering down of a teambuilding effort to the lowest organizational levels considered as needing to be involved in the teambuilding effort. Any new ideas that require changes in the culture of the organization would be thoroughly explained at this time, and participants in the lower-level teambuilding would be expected to provide input regarding how they envisage objectives at their level might be formulated consonant with the objectives of the organization.

After the induction has been completed, which could take a rather long period of time in an extremely large organization, follow-up "booster shots" of teambuilding would be necessary for top management and eventually filtered down through the organization. New insights from different external change agents might be utilized or a continuing relationship could be established with one or more external change agents for the purpose of keeping up the momentum in the OD effort and injecting new ideas in the teambuilding process. These booster shots could be held quarterly, semi-annually, or annually. Their frequency would depend upon the perceived health of the organization and its ability to absorb change. Ultimately, it is hoped that team skills would be transmitted throughout the organization, resulting in a new mode of managing having become the norm. It is important to note that follow-up must be continued until the organization has internally generated its own ability to sustain the momentum in the change effort.

Conclusion

As Huse has suggested, any organization depends on the cooperation of a number of people if its work is to be carried out effectively. We have much to learn about teambuilding, but it represents a stage in the progress of organizational development beyond the widespread use of the T-group in industrial and other settings that characterized the 1960s and early 1970s.[62] Complex organizations that dominate the American scene today clearly need the advantages that can be obtained when employees at all levels extend themselves to one another for the accomplishment of work. Additional innovations in social technology are required for the 1980s in order to unblock human energy so that managers are shown ways in which they can extend their resources to one another for the accomplishment of work. We already know enough about teambuilding to realize that it has great potential for the improved management of human resources.

Notes

1.   Anthony J. Reilly and John E. Jones, "Team-Building," in J. William Pfeiffer and John E. Jones, Eds., *The 1974 Annual Handbook for Group Facilitators*, University Associates, La Jolla, CA., 1974, p. 127.

2.   In this chapter teambuilding is focussed upon building teams of managers and/or professional salaried employees rather than on teams of hourly workers. There is an extensive literature on that subject that can be consulted by readers interested in the experiences reported at Volvo, Saab, Gaines' dogfood plant, in Japan, and elsewhere. See the following: Pehr G. Gyllenhammar, *People at Work,* Addison–Wesley, Reading, MA, 1977; Shigeru Kobayashi, *Creative Management,* American Management Association, New York, 1971; Thomas G. Cummings and Edmond S. Molloy, *Improving Productivity and the Quality of Work Life,* Praeger, New York, 1977; Louis E. Davis and

Albert B. Chernes, Eds., *The Quality of Working Life,* Free Press, New York, 1975, Vols. I and II; Richard E. Walton, "How to Counter Alienation in the Plant," *Harvard Business Review,* Vol. 50, No. 6, November–December 1972, pp. 70–81; Charles H. Gibson, "Volvo Increases Productivity Through Job Enrichment, *California Management Review*, Vol. 15, No. 4, Summer 1973, pp. 64–66; Earl R. Gommersall and M. Scott Myers, "Breakthrough in On-the-Job Training," *Harvard Business Review*, Vol. 44, No. 4, July–August 1966, pp. 62–72; and Edgar F. Huse and Michael Beer, "Eclectic Approach to Organizational Development," *Harvard Business Review*, Vol. 49, No. 5, September–October 1971, pp. 103–112.

3. Reilly and Jones, *op. cit., idem.*

4. See, for example, Kurt W. Back, *Beyond Words: The Story of Sensitivity Training and the Encounter Movement,* Russell Sage Foundation, New York, 1972.

5. Billie T. Alban and L. Irving Pollitt, "Team Building," in Thomas H. Patten, Jr., Ed., *OD—Emerging Dimensions and Concepts,* American Society for Training and Development, Madison, WI, 1973, p. 33.

6. Richard Beckhard, *Organization Development: Strategies and Models,* Addison–Wesley, Reading, MA, 1969, pp. 27–42.

7. William B. Dyer, *Team Building: Issues and Alternatives,* Addison–Wesley, Reading, MA, 1977, pp. 3–24, 41–139.

8. See such competent handbooks of the literature as the following: Uri Merry and Melvin E. Allerhand, *Developing Teams and Organizations: A Practical Handbook for Managers and Consultants,* Addison–Wesley, Reading, MA, 1977, pp. 7–392; and William I. Gordon and Roger J. Howe, *Team Dynamics in Developing Organizations,* Kendall/Hunt, Dubuque, IA, 1977, pp. 147–202 and *passim.*

9. Alban and Pollitt, *op. cit., idem.*

10. The here-and-now should be contrasted with the there-and-then. The former refers to the existential present being experienced by a team or group whereas the latter refers to events, experiences, or happenings that took place in the past and usually among an entirely different group of people or with a different individual.

11. Alban and Pollitt, *op. cit.,* pp. 34–35.

12. *Ibid.,* p. 35.

13. *Ibid.,* pp. 35–36.

14. Herbert A. Shepard and Sheldon Davis, "Organization Development in Good Times and Bad," *Journal of Contemporary Business,* Vol. 1, No. 3, Summer, 1972, pp. 65–73.

15. Alban and Pollitt, *op. cit.,* p. 36.

16. Lawrence and Lorsch emphasize the importance of interface relations in OD, both for purposes of problem-diagnosis and action-taking. See Paul R. Lawrence and Jay W. Lorsch, *Developing Organizations: Diagnosis and Action,* Addison–Wesley, Reading, MA, 1969, pp. 23–83.

17. For a discussion see Edgar F. Huse, *Organization Development and Change,* West, St. Paul, 1975, pp. 71–82; and Pollitt and Alban, *op. cit.,* p. 37.

18. Gordon L. Lippitt, *Organization Renewal,* Prentice–Hall, Englewood Cliffs, NJ, 1969, pp. 69–71, 75–78; Harry Levinson et al., *Men, Management, and Mental Health,* Harvard University Press, Cambridge, MA, 1963, pp. 23–38; and Marvin Weisbord, "The Organization Development Contract," in Wendell L. French et al., Eds., *Organization Development: Theory, Practice, and Research,* Business Publications, Dallas, 1978, pp. 321–326.

19. Thomas H. Patten, Jr., "Team Building. Part 1. Designing the Intervention," *Personnel,* Vol. 56, No. 1, January–February 1979, pp. 19–21.

20. Lippitt, *op. cit.,* pp. 163–180.

21. *Ibid.,* pp. 240–270.

22. On stopping managerial game-playing see Dudley Bennett, *TA and the Manager,* AMACOM, New York, 1976.

23. Richard Beckhard, "The Confrontation Meeting," *Harvard Business Review,* Vol. 45, No. 2, March–April, 1967, pp. 149–155.

24. Jack K. Fordyce and Raymond Weil, *Managing With People: A Manager's Handbook of Organization Development Methods,* Addison–Wesley, Reading, MA, 1971.

25. See Edgar H. Schein, *Process Consultation: Its Role in Organization Development,* Addison–Wesley, Reading, MA, 1969, pp. 3–9 and *passim.*

26. Alban and Pollitt, *op. cit.,* pp. 38–39.

27. David Bowers and Jerome L. Franklin, *Survey-Guided Development: Data Based Organizational Change,* University of Michigan, Institute for Social Research, Ann Arbor, 1976.

28. Merry and Allerhand, *op. cit.,* pp. 195–210. See also John J. Sherwood and John C. Glidewell, "Planned Renegotiation—A Norm-Setting OD Intervention," in John E. Jones and J. William Pfeiffer, Eds., *The 1973*

Annual Handbook for Group Facilitators, University Associates, Iowa City, IA, 1973, pp. 195–202.

29. Jay R. Galbraith, *Organization Design,* Addison–Wesley, Reading, MA, 1977, pp. 243–262, 333–379.

30. Alban and Pollitt, *op. cit.,* pp. 38–39.

31. J. William Pfeiffer and John E. Jones, Eds., *A Handbook of Structured Experiences for Human Relations Training,* University Associates, Iowa City, IA, 1969, Vol. I, pp. 52–58.

32. The organization (ELM) is in the forefront of the OD field in developing and improving such exercises.

33. See "Consensus-Seeking: A Collection of Tasks," in J. William Pfeiffer and John E. Jones, Eds., *A Handbook of Structured Experiences for Human Relations Training,* Univeristy Associates, Iowa City, IA, 1973, Vol. IV, pp. 51–65; and "Kerner Report: Seeking Consensus," in J. William Pfeiffer and John E. Jones, Eds., *A Handbook of Structured Experiences for Human Relations Training,* University Associates, Iowa City, IA, 1971, Vol. III, pp. 71–78.

34. Paul M. Nemiroff and William A. Pasmore, "Lost at Sea: A Consensus-Seeking Task," in John E. Jones and J. William Pfeiffer, Eds., *The 1975 Annual Handbook for Group Facilitators,* University Associates, La Jolla, CA, 1975, pp. 28–34.

35. Donald T. Simpson, "Wilderness Survival," in J. William Pfeiffer and John E. Jones, Eds., *The 1976 Annual Handbook for Group Facilitators,* University Associates, La Jolla, CA, 1976, pp. 19–25.

36. The items on Forms A and B of this teambuilding questionnaire are apparently derived from Douglas McGregor, *The Professional Manager,* McGraw–Hill, New York, 1967, pp. 160–182.

37. Dennis P. Slevin, "Observations on the Invalid Scoring Algorithm of 'NASA' and the Similar Consensus Tasks," *Group and Organization Studies,* Vol. 3, No. 4, December 1978, pp. 497–507. Other objections to the very idea of group consensus can be found in Irving L. Janis, "Groupthink" in David A. Kolb et al., Eds., *Organizational Psychology: A Book of Readings,* Prentice–Hall, Englewood Cliffs, NJ, 1979, pp. 236–246.

38. Jay Hall, "Observations on the Invalid Scoring Algorithm of 'NASA' and Similar Consensus Tasks: A Response," *Group and Organizational Studies,* Vol. 4, No. 1, March, 1979, pp. 116–118; and Jay Hall and Martha S. Williams, "Group Dynamics Training and Improved Decision-Making," *Journal of Applied Behavioral Science,* Vol. 6, No. 1, January–February–March, 1970, pp. 39–68.

39. "Towers: An Intergroup Competition Exercise," in J. William Pfeiffer and John E. Jones, Eds., *A Handbook of Structured Experiences for Human Relations Training,* University Associates, Iowa City, IA, 1971, Vol. II, pp. 22–26; and "Tinkertoy Bridge: Intergroup Competition," in J. William Pfeiffer and John E. Jones, Eds., *A Handbook of Structured Experiences for Human Relations Training,* University Associates, LaJolla, CA, 1975, Vol. V, pp. 60–72.

40. "The 'Hollow Square' Experiment," in J. William Pfeiffer and John E. Jones, Eds., *A Handbook of Structured Experiences for Human Relations Training*, University Associates, Iowa City, IA, 1970, Vol. II, pp. 35–43.

41. Alban and Pollitt, *op. cit.,* pp. 39–40.

42. Robert Tannenbaum and Warren H. Schmidt, "How to Choose a Leadership Pattern," *Harvard Business Review*, Vol. 51, No. 3, May–June, 1973, pp. 162–172.

43. Eric Berne, *Games People Play,* Grove, New York, 1964.

44. Thomas Harris, *I'm OK—You're OK: A Practical Guide to Transactional Analysis,* Harper and Row, New York, 1967.

45. Dorothy Jongeward et al., *Everybody Wins: Transactional Analysis Applied to Organizations,* Addison–Wesley, Reading, MA, 1973.

46. Alban and Pollitt, *op. cit.,* pp. 40–41.

47. *Ibid.,* p. 41.

48. *Idem.*

49. *Ibid.,* pp. 41–42.

50. *Idem.*

51. Huse, *op. cit.,* p. 230.

52. *Ibid.,* p. 231.

53. *Idem.*

54. *Ibid.,* pp. 231–232.

55. *Ibid.,* pp. 232–233.

56. Thomas H. Patten, Jr., "Time for Organizational Development?", *Personnel,* Vol. 54, No. 2, March–April 1977, pp. 26–33.

57. *Huse, op. cit.,* p. 234.

58. *Ibid.,* p. 235.

59. Reilly and Jones, *op. cit.,* pp. 227–228.

60. *Ibid.,* pp. 228–229.

61. Beckhard, *Organization Development: Strategies and Models, op. cit.,* pp. 26–42.

62. Needless to say not all the literature on teambuilding is laudatory. See John J. Scherer, "Can Team Building Increase Productivity? or How Can Something That Feels So Good Not Be Worthwhile?" *Group and Organization Studies,* Vol. 4, No. 3, September, 1979, pp. 335–351.

chapter 5

THE MANAGEMENT OF CONFLICT

Teambuilding is used for many purposes, not the least of which is the reduction of interpersonal, intraorganizational, and interorganizational conflict. OD has, in fact, often looked upon conflict resolution as its special area of emphasis and OD specialists have reported considerable success in reducing conflict within management and other work groups. The goals of these endeavors have often been to help parties understand each other, increase trust, reduce stereotyped nonempathic thinking, and solve problems. Up to the present, these efforts have been primarily focused upon conflicts within organizations, ignoring collective bargaining.[1] The few attempts reported by OD specialists to influence collective bargaining processes either for intraorganizational or interorganizational reasons have failed to deal adequately with the dynamics and complexity of the bargaining process *per se*.[2]

In this chapter we examine the nature of conflict, focusing first upon the interpersonal and intraorganizational aspects because they are closely related and then upon interorganizational conflict and collective bargaining. By these means we should obtain an enlarged understanding of the ideas of consensus and teambuilding that builds upon the materials discussed in the last chapter. In discussing interpersonal and intraorganizational conflict it is worth mentioning both a didactic game created by Rausch and Wohlking[3] that has been found to be a particularly useful vehicle in interpersonal conflict resolution and an exercise created by the author (the Lindell–Billings Confrontation Role Play) that has proven valuable in dealing with intraorganizational conflict as well as with certain aspects of interpersonal conflict. In discussing interorganizational conflict later in the chapter in conjunction with collective bargaining conflict, another original exercise created by the author, namely, Permo-Chromatics, Inc.—A White Paper Exercise, will be discussed. The latter is especially relevant for helping managers learn about the use of the white paper in teambuilding across departmental lines and could be used as a warm-up exercise in strengthening a management team preparatory to collective bargaining. No exercises in bargaining *per se* are set forth or explained in detail in this book because the explicit use of OD in labor relations is a vast new area that would require a separate book to cover. Nevertheless, it is an obviously important area for the future application of OD and teambuilding, and the reader should be aware of its interconnection with the subject matter of this book because one of the new frontiers of OD in the 1980s is its application to labor relations.

OD and Conflict

OD specialists are used to dealing with problems in hierarchical organizations that have certain superordinate, overriding missions to which members of management desire to direct their time and attention. We perhaps assume that the impediments to consensus and mission-attainment are caused by misunderstandings, inauthentic relations, poor teamwork, and the like. Given our widespread belief that properly approached (i.e., with trust, openness, candor, authenticity, and the like) most problems yield to "win-win" solutions, we are unfortunately quite likely to find a good share of OD specialists are poorly equipped to deal with bargaining, the use of power, institutionalized conflict, or with what game theorists call zero-sum game situations (where everyone in conflict loses). Some of the standard (and most successful) tactics in distributive bargaining (such as bluffing, threats, feigned anger, and exaggeration of the degree to which one's own position is fixed) appear to be inconsistent with the conventional wisdom of OD. It should be noted that OD tries to convert "distributive" into "integrative" bargaining (two terms returned to later in the chapter) even where objective conditions of scarce resources make win-win solutions impossible.[4]

OD specialists, further, have often had little experience with relations between independent organizations and many, consequently, tend to approach both human and organizational problems in face-to-face terms. Thus, many of us frequently underestimate the importance of the social–political–economic determinants of conflict. Furthermore, since many of us have orientations that are psychological rather than sociological, we tend to assume that participants in conflict situations are free agents rather than representatives of organizations subject to role requirements and constituency pressures. To be sure, OD insights are likely to be most useful in the intraorganizational bargaining that accompanies the formulation of positions within a bargaining team and the "selling" or persuading of members of management or the union to accept the negotiated terms of the agreement. Yet even during the interorganizational bargaining that takes place at the bargaining table itself OD techniques should prove helpful in facilitating those aspects of the bargaining process that are truly integrative.[5]

The Concept of Conflict

Conflict can be placed upon the cooperation–opposition continuum, which is in important theoretical focus in conceptually understanding OD and teambuilding.[6] Conflict is neither "good" nor "bad" for an organization in any global sense. The reason is that not all conflicts are of the same kind. Some, for example, follow definite rules and are not typically associated with angry feelings on the part of individuals. Others may involve irrational behavior and the use of violent or disruptive acts by the parties. Therefore, we need to distinguish between those forms of opposition that are mild and competitive and those that are rancorous and destructive.

In conflict the parties do not follow a mutually acceptable set of rules and are not primarily concerned with winning. Instead, they are intent on reducing, defeating, harming, driving away, or possibly (in the extreme case of war) physically destroying the opponent. The means used are expedient; the climate is one of stress, anger, and/or fear.[7]

The opposite form of behavior from conflict could be viewed as problem-solving. Because unchecked conflict tends to result in destruction everywhere, we observe an entropic tendency toward conflict resolution. Conflict winds down to loss; problem-solving ends in the satisfactory achievement of the needs of the involved parties. Two values associated with problem-solving are that it can result in objectively superior decisions contrasted with those resulting from typical conflict methods and that it can make the unsolved parties feel like winners. People who feel like winners are likely to have more energy, creativity, and desire to perform in work organizations than losers.[8] Hence, conflict resolution has become and remains a central concern of OD.

We may summarize the characteristics of conflict as follows:

1. At least two parties (individuals or groups) are interacting.
2. Mutually exclusive goals and/or mutually exclusive values either exist or, what is functionally equivalent, are perceived by the parties as existing.
3. Interaction is characterized by behavior designed to defeat, reduce, or suppress the opponent or to gain a mutually designated victory.
4. The parties face each other with mutually opposing actions and counteractions.
5. Each party attempts to create an imbalance or relatively favored position of power vis-à-vis the other.[9]

The conflict process will culminate in results; the evaluation of those results as favorable or unfavorable depends on the measures used, the party making the judgment, and other subjective criteria.[10] A team may result from the resolution of conflicts; hence, it is most desirable to work through the differences before deep rancor results from the parties' opposition. We have seen that teambuilding is a human problem-solving process; therefore, teambuilding may be conceived of as solving one type of social conflict that has interpersonal, intraorganizational, and interorganizational manifestations. Caring about the conflict and learning how to cope so that it can be resolved are obviously indispensable skills for teambuilding.

The term conflict can also be approached another way and applied to the breakdown of decision-making such as when an individual or group experiences difficulty choosing among alternative courses of action. Some common decision problems may arise for intra-individual reasons. Other types of conflict arise not because individuals cannot make up their minds but instead from the differences between the choices made by different individuals in the organization. In the latter case, called intergroup conflict, the individuals are not in conflict but the organization as a whole is.[11]

The conditions necessary for intergroup conflict are three: the existence of a positive felt need for joint decision-making, a difference in goals, and/or a difference in perceptions of reality. Organizations typically react to conflict by engaging in four forms of behavior: problem-solving as previously discussed), persuasion, bargaining, and politics. In problem-solving, objectives are shared; the goal is to identify a solution that satisfies the shared criteria. In persuasion, individual goals may differ within the organization but objectives are shared at some organizational level; disagreements can be accommodated by referring to allegiance to the common goals. In bargaining, disagreement over goals is accepted as a defense of fixed interests; agreement is sought without persuasion. Politics, the fourth type of decision-making behavior, is a process in which the social situation is the same as in bargaining in respect to an acceptance of an intergroup conflict of interest. However, the scope of the area for bargaining is not regarded as fixed. In this way, opponents of lesser power do not allow relations to become bilateral but rather hope to expand the parties in conflict by bringing in potential allies and tipping the scales in the balance of power.[12] The clever use of politics in an organization is a useful technique for resolving intergroup conflict and, of course, well known to practicing managers.

It could be said that problem-solving and persuasion are "analytical" attempts to secure private as well as public agreement on the decisions around which the conflict is raging. Bargaining and politics are negotiatory processes that are less than rational. The more organizational conflicts represent individual rather than intergroup conflict, the greater the use of analytical procedures. It is thus recognized that the organization cannot reach an agreement because individual participants are unable to do so. On the other hand, the more organizational conflict represents intergroup differences, the greater the use of bargaining.[13]

The tendencies to resolve intergroup conflict through bargaining and to resolve individual conflict through analysis have different effects on organizations. Bargaining has potentially disruptive consequences as a decision-making process because it usually places strains on the distribution of status and power in an organization. Bargaining also acknowledges and legitimizes a heterogeneity of objectives in an organization. This legitimization removes a possible technique of control available to any organization, namely, goal identity and uniformity. Because of these problematic consequences stemming from bargaining, managements in organizations customarily perceive and react to all conflict as though it were in fact individual rather than intergroup in nature. As a result, almost all disputes in an organization will be defined as problems in analysis and the managerial reaction to conflict will be problem-solving and persuasion. These reactions will exist and persist even if they appear to be inappropriate. There is likely to be a greater explicit emphasis on common goals where they do *not* exist than where they exist. Bargaining if it occurs will be surreptitious and masked by an analytical framework or overlay.[14]

Interpersonal Conflict—An Exercise

We turn next to describing an exercise that is very useful in skill-building for solving interpersonal conflicts. This exercise, created by Rausch and Wohlking,[15] is particularly useful for requiring a group undergoing a teambuilding effort to analyze why a subordinate manager is in conflict with his organizational superior and to obtain some skill practice in how to manage the conflict. The focus is on interpersonal conflict but to some extent intrapersonal conflict is involved as well.

The exercise is built upon a situation where a manager (who is at least on the second level of supervision) has several managers reporting to him. One of these managers has been assigned the task of converting some information-handling operations in the department to electronic data processing. The superordinate manager has made the assignment to the lower-level manager and discussed it with the latter on several occasions. The boss has allowed the first phase of the work to overrun the deadline date by two months and then decides to follow up on the reasons for the delay.

The exercise is in the form of a didactic game[16] where each member of the teambuilding workshop is given a booklet to be used for analyzing the stages through which the superior and subordinate manager pass as they attempt to accomplish work in a situation of interpersonal conflict. The booklet provides a format for analyzing seven aspects of the interpersonal confrontation of managerial conflict: taking the first steps to encounter one another; achieving an early confrontation; analyzing the subordinate manager's reaction; dealing with defensiveness; dealing with evasiveness; dealing with withdrawal and preparing for disciplinary action; and dealing with a hostile response. The participants in the workshop proceed step-by-step through the exercise in small groups and as a team share their ideas about how to confront the recalcitrant manager and to do so in ways that attempt to keep him on the team.

The creators of the didactic game suggest the best ways of managing the conflict and offer a scoring mechanism. The participants are encouraged to conceive of a variety of ways of coping with the manager in question and have in their power all courses of action except discharging the recalcitrant manager.

The didactic game stimulates team discussion and enables team members to learn and criticize one another's style for managing interpersonal conflict. This is especially valuable, of course, for teambuilding. If several groups of teamed managers proceed through the exercise in the same workshop simultaneously, the final decisions made by each team can be compared with each group in the workshop, thereby providing the chance for teambuilding across all the groups present, a most educational and useful experience.

This particular exercise also permits analysis of intrapersonal conflict in respect to the subordinate manager. The didactic game suggests the manager's characteristic mode of reaction to accepting and fulfilling assignments has changed; one could speculate as to why, including considering changes in the manager's mental and physical health and other types of intrapersonal problems.

Intraorganizational Conflict—An exercise

Conflict between many managers in the same organization is yet another well-known type of conflict management problem. The prior exercise was intraorganizational but essentially of a one-on-one interpersonal type. What can be done about teambuilding among groups of managers intraorganizationally?

The "Lindell–Billings Corporation: A Confrontation Role Play," created by the author,[17] provides an intraorganizational experience that permits the team members to confront one another and develop skills in negotiation, managing intergroup conflict, and problem-solving. It is a vicarious learning vehicle that can be followed up by other exercises on live organizational problems or in other ways deemed appropriate, based upon the diagnosis of the OD facilitator.

Organizational development specialists have tools available for conducting confrontation meetings within live organizations and can draw upon managers' experiences, feelings, and goals for data when conducting a confrontation meeting. In teaching individuals OD techniques, the OD specialist often has a difficult time in building verisimilitude into learning vehicles and making the learning experience worthwhile and realistic. For example, it is difficult to teach individuals about the theory and practice of the confrontation meeting unless they can be placed vicariously in an organization and experience a confrontation both intellectually and social-emotionally. The "Lindell–Billings Corporation—A Confrontation Exercise" has proven to be a useful vehicle for realistic yet vicarious learning about intraorganizational conflict.

The exercise or role play is easy to perform and can be used by groups of 15 to 30 participants. The exercise can be conducted to include all phases of a "classical" confrontation meeting or reduced to only the first few phases if time pressures are a limiting factor in the OD effort.

The exercise is conducted by passing out the factual write-up and quickly moving into teams preparatory to a confrontation. After the participants read the write-up they usually become quite involved in their tasks as either top management, top management observers, the staff group, and the staff group observers. (The observer groups can be eliminated if the number of participants is small. Similarly, some of the top management and staff group roles can be eliminated if required by the size of the teambuilding group.)

It is necessary to assign only two roles, namely, who will be chairman of the corporation (i.e., Lindell) and who will take responsibility for reporting the staff group's concerns. These chairmen are responsible for getting their teams' views reduced to newsprint and reporting confrontation.

The OD process facilitator role-models the external consultant or change agent throughout the exercise. His behavior as well as the dynamics leading up to and reflected in the confrontation become valuable data that can be analyzed and debriefed after the confrontation is completed.

If the teambuilding workshop participants are thought to need a theory input on confrontation in the "warm-up" phase of the exercise, it is useful to improvise one or utilize one that is already available if it seems suitable for the group.

The Lindell–Billings exercise begins when the facilitator explains to the participants that they will engage in a confrontation meeting by playing assigned roles.

The OD teambuilding facilitator divides the participants into at least two teams. Team A (top management) consists of seven people in top management who are to be confronted as a group (Lindell, Billings, Mahoney, Thayer, Diamond, Gomez, and Jamieson). Team B (the staff team) consists of eight staff vice presidents. (These roles are shown on the Lindell–Billings Corporate Organization Chart, Figure 5.1.) If more than 15 participants are present, the remainder are divided and assigned to be observers of Team A and Team B. It is possible to have up to 15 observers, each assigned to observe one team participant but it is preferable to have fewer, with two being ideal.

The OD teambuilding facilitator distributes the Lindell–Billings Corporation—An Intraorganization Conflict exercise fact sheet and the Lindell–Billings Corporate Organization Chart to each participant. He allows participants five minutes to read these materials and gives participants one hour to prepare for a confrontation based upon their team roles. Their task is to reach a consensus within an hour regarding what they wish to communicate to the opposite team about the issues in the case (and how they feel about them) and to reduce the consensus to newsprint. If there are to be observers of the "top management" and "staff" teams, they are simply told to sit with the teams they are observing, making no inputs into the confrontation but prepared to report their observations on the behavior of assigned

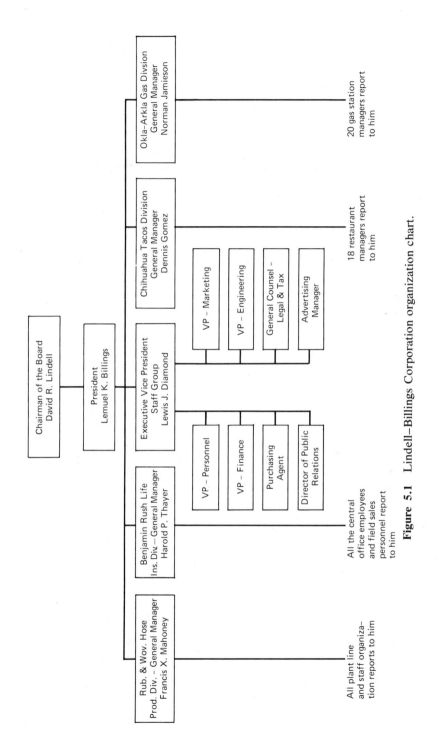

Figure 5.1 Lindell–Billings Corporation organization chart.

individuals and the team in a planned debriefing after the conduct of the exercise. The facilitator also asks the "top management" team to select who will play Lindell and the "staff" team to select a spokesman.

The facilitator tells the teams to begin and circulates among the teams to answer any questions and keep the exercise moving. He urges the respective teams to have their newsprint ready within an hour but to post it until the other team has also reduced their consensus to newsprint.

When the newsprint for both teams is completed, they are posted simultaneously. The teams are allowed five minutes to read them and then the chairmen of the top management team (Lindell) and of the staff team discuss the major points of their papers, answering any questions asked by participants. The facilitator acts as a moderator, if needed. The observers, if any, report on their observations of the individual and team behavior. The total reporting and debriefing takes approximately one hour.

The facilitator then asks the top management and staff teams to go back to their teams and work for half an hour on the task of deciding consensually what action they propose to take next, based on the confrontation over the aforementioned perceived issues. The courses of actions are also reduced to newsprint.

The teams convene for the final time and the posting and discussing of their newsprints is repeated. The second confrontation should take about one-half hour.

The facilitator leads the entire group in a discussion of the dynamics of the exercise from a design standpoint, emphasizing how the features of the confrontation meeting design can be applied to a wide range of managerial problems in work organizations that are experiencing intraorganizational conflict.

The fact sheet on the Lindell–Billings exercise and an organizational chart of the firm are shown next.

The Lindell–Billings Corporation—An Intraorganizational Conflict Exercise

---

David R. Lindell and Lemuel K. Billings are, respectively, chairman and president of the Lindell–Billings Corporation. The company was founded by Lindell's father as a manufacturer of rubber and woven hose products about fifty years ago. It has in recent years become a conglomerate and is regarded as one of the most aggressive miniconglomerates in the United States. It has, in the past decade, acquired a small life insurance company (the Benjamin Rush of Hartford, Connecticut), a chain of eighteen quick-service restaurants (Chihuahua Tacos), twenty ultramodern gas stations located off interstate highways (Okla–Arkla Gas), and is considering taking over the Ranchero Motel chain in the Southwest.

Lindell–Billings' top management consists of Lindell (a hard-driving fellow who came up through manufacturing in the rubber hose segment of the business), Billings (a shrewd financier who was chairman of the Benjamin Rush before moving to the parent corporation), the present general managers of the Rubber and Woven Hose Products Division (Francis X. Mahoney), Benjamin Rush Life Insurance Division (Harold P. Thayer), Chihuahua Tacos Division (Dennis

Gomez), Okla–Arkla Gasoline Division (Norman Jamieson), and the executive vice president, staff group (Lewis J. Diamond). This seven-man team works together well and is extremely entrepreneurial in its outlook.

Beneath the top management team are managerial groups that direct day-to-day operations of the various divisions. Lindell–Billings provides these managers with considerable autonomy but looks toward inputs from Lew Diamond's staff group when it is considering long-range business planning. The staff group provides services for all the divisions. Diamond's staff vice presidents and managers have expertise in depth in such fields as finance, personnel, engineering, marketing, purchasing, public relations, advertising, and legal and tax affairs. (The organization chart of the corporation is available. It should be emphasized that the staff group reporting to Diamond contains a number of highly competent and highly paid executives that have approximate status parity with the divisional general managers.)

Lindell and Billings have just pulled off a new financial coup that has Diamond's staff upset and concerned. Several are threatening to resign, report data to the Justice Department, Securities and Exchange Commission, or otherwise disrupt the business. On the other hand, the top management group (including Diamond) stands solidly behind Lindell and Billings. Lindell and Billings have retained an OD process facilitator from Midwestern State University to conduct a confrontation meeting with the staff group.

These are the issues that are bothering the staff group:

- Lindell and Billings gave a check for $39 million to wheeler-dealer John J. LaVerne for the purchase of the Ishpeming Copper Company, on the condition that he would deposit it in the National City Bank and leave it untouched for a specified period. LaVerne has a controlling interest in the Ishpeming Copper Company and is virtually answerable to no one.

- They then set up a "paper" organization known as the LB Copper Corporation, with the names of certain members of the staff group as dummy directors, and caused the LB Copper Corporation to buy Ishpeming Copper—not for cash but for $75 million in LB stock which was conveniently printed for the purpose.

- From the National City Bank, Lindell and Billings then borrowed $39 million to cover the check they had given to LaVerne; and as collateral for this loan they used the $75 million in LB Copper stock.

- They then sold the LB Copper Corporation stock on the market (first having touted it through their brokers) for $75 million.

- With the proceeds, Lindell and Billings retired the $39 million loan from the National City Bank and have reported $36 million as the parent company's profit on the deal.

With this information at hand, one group plays the top management team of Lindell, Billings, Mahoney, Thayer, Gomez, Jamieson, and Diamond; a second group plays the staff group's role. There may be some observers assigned to each group. The OD process facilitator will assist in carrying out the confrontation and instruct team members orally in their task(s) once they have read the case and thought about it.

Having examined intraorganizational conflict, we turn next to interorganizational conflict and the resolution of intraorganizational conflict as it relates to the management of interorganizational conflict. Those words may be confusing but our next topic is the management of conflict between unions and management or what could be termed cross- or transorganizational conflict.[18] In order to proceed with this discussion we first need to provide some background on the relationship of OD to models inclusive of unions. This subject is truly on the frontier of OD, as previously mentioned, but needs to be crossed if we are to extend the concept of teambuilding to far-flung corners of the realm of human resource management.

OD and Models Inclusive of Unions

All planned change is governed by some type of theoretical model that contains a set of value premises, propositions, or hypotheses about the major variables involved and a desired set of outcomes or results. In trying to understand the application of OD to a unionized setting it is important that an appropriate model be used. Although we may assume that the pressures for change operate on union and nonunion organizations alike, no OD change models have yet conceptualized any role for labor unions.[19] Indeed it might be said OD has little to say about the union at all.[20] There is even a velvet-gloved belligerence against unions in some of the OD literature.[21] The problem has gotten to the point where organized labor is expected to step up its campaign in the 1980s for Congressional investigations into what it considers "union-busting" law firms, consultants, and trade associations. Organized labor has, in fact, recently alleged that such opponents number 1,000 firms with more than 1,500 individual practitioners engaged in the full-time activity of preventing unionization efforts, a "business" with sales in excess of one-half billion dollars annually.[22] Thus, it is not surprising that many unions are highly suspicious of OD and OD practitioners, seeing them as *management* consultants in the narrowest possible sense.[23]

The lack of attention given to unionized situations by OD specialists may be partly the result of an erroneous impression that union–management relations are confined to the formal process known as collective bargaining. Yet there are a number of examples where the parties have chosen to supplement the bargaining process with more continual efforts at facilitating change. These include joint long-range union–management committees, quality of working life experiments, standing task forces on occupational safety and health, and similar efforts that suggest interorganization mechanisms for conflict resolution in limited domains.[24]

Union–management joint change efforts such as those enumerated would seem to be relevant to teambuilding. First, these efforts reflect departures from orthodox bureaucratic organizational designs. Second, they apparently take place in organizational climates where there must be a modicum of facing up to and exploring problems with a predisposition toward action based on experimentation and research. Third, the actions undertaken represent OD interventions. The actions are "integrative," involving issues where the goals of the union and management are not of an adversary nature. They may be distinguished from "distributive" issues, which are, of course, ones where the goals of the union and management are clearly incompatible.

Union–management relations may be regarded as but one form of interorganizational relations in contemporary conflict theory (in much the same way, strikes may be viewed as one form of collective action). The emphasis in this subject today is not on individuals but on organizations, which are viewed as open systems constantly "bargaining" with their environments. It is recognized that organizations have multiple goals, that there are real conflicts of interest over scarce resources (both within and between organizations), and that power is a primary method of settling conflict.[25]

Assumptions in a Union–Management Model

From within the fields of organizational behavior and industrial relations Kochan and Dyer have identified and interwoven three central concepts that provide a provocative model that conceptualizes and provides a basis for evaluating union–management change processes, namely, goals, power, and conflict. They also make a number of reasonable assumptions about the realities of union–management relations.[26]

First, it is assumed that employers and employees interact in an interdependent relationship that resembles a mixed-motive game situation. That is, some of the goals held by the parties are compatible and some are incompatible. When employees are formally represented by a union, the partial conflict of interests becomes institutionalized. Then a third set of interests, specifically the organizational interests of the union, enter the relationship. Each of these sets of interests (the individual's as both employee and union member, the employer's, and the union's as an organization) is accepted as legitimate. It is also assumed to be legitimate for each interest to pursue its own goals in interactions within this system of interdependent relationships.

The presence of a union implies that, in order to pursue their interests, employees have formed a relatively permanent structure that is protected and legitimatized by legislation. Consequently, it is also assumed that, unlike nonunionized situations, the relationship is characterized by a structurally based power-sharing arrangement.[27] Because power is shared between two organizations with partially incompatible goals, it is further assumed that structurally based conflict is a natural and inevitable phenomenon in the relationship.

The aforementioned assumptions imply that an interest group or "subsystem" approach must be used to conceptualize the dynamics of union–management change efforts as well as in determining their perceived effectiveness.[28] The reason for this implication is that since each interest group is expected to pursue goals important to it in interactions with the other, the effectiveness of a joint change effort must be defined as the extent to which the program is perceived to contribute to the attainment of goals valued by each subsystem (or interest group).

It is important to recognize always that the outcomes valued by each of the subsystems should be given equal weight by any outside observer or analyst who conducts, intervenes in, and/or judges the success of a union–management change effort. The goals of one party or subsystem should not be valued more than the goals of another.

It is also important to recognize that any subsystem, although perhaps appearing to be unified and possessing solidarity, beneath the surface may be a temporary and/or loose coalition reflecting internal compromises.[29]

Propositions in a Union–Management Model

The Kochan–Dyer model has been summarized into formal propositions in order to facilitate empirical testing of their theory. The model is composed of three stages or components that parallel certain logical sequences. The first stage discusses the stimuli for union–management change. The second change focuses on the initial decision to participate or commit the respective organizations to a specific change effort. The third focuses on maintaining commitment to the change effort (or constitutionalizing it over time).

Turning first to the stimuli for union–management change, we should note that since the collective bargaining process has long since been proven adaptable to changed conditions both unions and managements have historically been reluctant to collaborate in joint ventures established for organizational change outside of the bargaining process. Thus proposition 1a follows: the greater the *external* pressure that a union or management is experiencing, the higher the likelihood that the parties will be stimulated or motivated to consider alternative joint ventures. Proposition 1b states that the greater the *internal* pressures a union or management is experiencing, the higher the likelihood that one or the other will be motivated to consider alternative joint ventures. Proposition 1c states that the less effective the formal bargaining process is perceived to be in dealing with the issues over which pressures are being generated, the higher the likelihood that the union and management leaders will be motivated to search for alternative joint ventures for change outside of the bargaining process.

The parties having been stimulated to initiate a search for alternative means of improving their performance, the second stage of the change process begins, namely, that of reaching an initial joint decision to embark on some specific program of organizational change. The initial decision to join forces is difficult to reach because two parties that have partially conflicting goals and priorities must agree to proceed with change and are themselves likely to be unstable coalitions. Insofar as there is no overriding authority structure or goal shared by a union or management that is sufficiently specific to guide their decision-making (except perhaps survival), the conflict resolution strategies typically advocated in the OD literature (focusing on changes in interpersonal relations, problem-solving, or appeals to superordinate goals) are likely to be ineffective. Thus, proposition 2a: a joint commitment to embark on a specific change effort will be forthcoming only when both the union and management perceive the change as being instrumental to the attainment of goals valued by their respective organizations. Related to this idea is proposition 2b: a joint commitment to embark on a specific change effort will be more likely to develop when the parties are willing to negotiate and make compromises over the goals of the change effort. Proposition 2c is also pertinent: a joint commitment to embark on a specific change effort will be more likely to occur when coalitions or individual power holders within each organization do not attempt to block the organization from participating in the joint effort.

The final stage of the change model addresses the problems of institutionalizing the change program over time within the larger context of union–management relations. A number of propositions bear upon the continuation of such a change program. Proposition 3a suggests that the more the goals valued by the union and the goals valued by management are achieved in the initial phase of the program, the more likely it is that a mutual commitment to maintain the program will be achieved. Proposition 3b states that the higher the probability that the union and management will continue to achieve valued goals in the future, the more likely it is that a mutual commitment to maintain the effort will be achieved.

Continuation of the change can be affected by goal displacement or a change in the perception of the initial goal. Thus proposition 3c holds: the commitment to the change program will be less likely to continue if the initial goals of either of the parties toward the effort are displaced by goals of a higher priority. Proposition 3d states that the more the initial stimulus to the change effort subsides, the more difficult it will be to maintain the commitment to the effort over time.

Another facet of continuation of the change effort and institutionalization is diffusing the benefits of the change. Some means of spreading the benefits of the change throughout the organization will have to be worked out; otherwise the political pressures within either the union or management will explode and eventually kill the change effort. Thus proposition 3e holds: the more the benefits from the program are perceived to be equitably distributed among organizational members (both union and management), the more likely it is that commitment to the effort will continue over time.

No organization will participate in a change effort that may contribute to its own demise, particularly a union whose leaders are elected officials. Typically, union leaders want to be perceived by the rank-and-file as having been instrumental in obtaining positive payoffs from the change effort. This observation leads to proposition 3f: the more instrumental the role the union is perceived to play in the attainment of the benefits of the change effort, the more likely it is that the union will continue its commitment to the change effort over time.

Beyond these minimal conditions for continued participation, the parties will also want to perceive their involvement in a change effort as being a legitimate endeavor in terms of the overall union–management relationship. Commonly, this means that the change effort must be viewed from the start as a supplement to and not as a replacement for collective bargaining. Based on this reasoning, the following three propositions can be derived. Proposition 3g holds: the less the union members see the change effort as infringing on issues or areas that they believe should be handled solely within the formal collective bargaining process, the more likely it is that the union will continue its commitment to the program over time. Proposition 3h states: the less management perceives the program as threatening their managerial prerogatives, the more willing the employer will be to continue his commitment to the change effort over time. Proposition 3i states: the more successfully the jurisdictional ambiguities among the formal bargaining process, the formal grievance procedure, and the change effort are worked out, the more likely it is that the parties will continue their commitment to the program over time.

Finally, one salient reason for union leaders' hesitance to participate in joint programs is their fear of being perceived as having sold out to management. Three important propositions stem from this observation. Proposition 3j holds: the less the union leaders are seen as being "coopted" into performing roles indistinguishable from management, the more likely it is that the union will continue its commitment to the change effort over time. Proposition 3k states: the more the change effort is buffered from the strategic maneuvers of the formal contract negotiations process, the more likely it is that the parties will maintain their commitment to the change effort over time. Proposition 3l holds: the more union leaders continue to pursue aggressively their constituents parallel goals on the distribution of rewards through the formal bargaining process, the more likely it is that the union will continue its sustained commitment to the joint change effort.[30]

Implications of the Union–Management Model

Foremost among the implications of the Kochan–Dyer model is that OD specialists should recognize the basic differences between traditional organizational change situations and those in which unions are involved and should adjust their teambuilding and other interventions accordingly. Both union and management representatives are likely to adopt a highly instrumental attitude toward participating in programs of planned organizational change. Put another way they are likely to ask "What's in it for me?" and not participate initially or continue to participate in a change effort unless this politically pragmatic question is answered to their satisfaction.

In addition, the union–management situation rests upon structurally based power-sharing and conflict. OD specialists who insist upon arguing that the first step in developing a successful change effort is to establish a climate of high mutual trust may never make it in the union–management arena. Low levels of trust are probably characteristic in relationships between parties with incompatible goals or strong self-interest orientations. Because low trust is consistent with the objective circumstances of union–management relationships, it should be expected that the parties are likely to be wary of OD strategies for increasing trust levels through laboratory training or team-building. Yet, contradictorily, ways must be found to help the parties openly confront and resolve their conflicts. Clearly, improvements in relationships will not grow out of condoning suppression, smoothing over unresolved differences, or sweeping aggravating problems under the rug. The OD specialist should not belittle the time-tested techniques of collective bargaining and compromise in his interventions. Indeed these should be accepted and employed.[31] The problem is finding a way for the OD consultant to enter the collective bargaining arena without appearing as a naive or gullible gladiator.

Collective Bargaining and Consensus

It is clear that, to date, applied behavioral science, laboratory training, and OD teambuilding seem to have had little impact upon or use by unions or managements in the collective bargaining process in industry or in government.[32]

If we assume that, behaviorally viewed, collective bargaining in America is an institutionalized form of conflict resolution, then it is relevant to inquire why OD has not been used to an appreciable extent in the past decade as either a prelude or accompaniment to negotiating union–management contracts and resolving grievances. Perhaps more importantly, it is relevant to ask whether the accommodations to conflict reached through collective bargaining are on the same plane as a consensus developed under the conditions of trust, openness, risk-taking, authenticity, receptivity to feedback, and focus upon change that are held to be characteristic of OD. Lastly, it would be worthwhile to consider the possibilities of institutional change in union–management relations through use of OD-teambuilding in collective bargaining on a more broad-scale basis. These are our concerns in the remainder of this chapter.

Collective bargaining is defined for our purposes as negotiations between a union and management concerning wages, hours, and working conditions, which culminates in a written legally enforceable agreement commonly called a contract. Inasmuch as 99% of collective bargaining agreements in the United States today contain a grievance procedure, employee grievances are also negotiated by the union during the life of the agreement and constitute collective bargaining on a day-to-day basis. Grievance administration and settlement thus involve negotiation by the collectivity (the union) in the name of the individual (the employee). Unless otherwise noted in context, the chapter focuses upon the collective bargaining of a contract rather than the negotiation and settlement of grievances during the contractual life of the agreement.

Although the examples are limited, there have been cases where behavioral scientists were active in industrial relations and contributed to improving a union–management relationship. Perhaps one of the earliest of these extends back to 1948, when Elliott Jaques was involved very deeply in social science consultancy with Wilfred Brown at the Glacier Metal Company in Britain.[33] Another experience was reported by Muench, who eschewed the role of side-taker and arbitrator in a conflict and instead acted as a consultant, approaching each person and group with a relatively unstructured, open-ended psychotherapeutic-type session in which the primary concern was crystallizing issues, pinpointing areas of difference, and recognizing the feelings and attitudes which colored every issue.[34]

More explicit use of OD can be found in reports by Blake, Mouton, and their associates in the union–management intergroup laboratory using a confrontation design.[35] These researchers have also applied their grid organization development technique in industrial relations with considerable reported success in improving the interpersonal relations and climate in a firm.[36]

Lastly, Stern and Pearse have reported on the unilateral use of OD by a local union of the Amalgamated Meat Cutters and Retail Food Store Employees' Union to train negotiating committees on conflict resolution, improved communication, and the planning of change (i.e., negotiations strategy).[37] Their program differed from one of Blake's, which was bilateral (management and the union).

There are very few books on collective bargaining providing behavioral analyses that have a theoretical framework above the level of simple typologies or that give much consideration to OD or laboratory training techniques. Walton and McKersie,[38] however, use in part the kind of approach that would be familiar to behavioral scientists.

Four different types of systems are treated in their discussion. The first system of activities comprises competitive and conflicting behaviors over issues that are intended to influence the division of limited resources and is the familiar distributive bargaining of economics. The second system includes activities that increase the joint gain available to the negotiating parties. These are problem-solving behaviors and other activities that identify, augment, and influence the common interest of the parties. The focus here is upon issues and a joint approach (called "integrative bargaining") to their solution.[39] The third system comprises activities that influence the attitudes of the parties toward each other and that influence the basic relationship bonds between the social units involved. This system is referred to as "attitudinal restructuring" and comes closest to the domain of OD.

The fourth, and last system, includes the behaviors of a contract negotiator that are meant to achieve consensus within his own organization and, hence, is called "intraorganizational bargaining."[40] The latter aims at developing flexibility in the position of one party and the consensus of one party.[41]

Balance theory, reinforcement theory, and "working through" methodology are mentioned but not rigorously employed to analyze contract negotiations and explain how attitudes are restructured.[42] The relevant concepts are stated, illustrative anecdotes are mentioned and juxtaposed against concepts, and the authors think out loud about interconnections, all of which lead them to conclude the following:

> Integrative bargaining is a cognitive task, while attitudinal structuring is a socioemotional process. The process of integrative bargaining brings the parties together to solve specific problems and search for other areas of common interest.

> During integrative bargaining the parties move closer both substantively and attitudinally. First, because the demands of integrative bargaining require that the parties approach the agenda items from an objective point of view, the interaction can serve to structure positive attitudes between the participants. Under such neutral interactions (as far as attitudinal content is concerned), interaction leads to positive sentiments. Second, to the extent that the parties do more than engage in the interaction and succeed in identifying (or underscoring the salience of) areas of common interest, the participants will tend even more to be positively disposed toward each other.[43]

Although we need not accept the inevitability of neutral interactions leading to positive sentiments, it is quite clear that the authors do join problem-solving styles in collective bargaining with emotionally energizing concepts that make union–management consensus possible. The use of OD to capture this energy and harness it to build more trusting, open, authentic, and honest relations is perceived as a real possibility.

Collective Bargaining in Practice: Horse-Trading

It is difficult to generalize in collective bargaining because there is a variety of patterns available, ranging from the craft union model, applicable in the building trades, to the industrial union model, applicable in the automobile or steel industries, and the professional association model, applicable in public education. However, it appears that much of collective bargaining in industry where there is no overwhelming power on the side of the union or management centers around "horse-trading." This is essentially a technique intended to split the difference between the parties rather than resorting to a mutually opposed win–lose situation.

In horse-trading, both parties win something, and the bargaining involved does suggest an incipient but fairly low-level understanding. It saves face for the union and makes it possible for management to live with the union. By the same token, the union's willingness to trade off various of its demands will frequently save management's face. Thus, horse-trading as a strategy is perceived as better than the dog-eat-dog conflict of the pre-collective bargaining era in industry. Moreover, the astute manager who follows union politics and the perceptive union leader who studies managerial power plays and climate will learn a great deal about issues that are tradable and can make his life tolerable and even pleasurable or entertaining in the industrial arena.

Horse-trading is, however, antithetical to consensus because traditional collective bargaining institutionalizes perceived interest groups that function primarily on the basis of splitting the difference. When collective bargaining is institutionalized into a system supported by law, it rigidifies union–management relationships and results in a state of affairs that forestalls consensus. More specifically, continued collective bargaining over a number of years under the impetus of the union's search for job security and employee tenure results in contracts that are longer and longer and more and more specific regarding the details of wages, hours, and working conditions.

The administration of such complex agreements almost necessarily means that a bureaucracy will arise to handle matters. There will be a managerial bureaucracy acting to produce goods and services (and documenting its prerogatives to the last dotted i and crossed t) and a union bureaucracy reacting to these actions (with perhaps poorer records because it has fewer resources for keeping them but long memories living in the minds of experienced union members—living history books, if you will).

Yet if there is anything that is characteristic of the times, it is the multiplying evidence that people want to escape bureaucracy and will do so through revolt or through such calculated forms of opposition as undependable performance, goal displacement, or the formation of counterbureaucracies. The kinds of revolts that we have seen in recent years in response to bureaucracy are not so much based upon the rise of charismatic leaders with answers to all problems as they are caused by people's desperation to have their needs met in a more personalized way than is possible under the bureaucratic reign of rules. In collective bargaining, evidence for this revolt has been shown time and again in the rejection of agreements negotiated on the national level by employees in specific plants who have stridently voiced their concern that "big-table" collective bargaining is inadequate for meeting local plant needs because it is insensitive to those needs.

In view of these considerations it is perhaps timely to question whether we have been wise in the United States to institutionalize conflict through collective bargaining legislation and to almost uncritically applaud the results. More specifically, we should raise the question of whether there is a higher order of things than currently composed collective bargaining; if there is, can we get there in practical terms in the near future?

Making Consensus Possible

There are some ideas about group functioning and normative patterns applicable to moving collective bargaining from arm's length conflict-accommodation to open, authentic, trusting relations that make decision-making by consensus possible. Put another way by Marrow:

We consider the practice of management to be an art in the same way that the practice of medicine is an art. But there are scientific principles that must be used in the practice of both. Managing people is developing these principles today. Effective management now requires scientific knowledge of the principles of human behavior as they are applied in industrial organizations.[44]

Although normative patterns restated here were based upon limited research,[45] they seem consonant with much of the literature of applied behavioral science (see Figure 5.2).

More specifically, it is suggested that union and management collective bargaining teams that enter into and carry out negotiations should be willing to (1) give and take feedback, (2) express feelings, (3) develop acceptance, concern, and trust, (4) switch the focus periodically from the content of negotiations to the analysis of the group interaction process, (5) use the negotiations sessions for self-education as well as task concern, (6) experiment with new behavior, (7) share leadership power and influence, (8) enable all group members to participate responsibly, (9) work within an informal structure, and (10) commit themselves to working through to consensus rather than relying upon majority rule or sweeping messy issues under the rug. Beginning with these intentions will elevate collective bargaining beyond its present plateau. Moreover, all of these actions would be "good faith" bargaining and far removed from "unfair labor practices." Indeed the very language of prevailing labor legislation and the bureaucratic tangle of National Labor Relations Board decisions would be translated into behavior in union–management relations that was positive and fair, thereby transcending both law and bureaucracy by calling forth the social skills of the parties to solve their own problems.

Put another way, since institutions are concrete behavior patterns carried out by people, changing social institutions (such as collective bargaining) should begin by changing the behavior of the people who negotiate agreements and settle grievances. The way to do this seemingly is to use OD-teambuilding interventions.

Legal Biases in Collective Bargaining

The subject-matter of collective bargaining almost because of its nature seems to be necessarily union-oriented, perhaps because the mere fact of recognition of a union implies something that managements have historically not granted on a voluntary basis but only under compulsion and when the prevailing labor legislation required union recognition under stipulated circumstances. Thus one almost is inclined to feel that, over-simplified, the prevailing implicit concept of collective bargaining appears to be that management bargains and the union collects.

Because of the limitations of the concept it is difficult to view collective

Figure 5.2 List of Normative Dimensions Applicable to Union–Management Contract Negotiations

---

1. **Feedback** the process in which group members exchange reflections, observations, opinions, impressions, evaluations, and criticism regarding behavior of fellow members, including selves.
   a. Members should take an active part in the feedback process by both giving and receiving (accepting) feedback, even though it may be difficult at times.
   b. Members should not "block"[a] the feedback process.

2. **Feelings** the mutual and spontaneous expression and open acceptance of sentiments, emotions, and feelings on the part of group members and the avoidance of intellectualization.
   a. Members should encourage the expression of feelings from all group members, including themselves.
   b. Members should not "block" either their own feelings or those of other members.

3. **Acceptance Concern** includes the formation of trust in other members, the reduction of fear of others and of self, and the encouragement of acceptance of self and others; the common recognition among group members that each should have an equal chance to speak.
   a. Members should promote acceptance among all members of the group.
   b. Members should not block the development of acceptance or the acceptance concern as it exists in the group.

4. **Analyzing Group Interaction or Process** the analysis of past and present member interaction in order to discover its significance as a learning experience.
   a. Members should encourage and participate in the analysis of "group process," drawing upon data from the here-and-now, and should think of this as a goal within itself.
   b. Members should not block or discourage the analysis of group process.

5. **Goal and Task Concern** the attempt to set goals, provide data, materials, or tasks for the group to work on in the usual work-group sense. This is characterized by member attempts to overcome "datalessness" by bringing suggestions, bibliographies, articles, and ideas to the attention of other group members, in the hope that these data might serve as problems or tasks for the group to work on.
   a. Members should accept the goals and tasks (defined in 1, 2, 3, 4, and 6) of giving and receiving feedback, feelings and acceptance, analyzing group process, and attempting behavior experimentation.
   b. Members should not be concerned with a lack of content or tasks in the usual work group sense; they should not try to formulate goals to be worked on outside the T-group.

6. **Behavior Experimentation** the effort by the individual to change or alter any aspects of his behavior in the group in order to increase his learning experience, receive feedback concerning his new behavior, or facilitate the development of group sensitivity skills.
   a. Group members should be encouraged to "try on" (experiment with) new behaviors themselves and should permit others to do so also.

---

[a]"Blocks" are here defined as those verbal, psychological, or even physical behaviors which interfere with the development of group sensitivity skills.

Source: Adapted with special permission from *The Journal of Applied Behavioral Science*, "Trainer Interventions and Normative Patterns in the T Group," by George Psathas and Ronald A. Hardert Vol. 2, No. 2, pp. 157–164, copyright 1966, NTL Institute.

Figure 5.2 (*Continued*)

b. Group members should not block or discourage others or themselves from trying on (experimenting with) new behaviors.

7. **Leadership Behavior (member–member)** includes any attempt on the part of the group member to gain a position of power and influence (for himself) in the group or to support another's attempt to achieve power and influence.
   a. Group members should share in the leadership of the group.
   b. Group members should not attempt to "take over" as leaders through exercise of power, dominance, excessive verbal activity, or other means.

8. **Participation** all forms of member behavior that contribute to group process and are part of member interaction. Participation can be active (i.e., overt participation in a verbal or physical manner) or passive (i.e., just listening to others participate). Participation is a sign of accepting responsibility as a group member for the success of the group.
   a. Group members should participate during the life of the group.
   b. Group members should not "over-participate" or "underparticipate" (especially verbally) in the life of the group.

9. **Third Parties and Authority Problems** any tendency on the part of group members to maintain or support a third party as an authority figure in the group. However, power differences should be recognized.
   a. Members should be sensitive to the problem of authority as, when, and if it arises in the group
   b. Members should net depend upon, maintain, or expect any third party to be an authority figure in the group.

10. **Decision Making** refers to problems of decision making and group problem solving, the mode by which decisions will be made and procedures devised by the group for discovering and reaching consensus. Members should be actively aware of decision-making procedures.
    a. Decisions should be made through consensus of all members.

11. **Structure Concern** refers to the development of permanent roles, the maintenance of social structure, and the hope for "a continuing organization to distribute roles and maintain group interdependence."
    a. Group interaction should take place with-in an unstructured, informal organization.
    b. Members should not concern themselves with the usual development and maintenance of group social structure, as this concern can block the analysis of group process and the development of group sensitivity skills.

---

bargaining as conflict resolution, per se, without ideology and free from an adversary point of view. If it is viewed broadly as conflict resolution, it is very easy to drift into myopic thinking about the law and such formal devices for conflict resolution as conciliation, fact-finding, mediation, and arbitration. The tendency then is to continue drifting and look toward third parties for settling disputes. The parties in negotiations themselves are for some reason, perhaps economic interest, seen as unable to reach settlements. In the few cases where there is literature available on conflict resolution in industrial relations it stresses the resulting typological patterns[46] but not well-pinpointed dynamic causes. The one book in recent years that breaks new ground in conflict resolution has an OD slant to it and stresses the role of MBO in collective bargaining.[47] It deals with CBBO: collective bargaining by objectives.

One would look high and low to find books on collective bargaining that stress process because all are short on process and long on the law and legal technicalities. Managements and unions are typically seen as rational actors in an economic drama.

Students of industrial relations are taught to consider only the cognitive aspects of collective bargaining so that they can play their roles as cognitive actors. Yet, when it comes to trying to specify the process by which an agreement is reached in collective bargaining, mention is made of such activities as all-night bargaining sessions, news blackouts, and other seemingly irrational devices. In essence, it appears that in order to reach an agreement it is necessary for the entree of a type of tension release and emotionality whereby the relationships between the parties can break through the facades of everyday life and reach some degree of trust, thereby transcending legal technicalities.

The shallow interaction that takes place in the bargaining room prior to the deadline date of contract expiration and round-the-clock bargaining may be likened to the sessions of an eight- or nine-day training laboratory before T-grouping has had much of an effect in changing the interpersonal atmosphere. The buildup of tension as days pass and the participants in collective bargaining start to explore one another's personalities at the intrapersonal, interpersonal, and group levels leads to the kinds of things that take place in the midweek of a human relations laboratory and thereby provide a basis for moving ahead into higher-order relationships and, finally, signing an agreement. Consensus is finally reached through frenetic sessions of collective bargaining although it is a limited type of consensus, an accommodation or agreement to suspend disagreement for a while. Managerial protagonists can then go home and brag about how they fought the good fight; union negotiators can head back to the union hall and sell the agreement to the membership by underscoring how they bargained around the clock beyond a state of meta-fatigue for the boys in the local. In both cases the political constituency is served—at least seemingly.

Changing an Institution

As has been suggested several times above in the chapter, collective bargaining is the same as institutionalized conflict. It cannot be regarded as consensus. Nevertheless, long-term contracts (such as those for three years) reflect some trust between management and the union but not consensus. An agreement is valid only for a limited time period, which may be regarded as an accommodation, but the conflict will blossom forth again at the time of contract expiration. This is very much unlike a marriage contract, which need not be reopened every three years but is constantly being renegotiated through the interaction of everyday life and in many instances is regarded as a permanent type of consensus. To be sure, everyday grievance negotiations in a plant may be regarded as the proper analogy to the daily renegotiation of the contract as in marriage. However, the analogy of collective bargaining to a marriage is perhaps not a very good one because although renegotiation is being carried on in both instances there still is the requirement of a fundamental renegotiation of the total agreement in industrial relations.

Collective bargaining should also be viewed from the standpoint of several organizational levels, as suggested earlier, if we are to talk about the total relationship. At the specific level of contract negotiations or grievance settlements, collective bargaining depends very much upon the interpersonal relations of the negotiators. It is therefore at this level that OD and team-building have their greatest potential for moving collective bargaining from the level of horse-trading and limited conflict resolution to consensus. This is because institutional change in collective bargaining would be affected by the principals in contract negotiation and their behavior within the power spheres in which they behave. Once their behavior is changed, it should then become possible for the character of the relationship itself to change.

When collective bargaining is looked at not from the perspective of the bargainers but from that of the persons organizationally removed from it who are located in higher management or international union leadership positions, consensus seems to be apparent in union–management relations. Of course, at this level the degree of abstraction is very high and perhaps not very significant. Thus we find social scientists such as the late Elton Mayo making much of the convergence in thinking of unions and managements on industrial relations matters in many of his writings.[48] The examples could be multiplied.[49]

If the reasoning to this point has any meaning, it should suggest that collective bargaining as it is currently carried out in American industrial relations is antithetical to using the potential of the parties in collective bargaining for the achievement of consensus. In fact, it is at the very point at which collective bargaining breaks down that one finds possibilities for the achievement of consensus, namely, when the parties have been in a marathon session, worn one another down, dropped the facades of everyday life, and seem willing to negotiate in an environment of trust, openness, and authenticity.

Rather than exalting collective bargaining as the *summum bonum* of industrial relations, as we hypothesized the case to be with contemporary industrial relations experts in the United States, it is proposed that consideration be given to techniques that are based upon beliefs in the potentials of the parties to use themselves as human resources for resolving conflict. The legal structure and the use of third parties to the extent that they reinforce tendencies for limited conflict resolution (accommodation) should be regarded only as temporary way stations on the road to higher orders of human relationships.

An Exercise on the White Paper in OD

Few would disagree that creative solutions to the problems of collective bargaining are needed in America today. OD specialists should be alert to opportunities for making contributions to consensus-building in union–management relations. One such exercise that has value is Permo-Chromatics Products, Inc., which is a white-paper simulation[50] that is useful for managers undergoing a teambuilding effort in building their own solidarity and achieving consensus as a team. Once this is built, the managers can move into a more open stance with improved communications and prepare to function more effectively as a bargaining team. The exercise also deals with building trust among managers and lays a foundation whereby cognitive learning can take place concerning the formulation of a bargaining position. Skill training in collective bargaining by objectives, a subset of OD teambuilding, would then be utilized by the managers to enter bargaining sessions with the union. The combination of using Permo-Chromatics Products, Inc. with CBBO should provide managers with a new approach for developing both social–emotional and cognitive skills for effective bargaining.

The Permo-Chromatics Products Inc. exercise may also be used with union teams to help them build solidarity, achieve a consensus, and communicate effectively. There is one serious drawback in recommending a union group use the exercise, namely, the content of the exercise would have a lower appeal to them than to managers. More specifically, the content lacks a union flavor and is in a managerial setting. However, the implicit design in the exercise could be used as a model by union training and OD specialists in constructing a white paper exercise with content that has verisimilitude for a group of union officials.

For teams of managers and union leaders that are desirous of jointly using an exercise for teambuilding, Permo-Chromatics Products, Inc. could be applied for practice in building trust and reaching consensus. This utilization would be a vicarious experience that could then be followed by having the union and management teams work on live problems that need to be bargained.[51]

The idea of using a white paper exercise in the context of union–management relations has special merits. The white paper requires negotiatory give-and-take and builds skill in helping determine a sense of direction and a consensus. It should provide practice in working with the List of Normative Dimensions Applicable to Union–Management Contract Negotiations (Figure 5.2) discussed earlier in the chapter with which union and management negotiations must deal if they are ever to engage in negotiations in other than an adversary mode.

The Permo-Chromatics exercise consists of several parts which are used by the teams undergoing teambuilding. They are given (1) a cover letter signed by a consultant who was used to assist in developing the white paper; (2) a list of names of persons who prepared the white paper; (3) the table of contents of the white paper; and (4) the white paper itself. All these materials appear in the next several pages of the chapter. The content of the exercise follows.

Department of Organizational Behavior
and Personnel Management
Vandergrift University
Erskine, CT 13289

August 25, 1981

Mr. Leo T. Murray, President
Permo-Chromatics Products Inc.
927 S. Broadway
Albuquerque, New Mexico 48702

Dear Leo:

Enclosed is the white paper that was developed by your management team consisting of selected middle managers from finance, engineering, marketing, production, personnel, and administrative services as well as management representatives from the electronics controls, extruded products, and paper manufacturing divisions. Each of these executives worked closely with his or her subordinates in securing input for the white paper, and I now believe it is up to you and the vice presidents to take action. I believe the task force has worked hard and done a good job.

Joe Schwartz acted as internal consultant throughout the time I worked with the task force. I appreciate your making him available from the Canadian subsidiary for assignment to the task force because his knowledge of paper-making technology proved indispensable in thinking through some of our ideas about new organizational directions and profit-making opportunities.

It was a pleasure working with Permo-Chromatics and I will be available as an outsider to help on implementation of the white paper if you need me. I feel Joe can carry the ball to a large extent from here on and would assume you agree based upon the caliber of his contribution to our work as a task force.

Very truly yours,

Henry C. Baker

Henry C. Baker
Professor

A WHITE PAPER FOR PERMO-CHROMATICS, INC.

Our Position on Organizational Development

Prepared by the Task Force on
Organizational Improvement

Joseph R. Schwartz, Production Programming and Control
Manager, Canadian Operations (Task Force Chairman)
K. William Baggio, Laboratory Manager, Chemicals and Paper
Richard J. Becker, Manager of Financial Analysis
J. J. Collins, Assistant General Manager, Electronics Controls Division
Barbara Ellis, Manager of Plastics Technology
Fred K. Gibson, Manager of Sales and Marketing
Daniel S. Gould, Salaried Personnel Manager
Herbert Otterbein, Administrative Services Support Manager
C. P. Porter, Chief Engineer, Electronics
Frank W. Wilder, Production General Superintendent

I. Introduction

What follows has two purposes. One is simply to share with you some of our wilder fantasies, hoping that it will stimulate some of your creative thought processes. The other purpose is to explain the strategy we have adopted as a result of working on our task force and bringing our work to a conclusion.

As you are aware, we are starting what amounts to a very nuts-and-bolts crusade, examining needs, defining problems, working on many fronts at the same time, and assuming a little patching will not be sufficient.

We start by noting what we think are the overall major issues. These are a synthesis of all of the problems noted on the newsprints we used at our off-site meetings during early 1980 and our experiences in the company. They boil down to two major issues that are easily labeled. One is role clarification, meaning getting the people in individual positions and units of the organization to have a much better idea of what they do, who they relate to, and how they are to work alone and together. The second major issue is to improve the influence and communication processes throughout the organization. Quite obviously these two major issues are intertwined. Also we should note that they imply structural change. You may be wondering what happened to finances, product-line funding, and similar concerns. We regard these as secondary at the present time; in fact, resolutions to these problems flow or follow from some of the larger structural redesign we believe is needed ahead of us once we get started on the road to change.

Any white paper, diagnosis, or report has in it a number of beliefs. Sometimes these are not stated. We state ours as best we can in an attempt to be as clear and above-board as possible.

II. Assumptions

A. There is price pressure in the industries in which we compete that pushes us toward increased innovation and creativity in order to maintain our position in the market. Therefore, more effective use of people's resources is necessary for the future.

B. The anticipated need within the next three years for additional high-caliber personnel can be filled in great part by present employees. However, in general they need to increase their capacities as soon as possible in such areas as interpersonal relations, technical know-how, and managerial systems. This fact lends an urgency to encouraging personal and professional growth in all employees.

C. With anticipated change comes an increased need for maximum communication from top to bottom in the organization. Getting decision-making located close to information sources and implementing the ideas of groups and individuals maximizes communication. Also, developing a common corporate language to describe the planning process and other managerial methods facilitates communication.

D. In an organization capitalizing on technical and market changes, it is necessary to create a depth of experience and know-how among employees so that the organization is not simply dependent on a few key expendable persons. We have seen too much of this dependence in the past.

E. There is a growing need in general throughout industry to work for a company that takes human dignity and potential into account. Permo-Chromatics wants to be that kind of company.

III. Organizational Development and Participative Management

Is OD a fantasy or a tool for the real world? Our meetings with Professor Baker acquainted us with the idea of organizational development, although some of us had heard the term before.

We think Permo-Chromatics should adopt OD as an approach to foster and handle change. OD is not a particular program or programs. It aims to release human potential, insure productiveness, and stimulate the right kind of corporate growth.

One of our main problems at Permo-Chromatics has been a lack of participative management and that, in turn, may have been caused by a low level of trust. Accordingly, we see the key to the future success of the enterprise as being participative management, which we define as an opportunity for input by those who can make a valued contribution to a situation within a framework of defined responsibility *together with* authority to accomplish results. This is the kind of OD we need.

IV. A Diagnosis of Specific Problems Today at Permo-Chromatics

Employees below top management in key roles are confused, worried, and, at times, hostile about the future direction of the corporation.

We lack knowledge of/or do not perceive having:

A. Corporate Goals

1. A planned annual percentage of sales increase by product type.
2. In a rising cost market, a planned goal of cost reduction to maintain profits.
3. A capital improvements budget to provide for profit maximization.

B. Major Department (Functional) Goals

1. What specific domestic markets we plan to participate in and how aggressively we plan to participate in those markets?
2. Budget and cost systems.

3. A planned approach toward possible crew reduction to maintain profits.
4. A planned approach toward material and supply cost reduction.

C. Information Flow from the Top Downward Regarding the Following:

1. Marketing, acquisitions, sales, customers and competitors that would enable us to operate departments more effectively and productively.
2. Plans for expansion overseas by product line.

D. Clear Lines and Definition of Responsibility and Authority

1. Job definition related to positional versus personal responsibility and authority create conflicts and misdirection of efforts.
2. Base pay and additions to base (such as bonuses).

E. Opportunity for Employees to Participate in all the above and to Communicate Upward in Such a Way as to be "Heard"

Our contacts with subordinates confirm substantially a shared diagnosis of the problems identified above. We feel these problems are the real ones in the organization today.

V. Recommended Actions

A. If we have corporate and departmental goals, distribute them to all concerned.

B. Encourage a participative management style for all levels in Permo-Chromatics by getting input into all goal-setting from this date forward.

C. Develop personnel systems, policies, wage and salary administration, executive compensation, employee benefits, and health, safety, and space-planning measures that will help create an organization culture that facilitates the highest productivity and quality of work.

D. Develop and continually review the effect of present reporting structures, interplant and interdepartmental linkages, task forces, and organization functions. Such a review and resulting changes would ensure a dynamic response to production and human concerns.

E. Provide a Career Development Program that Offers the Following:

1. Clear managerial and technical advancement opportunities.
2. Systematic training and education toward achieving professional excellence for these ends.

F. Create an organizational climate where:

 1. Problems are solved, not "blame-fixed."
 2. Issues of relationships are confronted rather than buried.
 3. Objectives are clear and measurable.
 4. People operate with greater self-control and self-direction.
 5. People gain a greater sense of "ownership" of organization objectives.

VI. Climate—The Key to the Future

Professor Baker reminded us of an old Chinese maxim that states, in effect, that the thousand-mile journey begins with the first step. Accordingly, we on the task force, in the expectation that we are reading top management correctly, wish to elaborate openly on point F above. There are several key factors that need to be addressed in taking the first step in establishing an organizational climate where OD can operate. We single out four climate variables as follows:

A. Senior Management's Behavior

 1. Must be consistent in allowing other members of management to participate in decision-making.
 2. Must show that they believe there is more than one way (their way) to solve a problem.
 3. Must change manifestly to remove any sense of "pending doom" or subordinates being "nailed to the wall." This change will create a problem-solving climate where creative risks can be taken by all levels of employees.

B. Decision-Making: this pertains to how, what, and by whom decisions are made. This also is perhaps the long-range key to attaining many of the OD goals. Assigning the responsibility for decision-making cannot be done arbitrarily or mechanically. How, what, and by whom will emerge both informally and formally as individuals and groups become more self-directing, self-controlling, and demonstrate competence. The principle of decisions being made by those closest to the situation should guide the maturation of the process.

C. Necessary secrecy in a closely held company versus participative management: Any closely held company necessarily protects the owners through not publishing financial information on the total corporation balance sheet and other shareholder information. Such a policy should probably continue at Permo-Chromatics, but all levels of management need to reexamine whether people are getting the necessary information they need to make sound decisions. This extends to the hourly worker.

Although there is necessary secrecy, it should not be extended to secrecy in unnecessary matters. All employees should have the right to request and receive information needed to do their jobs.

D. Organization charts and performance review: A current organization chart and a three-year projection of crystallized organization concepts, if not specific jobs, should be published. A performance review system that emphasizes attaining corporate objectives and personal/professional goals should be used by everyone.

If top management is uninterested or unwilling to address these climate variables, then the task force despairs of making the progress in OD that can be made. We feel we have been open and that it is now up to top management to start showing trust in us for the long-range good of the company.

The exercise is conducted by asking one or more teams to read the white paper and prepare to discuss its content, the manner in which it was prepared, and its quality and likely effectiveness. One or more other teams are asked to set forth the criteria for a white paper. The teams then post their analyses of the Permo-Chromatics white paper and the criteria for an adequate white paper. The OD facilitator who uses this white paper exercise then thoroughly debriefs the groups and encourages an open discussion of how the white paper can be used for teambuilding, problem-solving, and reaching a consensus. Because the problems in Permo-Chromatics are interorganizational the content of the exercise leads readily into a dissection of teambuilding, trust among groups, solidarity, open communications, and many other issues that pertain not only to management but also to union–management relations.

The Permo-Chromatics exercise could also be used before or after a number of OD exercises that are built around win/win, win/lose, lose/win, and lose/lose game notions. Such well-known old standard exercises in OD as Win As Much As You Can,[52] Towers,[53] Prisoners' Dilemma,[54] the Lego Man,[55] the Lego Bridge,[56] and the like, help teams understand the value of conflict resolution, intergroup competition, bargaining, and forms of interaction that reduce the disadvantages of opposition and increase the advantages of moving toward cooperation.

The Permo-Chromatics exercise could also be followed by mock bargaining[57] over issues that are "live" in any specific union–management relationship. This could, in turn, be followed by building the most important of all teams—one that is seldom seen in the typical adversary industrial relations context—a union–management team.

Conclusion

The many facets of conflict management and several exercises for teambuilding at various personal and organizational levels were analyzed and presented from a systems standpoint in this chapter. The various personal/ organizational levels covered were the interpersonal, intraorganizational (or interorganization subsystems but within the same system), and cross- or trans-organizational, considering unions and managements that are linked by collective bargaining agreements to be separate organizations temporarily accommodated to one another.

Exception could be taken to labeling union–management relations as transorganizational on the theory that any union–management relationship is a miniature industrial relations system.[58] However, all bargaining relationships are subject to termination and must be renewed periodically.

The importance of goals and consensus was stressed throughout the chapter and provides a focal point for understanding the management of conflict. Collective bargaining by objectives (CBBO) holds much promise as a concept for elevating union–management relations to a plane where OD and teambuilding can be utilized. We turn in the next chapter to a closer look at concepts and techniques for team goal-setting, an enlarged conception of MBO for the 1980s.

Notes

1. George Strauss, "The Study of Conflict: Hope for A New Synthesis Between Industrial Relations and Organizational Behavior?" in James L. Stern and Barbara D. Dennis, Eds., *Proceedings of the 29th Annual Winter Meeting of the Industrial Relations Research Association, Atlantic City,* Madison, WI: Industrial Relations Research Association, 1977, pp. 331–332.

2. The best known example of this is found in Roy J. Lewicki and Clayton P. Alderfer, "The Tensions Between Research and Intervention in Intergroup Conflict," *Journal of Applied Behavioral Science,* Vol. 9, No. 4, July–August 1973, pp. 424–449. See also the comments on this article in the same issue of *JABS* by Bert R. Brown, "I. Reflections on Missing the Broadside of a Barn," pp. 450–458; Frank Friedlander, "II. The Innocence of Research," pp. 459–463; and Roy J. Lewicki and Clayton P. Alderfer, "Rejoinder From the Dual Third Party," pp. 463–568. Later in the chapter more successful interventions are reported but are not dissected in as great detail as the Lewicki–Alderfer effort, which is a rich contribution to the subject of OD failures.

3. Erwin Rausch and Wallace Wohlking, *Handling Conflict in Management: III,* Didactic Game Company, Cranford, NJ, 1969, 35 pp.

4. Strauss, *op. cit.,* p. 332. See also Richard E. Walton and Robert B. McKersie, *A Behavioral Theory of Labor Negotiations,* McGraw–Hill, New York, 1965, pp. 127–280.

5. Strauss, *op. cit.,* pp. 332–333.

6. For an elaboration see: Thomas H. Patten, Jr., "The Behavioral Science Roots of Organization Development—An Integrated Perspective." in John E. Jones and J. William Pfeiffer, Eds., *The 1979 Annual Handbook for Group Facilitators*, University Associates, La Jolla, CA, 1979, pp. 194–206.

7. Alan C. Filley, *Interpersonal Conflict Resolution,* Scott Foresman, Glenview, IL, 1975, pp. 2–3.

8. *Ibid.*, p. i.

9. *Ibid.*, p. 4.

10. *Idem.*

11. James G. March and Herbert A. Simon, *Organizations,* Wiley, New York, 1959, pp. 112–118.

12. *Ibid.*, pp. 118–130.

13. *Ibid.*, p. 131.

14. *Idem.*

15. Rausch and Wohlking, *op. cit.*

16. The conflict management didactic games create a framework for skill practice and for the exchange of ideas on how potential conflict situations can be turned into productive channels. Although didactic, they are designed to teach in a pleasurable, even entertaining, manner. The participants in a game are encouraged to discuss the defensive and other emotional reactions that arise: how to recognize them, deal with them, and turn them toward constructive problem-solving.

17. This exercise may also be found in Thomas H. Patten, Jr., "Lindell–Billings Corporation: A Confrontation Role Play," in John E. Jones and J. William Pfeiffer, Eds., *The 1975 Annual Handbook for Group Facilitators*, University Associates, La Jolla, CA, 1975, pp. 46–50. Certain facts in the exercise were based on a problem made popular by Robert L. Heilbroner (with changed names and locations), *The Worldly Philosophers,* Simon and Schuster, New York, 1953, pp. 202–203.

18. Probably the best recent lengthy conceptual treatment of conflict management can be found in Kenneth Thomas, "Conflict and Conflict Management," in Marvin D. Dunnette, Ed., *Handbook of Industrial and Organizational Psychology,* Rand McNally, Chicago, 1976, pp. 889–935.

19. Thomas A. Kochan and Lee Dyer, "A Model of Organizational Change in the Context of Union–Management Relations," *Journal of Applied Behavioral Science,* Vol. 12, No. 1, January–February–March 1976, pp. 59–60.

20. Edgar F. Huse, *Organization Development and Change,* West, St. Paul, p. 65.

21. See, for example, M. Scott Myers, *Managing Without Unions,* Addison–Wesley, Reading, MA, 1976, pp. vii–xxx, 47–106, 145–172; and Charles L. Hughes, *Making Unions Unnecessary,* Executive Enterprises, New York, 1976, pp. 5–10, 115, and *passim.* On one level Myers and Hughes are arguing for sound human resource management; on another, the message seems to be that applied behavioral science knowledge can be used to thwart unionization drives (and should be).

22. *Detroit Free Press,* January 23, 1980, p. 12-A.

23. Hughes, *op. cit., idem.* A major exception in the author's view would be managerial consultation on the Scanlon Plan and use of it as an OD intervention. For a discussion of the mechanics and effectiveness of the plan see: Carl F. Frost *et al., The Scanlon Plan for Organization Development: Identity, Participation, and Equity,* Michigan State University Press, East Lansing, 1974.

24. Kochan and Dyer, *op. cit.,* p. 61.

25. Strauss, *op. cit.,* pp. 332–333.

26. The materials which follow provide a digest of the model of Kochan–Dyer, *op. cit.,* pp. 62–72.

27. See also C. Brooklyn Derr, "Managing Organizational Conflict: Collaboration, Bargaining, and Power Approaches," *California Management Review,* Vol. 21, No. 2, Winter 1978, pp. 76–83.

28. See also D. Quinn Mills, "Managing Human Relationships Among Organizations," *Organizational Dynamics,* Vol. 3, No. 4, Spring 1975, pp. 39–41.

29. Kochan and Dyer, *op. cit.,* p. 63.

30. *Ibid.,* pp. 62–72.

31. *Ibid.,* pp. 72–74.

32. Some of the material in this section of the chapter appeared in Thomas H. Patten, Jr., "Collective Bargaining and Consensus: The Potential of a Laboratory Training Input," *Management of Personnel Quarterly,* Vol. 9, No. 1, Spring 1970, pp. 29–37.

33. One overview of this prolonged relationship is found in Elliott Jaques, "Social-Analysis and the Glacier Project," *Human Relations,* Vol. 17, No. 4, November 1964, pp. 361–375.

34. G. A. Muench, "A Clinical Psychologist's Treatment of Labor–

Management Conflicts," *Personnel Psychology,* Vol. 13, No. 2, Summer 1960, pp. 165–172; and "A Clinical Psychologist's Treatment of Labor–Management Conflicts: A Four Year Study," *Journal of Humanistic Psychology,* Vol. 3, No. 1, Spring 1963, pp. 92–97.

35. Robert R. Blake *et al.,* "The Union–Management Intergroup Laboratory," *Journal of Applied Behavioral Science,* Vol. 1, No. 1, January–February–March 1965, pp. 25–57; and Robert R. Blake and Jane Srygley Mouton, *Diary of an OD Man,* Gulf, Houston, 1976, pp. 173–223 and *passim.*

36. Robert R. Blake and Jane Srygley Mouton, "Some Effects of Managerial Grid Seminar Training on Union and Management Attitudes Toward Supervision," *Journal of Applied Behavioral Science,* Vol. 2, No. 4, October–November–December 1966, pp. 387–400; and their *Corporate Excellence Through Grid Organization Development,* Gulf, Houston, 1968, pp. 175–200.

37. Irving Stern and Robert F. Pearse, "Collective Bargaining: A Union's Program for Reducing Conflict," *Personnel,* Vol. 45, No. 3, July–August 1968, pp. 61–72.

38. Walton and McKersie, *op. cit., passim.*

39. *Ibid.,* p. 127.

40. *Ibid.,* p. vii.

41. *Ibid.,* pp. 350–351.

42. *Ibid.,* pp. 184–280.

43. From *A Behavioral Theory of Labor Negotiations* by Richard E. Walton and Robert B. McKersie, pp. 279–280. Copyright © 1965 by McGraw-Hill Book Company. Used with permission of McGraw-Hill Book Company.

44. Alfred J. Marrow, *Behind The Executive Mask,* American Management Association, New York, 1964, p. 122.

45. George Psathas and Ronald Hardert, "Trainer Interventions and Normative Patterns in the T Group," *Journal of Applied Behavioral Science,* Vol. 2, No. 2, April–May–June 1966, pp. 149–169.

46. For example, Frederick H. Harbison and Robert Dubin, *Patterns of Union–Management Relations,* Science Research Association, Chicago, 1947; Frederick H. Harbison and John R. Coleman, *Goals and Strategy in Collective Bargaining,* Harper, New York, 1951; and B. N. Selekman *et al., Problems in Labor Relations,* 3rd ed., McGraw-Hill, New York, 1964.

47. Reed C. Richardson, *Collective Bargaining by Objectives: A Positive Approach,* Prentice–Hall, Englewood Cliffs, NJ, 1977.

48. Elton Mayo, *The Human Problems of An Industrial Civilization,* 2nd ed., Viking, New York, 1960, and *The Social Problems of an Industrial Civilization,* Graduate School of Business, Harvard University, Boston, 1945.

49. For example, Alexander Heron, *Why Men Work,* Stanford University Press, Stanford, CA, 1948.

50. See Thomas H. Patten, Jr., "What is a White Paper?" in John E. Jones and J. William Pfeiffer, Eds., *The 1975 Annual Handbook for Group Facilitators,* University Associates, La Jolla, CA, 1975, pp. 195–198.

51. The Federal Mediation and Conciliation Service has been using a kind of OD package in recent years in a program called "Relationships-by-Objectives" to attain some of the same goals discussed here. For more information see John J. Popular, "U.S. Mediators Try to Build Common Objectives," *World of Work Report,* Vol. 1, No. 7, September 1976, pp. 1–3; and "U.S. Mediators Try a New Role," *Business Week,* No. 2377, April 21, 1975, p. 108.

52. J. William Pfeiffer and John E. Jones, *A Handbook of Structured Experiences for Human Relations Training,* University Associates, Iowa City, IA, 1970, Vol. II, pp. 66–70.

53. *Ibid.,* Vol. III, 1970, pp. 22–26.

54. *Ibid.,* Vol. III, 1970, pp. 60–63.

55. W. Brendan Reddy and Otto Kroeger, "Intergroup Model-Building: The Lego Man," in J. William Pfeiffer and John E. Jones, Eds., *The 1972 Annual Handbook for Group Facilitators,* University Associates, Iowa City, IA, 1972, pp. 36–43.

56. J. William Pfeiffer and John E. Jones, *A Handbook of Structured Experiences for Human Relations Training,* University Associates, La Jolla, CA, 1975, Vol. V, pp. 73–77.

57. *Ibid.,* 1979, Vol. VII, pp. 124–126.

58. John T. Dunlop, *Industrial Relations Systems,* Holt, New York, 1958, pp. 1–263.

chapter 6

MANAGEMENT BY OBJECTIVES AND GOAL SETTING

The advantages of cooperation in work organizations, among managements and unions, and in society as a whole should be patent from what has been previously discussed in this book. There is the further significance in teamwork—involving commitment and communal responsibilities—that, whenever feats of extraordinary endurance are required, the inspiration of a common ideal or purpose is the best way to help each individual to endure hardships. The heroic performance of the population of London during the Blitz of World War II and of the Soviet citizens in the siege of Leningrad demonstrates the persistence and courage that can be inspired among people. Moreover, a common purpose inspires not only physical endurance and fortitude but also unusual mental feats. For example, microbiologists agree that the extraordinarily rapid development of penicillin was possible only because groups of scientists in many countries were impelled to rise above all the questions of national pride or personal scientific credit and pool their efforts to make this efficient antibiotic available for individuals wounded in combat.[1]

Management by objectives (MBO) is a tool in OD that is (or should be) inextricably connected with teambuilding so that the work commitment of team members can be increased and their desire to excel in performance can be inspired. We hope for extraordinary accomplishment across the board but will probably settle for something less as long as the organizational mission or missions are accomplished. Ordinarily, mission accomplishment will not be the case unless individuals are interfacing effectively as teams and are sufficiently energetic to put forth the effort and extended commitment needed for results.

We have previously indicated that, in the model of organizational development through teambuilding, after a group has gone through the two phases of developing self-awareness and learning about teamwork and group decision making, they have become relatively "unfrozen" (to use Lewin's concepts once again) and are ready to take a new look at their jobs. They are interested in changing from one behavioral style to another and are often quite eager for knowledge of specific managerial skills that will enable them to become more effective and efficient managers. Also, they often feel a new surge of emotional energy and camaraderie that motivates them to approach the subsequent phases of teambuilding with enthusiasm and high motivation.

Someone once identified the six stages of management by objectives as consisting of: excitement; confusion; disillusionment; search for the guilty; punishment of the innocent; and rewards to the noninvolved. Although this is a whimsical if not cynical view of the MBO installation process, it possesses a certain verisimilitude that has its bases in contemporary industrial history in America. We are interested, naturally, in capitalizing on the excitement and enthusiasm of managers who have experienced some unblocking and the creation of self-awareness and team skills as a result of OD work. However, we want to avoid installing MBO in such a way that it initially has a very high profile but rapidly, through misapplication, is reduced to another paper program that eventually becomes discarded.

In this chapter we discuss a simple but adequate concept of MBO that should prove to be widely applicable. It has been tried by Lasagna[2] at the Wells Fargo Bank, is implicit in much of the MBO work at leading firms as reported by the Conference Board,[3] and seems compatible with a wide range of MBO installations, judging by reported and published accounts, especially of Morrisey,[4] Mali,[5] Raia,[6] McConkey,[7] and Odiorne.[8]

MBO as a Planning and Control Process

MBO may be viewed as either an overall management system or a sound manner for structuring employee performance reviews. There is perhaps a middle ground between these two polar concepts of MBO and that is found when we consider MBO as a planning and control process.[9]

We might begin by remarking that MBO can be amorphous and flexible and that if we look back on its history, it was discovered by its absence. In other words, MBO came into existence when it was found that a lack of planning and control usually meant extensive and disruptive organizational and managerial problems that, in turn, required a great deal of managerial time, energy, and attention for correction.

MBO can become a system of its own or simply be used in a work organization without changing any existing systems. Unfortunately, many individuals have "sold" MBO as a particular kind of paperwork system with many pretty forms and other formal reports that, in the final analysis, are unnecessary.[10] Perhaps the most important consideration in an MBO system is the realization that it can help a person in a managerial or professional position to know for sure what he is doing on the job and how to gauge his success in his work.

There are many options to MBO that are worth passing consideration. First, there is management-by-crisis, which is unfortunately charteristic of many work organizations in America, particularly those parts of the business closely connected with production and sales, which are subject to many immediate pressures. Work in these organizations often seems to involve movement from crisis to crisis, and the type of behavior required may, in fact, appear to be exciting and pleasurable to those individuals who like to "fight fires." However, in a broader sense management-by-crisis is dysfunctional and inconsistent with notions of sound planning and control over the organization's destination and the manner in which work is done.

Management-by-charisma is another option to MBO; as Collins and others have pointed out, entrepreneurs often manage by charisma.[11] Today many small businessmen are still the owner–operators of their companies; they often have employees who are extremely loyal to them and perform at very high levels of competence. Yet when the crunch comes in the market or economy, we often find that management-by-charisma is typically accompanied by inadequate planning and control, resulting in inadequacies that doom the business.

Another alternative to MBO is management-by-abdication, which may be viewed as a misapplication of Theory Y or, put another way, Theory Y gone wild. As Tannenbaum and Schmidt have shown in their classic work,[12] there are many ways of managing and coordinating the work of subordinates. Importantly, involving subordinates in decision-making does not suggest that the manager should abdicate his responsibility to manage, although we do find situations where managers have misconstrued what is meant by participation and *have* improperly abdicated their responsibilities.

Perhaps the last option to MBO is management-by-good-news only. This idea refers to the classic situation where the manager insulates himself from the work situation sufficiently so that by communicating with his subordinates he has left the impression that he operates on the premise of "don't bring me your problems; bring me your solutions." He does not want to hear bad news, and those managers and subordinates who bring him what he does not want to hear are likely to find themselves regarded as messengers of evil tidings. As in the classical tale, the messenger who does this is killed, however irrational that may seem. Thus, the problem is disposed of; the manager can lapse into lethargy once again until, finally, his errors accumulate and cause his downfall.

Among the advantages of MBO is that it can become a disciplined way of managing, involving a rational cycle of planning and control. This cycle is enhanced when it is regarded as not merely a rational process but one that brings together people who are energetic, open, confronting, and able to make their individual human resources available to one another. As a result, MBO can help managers to manage more and fire fight less, which judging by what appears in management textbooks, is desirable managerial behavior.

MBO helps management move the focus of its attention from activities or the "how" of carrying out work to actual results expected on the job. MBO allows employees to work together and managers to supervise in a supportive mode. Likert makes much of this point in his research.[13]

In addition, MBO permits meaningful manager development because MBO focuses attention on the planning and control of work assignments and encourages the superior to work with the subordinate through coaching and counseling to assist the latter in growing on the job and reaching his potential. As we have seen, MBO provides a constructive basis for performance review. Last, MBO can be integrated with pay planning and administration, which is covered later in the book, or it can stand by itself as a management system with less of a direct connection with compensation determination.

It is important to bear in mind that administering, planning, and controlling the organizational budget is not tantamount to MBO.[14] We have been acquainted with several organizations in which someone at a high managerial level rejected MBO because the corporation operated according to an annual profit plan and it was thought that the existence of it precluded a need for MBO. Budgets in these organizations were constructed based on the profit plan; the budget-making process was considered sufficient, making MBO redundant. However, many critical things in the managerial job are not included in the budget, particularly the tasking of the manager in relation to specific measurable work that is most intimately known to be needed by his organizational superior. However, in a different way the proper use of MBO should actually help a manager work within the budget or in concert with any other system in the organization, such as PERT-CPM, PPBS, or the like. Zero-based budgeting, given great stress by President Jimmy Carter, is fundamentally based on MBO.[15]

Defining MBO

In defining MBO we should probably pay less attention to semantics than to the manner in which MBO orginated. We generally regard the origins of MBO as traceable to the work of Drucker at General Motors during the 1940s. An investigation he made at that time indicated that the success of General Motors as a work organization was attributable to the fact that managers knew the requirements of their job assignments and had specific goals toward which they were working.[16] Odiorne, who subsequently studied under Drucker, became an important popularizer of MBO and further extended it so that it became operationally clearer to personnel directors, training specialists, OD experts, and human resource development technicians. One highlight of Odiorne's research on MBO was the finding that supervisors and subordinates agreed only about 25% of the time on what the subordinate's objectives were when the two were asked to identify objectives. This disparity caused Odiorne to think through what could be done to bridge the gap through the diffusion of knowledge about MBO.[17] In his recent career he has extended the MBO concept to many other aspects of industrial management.

In the past two decades MBO has been widely applied and is well known throughout the world. Sometimes it is called work planning and review (as at General Electric), or goal-setting, target-setting, or some other term that organizations feel more acceptable or descriptive in their own work culture. MBO has been applied in both the private and the public sectors.[18]

When we discuss MBO we are referring to goal-setting for one year ahead. For us goals and objectives are synonymous. In MBO the emphasis is on the short-range, meaning one year, rather than the long-range. However, MBO can be linked to long-range plans and has been. We believe that the greatest practical or operational value of MBO is using it over an annual period rather than tying it to long-range planning, meaning plans that extend beyond twelve months.

If MBO is looked upon as a superior planning and controlling system, it should become apparent that in most organizations what is wrong with planning and controlling is that it's left solely to managerial personnel who have organizational titles that include the words planning and controlling. If the corporate controller advises a manager that he is out of control, it is probably already too late for that manager to take the most desirable course of action. He must remedy a problem situation and perhaps clean up a mess or stop losses. Also, because the situation is out of control there is a tendency to reward or punish managers who are respectively on-target or off-target.

MBO encourages managers to be pro-active rather than re-active and to assume within their own work domain a greater degree of control and direction-setting for planning and controlling the work than is the case when planning and controlling are regarded as the primary responsibility of some other part of the business. An effective MBO installation can probably cause reorientation of the outlook of the director of production control, financial control, material control, and the like.

On the other hand, MBO sometimes does not give a timely measurement and itself falls down from the planning and controlling standpoint. This is particularly the case when the type of MBO installed is a complex paper system and falls under its own weight because of excessive formality and only lip-service support for the system. This misapplication reminds us that MBO should not be a task or a program to be done but rather a process to be lived, a new way of life, or a new way of managing that has great potency to it.

When MBO is operating as a sound planning and control system, it may be compared to a thermostat. In other words, planning is choosing out of the environment, like selecting a certain temperature for a room. Controlling is measuring whether or not your choice has been implemented as by checking the actual room temperature or a thermometer and taking the appropriate action if your choice has not been implemented. The analogy is apt because it denotes the fact that the MBO is a monitor—a tool for measuring and appraising that is itself neutral.

A Universal Model for MBO

Based on the discussion to this point in the chapter, it should be plain that I have in mind a fluid, amorphous model of MBO. I see MBO as belonging in an organization that has sufficient autonomy and personnel, budgetary, and policy integrity that the model can operate relatively freely from imposition of an excessive number of external constraints. Hence MBO should be installed in a relatively autonomous organization (or autonomous organizational element in a larger system) so that it can have some degree of free reign.

It has been suggested that MBO be installed in an organic family unit that has sufficient integrity to allow the MBO effort at least at the outset a chance for success. It is also necessary to make the utilization of MBO voluntary; this may seem like a radical thought. Yet there are few managers who will resist a useful planning and control system, although some might. Rather than force those individuals to accept MBO, it is far better to act opportunistically and follow the path of least resistance in the installation. Successful applications by managers who use it will probably result in a certain amount of boasting. The resulting peer pressure will coax the reluctant manager to give MBO a trial.[19] The installation and success stories of MBO may then become individual fires in an organization, which, much like a forest fire, if the wind is blowing properly, will cause the fires to coalesce and result in a great conflagration, which in terms of the end-result will mean organizational installation of MBO. If MBO does not catch fire, it is preferable to let it function where it is wanted rather than force it on the reluctant manager through the application of pressure from the top.

The model of MBO that I advocate has in rudimentary form been discussed elsewhere in my work on manpower planning.[20] However, I do not advocate the use of forms, administrative procedures, films, and other flashy paraphernalia, which amount to unnecessary expense and lay the groundwork for MBO's becoming at the outset a mere paper program. Instead, I advocate using plain pieces of standard 8½ by 11 inch paper in which the output of the manager involved in the MBO installation is simply the piece of paper with five or six carefully worded "critical" objectives.[21] The output is to be a working document and is not intended to be a museum piece for the file or a long laundry list of wishes. It is important that there be only five or six "critical" objectives rather than a long number of objectives that are either incapable of accomplishment or substantially irrelevant.

The MBO system should move from one organizational level at a time beginning from the top down.[22] It involves negotiation and renegotiation and importantly an atmosphere of trust.[23] It logically should follow an OD team-building effort, as has been previously described. In moving from level to level MBO should be dyadic and didactic, that is, involve individuals working as pairs in a teaching–learning mode. Ideally, there should be collaborative MBO or team MBO operating in the organizational environment so that the dyadic and didactic work is not done in isolation and that managers who interface directly know what their counterparts are expected to do and have shared in the goal-setting process.

It is very important that MBO involve the boss first and thereby eliminate the proverbial "they" in organizations, who are always people at a higher organizational level that appear to be in the position of forcing others at a lower organizational level to accept something they really do not want.[24] The "they" are thought to be out of touch with reality and not really understanding of problems and issues at the work level. MBO should thus require "mission statements" in writing; these are a kind of more vague and general type of objective set by top management so that the objectives of managers at lower levels can have meaning within a broad organizational context.[25] Mission statements can eliminate the proverbial "they" alibi for misunderstood communications.

Sometimes MBO makes use of a "third party facilitator" who is not part of the problem and can work with the dyad and the teams in goal-setting. In prior chapters on teambuilding I indicated how a third party, who may be either an internal or external change agent, can function to assist others in relating to one another (thereby improving interpersonal processes) or in calling attention to inadequacies in dealing with the task itself (which involves working on content).[26] Last, the system adheres to a timetable for reviews so that once the MBO system is started the boss and the subordinate meet periodically as needed to review progress and perhaps change the objectives in line with the emerging situation. This informal contact, which may be initiated by the boss or the subordinate, goes a long way toward making MBO a new way of life that can be handled informally but has its formal aspect as well.

Mission Statements as Broad Guides

I have already mentioned that MBO requires mission statements in writing. These statements translate longer-range plans into shorter-range kinds of objectives that are suitable for MBO. Mission statements aid in the synchronization of effort and form a sort of umbrella over the organization. They function to help managers and other employees think ahead and set objectives that are challenging and meaningful for the next year rather than merely repeating what they did last year.

The purpose of the mission statement is to link and give direction downward in the organization while allowing ample freedom for subordinates to draft their own objectives within these boundaries. Again it can be seen that a team MBO approach helps in both directions by opening up communication among all the affected parties to improve work planning and control.

A mission statement may be as long as three or four paragraphs, but it should be considered that the key readers of the statement are subordinates, not persons outside the organization or otherwise removed from the mission who would have trouble understanding it. Hence the mission statement need not be overly detailed and can be drafted in a way that taps into the institutional understandings of the persons to be receiving it. They definitely should not be documents produced "for the record" and drafted with the intent of being "Pearl Harbor" files.

Mission statements must be rewritten each year or at least as often as needed when the direction at the top of the organization shifts. Such shifts can be expected because of changes in technology and inventions, markets, the economy, legislation, world politics, and the like.

The mission statement requires distinguishing between what Pareto has called the "critical few" from the "trivial many."[27] We might say that a good manager is one who consistently identifies the critical few objectives in his domain and attains them. For him the "trivial many" objectives are delegated to others, ignored, accomplished by happenstance or, if necessary, left undone. Thus we can distinguish those goals on which a manager really should be spending his time and energy from other, lesser goals that might be nice to accomplish but are not critical in a particular time frame. Many poor managers unfortunately carry the trivial many into management and become overly concerned and indeed sometimes obsessed with matters of minor importance. In their behavior they demonstrate that they do not really understand how to manage.

Figures 6.1, 6.2, and 6.3 (from Refs. 28, 29, and 30, respectively) are samples of umbrella statements that are sufficiently broad as to mission but still adequate to allow subordinate managers to sense where the organization

Figure 6.1   Sears Roebuck Mission Statement

- Sears is a family store for middle-class, homeowning America
  It is the premier distributor of durable and nondurable goods that have their acceptance in function rather than fashion
  It is not a fashion store, nor a discounter, nor an *avant-garde* department store.
- Sears will reemphasize quality, be competitive at the lower end of product lines, and renew attention above the bottom prices to the "good–better–best" standards that Sears made famous.
- Sears' product mix of 70% durable goods and 30% apparel is about right.
- Sears' sales should grow about as fast as the rate of inflation in general-merchandise goods plus real growth in GNP.

Source: Adapted from Carol J. Loomis, "The Leaning Tower of Sears," *Fortune*, Vol. 99, No. 13, July 2, 1979, pp. 83–84.

Figure 6.2   Avis Rent-A-Car Co. Umbrella Statement

- "We want to become the fastest-growing company with the highest profit margins in the business of renting and leasing vehicles without drivers."
- Avis should:
    Reject acquisition of related business such as motels, hotels, airlines, and travel agencies.
    Spin off limosine and sightseeing companies already owned.
- Executive desk signs
    "Is what I'm doing or about to do getting us closer to our objective?"
    Unremitting concentration on mission and objectives.

Figure 6.3   Military Umbrella Statement—World War II

- Hold Japan in the Pacific.
- Crush Germany in Europe.
- Crush Japan.

is heading. Figure 6.1, an example from Sears, Roebuck[28] is probably the broadest statement of all, which may be the most difficult for subordinate managers to relate to. Figure 6.2 was discussed by Townsend in his *Up The Organization*[29] and is a reasonably specific statement about the Avis-Rent-A-Car Company that helped it to derive a clear sense of direction when it was drifting. Figure 6.3 is allegedly the logic that was developed by Eisenhower during World War II, as reported in *Crusade in Europe*.[30] Again this is a very general statement, but in terms of the strategy of the United States and its Allies for winning World War II, it clearly decided the strategy to be employed in winning the war. It also answered many of the questions as to whether the first goal should be the defeat of Germany or of Japan or whether these should be simultaneous goals.

In distinguishing between a mission statement and an objective the following clarifications can be made. A mission statement applies to many managers, sets broad direction, is difficult to measure, and is done in a joint session involving groups or teams. Figures 6.1 through 6.3 satisfy these criteria.

An objective or goal, on the other hand, has applicability to an individual, or singular accountability. It is specific in terms of end results. It is easy to measure on a timely basis. It is dyadic rather than developed in a written fashion in a joint session with a large number of people present. Again, I emphasize the importance of dyadic objectives' being consistent with those of the members of a particular team but recognize much one-on-one superior–subordinate work must be conducted as well.

Objective Statements as Specific Goals

Elaborating more on the characteristics of a well-written objective, it is important to spell out relevant criteria.[31] First, an objective should contain between ten and thirty words but not the "how" and "why." It is negotiated with the boss; it is agreed that the subject matter is critical and not trivial and delegable. An objective is easily changed when there is reason to do so, and the manager and his boss can rapidly move from one clear and important direction to another. The standards implicit in the objective are set at levels that are neither too high nor too low. The goals agreed upon are within the manager's position responsibilities and do not extend beyond the purview of his job. It is not particularly meaningful to have pie-in-the-sky goals or objectives that encompass responsibilities beyond one's organizational level. The measures of goal accomplishment should be clearly agreed upon and negotiated so that both the boss and the subordinate have a chance to make their inputs and exchange ideas about what is the appropriate objective.

There are some additional practical guides that can be considered in setting goals. As previously mentioned, it is important that the goals focus on key results or outputs, that is, the critical work in the manager's area of responsibility. A good way to begin defining these key results or outputs is to consider what can be improved. Examples might be an increased speed of service, reduced turnover, or lower costs. Naturally, it is assumed throughout that the boss and the subordinate have been sufficiently loosened up to be communicating interpersonally in an effective way and want to address themselves to improved management.

Having defined key results, it is useful next to set priorities and tailor these to the organizational component as well as the surrounding organization. This procedure again suggests the importance of the dyad's working with teams so that the goals that are identified are consonant with those of others.

In setting priorities about five or six result areas (rarely more than that) should be selected. These should be written on one sheet of plain paper in the rough and form a basis for discussion in terms of prioritization.

Next, the goal should be defined in terms as measurable as possible and then put in writing. Insofar as possible relevant percentages, completion times, and weights should be specified. Stress should be on the what and when, not the why and how. Figure 6.4 suggests how objectives can be stated. Each is as specific as possible with a minimum amount of verbiage

Figure 6.4 MBO—Examples of Well-Written Objectives

- Hire three well-qualified black professional-level (exempt) employees by June 15, 1982.
- Achieve sales growth of 14% to $19 million, as set forth in detail in the sales budget (SML 13, Dated October 1, 1981). These sales to be achieved within the expense budget stipulated.
- Reduce the expense of TDY during fiscal 1982 by 30% (compared to fiscal 1981) and increase the number of on-site inspections worldwide by 10% (compared to fiscal 1981).
- Improve the speed of order analysis to achieve daily order summaries by product line by March 1, 1982.

and indicates a deadline date. It is a matter of managerial judgment and good faith between the parties as to whether these particular objectives are challenging, critical, and relevant in a particular organization. Whether good faith and authentic interpersonal give-and-take will ensue depends on the foundation of trust between the parties and whether OD teambuilding has been successful.

Types of Objectives

In identifying objectives and putting them in writing, there are ways that sets of bosses and subordinates can carry out the MBO goal-setting process that have been proven to be helpful. Odiorne many years ago suggested categorizing objectives in order to stimulate thinking about one's work and what one ought to be doing.[32] Thus we might have regular or routine, ongoing, administrative objectives that are repetitive but nevertheless important. Many jobs in the lower levels of management or in specific functional fields in business have an abundance of regular objectives. In the general accounting function, for example, there are innumerable reports that must be prepared accurately and in a timely manner for decision-making in the business. These are regular reports that include regular goals as far as a particular manager is concerned.

There also are problem-solving objectives, and these are concerned with regular responsibilities that may have gone wrong and with unanticipated changes that are affecting routine work for the first time. There are innovative or creative objectives, that are useful for setting new objectives and perhaps for taking a novel approach to problem solving. Last, there are personal objectives, which Odiorne considers a part of MBO but I do not. Each of these categories of objectives is worth further elaboration.

As mentioned, regular objectives focus on important work that is underway; they involve the commitments of time, energy, and human and other resources. They often can be observed and controlled by reports of various kinds. When regular objectives are not easily accommodated by the smooth functioning of routine processes, they may give rise to problem-solving objectives, to which we turn next.

A problem-solving objective arises when there is a discrepancy between what is expected and what is obtained. If MBO is a planning and control system, by its very essence it should be quite clear that problem-solving goals can be dealt with effectively through MBO. Also, a problem-solving objective can be identified whenever we find that a regular responsibility has gone wrong and the organization is agonizing because important routines are no longer fulfilling their purpose. Sometimes planning is off-target, and control mechanisms quickly show there is a problem area in much the same way that the thermostat registers a drop or rise in the temperature in a room.

Innovative or creative objectives are those that the highest-performing managers seem to cope with the best. A manager who asks himself if he can manage better, smarter, or cheaper often forces himself into thinking about his job in new ways. He must also consider whether he wants or is able to divert his and his subordinates' energy to handling these innovative goals. In some organizations there are staffs that are charged to be innovative (such as a product planning staff). Yet every manager has within the purview of his own job the potential for making an innovative contribution by setting such goals. If he constantly asks himself what is new and inquires about better ways of operating, he is likely to find himself moving in the direction of innovative objective-setting.

Personal objectives are related to management-by-objectives but organizations normally do not include these in the MBO system. Kellogg has suggested that the career planning or the self-development of an employee is a valid objective but has demonstrated that career planning and personal ·development are really an implicit aspect of working in a large organization and touched upon whenever decisions are made in the field of personnel management.[33] Nevertheless, it can be agreed that every individual should have some objectives for himself so that he is able to make peace with himself and keep himself alert and active over the course of his employment. It is dubious whether MBO should include these personal objectives in any formal way because MBO is a business-oriented rather than a personal-oriented system.[34] Yet it cannot be doubted that commitment begins with the satisfaction of personal objectives, or ends with failures to meet personal objectives. Apparently creative people are those who are most self-actualized and capable of rising above or somehow working within the system- and boss-imposed activities of the work organization to attain their personal goals.

Problem-Solving and Decision-Making in MBO

So far MBO has been outlined in procedural and conceptual terms that relate to both the goal-setting and results-measuring processes. In discussing problem-solving goals in MBO decision-making was omitted but is now considered because, once problem-solving goals have been identified the manager usually finds he can benefit from a disciplined way of solving problems. One of the most useful models for problem-analysis and decision-making is that reported by Kepner and Tregoe; it has considerable application in setting and attaining problem-solving objectives.[35]

Once a problem has been identified it is important that a decision be made among alternative possible solutions. Sound decision-making requires solving the real problems that are reflected in the discrepancies between the expected and the actual in a work context.

Decision-making thus has a very heavy rational overlay to it; it is easy to ignore the emotional components of the process involving dyads or teams. In OD we are interested in both the rational and the emotional, and we need to examine how these two components can be implemented together. However, first let us turn to and review the rational processes normally associated with decision-making.

There are a number of steps that have been well identified in choosing alternative courses of action. Kepner and Tregoe, as well as many other authors, have identified patterns that approximate the scientific method in terms of inquiring about cause and effect relationships that reveal problems.[36] The first step is to define the problem, which is often the most difficult part of the problem-solving and decision-making process. Let us take the example of a problem where a secretary in a work organization wants a new typewriter. The real problem may be that it is actually needed or it may be that it is only regarded as a status symbol, one that is needed because someone else received one. In other words, the secretary may want a new typewriter for valid or invalid reasons. The manager must determine the validity of the reasons and then choose a course of action to solve the problem.

The second step is to obtain the data that are needed to make the decision. For example, the manager may ask about the status of the current typewriter to determine if there is a malfunction or whether there are other reasons connected with the request for a new typewriter.

The manager may next develop alternative solutions to the problem. He may decide to buy a new typewriter, fix the existing typewriter, or ask the secretary to exchange the typewriter with someone else.

Each solution to the problem would then be evaluated in terms of relevant criteria. For example, in deciding upon the typewriter problem it may be important to consider which is the quickest, the cheapest, and most convenient solution as opposed to a solution that might be based on other criteria.

The last action is to make the decision itself. At this point a choice is made among the various alternatives in light of how they satisfy various criteria that apply to the problem. Of course, a decision can be made to do nothing, which in itself is really a decision. Or a decision may be made to do something; in this case, there is a concrete action that takes place. Perhaps a new typewriter is purchased.

Social and Emotional Components

The rational components of the decision-making process are thus not too difficult to specify, although the exact number of steps depends on which theory is being used. All authors of textbooks tend to emphasize the rational components; however, from the perspective of OD, we know that this is not the entire story. The emotional components, that is to say, the ways problems are solved, have important consequences for the motivation of employees and the degree of commitment that they have to implement solutions, as well as an important bearing on innovation and the quality of the solution.

In OD we need to augment the rational approach to decision-making in reference to problem-solving goals and MBO by examining the various emotional alternatives. Emotional alternatives can be categorized as abdication, polarization, difference-splitting, and consensus, or reaching a decision on the basis of negotiation.[37] Weisbord has presented a very interesting and useful model for looking at these emotional components in decision-making, which I have adapted in explaining some of the dynamics of MBO implementation.[38]

In addition to the emotional components themselves, it is important for a manager to realize that he should consider the type of employee involved in the problem-solving process so that the decision selected is acceptable. There are two different types of managerial subordinates, namely, the goal-oriented type of individual who wants a Theory Y boss and the task-oriented person who accepts a Theory X boss. Each will have a different emotional makeup that is connected with problem-solving and decision-making.

The existence of different types of managerial subordinates and the emotional components of decision-making raises once again the question of managerial style treated earlier in the book. A manager might well ask himself if he wants both polar types of employee. Can a task-oriented subordinate become goal-oriented if the boss uses MBO properly? Can a rational tool such as MBO be used in concert with emotional alternatives to gain motivational commitment and improve the innovative quality of problem-solving and decision making? Figure 6.5 indicates the polar types of subordi-

Figure 6.5   Polar Types of Subordinates*

Goal-oriented manager	Task-oriented manager
1. Seeks feedback and wants evaluation of performance based on results.	1. Avoids feedback and evaluation. Seeks approval on a personal basis.
2. Considers money a reward for good work rather than an incentive to work harder.	2. Wants every dollar he can get: "a dollar collector who is an injustice collector."
3. Performs best on jobs that can be improved. Creative. Satisfaction comes from solving problems.	3. Prefers routine non-improvable assignments. Does not act creative, satisfaction comes from finishing tasks.
4. Seeks goals with moderate risks. Will accept responsibility for attainment or failure.	4. Seeks goals with either very low or very high risks. Needs alibis. Resists measurement.
5. Has high drive and energy directed toward goals.	5. May or may not have high drive. Energy is not goal-directed.
6. Initiates action and dislikes "microscopic supervision."	6. Follows others' directives almost mindlessly.
7. Adjusts level of aspiration to realities of success and failure.	7. Maintains high or low level of aspiration regardless of results.

*The idea of goal-oriented and task-oriented managers is related to some ideas of Clayton Lafferty reported in Dale D. McConkey, *No-Nonsense Delegation.* AMACOM, New York, 1974, pp. 75–78.

nates and characteristic forms of behavior that they manifest in typical problem-solving MBO and decision-making.

The first type of emotional alternative in decision-making is abdication, as shown in Figure 6.6. The figure is largely self-explanatory, but the important point is that in the ''abdication'' model of Tannenbaum and Schmidt,[39] the boss prevents the work group or team from deciding and making inputs and himself makes the decision, with the obvious consequence of weakening subordinates' motivation and lessening the chances of obtaining innovative solutions. Instead of managing in a team mode he has abdicated his responsibility for marshalling human input.

Figure 6.7 indicates what happens in polarization, where the boss and the subordinate have a conflictful relationship and the interaction between the two results in a stalemate. Motivation and innovation suffer in both cases.

Figure 6.8 indicates the emotional alternative of difference splitting, which could be considered 5,5 in the managerial grid or tantamount to what often happens in collective bargaining. In these situations there is some attempt to negotiate, but the solutions are never really agreed upon. Thus, the decision is split in a way that is considered equitable but actually is almost nonsensical. The results in motivation and innovation are not entirely disastrous, but they hardly tap the human resource and possible contributions of the parties concerned.

Figure 6.9 is the emotional alternative of consensus or MBO negotiation. In this alternative it can be seen that there is an extension of human resources between the parties and an active process of dialogue, coping, searching, confronting, and coming to an agreement as to a course of action that has the most beneficial effects for motivation and innovation. Lippitt has indicated quite clearly how this process of dialogue and confronting can result in solutions to problems and decisions that are optimal.[40]

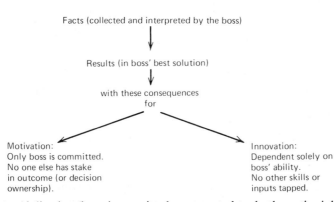

Figure 6.6 Abdication (boss is permitted or expected to do the entire job). (Model developed by Marvin R. Weisbord, based on work of Rensis Likert. Used by permission.)

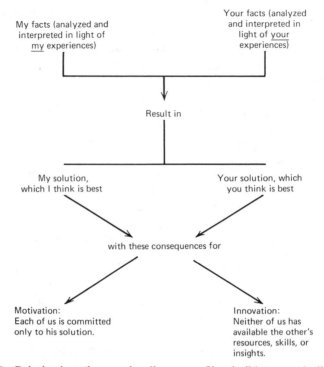

My facts (analyzed and interpreted in light of my experiences)

Your facts (analyzed and interpreted in light of your experiences)

Result in

My solution, which I think is best

Your solution, which you think is best

with these consequences for

Motivation:
Each of us is committed only to his solution.

Innovation:
Neither of us has available the other's resources, skills, or insights.

Figure 6.7 Polarization (boss–subordinate conflict builds around divergent interpretations). (Model developed by Marvin R. Weisbord, based on work of Rensis Likert. Used by permission.)

Exercises in MBO

In this chapter I have been discussing MBO and have now set forth as much information about the process and the theory as is probably necessary for the reader to understand a simple, flexible, and practical planning and control approach to MBO. But after learning what MBO is, how can this information be used to design and work with a team undergoing a workshop in teambuilding to acquire skills in MBO? The remaining exercises and figures in this chapter are useful formats that can be tried out in an MBO workshop. I next explain these figures and discuss some exercises that have practical value in an MBO workshop.

Figures 6.10 through 6.12 provide information on three exercises on MBO that should help an OD facilitator in moving from theory inputs on MBO into a workshop mode.

Figure 2.1 contains the teambuilding design from which we are working. MBO is covered in three separate modules, and the workshops correspond to these.

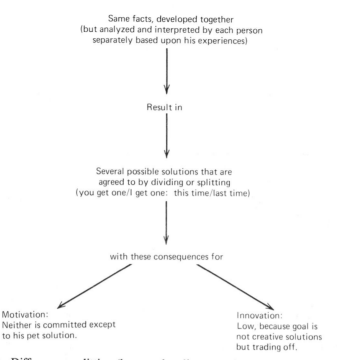

Same facts, developed together
(but analyzed and interpreted by each person
separately based upon his experiences)

Result in

Several possible solutions that are
agreed to by dividing or splitting
(you get one/I get one: this time/last time)

with these consequences for

Motivation:
Neither is committed except
to his pet solution.

Innovation:
Low, because goal is
not creative solutions
but trading off.

Figure 6.8 Difference–splitting (boss–subordinate trade–off as a means of settling painful or strained process of problem–solving). (Model developed by Marvin R. Weisbord, based on work of Rensis Likert. Used by permission.)

Figure 6.10 describes how the OD facilitator may instruct the teams in getting started in MBO goal-setting. The instructions are self-explanatory and provide an interesting and involving way to start the MBO process, beginning with dyads.

Figure 6.11 contains an exercise on problem-solving and innovative goals that gives the participants experience in working with teams. It too is usually regarded as an interesting and involving experience that provides meaningful skill practice. The goal-setting guide is also simple to use. I have found that teams who complete this exercise often receive extremely valuable input from team members that not only is applicable to the back-home job but also reinforces the commitment to use one another's resources and reach group decisions by consensus. The experience also provides a chance to try out new behaviors related to trust, interpersonal relations, communication, leadership/followership, and the like.

Figure 6.12 augments the workshop experience in tackling problem-solving and innovative goals by providing the team with a chance to learn from one another about decision-making processes. The movement through

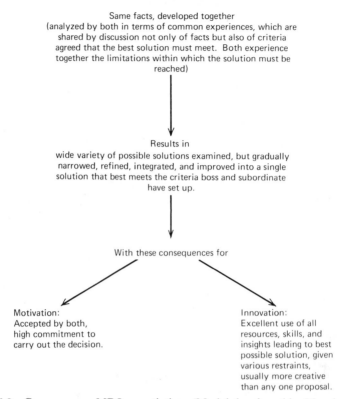

Same facts, developed together
(analyzed by both in terms of common experiences, which are
shared by discussion not only of facts but also of criteria
agreed that the best solution must meet. Both experience
together the limitations within which the solution must be
reached)

Results in
wide variety of possible solutions examined, but gradually
narrowed, refined, integrated, and improved into a single
solution that best meets the criteria boss and subordinate
have set up.

With these consequences for

Motivation:
Accepted by both,
high commitment to
carry out the decision.

Innovation:
Excellent use of all
resources, skills, and
insights leading to best
possible solution, given
various restraints,
usually more creative
than any one proposal.

Figure 6.9 Consensus or MBO negotiation. (Model developed by Marvin R. Weisbord, based on work of Rensis Likert. Used by permission.)

these three exercises should help a group see how MBO can be applied in dyads and teams and in situations calling for the combined use of rational and social–emotional skills. The delicate interplay between the rational and nonrational becomes increasingly meaningful by the time the exercise in Figure 6.12 is completed. Moreover, team participants gain further understanding of what "learning how to learn" means as a result of these exercises.

The Limitations of MBO

In this chapter MBO has been presented in an uncritical manner. I have stressed how and when it can be used for improved planning and control in management while utilizing human resources in an involving and participative manner. It would be naive to assume that MBO is easily translated from concept into action. We need to consider its limitations for obtaining desired levels of individual and team performance. In addition, there are overall system problems in MBO that must be examined from an organization-wide

Figure 6.10a   Exercise on Goal-Setting

Using the Goal-Setting Guide, go into your team and complete the guide as well as you can for your present job in about 15 minutes. Think of the mission statement of your organizational component (if there is one) in specifying your goals, the measurement or indicators of goal attainment, and the statement of actual or expected results. Concentrate on five or six critical objectives. Choose some that are difficult to measure and some that are easy to measure.

Once you have prepared the Goal-Setting Guide, you will be asked to discuss the goals with someone in your team in a dyad. He will act as your boss and ask questions about the information on your Guide. Then roles will be reversed and you will act as his organizational superior, asking questions about his Guide. This should take about 45 minutes.

In this and subsequent exercises, the OD facilitator will be circulating about the training location listening to various dyads discussing their MBO Goal-Setting Guides. At the end of the exercise, all will reassemble to debrief what took place and discuss a few of the goals on which the various dyads worked.

Figure 6.10b   Goal-Setting Guide

Goals for period ending: _____

	Objective	Measurement	Expected or actual results*
1			
2			
3			
4			
5			
6			

*Results are what actually happen over time while trying to attain objectives, and they are expected to be organizationally beneficial.

Figure 6.11   Exercise on Problem-Solving and Innovative Goals

You are asked to return to your teams (not dyads, as in the goal-setting exercise) and, working individually, identify one problem-solving and one innovative goal that you have for your present job. This task may take up to 15 to 20 minutes.

Then discuss in your team the problem-solving and innovative goals that were generated by group members. This task should take about 30 to 45 minutes. Discuss these goals in depth with each other and come to a conclusion as to one problem-solving and one innovative goal that you want to report back to the other teams.

Throughout these team discussions you should focus on managerial problems that are within the purview of the job responsibilities of the members of the team rather than broad-gauge or overall management problems that are part of the larger system or organization. The latter problems and innovative solutions to them probably do not involve managers in the team in the normal conduct of their work. Some can only be solved by top policy changes, organizational metamorphosis, or other changes that are not controllable by you.

All the teams will reassemble, and we will debrief the various goals reported. (For goal-setting guide, see Figure 6.10b.)

perspective, which we return to after examining individual and team performance concerns.[41]

As Kleber[42] has dramatically pointed out there are at least forty well-known problems that can thwart the success of an MBO system. As Schuster and Kindall[43] have observed in the only large-scale research on MBO utilization reported to date (which involved a sample of Fortune 500 com-

Figure 6.12a   Exercise on Decision-Making

Your task is to select for in-depth analysis one of your own problem-solving or innovative goals discussed yesterday in your team. If you believe that you have exhausted possibilities in analyzing your main problems, choose a fresh problem that you may not have thought of yesterday. Do not choose a simple problem that you have already solved. Select a challenging one within the scope of your present job that is likely to interest other team members, if possible. However, do not select a problem that totally transcends the scope of your job, i.e., do not work on your boss' problems or his boss' problems or overall systemic problems beyond the purview of your job.

Think over your own problem by applying the decision-making model. Then analyze it by using the sheet, "Evaluation of Proposed Solutions." This should take about 20 to 25 minutes. Next, join your team for an in-depth discussion of each member's decision analysis. Of all the decisions discussed, write one up on newsprint in the problem-solving and decision-making format. The decision chosen for the write-up should be based on the consensus of the team. The discussion of the problems and solutions in the teams should take about one hour. Each team will present one problem and solution, and seminar participants will debrief these. The presentation and debriefing should take about 45 minutes.

Frequently in this exercise we find that seminar participants acquire new insights into a problem, its symptoms, and the most plausible solution. As a result, it is important to choose a meaningful problem and attempt to work it through with the help of your team, drawing on the resources of everyone in the team. In this way you will obtain an exposure to MBO as a disciplined way of focusing on real problems in *your* work; and you will see how much effort is required in selecting the "critical few" from the "trivial many" problems. Also, in the process of working through this exercise you should see once again how the resources of other executives can help you and improve the quality of problem analysis and decision making.

Figure 6.12b Problem-Solving and Decision-Making Model for MBO Exercises

1. Identify the problem area.
2. Define what is actually happening in the problem area.
3. Define the planned or expected state of affairs in the problem area, i.e., what results or benefits you expect.
4. Examine the causes of the problem.
5. Select the most likely cause or causes (if possible).
6. Work through an evaluation of proposed solutions using the format below.
7. Choose the best solution.
8. Identify the risks, if any, of implementation of the best solution.
9. State any time controls or time limits that are pertinent to the problem and its solution.

Criteria (estimate high, low, or medium)

Proposed solutions	Contribution to objectives	Cost	Feasibility	Side effects (Desirable and undesirable)
1.				
2.				
3.				
4.				
5.				
6.				

panies) the process is more revered in the discussion of its value than in its practical implementation, judging by the fact that only 10 out of 181 reporting companies (a mere 8.3%) actually had a viable MBO performance review system in operation at the time the research was conducted. Nevertheless, it is assumed that under MBO if subordinates are involved in setting their own objectives, they will probably be more enthusiastic and committed to seeing that the objectives are accomplished than they would be under other types of performance review/employee control systems. It is also probable that if the objectives are properly determined (made attainable and challenging) and stated in written form (that is clear, specific, and measurable), then the evaluation at the end of the period will be more objective and provide less chance of disagreement between boss and subordinate than seems to be the norm in industrial practice. Finally, under MBO, during the time between the setting of objectives and the evaluation at the end of the period, both subordinate and boss can presumably use MBO as a communications, time-management, and delegation device to keep mutually informed, solve problems, and make decisions about the work.

Probably one of the greatest limitations of MBO is the extent it pays off for "doing," not "being." The focus should obviously be on results. However, if the MBO results are directly tied to an individual pay adjustment, certain problems may arise.

In respect to compensation itself, most practicing managers and compensation specialists would probably agree that differences in "measured" or "appraised" performance should be reflected in differences in employee paychecks. MBO, as stated above, pays off for "doing," not "being." However, there is a serious dilemma here that is reflected in the industrial engineering and personnel literature. Incentive plans for hourly-paid factory employees compensate employees for work results by comparing actual results to expected results. Hence, these plans require determination of expected results (called production standards) and methods of measuring actual results. Production—also called work—standards are normally a responsibility of industrial engineers and are developed by the process of work study. On the other hand, in most work organizations in America employee performance is not *measured* but rather is *evaluated* or *appraised*. Performance appraisal has thus become a formal method of evaluating employees that assumes that employee performance can be observed and assessed even when it cannot be objectively measured.[44]

We should not unwittingly confuse the measurement concepts of industrial engineering with the appraisal or evaluation concepts of personnel management. Furthermore, in compensating employees for performance, the organization applies various other pay policies in arriving at appropriate base compensation (on, for example, the timing between merit and promotional increases, maintaining salaries within ranges, exceptional policies for meeting market rates in high-demand occupations, and the like). Lastly, although we may not like to admit it because of conflicts with equal employment opportunity and affirmative action plans, organizations pay for personal contributions of an extraperformance nature such as length of service and age, personal appearance, an innovative attitude, employee cooperativeness and dependability as a consistent behavioral pattern, and employee efforts at self-improvement.[45] Thus, although racial and sexual discrimination in employment is unlawful—and perhaps declining—there is little doubt that managements still commonly appraise the other persona' employees in evaluating performance.

MBO probably helps to focus on objective results or ends, bu quality assessment captures subjective judgments about people anu they utilize means both ethically and administratively to attain objectives.

Many pay specialists believe means and ends are important in evaluating performance, provided the appraisal of means does not become overly focused on procedural details and the mechanical "how" of the work. They do not believe means are subsumed in ends. Beyond what has been previously mentioned, it should be added that employees are paid for commitment to the organization beyond the call of duty (extraordinary effort or loyalty perhaps). They are sometimes paid for being a resource, expert, or entity the company or agency can depend on year in and year out. Work organizations, in a sense, pay these employees in part to keep them on the payroll. They are paid both for "being" and "doing." These are the "thank God for" type of people, which may be another way of looking at commitment and loyalty as desired behaviors that require rewards.

Employees, particularly at the managerial level, are expected to be administratively efficient and effective and to have "the owner's eye" when it comes to controlling communication and travel costs, and the use of office or plant supplies, equipment, tools, and machines. Employees are expected to adhere to work rules and company or agency policies, including extending themselves to implement equal employment opportunity, provide smooth customer or client service, and cooperate enthusiastically with shifting managerial drives and campaigns. Pay and continued employment are intended to elicit these behaviors. Employees are often expected to contribute to the community, state, nation, professional associations, or other nonindustrial groups; they are given community service awards, corporate fellowships, perquisites, or status symbols as ego-enhancement awards for these contributions.[46]

The point is clear and the list could be extended: pay is for means, ends, and what for want of a better term are called "extras." Means and "extras" can be stated as objectives, but to do so in an exaggerated way would detract attention from specific projectized work goals that are the hallmark of MBO. Yet to ignore means and extras in pay determination is to place an unwarranted emphasis reminiscent of body kills, tons of bombs dropped, number of strategic hamlets pacified, and other goals in Vietnam that were perhaps indices of success but considerably less than the whole picture. The expected level of participation and contribution to performance as an employee usually exceeds goal-attainment in the narrow individual MBO sense.

From the team standpoint, MBO enters in where individual goal-setting ends. If dyadic MBO is working well, the boss and the subordinate may collaborate and communicate very clearly. However, several problems can be envisaged as shown in Figure 6.13. The customary one-on-one MBO

One-on-one

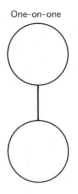

Departmental Organization

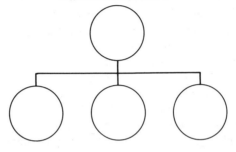

Departmental Organization (Teamed)

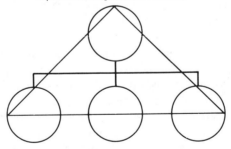

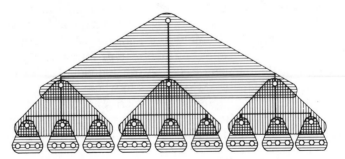

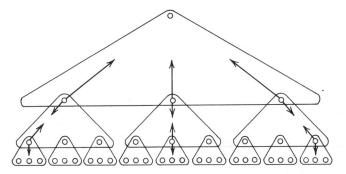

Figure 6.13 (*a*) A manager and employee dyad. (*b*) A manager and three employee subordinates, all one–on–one relationships. (*c*) A manager and three employee subordinates shown as one–on–one and as teamed. Manager is a linking pin. (*d*) Overlapping group form of organization where work teams consist of four people. (*e*) The arrows indicate the linking pin function. (**Source:** Adapted from Rensis Likert, *New Patterns of Management*, McGraw–Hill, New York, 1961, pp. 105, 113, from Thomas H. Patten, Jr., *Pay: Employee Compensation and Incentive Plans*, Free Press, New York, 1977, p. 129.)

situation is shown in 6.13*a*. The dyadic relationship could reflect any superior–subordinate set such as a manager and salaried employee. Figure 6.13*b* displays the typical organizational situation where the boss relates to subordinates one-on-one. The implication is that the subordinates may communicate with peers on their own level but goal-setting for each peer is carried out dyadically with the boss.

Figure 6.13*c* indicates that the three subordinates and the manager not only have dyadic relations but also team relations. From the MBO standpoint, the implication is that goals are set both by dyads and by teams. There is some synergy involved in this configuration that theoretically does not exist in Figure 13*b*. Figure 13*c* implies that once three sets of dyadic goals are tentatively worked out, the persons involved meet to discuss one another's goals so that they may decide how best the goals of the organizational unit (team) can be applied to meet the team goals. This discussion may involve considerable renegotiation of goals, the elimination of duplication and overlap, and the identification of ways everyone concerned can help each other. The fundamental superior–subordinate relationship in organizations is in no way undermined in this configuration. Lines of responsibility, authority, and accountability are as clear as ever in respect to MBO. The addition to the configuration is an OD teambuilding dimension. Individual and team contributions are discussed and will later be evaluated. This had been called collaborative MBO (CMBO) by French and Hollmann in a seminal article.[47] The configuration shown in Figure 6.13*c* could be a building block for an approach to individual pay and team pay as well as for individual and team goal setting. (Greater attention is given to CMBO and team pay in Chapter 8.)

Another aspect of this configuration is its connection to Figures 6.13*d* and 6.13*e*. Likert has discussed the top-to-bottom teambuilt organization shown in the former and the critical connecting points as managerial and supervisory linking pins. In team MBO the potential is unleased for managers (as suggested in Figure 6.13*e*) to work one-on-one and in teams at every level so that the resulting organization is teambuilt from the apex to the base, and base to apex.

Team MBO is one of the latest developments in the rapidly evolving field of human resource management. It is not without its problems in implementation but it appears to be a conceptual advancement over one-on-one "traditional" MBO.

In all likelihood the "means" and "extras" discussed in relationship to individual MBO are crucial for the success of team MBO. People are likely to extend themselves to one another if they are energetic individuals who care about how means relate to ends and are prepared to contribute the extra attention to team goals in a dependable and ethical manner. If the organizational culture emphasizes dog-eat-dog competition and rewards based on results alone, we should expect no interest in teamwork and an egocentric approach to work that destructively emphasizes the short run in one's own bailiwick. Thus, again we perceive the ways in which an OD intervention involving teambuiling is essential for a successful initial and enduring MBO installation.

Systemic Problems in MBO

MBO is not only a means for evaluating or appraising performance but also an approach to the management of a total organization. Indeed, it could be argued that MBO *is* management because the latter is by definition a purposive human endeavor.

In attending sessions of the International Management–by–Objectives Association I have formed some firm impressions about how pacesetting organizations solve systemic problems caused by the installation of MBO. It is important to recapitulate these here because they offer insight into how to keep MBO vital or how to revitalize a faltering or severely problem-ridden MBO system. Unless the total organization in which teams function is supportive of MBO and adopts it as "the" way of life in management, teams are bound to have difficulty in living by an MBO ethic. The comments that follow are geared to actions managers should carry out to keep an MBO system vital. They apply to the same extent to high-level, exempt, non-supervisory professional and administrative employees as well. First, every newly appointed manager should be provided with a minimum of two days' training on MBO, including the techniques for reducing goals to written measurable terms. Ideally, this training in concept and technique should be provided by the internal change agent (or better yet by a successful practicing manager who comes from the line or staff "cadre"). There should be annual clinics or workshops for experienced managers on MBO problems both for the purpose of keeping the MBO effort alive and visible and for constantly upgrading the skills of MBO cadre so that team MBO can become a reality.

Secondly, the MBO cadre should evaluate by random spot-checks how the overall MBO system is working in practice. This effort should be regular and on-going with the goal being a continuous effort to keep the program practicable given the changing environment and conditions in the world of work.

Third, the MBO cadre should report internally to all levels of management regarding their perceptions of how the MBO system is working out and request feedback on what can be done to make the system more operational, as well as what problems require solution. This provides an internal feedback loop that is important in any system.

Fourth, every manager should as a minimum have equal employment opportunity/affirmative action goals, employee development, and subordinate career planning goals in addition to business or agency goals built in his annual MBO plan. In addition, the "administrative skill" of every manager should be evaluated annually as a part of the MBO appraisal. These "administrative skill" assessments should constitute about 10% to 20% of the MBO appraisal and include an assessment of the use of "means" and "extra" contributions made by the manager, as those terms were defined earlier in the chapter.

Fifth, each manager should be required to have at least 20% of his goals each year be innovative, as that term was previously defined. This suggestion could be resisted on the grounds that for some jobs there is little opportunity for innovative approaches (or all the innovations involve additional budget and resources that are not available). Probably the greatest cause of managerial failure is obsolescence. MBO will wither and die without innovation; therefore, it must be deliberately built in the system.

Sixth, the chief executive officer should establish the concept of the written annual restatement and reformulation of the corporate or agency mission that underpins MBO. Lower-level managers in an organization perhaps cannot be expected to live by the same mission statement for too long. They are likely to scan the environment periodically and perceive incongruities that suggest the mission may have changed in part or totally and they either did not get the word or were left out. They may then stand pat, take on work that is unwanted, or perform work related to the same goals this year as last year until the mission signals from the top of the organization are made clear. All of these forms of organizational behavior suggest that they can best be avoided with the annual restatement or reformulation of the mission.

Last, the MBO system should periodically be evaluated by an outside consultant. These consultants (who should be varied frequently) should be prepared to report on how the particular MBO system studied could be improved technically, operationally, and conceptually.

Insofar as external consultants frequently advertise their availability for MBO installation and evaluation assignments, a few closing words on criteria for an adequate MBO consultant are warranted. These are worth specifying because the woods are full of MBO consultants!

An MBO consultant should have at least five years' experience in *all* phases of MBO, not merely its performance appraisal, compensation, or training aspects alone. The consultant should have made at least one full-scale MBO installation and lived with it for a minimum of three years. The MBO individual should be able to provide the client with specific examples of how each phase of MBO works. He should be able to provide references to prior clients and be open about successes and disappointments in prior implementations. Everyone has an occasional bomb-out! He should be personally acceptable to the client and personnel with whom he will be working. He should be willing to stay with the client sufficiently long to assist in implementation and surmount obstacles. Yet he should not create extended dependency of the client but instead when he exits the system, leave managers in the system with adequate knowledge of the processes and adequate skill in using them unassisted. Forms and paperwork should be kept to a minimum. Too many forms suggest a consultant more skilled in method than analysis. The hardest part of MBO is to enable people to be analytical about their work goals. Too often MBO has become a paper tiger that consumes its master. The goal should be for the MBO system to become a self-sustaining organizational way of life, a way of managing, a planning and control system that is capable of accommodating individual and team contributions.

Conclusion

MBO has taken management by storm in the past two decades.[48] Its history of successes is not unmitigated: there have been failures. The reasons for these have been discussed by Kleber[49] and Schuster and Kindall.[50] Yet another may be that MBO often is installed in organizations by people in top management for people in lower management who do not want it and lack the technical and social skills to implement it. In this book I try to overcome these shortcomings by not only starting the change process with a team-building OD effort but also integrating MBO theory, skill practice, and behavioral science knowledge when exposing the teams to MBO itself. In this way, MBO is perceived not as merely another new developmental fad for management but rather a way of getting the job done while helping managers grow. It becomes a way of "running" the job rather than an "override" on the regular way the job is being performed. Such overrides are likely to be reduced entirely to paper programs that are sooner or later headed for demise.

Notes

1. Hans Selye, *Stress Without Distress*, New American Library, New York, 1975, pp. 72–73.

2. John B. Lasagna, "Make Your MBO Pragmatic," *Harvard Business Review*, Vol. 49, No. 6, November–December 1971, pp. 64–69.

3. Walter S. Wikstrom, *Managing By- and With- Objectives* (Studies in Personnel Policy No. 212). New York: National Industrial Conference Board, 1968.

4. George L. Morrisey, *Management by Objectives and Results*, Addison–Wesley, Reading, MA, 1970; and his *Management by Objectives and Results in the Public Sector*, Addison–Wesley, Reading, MA, 1976.

5. Paul Mali, *Managing By Objectives*, Wiley, New York, 1972.

6. Anthony P. Raia, *Managing By Objectives*, Scott, Foresman, Glenview, IL, 1974.

7. Dale D. McConkey, *MBO for Nonprofit Organizations*, AMACOM, New York, 1975.

8. George S. Odiorne, *Management by Objectives: A System of Managerial Leadership*, Pitman, New York, 1965.

9. Morrisey, *Management by Objectives and Results*, *op. cit.*, pp. 15–18, 102–107 makes much of planning as being the "primary" and controlling the "other" function in MBO.

10. Lasagna, *op. cit.*, p. 65.

11. Orvis Collins, et al., *The Enterprising Man,* Michigan State University Press, East Lansing, 1964.

12. Robert Tannenbaum and Warren H. Schmidt, "How to Choose a Leadership Pattern," *Harvard Business Review*, Vol. 51, No. 3, May–June 1973, pp. 162–172.

13. Rensis Likert and Jane Gibson Likert, *New Ways of Managing Conflict*, McGraw–Hill, New York, 1976.

14. Morrisey, *Management by Objectives and Results*, *op. cit.*, pp. 89–94.

15. Logan M. Cheek, *Zero-Based Budgeting Comes of Age*, AMACOM, New York, 1978, pp. 11, 15, 22, 94, 142, 180–181.

16. Peter F. Drucker, *Concept of the Corporation* (rev. ed.), New American Library, New York, 1972, pp. 46–173.

17. Odiorne, *op. cit.*, pp. 54–55, 139–150. Also Odiorne, in *Management*

and the Activity Trap, Harper and Row, New York, 1974, p. 28, reports that in respect to subordinates' regular objectives, the average superior and subordinate failed to agree about 25% of the time; 50% of the time they failed to agree on what major problems exist and should be solved; and about 90% of the time they disagreed on what needed changing, improving, or modification.

18. Raia, *op cit.*, pp. 1–2.

19. Lasagna, *op. cit.*, pp. 65–66.

20. Thomas H. Patten, Jr., *Manpower Planning and the Development of Human Resources*, Wiley, New York, 1971, pp. 264–277.

21. Mali, *op. cit.*, pp. 37–39 discusses the "Pareto effect" after the Italian economist Vilfredo Pareto. The idea is that it is uneconomical to devote the same amount of time and attention to the trivial or inconsequential that one devotes to the critical. From the MBO standpoint the Pareto effect suggests managers should direct their attention to the critical tasks and delegate the trivial to others. The same point was made earlier by Juran. See Joseph M. Juran, "Universals in Management Planning and Controlling," *Management Review*, Vol. 43, No. 11, November 1954, pp. 748–761.

22. Odiorne, *op. cit.*, pp. 68–69 makes this point and many would agree. Yet others disagree. See Rodney L. Brady, "MBO Goes to Work in the Public Sector," *Harvard Business Review*, Vol. 51, No. 2, March–April 1973, pp. 65–74.

23. William B. Werther, Jr., and Heinz Weihrich, "Refining MBO Through Negotiations," *MSU Business Topics*, Vol. 23, No. 3, Summer 1975, pp. 53–59.

24. Theory X applied in a Theory Y way is a classical problem in MBO. The best article on this subject is: Harry Levinson, "Management by Whose Objectives?" *Harvard Business Review*, Vol. 48, No. 4, July–August 1970, pp. 125–134.

25. Morrisey, *Management by Objectives and Results*, *op. cit.*, pp. 19–32; and Lasagna, *op. cit.*, pp. 65–66.

26. Lasagna, pp. 68–69.

27. See note 21.

28. These missions seem implicit in Carol J. Loomis, "The Leaning Tower of Sears," *Fortune*, Vol. 99, No. 13, July 2, 1979, pp. 78–85.

29. Robert Townsend, *Up the Organization; How to Stop the Corporation from Stifling People and Strangling Profits*, Fawcett, Greenwich, CT, 1970, pp. 111–112.

30. Dwight D. Eisenhower, *Crusade in Europe*, Doubleday, Garden City, NY, 1949, pp. 26–28.

31. There is much guidance in the MBO literature on the best ways to write objectives. See, for example, Morrisey, *Management by Objectives and Results*, *op. cit.*, pp. 62–66; McConkey, *op. cit.*, pp. 52–62; and Mali, *op. cit.*, pp. 110–123.

32. Odiorne, *Management by Objectives: A System of Managerial Leadership, op. cit.*, pp. 98–138. These same categories are frequently referred to by other MBO specialists. See Lasagna, *op. cit.*, pp. 66–68; and Joseph P. Yaney, *Personnel Management: Reaching Organizational and Human Goals,* Merrill, Columbus, 1975, pp. 249–255.

33. Marion S. Kellogg, *Career Management*, American Management Association, New York, 1972, pp. 1–56.

34. It has been argued that organizational MBO is the macrolevel of individual career and life planning, which is MBO at the microlevel. See Dorothy Jongeward and Dru Scott, *Affirmative Action for Women: A Practical Guide,* Addison–Wesley, Reading, MA, 1973, pp. 253–286.

35. Charles H. Kepner and Benjamin B. Tregoe, *The Rational Manager*, McGraw–Hill, New York, 1965.

36. For a recent review of the problem-solving literature, see Kenneth R. MacCrimmon and Donald L. Taylor, "Decision Making and Problem Solving," in Marvin D. Dunnette, Ed., *Handbook of Industrial and Organizational Psychology*, Rand McNally, Chicago, 1976, pp. 1397–1453.

37. Likert and Likert, *op. cit.*, pp. 166–167.

38. Marvin R. Weisbord should be credited with the expanded conceptualization of these ideas in an unpublished paper. For more of his creative thinking see *Organizational Diagnosis: A Workbook of Theory and Practice*, Addison–Wesley, Reading, MA, 1978.

39. Tannenbaum and Schmidt, *op. cit.* pp. 162–165.

40. Gordon L. Lippitt, *Organization Renewal*, Prentice–Hall, Englewood Cliffs, NJ, 1969, pp. 123–141.

41. Some of the material that follows is from Thomas H. Patten, Jr., "Linking Financial Rewards to Employee Performance: the Roles of OD and MBO," *Human Resource Management*, Vol. 15, No. 4, Winter 1976–77, pp. 3–5.

42. Thomas P. Kleber, "Forty Common Goal-Setting Errors," *Human Resource Management*, Vol. 11, No. 3, Fall 1972, pp. 10–13.

43. Fred E. Schuster and Alva F. Kindall, "Management by Objectives Where We Stand—A Survey of the Fortune 500," *Human Resource Management*, Vol. 13, No. 1, Spring 1974, pp. 8–11. One of America's best informed consultants, Arch Patton, adds the following: "I am aware of only a few MBO success stories, and these usually concern rather uncomplicated businesses, such as cosmetics, packaged foods, and the like, that are small enough for the top man, to individually 'get his arms around.' The more typical make-and-sell company, in which success is keyed to the effective coordination of sales, manufacturing, engineering, and finance, finds the appraisal process involved in MBO a great deal more difficult. U.S. experience indicates that an MBO program is most effective when it provides the underpinning for an executive incentive plan. In fact, it is fair to say that MBO in the United States seems to require an incentive plan to provide the discipline for sound ongoing administration. Indeed, I know of no successful MBO programs among U.S. Companies that do not also have incentive plans." Arch Patton, "Does Performance Appraisal Work?", *Business Horizons*, Vol. 16, No. 1, February 1973, p. 89. Yet a recent book alleges that MBO is applicable to all levels of employees in a firm. See R. Henry Migliore, *MBO: Blue Collar to Top Executive*, Bureau of National Affairs, Washington, 1977.

44. Belcher makes a meaningful distinction in "measurement" and "appraisal" of performance that should be studied by anyone seriously concerned with the evaluation of employee work behavior. See David W. Belcher, *Compensation Administration*, Prentice–Hall, Englewood Cliffs, NJ, 1974, pp. 199–215.

45. *Ibid.*, pp. 216–226. Age discrimination is a different issue. Length of service, if extensive, implies age; and thus older employees in the same jobs as younger employees usually earn more. See Thomas H. Patten, Jr., "Merit Rating and the Facts of Organizational Life," *Management of Personnel Quarterly*, Vol. 7, No. 1, Summer 1968, pp. 30–38.

46. Robert I. Lazer, "The 'Discrimination Danger' in Performance Appraisal," *Conference Board Record*, Vol. 13, No. 3, March 1976, pp. 60–64, sets forth some of the basic parameters of the discriminatory use of performance reviews. Future court cases may very well show that MBO-types of performance when objectively administered are the most defensive of all varieties currently in use.

47. Wendell French and Robert W. Hollmann, "Management By Objectives: The Team Approach," *California Management Review*, Vol. 17, No. 3, Spring 1975, pp. 13–22. See also W. J. Reddin, *Effective Management By Objectives: The 3-D Method of MBO*, McGraw–Hill, New York, 1971, pp. 156–170, 144–155, and 171–179. He was probably the first specialist to give lengthy attention to one-on-one, team, and sys-

temic MBO, including the linkage of MBO to corporate long-range planning.

48. Charles H. Fox, "MBO: An Idea Whose Time Has Gone?" *Business Horizons*, Vol. 22, No. 6, December 1979, pp. 48–57, has given the funeral oration on MBO, as we enter the 1980s. To him, MBO has delivered less than it promised and its present value is to serve as a mode of what *not* to do in problem-solving and decision making! As could be expected, George S. Odiorne sees a promising future for MBO in "MBO: A Backward Glance," *Business Horizons*, Vol. 21, No. 5, October 1978, pp. 14–24. The reader may choose either crystal ball.

49. See note 42.

50. See note 43.

chapter 7

THE MANAGEMENT OF TIME

We have previously seen that MBO when viewed as a planning and control system acts as a discipline for managerial behavior. We also indicated that MBO is a communications device that can be a substitute for inadequate communication systems and function as a preventative of time-consuming meetings for problem-solving. Thus, there is an obvious but often neglected connection between MBO and time management and interpersonal communications. It may be said that when an adequate MBO system is installed and functioning properly that many time management and communications problems seem to go away.

It is only in very recent years that the literature of management has given much attention to the management of time. Perhaps the great interest in the subject can be attributed to Peter Drucker and some of his early books that gave passing but significant mention to time management in the context of other managerial activities.[1] Koontz and O'Donnell in their classic book on management also gave passing mention to time management.[2] The same is true of Terry.[3] Some of their thinking is discussed in the chapter.

In considering the management of time, particularly managerial time, to improve perspective it is worthwhile taking a new look at the resources available to management, that is, land, labor (in the sense of employees at all organizational levels), capital, entrepreneurship, and time, as Drucker first observed in 1954. Management has to do with the effective marshalling of all the various factors of production, and allocating them properly implies time although it may never be explicitly stated.

It is easy to see the connection between managing people and communicating with them and goal-setting. However, for some reason, until recent years, time was never singled out in the literature for specific attention.

Usually when time is considered, the attention given to it is based upon a notion that time is scarce and something has to be done to conserve it. When time is regarded as a scarce resource similar to the other factors of production, attention is often directed towards determining how to obtain more time or how to use time more effectively.[4] This focus, in turn, causes one to immediately think of the managerial skill of delegation; consequently, we find that discussions of time management almost inevitably lead to a consideration of effective and ineffective delegation.[5] Delegation with all its superior–subordinate teambuilding implications may, in fact, be the major key to improved time management, as subsequently explained in the chapter.

In this chapter we turn first to a discussion of time as a managerial resource and examine various ways in which managerial time can be analyzed and categorized. In addition to Drucker and Mackenzie, Oncken and Wass,[6] Adcock and Lee,[7] Lakein,[8] and others[9] have interesting insights into these matters. We then turn to what research has found concerning the utilization of time by managers. This is followed by a discussion of delegation of time and techniques for making more effective use of it. We also consider exercises on delegation problems and how to solve them, exercises on time-logging and scheduling, and suggestions for improving the use of time in team meetings. The latter is a particularly important consideration because it ties in with the notion of organizational development through teambuilding as a skill that managers should master in becoming more effective in dealing with peers in meetings and working collaboratively with them toward reaching a consensus when problem-solving. We also consider an exercise focused on being an effective participant in meetings and indicate that leadership when shared in group meetings can become an important time saver and a participative form of team work.

The Time Factor

Drucker has noted that the supply of time is totally inelastic. No matter how high the demand, the supply will not go up. Moreover, time is totally perishable and cannot be stored. Yesterday's time is gone forever and will never come back. Time is therefore always in exceedingly short supply not only for the manager but also for other busy people who have tasks to accomplish.[10]

Time is also a paradox because each of us already has had all the time there is. There simply is not any more time. Yet in working with organizations we frequently hear that few managers have enough of it. Evidence from research conducted by Patten and Dorey indicates that high-level managers undergoing a teambuilding OD effort report that newly-acquired skills in time management proved very important back on the job in becoming more effective in attaining organizational goals and in working with others.[11]

We often find that the higher an individual moves in management, the longer his day and his week seem to be.[12] Anecdotal evidence and reported experience suggest that managers often report to work before the regularly established starting hour and frequently remain after lower-level administrative and clerical personnel have gone home. Frequently these managers also take home a briefcase full of work in the evening and some develop the habit of coming to work on Saturday mornings or perhaps occasionally on

Sundays as well. It is true that some of these individuals may be "work-aholics" but many are individuals apparently well adjusted to life. They simply find that the demands of their work are such that they cannot accomplish all they desire during an 8 to 5 normal work day. These are the very individuals who are suffering from time management problems and feel under great stress and pressure because of time shortages.

Time is truly the scarcest resource; unless it is properly managed, nothing else can be managed. Thus Drucker advises being tough with one's time if one is a manager. Others suggest that managers not slip into the habit of postponing work on the theory that there is always tonight, this weekend, or the vacation that can be cut back a few days in order to accomplish work. Instead attention should be directed to the way the manager is behaving in carrying out his normal daily work so that there will be a renewal of his awareness of time utilization. Individuals such as Lee who specialize in time management indicate that in working with executives in OD and management development programs they spend initially a great deal of the program time in creating an awareness in managers of their good and bad habits in time utilization. Several of the kinds of instruments that heighten managerial awareness of time utilization have been developed by Lee.[13]

Time Proverbs

There are many managerial proverbs on time and these are worth passing attention because they are provocative when one considers at the same time how MBO can be used to combat the ineffective behavior implied in some of these proverbs. For example, one is that time management seeks its lowest level. In other words, the poorest time user in management drags all other managers and professionals with whom he works down to his level of time incompetence. He wastes their time, and they must use their scarcest resource ineffectively because he is ineffective.

It is often thought that time that is invested in planning enables managers to save time more generally. Although this is often true, if the planning does not have a basis in organizational goal attainment, such as can be the case in MBO, then the planning itself can become a monumental waste of time.[14]

Time is often connected not only with planning but also with controlling. Thus we find that if the manager's goal is control, it must be self-control first. Put another way, if the manager's goal is management, it must be self-management first. Self-management and self-control are practically identical. These proverbs suggest that a self-disciplined way of approaching one's work through individual time management is the basis for all meaningful time management.[15]

Another proverb is that nothing tells subordinates so much about what is important to the boss as the way he spends his time. Again we can see the connection between MBO and this proverb. For example, the manager who has no clear goals or the one who has several sets of conflicting goals inevitably sends signals to his subordinates that leaves them confused as to what they should really be doing, i.e., how they should be spending their time. Subordinates who frequently try to outpsych the boss will take cues from his time management in an effort to set goals and accomplish work for themselves that will be pleasing to him and perhaps foster their own careers and culminate in rewards. The lesson from this phenomenon for the manager is that the boss should spend his time on objectives that are important to him so that subordinates in turn will know how they should direct their energies. Naturally, an effective MBO system can go a long way in clearing up misconceptions about time utilization concerning who is supposed to do what in line with agreed priorities and allocated resources.

Still another proverb is that nothing is easier than being busy, but nothing is more difficult than being effective. In many organizations we find extremely busy people who are obsessed by the many activities they carry out on the job. They are "activity-oriented" people who often have long since lost sight of the forest because the innumerable trees surrounding them totally becloud their vision. Such employees when called up short on their performance are either bitter or dismayed when told that their performance is poor, inadequate, or just plain not wanted. They can point to their busy work and equate it with effectiveness. They often do not know the difference between the two; in fact, the manager is often to blame for not working with them on properly setting objectives.

Lastly, there is the proverb that advises choosing between doing a job right and doing the right job. In many ways this is similar to the problem of being busy but not being effective.[16] Again, it can be seen that MBO steers a course for the employee so that he should be able to know for certain that he is at least working on the right job even though he may not be totally effective in its performance.

Oncken and Wass have asked the following question: why is it that managers are typically running out of time while their subordinates are typically running out of work? They have developed some useful insights into the meaning of managerial time as it relates to the interaction between the manager and his boss, his own peers, and his subordinates.

Specifically, they deal with three different kinds of management time that are worth further discussion. There is, first, "boss-imposed time," which is used to accomplish those activities that the boss requires and that the manager cannot disregard without direct and swift penalty. Second, there is "system-imposed time," which is used to accommodate those requests to the manager for active support from his peers. Normally, this assistance must also be provided; otherwise there will be certain penalties, even though they may not be as direct or swift as would be the case with nonconformity with boss-imposed time. Third, there is "self-imposed time," which is the time set aside to do those things which the manager originates or agrees to do himself. A certain portion of self-imposed time, however, will be taken by the manager's subordinates and is called "subordinate-imposed time." The remaining portion is the manager's own time and is called "discretionary time." Self-imposed time is not subject to penalty because neither the boss nor the system can discipline the manager for not doing what they did not know he had intended to do in the first place.[17]

System-imposed time may be viewed as supervisory time because it refers to that time which the manager in his role as the supervisor of others must use to coordinate the efforts of his unit with those of persons managing other units located elsewhere in the organization. Boss-imposed time can be looked upon as employee time in the sense that this time refers to the kinds of behavior required by the manager as a subordinate employee of his own organizational superior. It also suggests that it is a kind of time that can be used most effectively when the boss and the subordinate communicate properly and understand one another because they have negotiated and worked upon mutually agreed objectives. Thus the connection between MBO and time management fits in this context as well.

In many respects self-imposed time can be looked upon as executive time because it is a kind of time that can be used one way by a manager who knows how to lead and in a completely different and ineffective way by a manager who is a poor leader. Managers with interpersonal relations problems often make ineffective use of the subordinate-imposed time component of self-imposed time because they cannot communicate and, consequently, use the time available inappropriately. By the same token, the effective manager who knows how to use the discretionary time component of self-imposed time can direct his energies toward proper planning and controlling of work assignments in the provision of personal supportive services and advice to subordinates who are having difficulties in their own problem-solving and decision-making work.

Although it cannot be proven, we hypothesize that the difference between the most effective and least effective executive in an organization is how he handles self-imposed time. The effective time-using manager finds a way to take care of personal goal attainment and his own career planning and life planning out of the lump of self-imposed time he makes available to himself. Inasmuch as I do not consider personal objectives as a part of an MBO system for the reasons mentioned in the previous chapter it can readily be seen that it is probably only in the proper handling of discretionary time that the astute manager can find the way to minister to his own needs for self development.

It is quite clear that the proper management of time necessitates that the manager obtain control over the timing and content of what he does. Since what the boss and the system impose on the manager are backed up by rewards and penalties, he cannot tamper very much with those requirements. Thus his self-imposed time becomes his major area of concern. This is why in the eyes of many experts on time management the manager's prime strategy for more effective time utilization is to increase the discretionary component of his self-imposed time by minimizing or doing away with the subordinate-imposed component. This is also the reason that, as previously stated, time management is often discussed simultaneously with the art and skill of delegation.

When the manager has been able to increase the discretionary component and reduce the subordinate component, he will then theoretically be able to use the newly-found increment to obtain better control over his boss-imposed and system-imposed activities. The reason for this is that most managers spend much more time on subordinate-imposed time requirements than they even faintly realize. Thus, a careful analysis by the manager of how his own unique behavior pattern of relationships with subordinates affects subordinate-imposed time is a highly worthwhile endeavor. In fact, it is the first step toward examining how subordinate-imposed time comes into being for a particular manager and what he can do about it. Probably some of the most apt examples of this sort of time-wasting can be found in the work of Oncken and Wass.[18] They clearly make the point that the first order of business is for the manager to enlarge his discretionary time by eliminating subordinate-imposed time. The second order of business is for the manager to use a portion of his newly-found discretionary time to determine that each of his subordinates possesses the initiative without which he cannot personally perform assignments, and then to see to it that this initiative is, in fact, taken. The third is for him to use another portion of his increased discretionary time to obtain and keep control of the timing and content of both boss-imposed and system-imposed time. The result of these activities should be that the manager will increase his leverage, which, in turn, will enable him to multiply the value of each hour that he spends in managing managerial time.

Principles of Time Management

We turn now to some of the guiding rules-of-thumb or principles that can be used as a general framework for considering time management. Unfortunately, many of the ideas concerning the improvement of one's handling of time are suggestions about utilizing gimmicks to this end. For example, it is sometimes suggested that a manager can save time if he gives up having a desk in the office, particularly in the case of production supervisors who should be presumably pounding the concrete on the plant floor rather than sitting at a desk or standing by a stand-up desk shuffling papers when the real needs are troubleshooting and supervising employees. Another gimmick suggested occasionally is for using travel time most advantageously by taking along a tape recorder for dictation purposes, such as when driving a car.[19] Although there is no managerial objection to this practice, it will hardly save a significant amount of time for the individual whose faulty use of time is attributable to ineffective managerial behavior. Also the highway safety and patrol experts may have their own ideas as how worthwhile it is to have a driver concentrating on his dictation rather than the road in front of him when he is traveling!

Adcock and Lee in an extensive search of the literature intended for finding principles of time management rather than simplistic gimmicks identified ten rules-of-thumb worth repeating here. They group their ten principles according to planning, organizing, and controlling, three of the main classical functions in the management literature.[20]

In respect to planning, there is first the principle of time analysis. Similar to many authors, Adcock and Lee believe that the individual's analysis of how he is spending his own time is a prerequisite to effective time management. Hence, they propose keeping a daily log of activities which records units of 15 to 30 minutes' duration over a span of at least two weeks as the essential first step in an analysis of time utilization.[21]

Figures 7.1 and 7.2 are formats that can be used for logging time. In Figure 7.1 a manager can schedule how he plans to use his time for a five-day period by blocking out each hour in an eight hour day. Obviously, the log could be subdivided in quarter and one-half hour units if desired. Figure 7.2 is an activity log that can be filled out daily and then compared to the time plan at the end of the five-day period to determine where the discrepancies lie. This comparison becomes useful after several weeks of analysis for identifying consistent time leaks and predictable usages of time that must be built in any realistic time schedule.[22] Some time-management specialists believe that no manager who is doing his job properly can schedule more than 50% of his time because if he is, he probably is not building in a sufficiently large component to be used for anticipating crises and other types of unexpected but justifiable interruptions in his plan. Thus there is a contradiction between extremely detailed time planning and planning that is sufficiently well done to allow for work accomplishment while allowing concurrently a reasonable opportunity for shifting one's attention depending upon pressing but unexpected needs.

The second planning principle is the principle of daily planning, which again can be assisted by the use of a time plan and time log such as those shown in Figures 7.1 and 7.2. As we have seen, inadequate planning has been repeatedly identified as a major cause of time mismanagement; and it is commonly thought that the daily planning of time will reduce this waste.[23] Most such plans consist of a list of work items and a time schedule for their accomplishment on the next day.

Customarily, it is thought that the plan should be made before the work day starts although some companies and agencies have built in so-called "quiet hours" that are used in the early morning for work planning as well as enabling the manager to start his day without repeatedly being called out of the office to a meeting or in other ways being interrupted from fulfilling his plan.[24] Thus the principle of daily planning formulated after business hours the previous day, or early before business hours on the same day, in concert with objectives and activities related to those objectives, is thought to be essential to the effective utilization of time.

It perhaps goes without saying that in constructing a daily plan, priorities

Figure 7.1 Time Plan

Week of _____

Hour	Monday	Tuesday	Wednesday	Thursday	Friday
8:00					
9:00					
10:00					
11:00					
12:00					
1:00					
2:00					
3:00					
4:00					

How will each activity contribute to the top priority objectives of the organization?

Figure 7.2 Activity Log of Time Actually Spent

Week of ____

Hour	Monday	Tuesday	Wednesday	Thursday	Friday
8:00					
9:00					
10:00					
11:00					
12:00					
1:00					
2:00					
3:00					
4:00					

need to be assigned to the items of work to be accomplished on that day, which is the third planning principle. However, the method of deciding the priorities is often either not well known or not practiced by managers. As we saw in the last chapter, some managers manage by crisis and set their priorities on the basis of whatever happens to land first upon their desks in the morning. Unfortunately, many issues and events that are urgent are not always important; and many issues and events that are important are not always urgent. Consequently, work items need to be classified according to urgency on a scale ranging from very important to unimportant. Once the items have been arranged according to urgency and importance, they can then be classified according to whether they can or cannot be delegated. The result would be that the highest work priorities are assigned to those items that cannot be delegated by the manager and are very urgent and very important.

Lakein has provided insight into methods of daily and longer-range time planning and prioritizing that deserve special attention. He suggests managers prepare a list of their plans (both for work and as related to their career and life planning) and evaluate them as A, B, or C. A are the items on the list that have a high value; B stands for those of the medium value; and C stands for the low-value items. Acknowledging there is some guessing inherent in the prioritizing, he believes that heuristically a start can be made this way in effective time planning. He believes items marked A should be those that yield the most value and that the person gets the most out of doing the As first and saving the Bs and Cs for later. Taking account of the time of day and urgency of the items, the manager can break them down further so that A items become A-1, A-2, A-3, and A-4 until the list is exhausted.

ABCs are relative, and an A task could drop in value upon closer examination and a C rise in value owing to changes in the environment or requirements of the business. Today's B could become a C or an A.[25] The judgment of the manager and his understanding of the job and MBOs help the manager decide on what work should be the focus of his attention. Obviously, it is not worthwhile to expend a great amount of effort for a task of little value. On the other hand, a project with high value could be worth a high degree of effort. Thus, only sound planning lets a manager reap maximum benefits from minimum time investments. The manager should concentrate on As, occasionally work on Bs (especially if on working on an A some progress can be made on a B), and be generally aware of Cs. For all practical purposes, the Bs and Cs are observed only to make sure their neglect will not confound the fulfillment of As. Also it is possible for Bs and Cs to be upgraded in priority.[26] Thus, in sum, closely connected with the principle of daily planning and deciding on priorities is then the principle of budgeting by priority. Simply stated, the time available in the work day should be budgeted for the accomplishment of those items of work and objectives that have the highest priorities.

The fourth planning principle is that of flexibility. Flexibility should always be a major consideration in the selection of plans regarding time. Stated simply, time should not be over- or underscheduled.

This point is worth elaboration based upon a previous comment above in the chapter concerning the scheduling of only 50% of the time in the work day of a manager. In formulating a daily plan, the manager should be aware of the limitations on the amount of time in a work day that he can reasonably schedule and maintain. The manager who plans every minute of his work day will find that his inflexible schedule cannot realistically be followed, and he invites frustration and the building up of stress. Any person in an important managerial position who schedules more than one-half his time is over-scheduling. At least one-half of his time can be expected to be taken up with crises, emergencies, and the pressures of everyday life in a large organization. This is particularly the case in a production or sales operation in the line organization where crises, problems, and problem-solving are the largest consumers of managerial time each day and where establishing longer-range objective-setting and control systems often seems to go by the wayside because there is no time for them.

Related to this advice, it should be recognized that on the average only 50% of a work day can be scheduled. However the work selected for accomplishment in the scheduled four hours of an eight-hour day should be truly worthy of that amount of time. For example, if during a lull, tasks that would normally take less than four hours of an eight-hour day are allowed to expand to fill the time available, in true Parkinsonian manner, poor time management habits will be acquired. The same strict discipline applicable to time management in normal times needs to be maintained over the use of time when slack periods occur in the work flow. Discipline, especially MBO discipline, is the safeguard that the manager needs to use in order to preclude the encroachment of work's expanding to fill the time available.

Turning to principles applicable to organizing work and the environment to become more efficient in the use of time, we should note that there are at least three. The first of these is the principle of delegation.

The principle of delegation of all possible work consistent with the limitations of the manager's job is essential to provide the time needed for the conduct of the manager's work, as we have previously seen. Establishing priorities for the tasks in the daily work plan consists also of deciding which of these can be delegated. Obviously, all work that can be delegated should be in order to free the manager for the accomplishment of that work only he can do.[27] To decide whether any item of work can be delegated the manager should follow some of the main ideas of delegation which we come back to later.

The second principle used in organizing work is the segmentation of similar activities into certain groupings for more efficient work accomplishment.[28] This principle may be called that of "activity segmentation." This means that work items that are similar in nature and require similar environmental surroundings and resources for their accomplishment should be grouped within divisions of the work day. Thus, it is useful to dictate one's letters in a time allocated for dictation, return one's telephone calls in a time set aside for this purpose, read one's mail in a designated block of time, and the like.

In conjunction with this principle another principle can be applied. This is the principle of control of interruptions. Adequate control and/or arrangement of activities by the manager to minimize the number and duration of unnecessary interruptions is essential to time management. Interruptions must be minimized, and one way to do this is to segment the activities by grouping. If the activities are segmented so that subordinates meet with a manager at a certain time daily, telephone calls are placed and returned in a certain time block, and "quiet time" is built into each day, then the efficiency of time utilization will improve correspondingly. The number of starts and stops on particular tasks will likewise be greatly reduced. Holding the number of stops and starts to a minimum materially improves the efficiency of accomplishing a task and itself saves time.

Lastly, there is the principal of minimization of routine work. This is a difficult principle to pin down and discuss in a meaningful way because some managers by the nature of their work have, as we saw in the previous chapter, a plethora of routine objectives governing their work. Other managers, typically those in purely staff positions, have positions and tasks that are concerned with specific projects rather than the responsibilities of a daily routine. The principle of delegation suggests the assignment of work to the lowest possible organizational level where it can be done effectively by people who know the work and have the authority or are given the authority to accomplish results. Much routine work concerned with regular or recurrent issues can be very well handled by experienced subordinates, provided the manager builds in a concept of management-by-exception, where those items of business truly not capable of being handled by subordinates are brought to him for his attention. He, in turn, can convene the managerial team; working together, they can come to a consensus decision on solution of these exceptional problems.[29]

Turning to the principles that apply to controlling, it should be noted that after planning and organizing the work there always remain plan implementation and daily follow-up. Thus the first principle is that of plan implementation and daily follow-up that, in effect, means the manager has moved from the mode in which he was previously functioning and has now taken on a new style, namely that of planning the utilization of his time and checking to see if the actual use of his time accords with the time plan. It thus can be easily seen that time-plan implementation is essential to the function of control. Control cannot be exercised unless there is a plan with which to compare actual and expected results. Following up, that is, adjusting of the plan, the schedule, and the performance to match objectives and conditions, is, in effect, controlling.

The last principle is that of repeated analysis, which takes cognizance of the fact that behavior, unless it is refrozen in a new mode which is a *bona fide* behavioral change, often results in regression.[30] Thus, a manager under the pressure of a crisis, manpower shortage, or other external force may find that his time management behavior deteriorates into ineffectiveness unless he constantly analyzes what he is doing and corrects any bad habits which may have developed. Also he must be sufficiently self-aware to check if he has reverted to previously ineffective time-management behavior. Thus time-usage analysis is advocated; normally a reanalysis using material such as those in Figures 7.1 and 7.2 can be helpful to this end.

In a research study, these ten principles of time management were found by Adcock and Lee to be widely ignored.[31] Specifically, the principal of daily planning, which may be the cornerstone of all other planning, was not found to be in general use. The majority of the respondents were found to establish priorities for their jobs and to budget time accordingly, but evidence indicated that only a small number actually followed their priorities when they were set. Also, a majority followed the principle of delegation; these were apparently the managers who had developed some kind of a trust level with subordinates such that they were willing to assign them responsibility and authority. Thus we again see the importance of a teambuilding OD effort that involves raising the interpersonal trust level if we are to have effective time management among managers.

Delegation

I have mentioned delegation several times in the chapter and now direct attention to it in some detail. In the simplest possible terms managing is getting things done through people; if we want, we might emphasize the "getting things done" or the "through people" aspects of that definition, depending upon our goal. If we emphasize "getting things done," we are likely to also think about MBO as a way of getting things done. If we stress "through people," we are likely to think about the effects of teambuilding OD on people, their energy, their resources, and the many values of having teams of managers interfacing smoothly for the accomplishment of work.[32]

Delegation is giving employees work assignments and thus amounts to deciding upon how objectives can be meaningfully sliced up in work assignments that specific employees are organizationally in the best position to accomplish. Put another way, we might say that managing and delegating are thus complements.

When delegation is not working properly, we have what we might call reverse management or "bottom up" management.[33] Oncken and Wass have pointed out in a humorous but insightful way how undesirable it is for managers to use their time so improperly that work assigned to subordinates is ultimately returned to the managers for their accomplishment when the level of assigned work is improper at the managerial level.[34] It was seen in the last chapter how goal-oriented subordinates are not likely to engage in reverse delegation, but the task-oriented subordinate who is willing to accept a Theory X managerial style is also the same individual who is sufficiently timid in problem-solving and decision-making that he is likely to be constantly demanding time of the manager for working through the solutions of problems that are in the normal purview of the subordinate's work assignments.

The effective manager is one who knows how to manage and delegate. We have often heard the comment: "don't bring me your problems, bring me your solutions." A manager who is experiencing reverse delegation might try this strategy on the task-oriented subordinate who is not performing at the proper level for his job. Naturally, the manager must work with such a subordinate to help him develop the skills, knowledge, attitudes, and behavior so that he can work in a Theory Y mode with subordinates. In order to get control over self-imposed time, it is important that the subordinate-imposed time component of that self-imposed time is carefully controlled. Thus the philosophy of "don't bring me your problems, bring me your solutions" is preferable and consistent with negotiatory MBO problem-solving. Yet one cannot move into being an effective delegator until one's subordinates are adequately trained to handle all the requirements of the delegated job. It is thus the manager's responsibility to provide or have provided to the employee the training a subordinate needs to satisfy acceptable standards of job performance.[35]

Figures 7.3 and 7.4 indicate two other time principles that are worth some

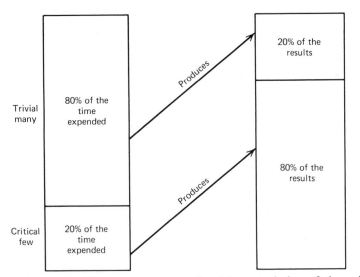

Figure 7.3 Time principle I. (**Source:** reprinted by permission of the publisher from *The Time Trap: Managing Your Way Out*, R. Alec Mackenzie, pp. 52 and 130, © 1972 by AMACOM, a division of American Management Associations. All rights reserved.)

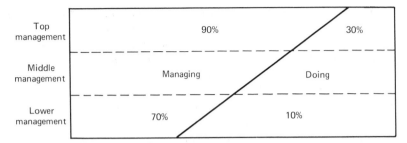

Figure 7.4 Time principle II. (**Source:** adapted from Mackenzie, *op. cit.*, p. 130, citing Ralph C. Davis, *The Fundamentals of Top Management*, Harper, New York, 1951.)

discussion and, according to MacKenzie, have an important bearing not only upon planning but also on delegating. Time principle I as shown in Figure 7.3 is based upon the work of Vilfredo Pareto, the 19th century Italian economist and sociologist. He stated that the significant items in a given group normally constitute a relatively small portion of the total items in the group. Inasmuch as a manager's most important problems as well as opportunities are concentrated in the way suggested by time principle I, the wisdom of focused effort is apparent.[36]

Juran first used the terms "vital few" (which I have called "critical few") and "trivial many" in applying the Pareto principle to a great variety of managerial situations.[37] In Figure 7.3 is illustrated a useful analysis of this principle. The percentages reflect the discovery by American project engineers who applied the Pareto principle to inventory control that 20% of the items normally comprise about 80% of the value of a given inventory.[38] Efforts made by managers to control the "critical few" elements brought results out of all proportion to the efforts expended. Thus, without necessarily overgeneralizing the meaning of time principle I, it is worthwhile to suggest that those managers who concentrate their energies on the critical few are likely to get very significant results from their work, whereas those who spend their time on the trivial many will have far fewer results and probably be considered less effective managers.

Management-by-exception is also based on the Pareto principle because this concept also suggests that managers are best advised to concentrate on the critical few and either delegate the trivial many to subordinate managers, postpone dealing with them, or perhaps, in selected circumstances, totally ignore the trivial many, except to recognize they exist and could become problems some day.[39]

Figure 7.4 is a useful way of looking at the managerial job in terms of the specific content of managerial work and the possibilities for delegation. For a manager to know how much he should delegate is often a difficult problem. We know that management level affects this problem in two ways. The first is that the ideal ratio between managing and doing (or carrying out operating functions) in terms of time varies directly with the level of management. The second is that the allocations of time to the specific managerial functions such as planning, organizing, and controlling, are not in fixed percentages but vary with the industry or type of organization, type of work force and managerial personnel, characteristics of both leaders and followers, and the nature of the situations or tasks involved.

The higher the level of management, the less time the manager should spend doing and the more he should spend managing. Mackenzie, using the work of Ralph C. Davis, suggests in Figure 7.4 the proportion of the manager's work recommended for doing and managing at various levels in the organization. Time principle II in Figure 7.4 shows that higher levels of management spend more time on classical managerial functions than they do in carrying out operations themselves. The lower levels of management, on the other hand, spend a very large proportion of their time on the operational side and less on managerial work *per se*. It can thus be seen that the higher levels of management have to give greater attention to delegating authority when managing whereas the lower levels of management, with greater operating responsibility, have large components of their own time necessarily dedicated to "doing" functions.[40] Again, I do not want to oversimplify or overgeneralize the significance of time principle II but simply suggest to the reader that higher levels of management should not "ride their specialties" in terms of the functional fields of business. They should instead be spending their time where the payoff is greatest for the total organization. This usually means concentrating their energy and time on the most important managerial decisions that are normally fewer in number, greater in time-span, and more planning- and goal-oriented than problems and decisions made in lower management.

Mackenzie has pointed out that a manager who does not delegate is not managing.[41] Because there are degrees of effectiveness, a more precise statement would probably be that a manager who cannot delegate effectively cannot manage effectively. This would then seem to mean that delegation, of all the skills of the manager, is probably the most indispensable.

Viewed another way, it might be said that the tasks of management are four. The first is managing a business or other organization. The second is managing managers. The third is managing workers and the work results that subordinates are supposed to attain. The fourth is managing time. It can be seen that the second and fourth tasks of management are clearly connected and that there are many benefits of delegation that affect all four of the tasks of management.

There are numerous benefits that flow from effective delegation. First, adequate delegation extends results from what a manager could do by himself to what he can control. This observation was noted by Drucker in his famous study of General Motors in the 1940s. It should also be noted that this benefit of delegation ties directly into the rationale for MBO in the sense that the latter assumes that the manager cannot and need not be involved in the microscopic supervision of subordinates' work. Yet the manager must necessarily know how to guide and direct them so that organizational goals can be attained.[42]

Effective delegation also releases the time that the manager might have to spend on other responsibilities for the conduct of distinctively management work.

Adequate delegation allows a manager more time to communicate upward in the organization because the chances are that his subordinates when properly trained and capable of handling delegation, can, in turn, handle their own jobs themselves, calling upon the boss only in exceptional circumstances where they for policy or other reasons need his distinctive input.

Effective delegation also develops subordinates' confidence in working toward objectives because it grants them the authority that they need in order to carry out assigned work. The assignment of authority carries with it an expectation in terms of accountability and responsibility that when assumed by the subordinate enables him to learn on the job and to become more effective in the managerial role.

For many years a popular belief in management theory has been that accountability cannot be delegated. If this were true, only the chief executive officer (or the board of directors) could be held accountable. Actually, accountability can be of two types: "prime" and "final."

Prime accountability is tied to the manager who must attain the MBO results. That is the individual nearest the action and from whom the results are expected. The manager with the final accountability is the delegator, that is, the higher-level manager who insures that the action of the subordinate is taken.[43]

Delegation breaks down because the second-level manager in the example cited above may not know how to give assignments and "let go" of the subordinate. He cannot resist constantly checking on whether the prime accountability is being properly handled; consequently, he does his subordinate's managerial job.

The proper handling of delegation results in each manager's performing the work that is proper for his organizational level. I have already commented on the value of employees' and managers' at various organizational levels performing work that is appropriate to their level of management.

Lastly, it should be recognized that delegation, when it operates properly, reinforces the concept that accountability for results rests permanently and unalterably at the top of the organization even though subordinate levels of management have been given work assignments and identifiable objectives that mesh with the objectives higher in the organization. Managers who fail to attain their goals must accept the responsibility for their failures as well as the praise for their successes and such rewards and penalties as are consequently meted out. However, in the case of failures managers cannot rightfully pass the buck downward in the organization.

Self-Awareness and Self-Management

Whether a manager chooses to reap the benefits of delegation depends upon the extent to which he has come to a realization that the key to effective management is effective self-management which links to MBO. For a manager to be capable of self-management, he must have decided to do something about the discretionary time component of self-imposed time that was discussed earlier in the chapter.

This would normally mean that in self-management he has decided to set objectives intelligently for his own organizational sphere, which from the standpoint of the ideas advocated in this book, would mean that he has gone through some kind of an organizational development through teambuilding effort. It would also mean that he has decided to assign priorities to tasks and activities, which, in turn, would give him greater control over the way that time is utilized. Finally, it would mean that he has decided to manage by exception and has taken the necessary steps to develop subordinates so that he is able to manage in this mode.

Specifically, he will have learned not to transmit work assignment instructions poorly and will have instead acquired the skill to transmit instructions in a participative manner so that subordinates thoroughly understand what is expected of them and have made input into the method by which goals can be attained. It means that he does not keep subordinates waiting for reviews of their work and does request their input into the conduct of assigned work. It also means that he does not interrupt subordinates' work unless the objectives have changed at higher levels in the organization, thus requiring his intervention to communicate those changes to the subordinates. It means that, although the manager will always be available for problem-solving discussions on objectives, he has ruled out the phenomenon of reverse delegation.[44]

Self-management, lastly, means that the manager will control by results and that he will gain control over any bad habits that exist in his own managerial behavior.[45] There are many bad habits that interfere with self-management and effective time management. Many managers need to learn to "single handle" many items that cross their desks in a day. This means not constantly shuffling the same paper in the in-basket when a decision can be made fairly early as to what should happen to the particular item that is there. Of course, there are occasions when items should be retained for further deliberation and consideration, but many items can be rapidly disposed of or turned over to a subordinate for this disposition. To do this implies that the subordinate has been trained and can accept delegation.

Another bad habit that needs to be examined is distractability. The effective manager should do one thing at a time and complete it rather than allow his attention to be constantly deflected from main assignments to what is "interesting" but perhaps trivial. He should avoid having a divided mind.

Setting realistic deadlines and meeting them is also important in self-management. Unfortunately, many managers do not have realistic deadlines and either set them unrealistically ahead or set up their lives so that the only way they can accomplish work is by artificial imposition of deadlines that have no particular meaning except as self-disciplining devices.

Following up on what happens is also crucial and is another way of referring to the control phenomenon. To not follow up is often to fail to carry out responsibilities.

Deciding what not to do and not doing it is also an important skill in managing.[46] This skill is often difficult for some managers to develop because they have an irresistible urge to make technical decisions in their former area of managerial specialism such as accounting, personnel, engineering, production, or sales. They would be well advised to resist this tendency.

Developing the ability to say no more often may be an impossibility for the energetic and results-oriented manager. Such individuals, because of their self confidence, are willing to charge in where others have failed or feared to tread. Again, managers should resist this temptation and instead develop delegation skills and train subordinates to carry out this kind of work.

Prominent Managerial Time Wasters

In discussing time management it is common to make long laundry lists of the different ways in which time can be wasted by managers. I will discuss a few of these, but the point is often made, as has been done by Mackenzie, that with a capable secretary[47] and the knowledge of how to work with her (or him) properly, a manager can make available to himself more time than he might have thought possible. Working effectively with secretaries and supporting technicians is really a separate subject beyond time management in general, but it is well worth considering by any manager who does not know how to relate effectively to a secretary or lacks a proper understanding of how genuinely helpful a professional can be.

In general, there are several prominent managerial time wasters. These are shown in Figure 7.5. First is the lack of planning, which was discussed above. Second is the lack of priority setting, also previously discussed. Third is the lack of delegation, about which no more shall be said. Fourth is overcommitment, which may be caused by improper delegation or by the inability to say no to work that should not be accepted by the manager. Overcommitment also is seen in the behavior of "workaholics."

Management-by-crisis is the fifth prominent time waster because it would not have been necessary to devote any time to putting out fires had adequate planning taken place initially. It should be noted that some crises cannot be headed off by adequate planning, but many can be, and in management-by-crisis none are. A sixth time waster is seen in an excessive number, and particularly, the protracted length of meetings. Meetings are discussed subsequently.

Figure 7.5 Prominent Managerial Time Wasters

• Lack of planning	• Haste
• Lack of priorities	• Routine and trivia
• Lack of delegation	• Paperwork and reading
• Overcommitment	• Visitors (open door) and "war stories"
• Management by crisis	• Indecision and procrastination
• Meetings	• Telephone (message machine)

A seventh time waster is haste in decision-making, which often results in improper decisions that later require reversal or correction because of faulty problem-solving and decision-making. An eighth time waster is excessive concern with routine decisions and trivia that the manager does not realize should be handled by someone else.

A ninth time waster is excessive paperwork and unnecessary reading. It is certainly true that much managerial work involves studying reports, technical publications, and the wide range of written materials that cross the manager's desk. Paperwork is probably the bane of our age, but there is not much that can be done about it. Many managers take courses in rapid reading in order to increase their skill in going through the paperwork, but this is not the solution to a serious problem among managers in American society. Perhaps resisting the temptation to send others information copies of letters and reports and building a work culture norm to reduce the passing of needless and peripheral information would partly solve the problem of excessive reading.

The tenth prominent managerial time waster is visiting with peers or others when there is no clear purpose in doing so. Thus the open-door policy that some managers advocate, although perhaps beneficial in suggesting to others that the manager is accessible, can prove to be dysfunctional from the time standpoint if others assume that this is an invitation to drop in and kill time. There certainly is value in informal contact and the open door policy is not a waste of time for everyone. However, the telling of "war stories" and killing time have no place in management.

The eleventh time waster is delay. Indecision and procrastination are sometimes necessary to arrive at a proper analysis of a problem or in arriving at a decision. Yet sometimes decisions are tardy and very irrelevant because they come so late and are out of phase with work that needs to be done.

The last prominent time waster is the improper use of the telephone. Although it is possible to expand on this subject at great length, probably all that needs emphasis is that the telephone should be regarded as a message machine rather than a device for visiting and for carrying out activities that have no apparent bearing upon managerial work. If the OD effort has changed the work culture and elevated the trust level, much wasted time on the telephone used for ice-breaking and laying the groundwork is not repeatedly necessary as a prelude to business content conversations. Managers will appreciate direct open conversations and be prepared to communicate in kind.

The above discussion by no means lists all the prominent time wasters but it should be suggestive and help stimulate thought.[48]

Making Meetings Move

I referred above to meetings as a time waster; in reality, however, meetings are necessary in order to conduct managerial work. The issue here perhaps is the difference between an efficient and inefficient meeting. At the outset it should be noted that if MBO is working properly many communications problems in an organization are already solved and meetings avoided. Those meetings that are required can probably be shorter and may consciously be steered so that they have a duration of perhaps an hour to an hour and a half. If those attending the meeting have already had a teambuilding experience, many interpersonal clashes have probably been resolved already and meetings can become more purposeful and productive.

In order to make meetings move and fully utilize the human resources present, the purpose and content of the meeting should be clear.[49] These are often clarified by the existence of a carefully thought through agenda agreed upon in advance of the meeting and perhaps only slightly altered at the time of the meeting if it is decided that alterations will help the organization get its work done.

Meetings also are improved when those who are present are self-aware and avoid "shooting from the lip" instead of preparing well for the meeting

Figure 7.6 Exercise on Time Management

Complete the "Self-Checklist on Delegation and Time Management," which takes about 5 minutes. Then go into your Base Group Teams and discuss commonly agreed-upon problem areas that are "Definitely a Problem." This should take about 30 minutes. Then reassemble in the seminar, at which time there will be a discussion of commonly identified problems and other novel problems that the group members wish to bring up. There is no specific reporting task that requires using newsprint to feedback information to all seminar participants.

You might ask yourself the following questions for stimulation:
- How often on the job do you handle the same letter, memorandum, or other paperwork that crosses your desk? Once? Twice? More often?
- Have you "let go" of work in your former technical or functional specialty that you continue to consider substantively "interesting" or perhaps "sensitive" and do not typically delegate?
- Do your subordinates tend to delegate upward because of their perceptions of your day-to-day managerial behavior and continuing nonmanagerial "interests"?
- What do you think of meetings and the effectiveness of your behavior as a meeting member when participating in a meeting? Have you ever stopped a meeting and asked members to question the group "processes" that are affecting "content" or task accomplishment in the meeting?

Figure 7.6 (*Continued*)

Self-Checklist on Delegation and Time Management

No Problem	Might be a Problem	Definitely a Problem	
_____	_____	_____	1. You prefer to make your own phone calls rather than ask your secretary to make them.
_____	_____	_____	2. Several long-range projects are postponed until you "get time."
_____	_____	_____	3. Subordinates often interrupt you for help and advice.
_____	_____	_____	4. Most of your subordinates feel they should bring problems to you rather than make decisions themselves.
_____	_____	_____	5. You spend part of your working day doing things for others they could do themselves.
_____	_____	_____	6. As much of your time is spent on details as on planning and supervising.
_____	_____	_____	7. You reserve those details for yourself that you particularly enjoy, even though someone else could do them.
_____	_____	_____	8. You feel you must keep a close tab on details to have a job done right.
_____	_____	_____	9. You lack confidence in subordinates, that is, you are afraid to risk giving them more responsibility.
_____	_____	_____	10. You are a perfectionist about details that do not affect the final outcome of a project.
_____	_____	_____	11. In delegating a job, you often fail to furnish full information the first time.
_____	_____	_____	12. After delegating a project, you grow apprehensive and hover over the subordinate who's doing the job.
_____	_____	_____	13. Your people are unprepared to take on more responsibilities—either because of lack of training, self-confidence, or ability.
_____	_____	_____	14. You take work home almost every night.
_____	_____	_____	15. You rewrite most written communications prepared by subordinates for your signature because you do not like their choice of words.

Figure 7.7 Effective Managerial Behavior in Meetings

Much has been written about how a manager can make his most effective contributions in a problem-solving or policy-setting meeting. The decisions that are arrived at as a consequence of these meetings often have long-range and durable effects on the parties who make them and on the client(s), employees, or publics who must work through the consequences of the decisions.

David Halberstam wrote a Pulitzer Prize winning book on the involvement of the United States in the war in Vietnam. His perceptions of the war are not shared by everyone, but they are well formulated and provocative. The quotations below are from his book, *The Best and the Brightest* (Greenwich, CT: Fawcett Publications, 1972) and refer to the managerial behavior in meetings of Robert S. McNamara, Secretary of Defense during almost the entire span of the Kennedy–Johnson administrations in the 1960s.

As you read these excerpts try to formulate your views on what constitutes effective and ineffective managerial behavior in the instances described. How could the behavior be changed to be more effective? What is your personal concept of "effectiveness" as a meeting member?

"Those who attended the meetings learned to play the game; the McNamara requests to speak freely were not to be taken too seriously. He would telegraph his own viewpoint, more often than not unconsciously, in the way he expressed the problem, and in particular he would summarize in an intimidating way, outlining point by point, using the letters of the alphabet, A through J, if necessary, and his position always seemed to win out in the summation. If you dissented or deviated, he listened, but you could almost hear the fingers wanting to drum on the table; if you agreed and gave pro evidence, he would respond warmly, his voice approving in tone. Gradually those who disagreed learned their lesson, and just as gradually he would reach out to men who were like him until he was surrounded by men in his own image. Those who knew him well could tell when he was angry, when he was going to explode. He would become tense, and if you looked under the table you could see him begin to hitch up his pants, a nervous habit, done because he knew he could not control his hands if they were on the table. The more restless he became, the more his antagonist assaulted his senses, the higher the pants would get, showing thick hairy legs. On bad days the pants might reach to the knees, and then suddenly he would talk, bang bang bang. You're wrong for these reasons. Flicking his fingers out. One. Two. Three. . . He always ran out of fingers." (pp. 288–289)

"When it came right down to it, McNamara had doubts about the bombing (of Vietnam) in his mind, but those doubts were not reflected in the meetings. He was forceful, intense, tearing apart the doubts of the others, almost ruthless in making his case; those around him were sure that he was being encouraged by the President (Lyndon B. Johnson) to do this; he was too much the corporate man to go as far as he did without somehow sensing that this was to be his role. He was (George) Ball (Under Secretary of State for Economic Affairs) found, quite different in private sessions than in the major meetings where Johnson presided. When Ball prepared paper after paper for Johnson, he would first send them to the other principals, and occasionally McNamara would suggest that he come by and talk the paper over before they went to see the President. Ball would find McNamara surprisingly sympathetic, indeed there seemed to be a considerable area of agreement. Sometimes (the late) John McNaughton (Aide to McNamara, expert on arms control, and former Harvard Law School professor) was present and McNamara would note that McNaughton was in general agreement with Ball, that he had great doubts about the course they were following. So Ball often left feeling that he had made some impression, that he had stirred some doubts in McNamara, that there was the beginning of an area of agreement. But then, in the real meetings, with Johnson present, it would be quite different: McNamara, the ripper now, his own doubts having disappeared, could not afford to lose an argument, or even express partial doubt; partial sympathy for Ball might hurt his own case. So he plunged forward, leaving Ball somewhat surprised and dominated by his force, his control and his statistics. McNamara may have realized that there was an enormous element of chance to what he was proposing, that he was only for it 60–40, but it seemed at the meetings that he was for it 100 percent. There was never anyone better at a meeting; it was a performance, really—programmed, brilliantly prepared, the right points fed in, in just the right way. It was done without emotion, that was a key point, it always seemed so objective and clear; and yet it carried conviction. Conviction and certitude without emotion. When he finished everyone knew what to do. The modern man." (pp. 625–626)

---

and having due respect for the views of others. There is an extensive literature on how a meeting can be set up mechanically to be most productive.
These materials should be consulted for useful guidance.[50]

Lastly, meetings that are most effective are probably those that encourage individuals to be team-aware as well as self-aware. Thus if someone in
the meeting stops the meeting occasionally to shift from an analysis of the
task or content of the meeting itself into the interpersonal processes that are
operating to facilitate task accomplishment, then those meetings are likely to
be most productive. There is an extensive literature in applied behavioral
science that indicates how managers become more effective once they have
learned how to learn from peers and are capable of dealing with both process
and content in meetings.

Exercise on Time Management

There are various ways to proceed in helping managers become better managers of their time. Figures 7.1 and 7.2, discussed earlier, can be reproduced
and given to managers for their individual use in planning and logging their
time over a two-week period. They can then make appropriate comparisons
between time planned and time used and take corrective action as needed if
they have difficulty in deciding upon a course of action to improve their
utilization of time.

Figure 7.6 is an exercise on time management which can be used in
teambuilding. The instructions for the exercise are shown although there are
other ways of conducting the exercise which may occur to the OD specialist.
The check list accompanying Figure 7.6 lists 15 common problems in delegating and time management that are reported to be commonly found among
managers. The exercise gives each manager in the teambuilding program a
chance to indicate, with respect to each item on the checklist, whether he
thinks he has no problem, a possible problem, or a definite problem. When
he shares this information with the members of his team he is likely to find
that others have or have had similar problems and in the ensuing discussion
of the problems it is quite possible that participating managers will learn how
others are coping with the problems.

Figure 7.7 can be used as a handout to stimulate a discussion on effective
managerial behavior in meetings by asking a group to read a case that is of
general interest and then discuss its implications for the behavior of subordinates. The case concerns a very well known public figure who was also a top

} Exercise on Delegation: Sharing Ideas on Improving Managerial
⸻s
───

eam member to consider how he typically handles the delegation of work assignments
nates at the present time and how he thinks he could improve the way he delegates
work. Then ask each group member to share his thinking with the team. Ask someone on the
team to record on newsprint the main ideas about how delegation techniques could be improved. Then debrief the teams around the room to determine common ideas about how they
can increase their skills in delegation.

Do the participants tie in the values of MBO to proper delegation and the management of
managerial time?

───

corporate executive. The excerpt is taken from two portions of a book that
are separated by a number of pages and portray former Secretary of Defense
Robert S. McNamara and his behavior in a way that is very interesting to a
typical managerial group. In order to cover this case exercise it is suggested
that the participants read the case and when prompted by the OD facilitator
express their views on what they see as effective and ineffective managerial
behavior in meetings. The case has many implications for teambuilding,
creating an open organizational climate, formal and informal relationships
between different levels of management, and the proper use of managerial
time to accomplish meaningful work. The facilitator can steer the discussion
to determining personal concepts of effectiveness as a meeting member if he
so desires and can redesign the session so that the individual teams in atten-
dance can use newsprint to report a consensus in their team on what should
be modified to yield effective behavior in a meeting. The case obviously
focuses more upon process than content and does not require any special
knowledge of the content of the situation to become an eminently discuss-
able learning vehicle.

There is one other exercise that can also be used in time management,
particularly if the main problem of the team is poor delegation skills. Figure
7.8 provides the instructions for the conduct of this exercise, which invites
an open discussion of delegation problems and the sharing of ideas about
how team members can become improved delegators. The length of time
needed to conduct and debrief would vary from group to group, as do most
of the exercises on time management discussed in this chapter.

Conclusion

In this chapter we have considered how the management of managerial time
is connected with organizational development through teambuilding and
MBO. This has led us into an analysis of many related topics such as delegation, interpersonal communications, and organizational reward and penalty
systems themselves. We can conclude that time is an important resource in
management and that its utilization is of vital concern.

In the next chapter our attention is directed specifically to the connection between OD, MBO, and the financial and nonfinancial reward and penalty systems in work organizations. In this way some important connections touched upon earlier in the book can be traced and hopefully the loop in our model of an organizational change strategy can be closed.

Notes

1. Peter F. Drucker, *The Practice of Management*, Harper, New York, 1954, pp. 14–15 and *passim*; and his *The Effective Executive*, Harper and Row, New York, 1967, pp. 26–27. See also Roy Rowan, "Keeping the Clock from Running Out," *Fortune*, Vol. 98, No. 9, November 6, 1978, pp. 76–82 for a current overview.

2. Harold Koontz and Cyril O'Donnell, *Principles of Management*, 3rd ed., McGraw–Hill, New York, 1964, pp. 27–28.

3. George R. Terry, *Principles of Management*, 4th ed., Irwin, Homewood, IL, 1964, pp. 50–57.

4. R. Alec Mackenzie, *The Time Trap: Managing Your Way Out of It*, AMACOM, New York, 1972, pp. 2–3.

5. See Mackenzie, *op. cit.*, pp. 122–142 in addition to such major works on the surprisingly neglected subject of delegation as Dale D. McConkey, *No-Nonsense Delegation*, AMACOM, New York, 1974; and Lawrence L. Steinmetz, *The Art and Skill of Delegation*, Reading, Addison–Wesley, MA, 1976.

6. William Oncken, Jr. and Donald L. Wass, "Management Time: Who's Got the Monkey?" *Harvard Business Review*, Vol. 52, No. 6, November–December 1974, pp. 75–80.

7. Robert L. Adcock and John W. Lee, "Time, One More Time," *California Management Review*, Vol. 14, No. 2, Winter 1971, pp. 28–33.

8. Alan Lakein, *How to Get Control of Your Time and Your Life*, New American Library, New York, 1973.

9. Included here are such representative book-length treatments over the past two decades as Joseph D. Cooper, *How to Get More Done in Less Time*, Doubleday, Garden City, NY, 1962; Ross A. Webber, *Time and Management*, Von Nostrand and Reinhold, New York, 1972; Mark L. Stein, *The T Factor*, Playboy Press, Chicago, 1976; and Jack D. Ferner, *Successful Time Management*, Wiley, New York, 1980.

10. Drucker, *The Practice of Management*, *op. cit.*, pp. 346–347.

11. Thomas H. Patten, Jr. and Lester E. Dorey, "Long Range Results of a Teambuilding Organizational Development Effort," *Personnel Management Review*, Vol. 6, No. 1, January–February 1977, pp. 44–45.

12. Mackenzie, *op. cit.*, p. 8.

13. Others also stress awareness-heightening. See Mackenzie, *op. cit.*, p. 5; Webber, *op. cit.*, pp. 11–19; and Stein, *op. cit.*, pp. 11–26.

14. Drucker, *The Practice of Management*, *op. cit.*, pp. 346–348; and Mackenzie, *op. cit.*, pp. 38–46.

15. Drucker's famous chapter "Management by Objectives and Self-Control" probably set the framework for this concept as well as for MBO itself. See his *Practice of Management*, *op. cit.*, pp. 121–136. See also Mackenzie, *op. cit.*, pp. 15–37.

16. Mackenzie, *op. cit.*, pp. 38–49.

17. Oncken and Wass, *op. cit.*, pp. 75–76.

18. *Ibid.*, pp. 77–80.

19. Mackenzie, *op cit.*, p. 118.

20. Adcock and Lee, *op. cit.*, p. 29.

21. Time logging has been advocated by Drucker and a bevy of experts on time management. See John J. Tarrant, *Drucker: The Man Who Invented the Corporate Society*, Cahners, Boston, 1976, p. 65; Mackenzie, *op. cit.*, pp. 20–22, 148–149; Cooper, *op. cit.*, pp. 12–41; and Ferner, *op. cit.*, pp. 19–20, 207–208.

22. Time leaks and "time robbers" are frequently discussed. See Ferner, *op. cit.*, pp. 33–37; and Lakein, *op. cit.*, p. 16.

23. Mackenzie, *op. cit.*, pp. 20–21.

24. *Ibid.*, pp. 46–47.

25. Lakein, *op. cit.*, pp. 28–29.

26. *Ibid.*, pp. 69–83, 100–108.

27. McConkey, *op. cit.*, pp. 64–79.

28. Webber, *op. cit.*, pp. 60–72; and Adcock and Lee, *op. cit.*, p. 30.

29. Adcock and Lee, *op. cit.*, *idem*.

30. *Ibid.*, p. 31.

31. *Ibid.*, pp. 31–32.

32. Mackenzie, *op. cit.*, pp. 122–123.

33. *Ibid.*, pp. 137–138.

34. Oncken and Wass, *op. cit.*, pp. 75–80.

35. Mackenzie, *op. cit.*, pp. 137–140.

36. *Ibid.*, pp. 51–52.

37. Joseph M. Juran, "Universals in Management Planning and Control-ling," *Management Review*, Vol. 43, No. 11, November 1954, pp. 748–761. See also Joseph M. Juran, *Managerial Breakthrough*, McGraw–Hill, New York, 1964.

38. For more on the so-called 80/20 principle see Paul Mali, *Managing by Objectives*, Wiley, New York, 1972, pp. 37–39; and Lakein, *op. cit.*, pp. 70–73.

39. Mackenzie, *op. cit.*, pp. 53–54.

40. *Ibid.*, pp. 129–135. See also Webber, *op. cit.*, pp. 31–42; and Stein-metz, *op. cit.*, p. 27.

41. Mackenzie, pp. 126–127.

42. *Ibid.*, pp. 122–123.

43. McConkey, *op. cit.*, pp. 13–15, 135–138 distinguishes conceptually between prime and final accountability.

44. Mackenzie, pp. 126–142. For augmentation of these ideas see McCon-key, *op. cit.*, and Steinmetz, *op. cit.*

45. The time management literature is replete with suggestions about how to control bad habits. See Mackenzie, *op. cit.*, pp. 61–112; 143–153; 173–176; Webber, *op. cit.*, pp. 154–161, 43–59; Lakein, *op. cit.*, pp. 149–160; and Cooper, *op. cit.*, *passim.*

46. Deciding what not to do and to adhere to the negative decision is also a theme in the time management literature. See Mackenzie, *op. cit.*, pp. 54–56, and Lakein, *op. cit.*, 84–88.

47. Again this is a time-management theme, with the boss and secretary sometimes called a "team of two." See Mackenzie, *op. cit.*, pp. 154–172.

48. Mackenzie, *op. cit.*, pp. 1–14 and *passim.*

49. This too is a time-management theme. Again see Mackenzie, *op. cit.*, pp. 98–112; Webber, *op. cit.*, pp. 51–53; and Michael Doyle and David Straus, *How to Make Meetings Work; The New Interaction Method*, Playboy Press, Chicago, 1976.

50. See George M. Prince, "How to Be a Better Meeting Chairman," *Harvard Business Review*, Vol. 47, No. 1, January–February 1969, pp. 98–108; and his "Creative Meetings Through Power Sharing," *Harvard Business Review*, Vol. 50, No. 4, July–August 1972, pp. 47–54. See also Roger A. Golde, "Are Your Meetings Like This One?," *Harvard Business Review*, Vol. 50, No. 1, January–February 1972, pp. 68–77.

chapter 8

OD, MBO, AND REWARD SYSTEMS IN ORGANIZATIONS

Throughout this book there has been discussion of management and employee motivation and the incentive to perform at work. I have suggested that reward systems should be structured and administered so that they elicit desired performance and teamwork.

Intervention Based on Trust

If we shift our attention from MBO to the inner workings of an organization, we find that interpersonal trust is an important ingredient for effectiveness in goal-attainment, MBO installations, and compensation allocation.[1] Levinson,[2] Gibb,[3] Zand,[4] Fox,[5] and many behavioral scientists have discussed the importance of trust, and it is useful to consider, in greater depth, their thinking.

Broadly, they are stating that management would like to trust that employees will give a fair day's work for a fair day's pay. Similarly, employees would like to trust managerial communications, policies, procedures, and practices not only in the domain of compensation but throughout the various areas of personnel administration. Mutual dependence or recognition of interdependence would thus appear to rest on trust.

One of the major reasons for the failure of MBO in many organizations is that management fails to recognize the political character of the MBO implementation process and destroys trust. MBO is indeed logical and systematic, but it must also deal with a number of factors, including power and authority, the organization form, and the values and expectations of people. The scuffles and corporate political infighting that grow out of an MBO installation can be very unsettling to employees, giving rise to feelings of job insecurity and fears concerning fair treatment and reward allocation.[6]

Gibb has remarked that the central and primary leverage dynamic of the growing organization often appears today to be fear and its antithesis, trust.

Growth occurs when one moves from fear toward trust. Over the long run, increasing trust is the primary determinant of sustained creativity and productivity.[7]

Trust has a strong bearing on an individual's willingness to commit himself to the attainment of organizational objectives and to engage in a meaningful dialogue on those objectives. Dialogue, in turn, is a basis for understanding one's responsibilities and performance expectations. Similarly, trust is an important and necessary condition for the creative and innovative exercise of capability. Finally, trust is an important aspect of an individual's willingness to accept change in general and change of his personal behavior in particular.

Mutuality of trust is brought about by example, by the encouragement of meaningful relationships, and by the expression of empathy and warmth in interpersonal dealings. Trust appears to develop more readily when there is opportunity for meaningful social interaction between superior and subordinate and when a subordinate believes his boss can control the situation at the next managerial level.[8] Such control would, on the face of it, seem to be facilitated by the installation of an MBO system.

It is probably impossible to carry out effective and efficient pay planning and administration in an organization where trust is absent from the work culture and the predominant emotion is fear. Fear of loss of employment through layoff or capricious termination, fear of unfair treatment in pay matters, and fear of personal powerlessness due to the way pay is administered are some of the main blocks to unleashing an employee's energy to work. OD interventions are needed to build trust where little or none exists. Unionization drives and collective bargaining are often a response to the above-mentioned conditions, in an attempt to reduce fear and insecurity when managements are hard-nosed, unresponsive, or uninformed.

Specifically, minor unilateral adjustments by management in the treatment of employees probably have little effect on the trust level within a work organization. Hence the characteristic top management exhortation to rank and file employees to "trust the company" is often received with cynicism. In the very way it structures work, authority, and rewards, management excludes lower-level employees from the trust bond it may have in the managerial ranks while simultaneously asking subordinates to submit to its discretion in handling their interests and destinies. In other words, management is saying, we do not trust you, but we ask you nevertheless to trust us![9]

The compensation specialist who perceives himself as having made OD interventions whenever he modifies the organizational reward system should realize that trust is the foundation for successful intervention. Trust is really interpersonal and intergroup acceptance carried to its logical end point. Hence, the broad goal of acceptability should never be ignored in planned change of the reward system. Acceptability, in turn, requires openness in pay transactions and accurate communications. For these reasons, the up-to-date compensation specialist requires an OD perspective on his work as well as the intellectual curiosity to stay abreast of developments in applied behavioral science over the course of his career in the pay field.

"If you want the mice to run differently, move the cheese around" is, however, fast becoming the rationale of compensation specialists who see cheese as pay and MBO as the control mechanism to stimulate running. Put another way, MBO is increasingly being viewed by pay planners and administrators as part and parcel of CBO, compensation-by-objectives; in fact, the term CBO has already been coined and used, although it has not yet slipped into general currency.

What are the implications of equating MBO with CBO? Should MBO be strictly demarcated from compensation decisions? There is much new and old thinking that argues for such separation. Should MBO be integrated with pay planning and administration to become CBO? There is some new thinking in the field that suggests it should; one school of thought argues for tight mechanical integration whereas the other urges a looser judgmental, managerial, or organic integration. More fundamentally, should the entire issue of MBO–CBO be reexamined so that the hoary field of wage and salary administration and fringe benefits is viewed as an organizational development (OD) intervention focused upon building a trusted reward system in which goal setting, performance review, monetary and nonmonetary rewards, the work itself, and participative teamwork are properly interrelated? This complex question is at the heart of improved organizational management and deserves serious consideration if we are to make a start in settling the MBO–CBO controversy. Let us review where we are conceptually and let me spell out in greater detail than I have previously in the book my OD → MBO → RS model and its underlying logic. Such a review can now be provided because the reader should be able to determine our direction in the final stages of teambuilding. Bottom-line results and, fundamentally, organizational goal attainment should be our primary interest.

Intervention in the pay planning and administration systems in a work organization is a particularly potent technical intervention in the management of human resources. Teams and their compensation should be considered in pay plans if we are to attain the fullest results from an OD effort.

Why OD Is More Basic than MBO

Despite the growth of OD, many personnel administrators, human resource experts, training directors, and pay specialists are not fully comfortable with the concept because they do not have a context for understanding it and often cannot relate it to MBO, the reward system, and all the other innovations in the personnel field coming along these days. The organizational iceberg, devised by Herman, provides a graphic way of viewing OD in context and makes it possible to see where MBO and the reward system fit in.[10]

Figure 8.1 depicts the organizational iceberg and indicates that there is a

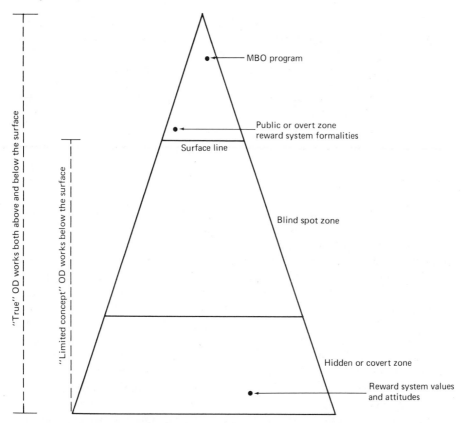

Figure 8.1   The organizational iceberg. (**Source:**   Patten, *Pay: Employee Compensation and Incentive Plans*, *op. cit.*, p. 564.)

surface line. Like all icebergs, probably only 8% to 12% of the organization is above the surface. Included here are the "public" or "overt" manifestations of the iceberg. Examples of these parts would be organizational charts, job descriptions, statements of functions, collectively bargained agreements, manuals of personnel policies, statements of objectives and goals in the MBO program, the formal salary administration program, and the like.

As Herman has pointed out, traditionally, in most organizations when a serious operating problem is encountered, management, consultants, and others interested in improving the functioning of the organization have tended to concentrate their attention in the overt area. Someone might get the bright idea that "we ought to have an MBO program" to solve the problem, and MBO is then decoratively placed on the tip of the iceberg. MBO thus becomes a formal change, and its success depends upon what goes on beneath the surface line. In OD it is important to pay heed to other dynamics in addition to (not instead of) formalities on the top. Let us turn to these next.

If we look at the bottom of Figure 8.1, we see that "hidden" or "covert" aspects of the iceberg are those that are far beneath the surface. Thus, in organizations we find the following: power and influence patterns; differences among departments as to their conceptions of the relative importance of their roles and missions; patterns of competition and alliances, such as to obtain larger budgets or expand programs; individual needs and feelings; and the like. It should be obvious that MBO has little or nothing to do directly with this important part of the iceberg, and yet what personnel or training director will deny that the dynamics of his job are not centered more in this part of the iceberg than in the formalities reflected on the top? However, we often find that this part of the personnel job is least satisfactorily carried out. Precisely because it is often bungled, the immediate response to failures in the covert zone is to move things around in the overt sector in the hope that the covert problems will somehow go away.

In the middle of the iceberg is a blind spot that, in terms of social psychological space, is somewhere between those rational things that we deliberately contrive in order to manage organizations (such as MBO again), and the social–emotional infrastructure upon which the buoyancy of the iceberg depends to some extent.

This blind spot has to do with other people's perceptions of the health and effectiveness of the organization, such as the views of the general public, the body politic, another agency or outside group, subparts of the same organization, and the like. The perceptions involve such thoughts as how the public feels about the organization's success in attaining objectives, its cooperativeness, resiliency, relevancy, extent of bureaucratization, and similar matters. Quite often public relations programs are launched in the hope that the blind spots will be dealt with, but the fight to change perceptions and build favorable images is most often a continuing effort or a campaign that never is permanently terminated.

It should be noted that some personnel and training directors who have been exposed to organizational development programs often think that OD works solely below the surface (as reflected on the left of Figure 8.1). Therefore, in their own minds they often give up trying to understand the nine-tenths of the iceberg below the surface, concentrating instead on the one-tenth above the surface that can be dealt with rationally. However, "true" OD works both above and below the surface and is all-encompassing. In this sense, MBO can be viewed as a part of "true" OD—and should be seen in this close connection.

The reward system is shown in Figure 8.1 as both above and below the surface. Those parts above could include, for example, all the formal compensation planning and administration programs, whereas those below would comprise all the values and attitudes about pay and performance expressly stated or implicitly held by employees, many of which would have been included in the formal pay programs.

What Is MBO?

Although both concepts are fairly new, MBO antedates OD in the literature of personnel administration.[11] Drucker was lecturing on MBO in the post World War II period at New York University and unified his early thinking as early as 1954.[12] As we have seen, Drucker's original statement was brief and based in part on his study of General Motors Corporation during the 1940s in which he saw managing by objectives as the explanatory variable in GM's economic success (rather than styling, efficient plants, a strong dealer setup, effective cost controls, flexible organization, planned managerial succession, or well-administered executive compensation plans, all of which were necessary but not sufficient conditions).[13] His thought was that no individual in a large-scale organization could direct all the *activities* of his subordinates. Yet if he could control the *results* of their work by a system built around understood goals, he could manage very well. GM had grasped this concept and built it into its *modus operandi*. In recent years, as we have seen, various organizations have called MBO goal setting, target setting, management by results, or work planning and review, but the ideas are very much alike.

Authors such as Humble[14] and Reddin[15] have taken interesting tacks from basic MBO, but Odiorne[16] has probably become the foremost interpreter and expositor of MBO; he has applied the concept to selection-by-objectives,[17] discipline-by-objectives,[18] and other aspects of personnel administration,[19] which suggests the versatility (if not the universality) of the concept. Similar to OD programs, most MBO experts seem to concur that MBO programs should begin with top management and cascade downward.

Odiorne's conceptualization of MBO is extremely clear and fits in well with many other experts' understandings of OD by displaying how one of the most potent systematic tools of personnel administration functions to focus total human energy in a rational and organizationally desired direction.

Odiorne believes MBO is a system that by defining outputs applies the latter as criteria to judge the quality of activities (behavior by employees) and to govern the release and effectiveness of the inputs. MBO is thus not only a method of performance review but also a management system. Thus, management itself can be defined as management by objectives. Figure 8.2 clarifies these interconnections.[20]

Starting with the left and moving to the right, we consider inputs first. They may be defined as resources committed to an idea to transform it into a going concern or entity. Typical inputs are, as shown, capital, labor, materials, and human knowledge and skills.

Activities are the behaviors of people in organizations, the actual work that they perform as brought about by their conduct in the work organization. Typical activities are shown in Figure 8.2. They are supposedly carried out to add value to the inputs. Sadly, for many people they become ends in

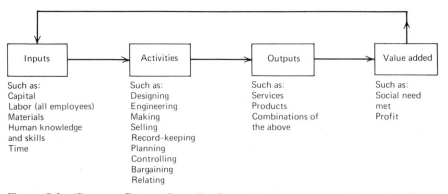

Inputs	Activities	Outputs	Value added
Such as:	Such as:	Such as:	Such as:
Capital	Designing	Services	Social need
Labor (all employees)	Engineering	Products	met
Materials	Making	Combinations of	Profit
Human knowledge	Selling	the above	
and skills	Record-keeping		
Time	Planning		
	Controlling		
	Bargaining		
	Relating		

Figure 8.2 (**Source:** Patten, *Pay: Employee Compensation and Incentive Plans, op. cit.*, p. 566.)

themselves; people that acquire "trained incapacity" or "competence" with trivia, sometimes becoming so ultraspecialized and punctilious that they end up knowing everything about nothing. All of this results, of course, in serious goal-displacement behavior in many organizations. They are engulfed in the activity trap.

Outputs are the services and products that come out of the system. They should be more valuable than all of the inputs used up in their making. They allow us to compute a value added.

Value added is the profit, the need being fulfilled, and the purpose for the input's being committed and the activities' being carried out. The values added are used in two ways, either separately or in combination. They may be fed back into the system, such as profits ploughed back for further expansion of the business; or they may be distributed to the beneficiaries of the system (the sources of input) in the form of dividends, learning satisfactions, benefits, needs met, and the like. These thoughts are reflected in the feedback arrows shown on the top of Figure 8.2.

Unfortunately, MBO is often accompanied by typical systemic problems.[21] For example, some managerial and administrative employees become input-obsessed and cannot realistically estimate what can be done with limited inputs or inefficient activities. Interestingly, output-obsessed managers who overestimate what can be accomplished with limited inputs, or promise more than what they can reasonably expect to deliver, are more common than managers who cleverly set easily attainable goals and use MBO as a cop-out for working harder and smarter. However, perhaps most common of all is the activity-obsessed person who has transformed means into ends. It is sad to see such behavior often defined as a peculiar kind of competence and such persons referred to in bureaucratic jargon as "excellent technicians" when in reality they are wasting the most precious resources of all—themselves, their time, and other people and their time in a misunderstood charade equated with "work." MBO can clearly forestall this type of dysfunctional behavior.

MBO need not spawn these systemic problems. Indeed, a properly installed and controlled MBO system should provide an organization with unremitting attention to purpose, clarify ambiguities in roles between superiors and subordinates, help employees perform at high standards, and improve management across the board.[22]

Mahler has suggested the nature of behavioral shifts among employees that stem from an adequate MBO–OD effort where the dysfunctional consequences have been avoided.[23] These dimensions are shown in Figure 8.3 and are probably self-explanatory. In general, an MBO–OD installation and implementation moves an organization from one in which authoritarian styles prevail to one that is more open, trusting, human, and rewarding.

When individuals in a work organization have undergone some change through a teambuilding effort and committed themselves to new values, it becomes possible for them to not only accept MBO but also to desire genuinely a rational approach to the management of work. People who have been loosened up by an OD program that dealt initially with issues of self-awareness and skill acquisition in how to become an effective team-member and managerial meeting-attender become less defensive and more problem-

Figure 8.3   Behavioral Outcomes of an Effective MBO–OD Effort
$- - - - - -$ Behavioral shift $- - - - - - \rightarrow$

1. Low individual commitment to achieving needed performance results.	1. High individual commitment.
2. No teamwork—both individual and group behavior is highly egocentric.	2. Effective teamwork—effective problem-solving against higher order goals.
3. Personal goals not related to organizational goals.	3. Personal goals related to organizational goals.
4. Individuals working against low standards or none at all.	4. Individuals working against high standards.
5. Ineffective supervisory–subordinate relations (motivation by fear, close supervision, and withholding information).	5. Effective supervisor–subordinate relations (supervisor delegates and encourages participation; subordinate accepts responsibility; trust, openness, candor, and self-supervision).
6. Jobs restricted—satisfactions limited.	6. Job enlarged, enriched, expanded. Increased job satisfaction.
7. Plateau or regression in growth of abilities and self-confidence.	7. Steady growth in abilities and self-confidence.
8. Data on abilities and performance not available or misused.	8. Data available on abilities and performance; data contributes to effective utilization and motivation.

Source: Patten, *Pay: Employee Compensation and Incentive Plans, op. cit.*, p. 568.

solving oriented in the attention they give to work. They are likely to expend
the effort and energy needed for thoroughgoing problem-analysis. They will
wholeheartedly accept a rational tool such as management-by-objectives so
that all of their energies and behaviors flow together in a common direction.
Concerted action is thus possible because the behavioral infrastructure is
open and people are willing to draw upon their resources and make them
"available" (to use Sherwood's felicitous term)[24] rather than hide them.

OD–MBO Mutual Impacts

When a work organization begins to conceive of MBO as its management
process rather than merely another improved control technique, the need for
OD increases rapidly and dramatically. Employees who are to use MBO may
lack the behavioral skills and competence needed to function effectively in
the new mode. Consequently, as the management of an organization attempts
to shift into an MBO mode it very soon realizes that it must come to grips
with both MBO and OD in some significantly different ways. Inherent in
such a shift is the commitment to (1) manage for results by objectives and (2)
develop the effectiveness of the organization through a planned change and
growth process in which the desired results are clearly stated.

   Also inherent in the shift is the change in emphasis from individual to
organizational results, which itself creates considerable pressure for OD
skills. Specifically, there are individual, work group, and intergroup concerns that need to be managed, most of which are basic OD issues. In this
context, too, there is a much greater need for defining the results to be
achieved by the organization. In turn, there begin to surface differing perceptions of what the results really are. Ultimately, MBO becomes a group
process rather than a mere one-on-one boss–subordinate process in which
the writing of objectives is central. Basic group skills that are necessary for
group or team goal setting are (1) problem solving, (2) management of the
helping relationship, individual differences, and accountability, and (3) planning. Put another way, it is actually in the people of an organization that
MBO and OD meet, when employees function as groups or teams to achieve
organizational results through an MBO process.[25]

   The most significant recent development in MBO, which recognizes the
interdependent nature of most jobs, particularly at the managerial and
supervisory levels, is now known as CMBO (collaborative MBO).[26] One way
to describe how CMBO differs qualitatively from a one-on-one approach in
MBO is to contrast the latter with the emerging field of OD, which has a
strong emphasis on team collaboration. Figure 8.4 depicts the chief differences between an individual and team orientation to MBO. Traditional MBO
concentrates on the individual, on goal setting for the person, on rationality,
and on end results. As practiced, this type of MBO is often a universal
solution in search of a problem. In contrast, OD focuses on how individuals
perceive the functioning of their teams and the organization, on nonrational-

Figure 8.4 Objective Setting in Different Versions of MBO

Degree of subordinate influence on objectives	Very little	Some	Moderate	Considerable
	1a	**1b**	**1c**	**1d**
Individual orientation	Superior prepares list of subordinate's objectives and gives it to subordinate.	Superior prepares list of subordinate's objectives; allows opportunity for clarification and suggestions.	Subordinate prepares list of his objectives; superior–subordinate discussion of tentative list is followed by editing, modification, and finalization by superior.	Superior and subordinate independently prepare list of subordinate's objectives; mutual agreement reached after extensive dialogue.
	2a	**2b**	**2c**	**2d**
Team orientation	Superior prepares individual lists of various subordinates' objectives; hands out lists in group meeting and explains objectives.	Superior prepares unit and individual objectives; allows opportunity for questions and suggestions in group meeting.	Superior prepares list of unit objectives which are discussed in group meeting; superior decides. Subordinates then prepare lists of their objectives, discuss with superior; individuals' objectives discussed in team meeting with modifications made by superior after extensive dialogue.	Unit objectives, including team effectiveness goals, are developed among superior, subordinates, and peers in a group meeting, usually by consensus; superior and subordinates later independently prepare lists of subordinates' objectives, reach temporary agreement; subordinates' objectives finalized after extensive discussion in team meeting.

Source: Wendell L. French and Robert W. Hollman, ''Management By Objectives: The Team Approach'' Copyright © 1975 by the Regents of the University of California. Reprinted from *California Management Review*, Vol. 17, No. 3, p. 14, figure 4.

ity, as well as rationality, and on means as well as ends. In addition, OD has a recurring component of system diagnosis that appears to be absent or only minimally present in the traditional forms of MBO that focus essentially on the dyadic superior–subordinate performance review. Although the details of the CMBO process need not concern us here, they have been thought out.[27] As yet they have not been connected with compensation decisions, although there is no reason why they could not be.[28] Likert and Fisher favor group decision-making on compensation decisions.[29] Pay under CMBO would involve team bonuses as well as individual pay adjustments. Such a pay plan would be the ultimate in OD, MBO, and Reward System integration and will perhaps become diffused among pace-setting firms in the U.S. in the 1980s.

People at work in their organizational roles in healthy organizations are likely to try to communicate as effectively as possible. The identification of organizational objectives up and down the line and across through the staffs and among scattered and interfacing organizational components becomes possible under CMBO; what has been called the prevailing managerial style, or organizational culture, or the way of life in an organization, can become transformed. In summary, once the social–emotional learning has taken place it becomes possible for the rational to function more effectively because the misdirected or undirected social–emotional resources that often prevent goal attainment are reduced if they have not, in fact, vanished.

Consistent with the aforementioned, I must emphasize the importance of the compensation planning and administration system as it relates to organizational development and management-by-objectives. In the last decade and a half there has been a resurgence of serious scholarly interest in the systematic study of pay; new ideas about motivating employees through compensation planning and administration (what is subsequently discussed below as "rewards theory") were being announced in the literature of the behavioral sciences throughout the 1970s and can be expected to be stressed even more in the 1980s. With the relative decline in numbers of blue-collar workers and the rise in numbers of managerial, technical, and professional employees in the American labor force, the need for adequate compensation planning and administration for high-talent manpower has become very apparent. This labor force shift signals many future problems and opportunities for human resource management that need to be confronted now.

Theory of Reward Systems

As previously mentioned, until very recently applied behavioral scientists have seldom given reward systems the detailed attention that they deserve, even though they are often mentioned in passing in discussions about OD. Explanations of OD and MBO sometimes lead practitioners to think that the discussion is essentially utopian and out of touch with the real world of rewards and penalties, particularly pay administration. Indeed, a fair number of discussions of OD and MBO are not firmly grounded, but many prominent writers make explicit reference to pay matters and suggest that money as a motivator to perform in work organizations be looked upon more sophisticatedly than it has been by economists and industrial engineers. I next attempt to tighten up their thinking on OD, MBO, and rewards still further by reviewing some important new contributions of Belcher[30] and by pointing the way and charting what already has been done in laying a new foundation for systemic intervention and for organizational change.[31]

In the emerging behavioral science theory of rewards, we find a confluence and synthesis of contributions from exchange, expectancy, and equity theory. As a result, rewards for work are defined as all those things, tangible and intangible, that the employee receives as a consequence of the employment exchange. By the term "employment exchange" is meant the transaction between the employer and employee where contributions of the organization are rewards to the individual and contributions of the individual are rewards to the organization. Contributions include many inputs that are made with the intention of making recognizable or relevant payments in the exchange process.

In other words, a double input/output system operates. To both parties in the exchange, outputs must exceed inputs if the individual employee and the organization are to survive and achieve their goals. Put another way, employees must perceive their rewards as greater than their contributions; organizations must perceive rewards provided employees as less than the contributions of employees. Otherwise, there can be no "exchange."

Defining rewards in this way suggests that there are various kinds of rewards and that work organizations often supply a greater variety of rewards than they may realize. Organizations are, of course, usually aware that they are providing economic rewards and that these economic rewards are limited by organizational resources. They may or may not be aware that they are providing many other kinds of rewards, only some of which are limited by organization resources.

We find, in fact, that the variety of rewards from the employment exchange is almost endless. There are several ways of classifying them. Herzberg, for example, discussed only two factors that allegedly relate to satisfaction at work and, from our standpoint, may be viewed as rewards, namely intrinsic rewards and extrinsic rewards.[32] The extrinsic rewards are those provided by the work organization and consist of variables other than the work itself, such as supervisory style, quality of interpersonal relations, amount of salary, personnel policies, physical working conditions, and job security. These extrinsic rewards are hygienically beneficial to the employee, to use Herzberg's peculiar terminology. Intrinsic factors that satisfy the individual and motivate and reward him consist of the work itself and other variables quite closely connected with on-the-job performance, such as the achievement of an important task, responsibility at work, recognition for work, and opportunity for advancement.

Dubin has classified rewards as economic and noneconomic by identifying financial and nonfinancial pay.[33] According to Dubin, effective motivational systems in industry always define their rewards for acceptable individual employee behavior in terms of organizational reward systems. The payoff is in money (or financial pay), power pay, authority pay, and status pay. Financial payoffs for working become an important way of stating the value of an employee's work. If one employee earns more than another, his productive efforts may be presumed to be more valuable. This concept underlies merit pay (or varying employee compensation for individuals on the same job who perform at different levels of competence), salesmen's compensation, hourly employee incentive plans, and certain forms of executive compensation. The concern with money as a measure of an employee's value to a productive enterprise is thus the keystone to (and Achilles' heel of) all financial incentive plans.[34]

Performance on the part of an employee that meets or excels standards set by management may also be rewarded by giving an employee an opportunity to perform more important functions at work or to assume the exclusive control of some functions; in this case, the reward is power. Such behavior may lead to the assumption of a decision-making position in the supervision of the work of others; the reward for the employee in this instance is authority. Finally, socially appropriate behavior as defined by management in the work organization may be accorded the reward of higher positional rank; the reward here is status pay. It is in this sense of broad types of reward that the payoff of motivational systems may be said to be general rather than specific. Money alone as a financial incentive rarely—probably never—can fulfill the systemic functions of power, authority, and status pay, as has been demonstrated in many behavioral science research studies over the past two decades.[35]

Turning back to the issue of the classification of reward systems in general, it thus becomes clear that the student and practitioner of OD is provided useful information either when he or she classifies rewards as economic and noneconomic or as extrinsic and intrinsic. The former classification, because it emphasizes what to most of us are the primary rewards from work, is very meaningful. The latter classification involving the extrinsic/intrinsic distinction is useful because it emphasizes that many rewards from work are provided by the individual, his interests, and his perceptions and may, in a certain sense, be cost-free to the work organization.

Belcher has advanced our thinking in rewards theory by making a further distinction that enables us to conceive of "membership motivation" and "performance motivation."[36] He believes that rewards available from work organizations can be divided into three types based upon their differing purposes:

"Job rewards" are those attached to a particular job and include many economic and noneconomic payoffs to job incumbents. For example, there are base wage and salary; then there are the power, status, and authority concomitants of each job. The latter might include a supervisory title as well as authority in assigning work and directing the activities of persons in subordinate work positions.

"Performance rewards" are economic and noneconomic payoffs allocated on the basis of differential performance in a job or position. These rewards would include such economic adjustments as merit increases, bonuses, and promotional increments as well as power, authority, and status recognition associated with visible and approved patterns of employee work behavior. Performance rewards stimulate "performance motivation" or the will to work effectively and efficiently, which can, in turn, often be made operational in an MBO context.

"Membership rewards" are those economic and noneconomic advantages that an individual receives simply for being on the payroll and, therefore, a member of the organization. These membership rewards include the range of fringe benefits that provide income continuity to an employee in terms of adversity (and, therefore, protect the employee and his family from economic setbacks when experiencing the contingencies of life).

Basic job rewards can be said to provide an employee with income primarily whereas membership rewards tend to provide other forms of economic benefit useful for security in times when the employee is not or cannot be at work. Job rewards and membership rewards appeal to broad membership motivation. Among the nonfinancial membership rewards are affiliation with a prestigious employer, from occupancy of a prestigious position, as well as a number of personally satisfying and ego-fulfilling sources of gratification wanted or needed by the individual.

In summary, rewards are what the individual receives from the employment exchange for the reciprocal process characterized as a double input/output exchange of contributions and values. The importance of the exchange to the employee depends on the degree to which he wants or needs the rewards available to him in the exchange. Almost any item the individual needs or desires can be a reward. The two requirements are that he recognize the reward and perceive it as relevant.

The employment exchange may involve only one reward or it may involve many. The more rewards available, the more likely it is that the exchange will be binding and important to the individual. As we have seen, most employment exchanges entail many important rewards. In particular, the employment exchange provides the way in which the individual finds his place in society.

Reward Systems as Systems

We turn from rewards theory to rewards systems *per se*. For the sake of illustration, financial pay is stressed in the following analysis. I have in mind particularly the administration of pay increases of all types, such as merit increases, bonuses, and promotional increments. However, I am also mindful of pay decrements as well as the administration of managerial placement and succession plans, the reward of special developmental assignments, the various forms of recognition and withholding recognition, and all other status, authority, and power rewards and penalties as parts of total organizational rewards systems. Again, this is not the place to repeat the salary administration mechanics of the pay plan that need specific linking with OD and MBO (and that, incidentally, are also rewarding or punishing in function) because knowledge of these is available for review in the technical literature of personnel administration.[37] Yet I mention salary administration as a reinforcer of employee behavior in order to explicate my OD → MBO → RS model for organizational change.

Pay is typically regarded as performing a number of behavioral and technical functions that contribute to organizational effectiveness. Pay is primarily considered a reward that can be used to make employees feel satisfied with their job, motivate them, gain their commitment to the organization, and retain them. Questions about the impact of pay in this context get into psychological knowledge that has only recently been made available through research. However, it should be emphasized that a pay plan must fit the characteristics of an organization if it is to be effective.

Lawler has noted that pay systems exist in the context of organizations and that the characteristics of organizations must be taken into account when pay systems are developed.[38] The kind of organizational climate that exists very much limits the kind of pay practices that an organization can use. Conversely, a pay system can change the climate and become an agent of change. Put another way, money speaks, and administered in a traditional way, it can say that a stated move toward participative management is not sincere. Administered in new ways, money can say that a real change is taking place. Thus, the pay plan can be viewed as a stimulant or lever to effect change in the organization.

There are at least two ways organizations and pay plans can be matched, according to Lawler. First, the task can be viewed as a problem of choosing the correct pay plan for an organization, taking into account the characteristics of the organization as it is presently administered. Second, instead of fitting the plan to the organization, management can change the organization to fit the pay plan, which is what has been emphasized in this chapter. Thus, the pay plan can be viewed as a stimulant or lever to effect change in the organization. Consistent with contemporary concepts in personnel administration, it is suggested that the pay plan be accommodated to the organization and used together with OD and MBO in an integrated manner. I advocate, even more specifically, using a Skinnerian variable-ratio intermittent-type schedule of reinforcement in administering financial payoffs.

Why bother at our present stage of behavioral science knowledge in integrating OD, MBO, and reward systems? There are several compelling reasons. In my consulting relationships and in those of friends, we have noticed that if the consultant is called in to look at a pay system problem he often cannot solve it because the goals of the compensation plan are unclear or absent. If a client is asked to clarify or explain an organization's approach to MBO, the client and change agent soon find that the compensation system is unconnected with organizational goals. Or, if an intervenor is asked to install MBO, he often finds large numbers of managers who cannot communicate or deliberately and defensively build protective walls to keep their managerial peers away. He sees a primary need for OD and, particularly, a need for the installation of trust, although he might not conceptualize the problem precisely that way unless he has ever considered the fundamental importance of trust-formation in OD efforts. Or, lastly, one may (rarely) experience an organization where OD has improved the climate but all that new-found managerial and employee energy has to be harnessed in an organizationally desired direction and properly compensated.

From the standpoint of the ideas set forth in this chapter, it is important to stress that pay as it is planned and administered must be consonant with organizational development and planned organizational change as well as MBO. In other words, if the way people are rewarded or penalized in terms of pay is not consistent with the behavior that they reveal as determined in the course of OD teambuilding programs or when trying to fulfill goals set as MBO targets, then something must be done about the pay system, the OD effort, or the operation of the MBO system.

Put another way, the underlying behaviors and the pay infrastructure must be in concert. Furthermore, when this thought is extended to MBO, it need only be added that the way employees are rewarded or penalized in pay must also be consistent with the extent to which they are effective in stating and accomplishing their managerial objectives. In summary, OD, compensation, and MBO are closely interrelated in theory and should be in OD strategy and tactics. Furthermore, they must be made compatible with one another if a work organization is to continue as an ongoing entity and we are to tap greater amounts of human potential in order to accomplish work and truly reward employees for their contributions.

Optimal Pattern for Change Integrating Rewards

If there is a reason to attempt the integration of OD, MBO, and the reward systems, is there also an optimal pattern for doing so? I believe that there probably is an optimal pattern for changing an organizational culture and employee behavior, and it is shown in Figure 8.5.

The optimal pattern is to introduce first an OD program (using a thrust toward teambuilding and creation of greater self-awareness), then MBO, and, finally, build or revamp the reward systems, particularly the pay or direct compensation aspects, at about the same time MBO is launched so that after the first year's experience with MBO is obtained, pay decisions can subsequently be made to accord with rewarding and penalizing employees based upon results from the MBO program.

Figure 8.5 Schematic Diagram of Changing Organizational Culture and Employee Behavior

OD	Optimal pattern MBO	Reward system (RS)
Social-emotional blockages overcome Start with teambuilding	Rationality limitations overcome Install MBO	Vary pay, promotion, recognition based upon standard-fulfilling performance directed toward organizational objectives
①	②	③

Alternate Patterns

Pattern	Comments
OD ——→ RS ——→ MBO:	No goal-oriented behavior specified; pay not necessarily performance related.
MBO ——→ RS ——→ OD:	Possible, but performance potential still blocked; satisfactory upon recycling because optimal pattern is now possible and attained.
MBO ——→ OD ——→ RS:	MBO potential reduced; organization may not be ready for OD: successful OD effort may cause reappraisal of MBO; pattern is thus wasteful; reward system remotely connected.
RS ——→ MBO ——→ OD:	RS changes realigned without goals or changed behavior; exact reversal of the optimal pattern.
RS ——→ OD ——→ MBO:	Pay changes capricious and separate from OD; no apparent connection in theory or practice with a rational pay on performance.
MBO ——→ RS (no OD):	An OD challenge in itself; may be better than doing nothing and lead to realization of need for OD.
RS ——→ MBO (no OD):	Ditto.
OD ——→ RS (no MBO):	Rational goal-setting omitted, which is undesirable.
OD ——→ MBO (no RS):	Why not reinforce with pay planning and administration?
MBO ——→ OD (no RS):	Possible way of starting, but is floundering and wasteful if we can identify an optimal pattern.
RS ——→ OD (no MBO):	Pay changes capricious and separate from OD; no apparent connection in theory or practice with a rational change strategy.
OD (no MBO or RS):	Good for self-awareness and fluidity in behavior, but what was the organization developed *for?*
MBO (no OD or RS):	Useful exercise in deciding on what we are to do, but how much of us as total human beings was involved?
RS (no OD or MBO):	Were human feelings and concerns considered? How will the desired behavior be reinforced? Is the most technically perfect system praiseworthy when it is not built into organizational objectives and when employees are passive role players?
OD ——→ MBO ——→ RS:	Appears optimal.

Source: Patten, *Pay: Employee Compensation and Incentive Plans, op. cit.,* p. 570.

We should start with an OD effort, if we are to start at all, recognizing that OD is not appropriate or practicable for many organizations because management may not be ready for it. OD should, of course, never be force-fit. It may be best to let management alone and allow the level of aggravation to build up before the change agent considers that the time is ripe for a successful OD intervention.

On the other hand, training and OD directors on the employer's payroll who are acting as internal agents of planned social change may not have the choice open to an external consultant and cannot "wait" until an organization is ready to start with OD. In this case, it often makes sense as an OD strategy to begin with an OD program because the latter is usually perceived as a lower threat to managers than an OD teambuilding intervention. However, the internal change agent or OD specialist should realize that starting with MBO is more likely to be strategically than optimally effective in a long-run overall organizational improvement effort. Specifically, if he starts with MBO, he may find that the MBO program runs out of gas or is relegated to a pretty book or series of forms stuffed in the manager's lower desk drawer, available for inspection on request but hardly a governing day-to-day consideration in the manager's work planning or job performance.

Alternatively, when the organizational change effort begins with MBO, it may make managers more open than before and cause them to squabble, identify a few of the real organizational problems, and desire rolling up their sleeves to get some serious work done, both being important types of work associated with job tasks and with interpersonal relations. If the training director or OD facilitator senses that such a relatively low-profile intervention can thus be heightened and extended, he can then move from a false or weak start in MBO to a teambuilding OD effort. Soon thereafter, he can launch a true MBO program—or so-called "second-generation MBO"—when management has dealt with its internal teambuilding problems; the internal change agent, if he is fortunate, may be able to follow up with changes in the reward systems. Thus, a very practical strategy for the training director who functions as an internal consultant may be the following four-step approach:

$$\text{MBO} \longrightarrow \text{OD} \longrightarrow \text{MBO} \longrightarrow \text{Reward System}$$

Yet there is a better way.

The optimal pattern and all the practical alternatives are described in Figure 8.5 and should be self-explanatory in the main. However, a few words of elaboration are in order.

In Figure 8.5 I have taken the alternative variables in the change strategy three at a time, two at a time, and one at a time and commented on what I predict can be expected for each pattern. There are several underlying assumptions, and these have already been explored in this chapter, where I set forth a theory of rewards, various conceptions of human nature (discussed in

Chapter 3), and views of OD and MBO. Yet there is value in elaborating on these assumptions here and discussing the alternate patterns that should be most useful in the future.

The first assumption is that individuals function most effectively at work when they are allowed to contribute fully on the social–emotional and rational levels and feel open and unblocked. This has been suggested before in the book. Thus it is proposed that an organizational change strategy be built upon a humanistic orientation and composed at the outset of an open encounter in the format of a teambuilding design.

As can be seen in examining the alternative patterns of variables three at a time, if we begin with a rational or technical intervention (such as MBO or improvements in the financial reward system) without enabling individuals to benefit from unfreezing through teambuilding, a great deal of momentum for thoroughgoing change is probably lost. On the other hand, there may be an opportunity to work on changing all three aspects of the optimal pattern simultaneously by concentrating most of the intervenor's energy on one phase of the pattern before moving on to the other two but nevertheless maintaining the others in synchronization. Thus, although there is value in considering the variables separately and sequentially for analytical purposes, in reality we could work on more than one front simultaneously. The important consideration is obtaining a green light on the strategy and recognizing where to begin in implementing the model.

The second assumption is that any attempt at strategic organizational change must deal with the basic dynamics of organizational behavior. Efforts should be directed toward fundamental improvement of the organizational culture rather than mere cosmetic changes or grafting new ideas on old structural bodies which will sooner or later reject the grafted organ. The OD literature is replete with case histories of cosmetic interventions that lasted only as long as could be expected from a fad. Indeed, there is accumulating evidence that many of the touted MBO installations of a decade or more ago had not even weathered the storms of organizational change and turbulence prior to the 1974–75 recession.[39]

The third assumption recognizes that although individuals may be functioning at different levels of the Maslovian needs hierarchy, they are still responsive to rewards and penalties, including pay, and have their self-esteem to some extent linked to pay decisions that affect them. From the standpoint of rewards theory, a case can easily be made that human needs in industrial society, regardless of the need level of the individual person, can be monetized because money can be used to purchase food and shelter, obtain entry into a social system and community, and contribute to one's self-concept and ego; money can even permit self-actualization, because it provides freedom for coming and going as one pleases and, if there is enough of it, obtaining total control over the manner in which time is utilized if one no longer has to "work."

I advocate the optimal pattern shown in Figure 8.5 because it begins by unblocking managers and employees, makes them receptive to a rational approach to management (such as MBO) with a reduced likelihood of engaging in the many types of dysfunctional behavior that can undermine the success of an MBO installation, and builds the rewards systems in such a way that organizationally desired behavior is reinforced and rewarded at the same time that performance inadequacies are spotted, admitted to, and dealt with. The alternative patterns described in Figure 8.5 have to greater or lesser degrees notable shortcomings, as pointed out under the comments column.

Skinnerian Theory

Reward theory and the operations of reward systems need to be connected better than they have been with Skinnerian operant conditioning or reinforcement theory, as mentioned earlier. Skinner himself has stated that his theory has important applicability for industrial practice, particularly the granting of intermittent rewards on a variable-ratio schedule.[40] I cannot here develop Skinner's thinking in any detail but brief elaboration is worthwhile. There is little doubt that what Skinner advocates is consistent with the OD → MBO → RS model that has been sketched.

The fundamental idea behind reinforcement and behavior modification is that a reinforced or rewarded behavior tends to be repeated. Nonfinancial rewards such as verbal praise ("Nice job, Chuck" or "Fine piece of work, Bill"), and actual rewards such as pay increases or being bought a drink or a lunch are examples of rewards used as positive reinforcers, assuming the receiver perceives them that way.

When used at the right time and in the right quantity, reinforcers increase the probability of a behavior's being repeated and, consequently, learned. Reinforcements can be used to overcome work behavior deficiencies, such as failures to meet deadlines or give up games (in the transactional analysis sense), to maintain present levels of work performance, or, more commonly, to shape expected behavior in carrying out job assignments. Reinforcements, in other words, need to be connected with MBO efforts and results.

The general rule for using the reinforcement approach apparently is that a particular new behavior must be shaped by approximation or through small steps and that the reinforcer must follow immediately when a behavior approximates the goal. After the new behavior is fully approximated or achieved, the scheduling of the reinforcement must be at intervals rather than after every instance in which the behavior is exhibited. Thus the repeated application of verbal praise ("Good job, Harry") loses its effectiveness as a reinforcer because of overuse. This is why praise must not be given every time an employee completes a task. The use of praise as a reward needs to be reappraised.[41] In addition, status, power, and authority pay should be used when possible as intermittent variable ratio rewards.

Another reason verbal praise may not be effective is that some employees do not respond well to it. They might respond much better if they received a different kind of reward such as a salary adjustment or recognition in the form of a story in the house organ or company newspaper. Finding the appropriate form of reinforcement is thus very important. Age, sex, job- and status-level, and personal interests affect the kind of reinforcement to which a person will respond. Yet it is important to note that it is the individual's *performance* or *behavior* rather than his *person* that should be reinforced. MBO helps in clarifying what types of on-the-job behavior will be considered in terms of rewards and penalties.

Closely related to reinforcement is the extinction of behaviors. In the latter case, the reward for the performance is purposely held back or discontinued. The individual perceives that his behavior is undesirable and allows it to subside or become extinct.[42] Postponing or reducing the amount of a merit increase or diversion of supervisory recognition from attention-getting but unwanted employee contributions can extinguish certain forms of behavior in employees who are motivated by these specific types of tangible and intangible rewards. Again, we can see where MBO results would be useful in extinction.

Integrating Financial Compensation Systems

In the 1970s great strides were made in working out specific techniques for making pay-for-performance systems operational.[43] However, the idea of paying employees for teamwork *per se* has been implemented to a far lesser degree than paying them as individual contributors. Two exceptions to this generalization are notable.

Pace-setting companies have for many years offered supplemental compensation plans that make bonuses available to eligible managers so that they can receive pay beyond base salary. The allocation formulas used to make bonuses available to subsystems in organizations normally are not grounded upon teamwork and do not focus upon teams of interacting managers in the sense that word has been used in this book. To be sure, organizations allocate bonus amounts to units that may formally be looked upon as teams, although they are in reality simply executives or managers on the same level in a certain division, department, or other organizational components that are profit-centers. The synergistic possibilities of linking team-building and pay in a carefully worked out OD design have not as yet been explored to an appreciable extent in American industry.

The Scanlon Plan and variants on it that focus upon plantwide productivity improvement may be viewed as a second exception to the assertion that pay based upon teamwork does not exist.[44] The Scanlon Plan through various organizational mechanisms encourages employees to participate in problem-solving and to improve productivity by making suggestions. Pay-outs are made not to a specific individual who made a proposal but to all employees covered by the Plan in a particular establishment. One could argue, as a result, that the Scanlon Plan focuses upon plantwide teamwork and comes closest to the notion of "teamwork pay" for both the rank-and-file employee and manager.

More than a decade ago it was thought possible that during the 1970s there would be a greater growth of group compensation practices and even such far-out ideas as permitting work groups to divide the budgeted or allocated salary dollars among the members. Professional baseball players work, of course, under a system of highly differentiated, individually negotiated salaries during the regular season. However, the teams that participate in the World Series vote equal shares to all members![45] Yet the 1970s were preoccupied with essentially mechanical questions of determining bonus awards,[46] the exchange of information on incentive plan design features,[47] how far down in staff management bonuses should be extended,[48] and similar issues. Hands were wrung over the need for pay systems to reward the management group for overachievement and to penalize them for underachievement.[49] Very little was written about teamwork pay for the rank-and-file.

The brightest signs of changes to come were pay plans that featured employee participation in the design of the compensation program. Some firms decided to break up the standardized corporate benefits package and allow employees to choose the "membership rewards" they most valued from a cafeteria or smorgasbord selection composed of group insurances, pensions, longer or shorter vacations, educational assistance plans, stock and savings programs, and the like. Such cafeteria plans, although not widespread, did signal employers' interest in permitting employees to tailor-make (within limits) each year a personalized benefit package.[50] The net effect was often intended to make employees feel more like they were on the team, in charge of their destinies, and being treated as individuals. The teambuilding results cannot be assessed at this time because the plans are new.

Perhaps the most notable development in compensation in the 1970s that is a harbinger for the 1980s is the thinking done by Lawler. He has suggested that reward systems be designed by stages when new plants are opened to take advantage of concepts such as employee participation in pay plan formation, the use of peer judgments in making pay adjustments, and, perhaps, eventually the installation of a team pay and individual pay component in the paycheck.[51] Lawler's ideas are being tested at several locations in the U.S. where organizations are in a startup stage. Usually, it is easier to make reward system changes when an organization is new and has no established traditions it must follow. Therefore, studies of these innovations in reward systems should provide a meaningful data base for the design of OD–teambuilding interventions in the years ahead. Coupled with the technology of CMBO that has been carefully set forth by French and Hollmann,[52] the application of knowledge gleaned from studies of reward systems in new plants has great potential for improving known existing systems that have been described in some detail elsewhere.[53]

Yet there is no doubt that much work remains to be done on teambuilding/reward system integration for employees at all organizational levels. Probably one of the most massive and far-reaching compensation experiments in American management is presently taking place in the Federal Government. It is an effort to create new rewards in pay-for-performance for top executives who are used to a more passive pay system of lock-step rewards totally unconnected with team effort. The results of the Federal Government's drive to turn the top of its organization around for new directions in improved productivity and efficiency is being closely watched by managers and OD experts throughout the nation.

Exercise on OD, MBO, and Reward Systems: Precepts Package

At the end of every seminar/workshop, participants desire some closure on the concepts and ideas explored. Thus, there is usually a need to pull everything together and reduce it as far as possible to practical guides for action back on the executive's job.

The "precepts package exercise" attempts to provide precepts (or rough rules of thumb) that have either a full or partial basis in behavioral science research for consideration for adaptation in the organization in which program participants work. The precepts should be regarded as starting points for action rather than the final word. As such, precepts can be useful in the day-to-day work of executives and furnish closure after a complex learning experience.

We also call the "precepts package exercise" the MANDOERS exercise because the letters selected suggest that managers who do their work effectively must make efficient use of the rewards systems available to them.[54] MANDOERS is thus an acronym for

- *MAN*agement *D*evelopment of subordinates
- *O*rganizationally *E*ffective behavior by the executive
- *R*ewarding *S*ubordinates in a way that motivates them to perform.

The exercise involves breaking seminar participants into three or more teams. At least one team works on organizationally effective behavior, one works on employee and management development, and one works on the administration of rewards. (A resource person who has current knowledge on pay and personnel policies in the employing organization should be present in the latter group.) The exercise takes an hour to an hour and one-half to complete.

Figure 8.6 explains the mechanics of the MANDOERS precepts package exercise that the OD facilitator follows. The latter instructs the teams to read the three sets of precepts for the purpose of thought stimulation, review, or

Figure 8.6 MANDOERS Exercise

You are assigned the following task. Reach a consensus and be prepared to report back on

1. What are the main problems in organizational effectiveness (*or* employee and management development *or* the administration of rewards) in your present organizational components?
2. How do you propose to deal with these problems personally in the next twelve months?
3. What levels of success do you predict, and how will you measure them?

Each group concentrates on only one of the main topics assigned. Read the attached precepts and then begin the assigned task. The precepts attached are then handed out.

Precepts for Organizationally Effective Behavior

Every executive or manager should:

1. Establish and communicate organizational objectives.

   - Develop organizational objectives consistent with those of the organization of which he is part, and be sure his superiors are in agreement with them.
   - Communicate all objectives to subordinates to the greatest extent practical.
   - Quickly adjust objectives to meet changing needs.
   - Establish criteria for determining the progress of subordinates in meeting their objectives.

2. Establish an organization that is simple in concept, responsive to new requirements, and that clearly defines individual responsibility.

3. Develop competent staff.

   - Staff his organization with capable people, develop superior replacements for all positions, and initiate action to replace employees not adequately discharging their responsibilities.
   - Provide opportunities for each employee to realize his full potential through regular review of achievements and shortcomings and guidance to improve performance.

4. Ensure organizational effectiveness.

   - Perform completed staff work and develop recommended solutions for all problems brought to the attention of his superior.
   - Understand line and staff relationships and use staff effectively.
   - Encourage innovation by developing an atmosphere within which employees will freely contribute ideas.
   - Hold administrative procedures and controls to a minimum.
   - Seek changes in policies and procedures when improved efficiency will result.
   - Reward subordinates in accordance with their contributions and performance.
   - Communicate employee attitudes to organizational superiors, and resolve employee complaints quickly.

5. Represent the employing organization to the public.

   - Show enthusiasm for the employing organization, its products, and/or its services.

Figure 8.6 (*Continued*)

- Use discretion in making public statements about the organization.
- Make no commitments that cannot be fulfilled.
- See that outside inquiries or complaints are handled promptly and well.

Precepts for Developing Subordinates

Every executive or manager should:

1. Treat each employee's development as a highly individual matter.

   - Recognize individual differences.
   - Vary developmental methods to suit the individual.

2. Recognize every person's development is ultimately self-development.

   - Understand that development is not something you "do" to a person.
   - Avoid trying to live the other person's life for him; encourage him to get in touch with himself and work toward goals.

3. Allow employees to express themselves at work by not forcing them to conform to a mold.

   - Recognize there are many successful and organizationally acceptable ways to accomplish work.
   - Build upon the employee's personal strengths to the extent practicable.

4. Use the person's present job and day-to-day work assignments to develop him.

   - Plan how to "stretch" people and do it; exhaust the learning opportunities in the present job.
   - Do not emphasize the promotional ladder and next job as the sole ways to development.

5. Provide an atmosphere of equal opportunity for development.

   - Allow everyone to grow.
   - Avoid artificial barriers of sexism, racism, and ageism.
   - Recognize that moral values beyond the work place enter into development.

6. Recognize the distinction between "man" or "woman" as the individual contributor and "manager" as the supervisor of the work of others.

   - Provide opportunities for the growth of individual contributors who appear to lack interest or skill in supervising others.
   - Provide managers with wide discretion in problem-solving and decision-making within the scope of their assignments.
   - Take risks and tolerate some errors until subordinates have learned their jobs well.

7. Hold subordinate managers responsible for the development of people reporting to them.

   - Do not abdicate developmental responsibilities to the personnel office.
   - Inquire about developmental activities carried out by your subordinates from time to time.

Figure 8.6 (*Continued*)

8. Provide open, honest feedback on job performance.

   - Level with employees.
   - Accept feedback from subordinates.
   - Formalize the feedback process by reducing it to writing at least some of the time.

Precepts for Rewarding Subordinates

Every executive or manager should:

1. Reward employees consistent with the accomplishment of their goals.

   - Use pay as a lever for performance.
   - Recommend pay changes, status changes, and forms of formal recognition based upon performance.

2. Communicate performance results formally and informally.

3. Assure that every employee reporting to him is properly classified and compensated.

   - Take the initiative in seeking changes in classification and pay where warranted.
   - Keep job descriptions up-to-date and properly applied.

4. Determine if financial rewards beyond base salary can be installed in the organization.

   - If possible, incent all key managerial and professional jobs.
   - If possible, restrict the remuneration of people in less important jobs to base compensation and fringe benefits.

5. Insist upon and fairly administer an "exceptional" pay policy.

   - Seek exceptions to policies and rules where equity and/or outstanding performance are involved.
   - Do not overapply an exceptional policy.

6. Help weak performers improve and take corrective action as needed in rewards and penalties.

   - Remove weak performers from their positions if after substantial attempts at coaching and counseling, they still fail to meet job standards.
   - Use the alternatives of demotion and discharge with care and discretion, considering the phasing of such transactions with attrition, outplacement possibilities, special early retirement possibilities, medical retirements, and the like.

7. Be prepared to explain decisions on rewards and penalties to employees and provide them with authoritative and honest information on the administration of rewards and penalties.

closure. He then assigns tasks to the teams, facilitates the exercise, and debriefs it.

Conclusion

In discussing the strategic model for change involving OD, MBO, and rewards systems I hope to have avoided the trap of assuming individual managers or employees to be interchangeable parts. I do not believe this. I believe instead that the kind of person who would respond to the optimal pattern for changing an organization's culture will be someone who has a high need for achievement and a personal will to manage in a humanistic way. I have elaborated on this at length elsewhere[55] but the same thinking applies to the discussion in this chapter.

I believe that we have now entered an era of social responsibility in America where the management of complex large-scale organizations is expected to turn those organizations into open societies where mobility is possible for all persons who perform. I and many others believe that OD, MBO, and the reward system must be built upon socially responsible personnel policies and that these, in turn, should assure that people with high needs for achievement and wills to manage eventually find their ways into managerial positions. It is doubtful that the optimal pattern can be made operational if the human resources intake into managerial positions is inadequate for the tasks and challenges that are there and there is an absence of equal employment opportunity and affirmative action.

The long-heralded new day in OD may be upon us as we move into more comprehensive strategic change models that consider the most potent and moving variables as being interrelated and ideally sequenced. Certainly, one of the outcomes of this new day will be to view OD, MBO, and reward systems not as opponents and unrelated interventions but rather as complements for improving life in work organizations and as levers for change that can be handled by people.

Notes

1. Parts of this chapter have been published before, but this chapter is a substantial updating and synthesis of the author's thinking on the subject from the perspective of the 1980s. Previous sources are the following: Thomas H. Patten, Jr., "Linking Financial Rewards to Employee Performance: The Roles of OD and MBO," *Human Resources Management*, Vol. 15, No. 4, Winter 1976, pp. 2–17; "Intervening in Organizations Through Reward Systems," in John E. Jones and J. William Pfeiffer, Eds., *The 1977 Annual Handbook for Group Facilitators*, University Associates, La Jolla, CA, 1977, pp. 195–207; *Pay: Employee Compensation and Incentive Plans*, Free Press, New

York, 1977, pp. 559–591; and "MANDOERS: Organizational Clarification," in J. William Pfeiffer and John E. Jones, Eds., *The 1978 Annual Handbook for Group Facilitators*, University Associates, La Jolla, CA, 1978, pp. 71–76.

2. Harry Levinson, *The Great Jackass Fallacy*, Division of Research, Graduate School of Business Administration, Harvard University, Boston, 1973, pp. 87–88.

3. Jack R. Gibb, "TORI Theory: Consultantless Team-Building," *Journal of Contemporary Business*, Vol. 1, No. 3, Summer 1972, pp. 33–34; see also *idem*, "Climate for Trust Formation," in *T-Group Theory and Laboratory Method*, Leland P. Bradford et al., Ed., Wiley, New York, 1964, pp. 279–309; and Jack R. Gibb and Lorraine M. Gibb, "Role Freedom in a TORI Group," in *Encounter*, Arthur Burton, Ed., Jossey-Bass, San Francisco, 1969, pp. 42–57.

4. Dale E. Zand, "Trust and Managerial Problem Solving," *Administrative Science Quarterly*, Vol. 17, No. 2, June 1972, pp. 229–239.

5. Alan Fox, *Beyond Contract: Work, Power, and Trust Relations*, Faber and Faber, London, 1974, pp. 67–76.

6. George S. Odiorne, "The Politics of Implementing MBO," *Business Horizons*, Vol. 17, No. 3, June 1974, p. 13.

7. Gibb, "TORI Theory: Consultantless Team-Building," *op. cit.*, pp. 33–34.

8. R. L. Ford, "Appraising Performance for Individual Development," in Milton L. Rock, Ed., *Handbook of Wage and Salary Administration*, McGraw–Hill, New York, 1972, pp. 5–64.

9. Fox, *op. cit.*, p. 76.

10. This discussion is from Patten, *Pay: Employee Compensation and Incentive Plans, op cit.*, pp. 563–565. The organizational iceberg idea was suggested in Stanley M. Herman, "What Is This Thing Called Organization Development?" *Personnel Journal*, Vol. 50, No. 8, August 1971, pp. 599–602.

11. This discussion is from Patten, *Pay: Employee Compensation and Incentive Plans, op. cit.*, pp. 565–568.

12. Peter F. Drucker, *The Practice of Management*, Harper, New York, 1954, pp. 121–136. Other early work in MBO can be seen in three books by Edward C. Schleh, *Successful Executive Action*, Prentice-Hall, Englewood Cliffs, NJ, 1955; *Management by Results*, McGraw–Hill, New York, 1961; and *The Management Technique*, McGraw–Hill, New York, 1974.

13. See Peter F. Drucker, *Concept of the Corporation*, Day, New York, 1946, pp. 46–251.

14. John W. Humble, Ed., *Management by Objectives in Action*, McGraw–Hill, New York, 1970.

15. W. J. Reddin, *Effective Management by Objectives: The 3-D Method of MBO*, McGraw–Hill, New York, 1971.

16. George S. Odiorne, *MBO II: A System of Managerial Leadership for the 80s*, Fearon Pitman, Belmont, CA, 1979.

17. George S. Odiorne and Edwin L. Miller, "Selection by Objectives: A New Approach to Managerial Selection," *Management of Personnel Quarterly*, Vol. 5, No. 3, Fall 1966, pp. 2–10.

18. George S. Odiorne, "Discipline by Objectives," *Management of Personnel Quarterly*, Vol. 10, No. 2, Summer 1971, pp. 13–20.

19. See George S. Odiorne, *Management by Objectives: A System of Managerial Leadership*, Pitman, New York, 1965; *Training by Objectives: An Economic Approach to Management Training*, Macmillan, New York, 1970, and *Personnel Administration by Objectives*, Irwin, Homewood, IL, 1971.

20. Adapted from George S. Odiorne, "Management by Objectives—The Current State of the Art" (Paper presented at the National Conference of the American Society for Training and Development, New York, New York, May 26, 1971), pp. 1–4.

21. For a well-known critique of problems in MBO applications see Thomas P. Kleber, "Forty Common Goal-Setting Errors," *Human Resource Management*, Vol. 11, No. 3, Fall 1972, pp. 10–13.

22. Odiorne, *op. cit.*, "Management by Objectives—The Current State of the Art," pp. 4–6.

23. Adapted from Walter R. Mahler, "MBO—The Achilles' Heel of Most OD Efforts" (Paper presented at the National Conference of the American Society for Training and Development, New York, May 24, 1971), pp. 1–3.

24. John J. Sherwood, "An Introduction to Organization Development" in J. William Pfeiffer and John E. Jones, Eds., *The 1972 Annual Handbook for Group Facilitators*, University Associates, La Jolla, CA, 1972, pp. 153–156. The full definition is "Organization development is an educational process by which human resources are continuously identified, allocated, and expanded in ways that make these resources more *available* to the organization, and, therefore, improve the organization's problem-solving capabilities," p. 153 (italics added).

25. Ellis D. Hillmar, "Where OD and MBO Meet," unpublished paper, 1974, pp. 5–9. For a more extended discussion of this see Thomas H. Patten, Jr., "OD, MBO, and The Reward System," in Thomas H. Patten, Jr., Ed., *OD—Emerging Dimensions and Concepts*, American Society for Training and Development, Madison, WI, 1973, pp. 9–31. See also William H. Mobley, "The Link Between MBO and Merit Compensation," *Personnel Journal*, Vol. 53, No. 6, June 1974, pp. 423–427.

26. Wendell L. French and Robert W. Hollmann, "Management by Objectives: The Team Approach," *California Management Review*, Vol. 17, No. 3, Spring 1975, pp. 13–22.

27. *Idem.*

28. Others writing about the functional equivalent of CMBO include the following: Richard E. Byrd and John Cowan, "MBO: A Behavioral Science Approach," *Personnel*, Vol. 51, No. 2, March–April 1974, pp. 42–50; and William W. George, "Task Teams for Rapid Growth," *Harvard Business Review*, Vol. 55, No. 2, March–April 1977, pp. 71–80.

29. Rensis Likert and M. Scott Fisher, "MBGO: Putting Some Team Spirit into MBO," *Personnel*, Vol. 54, No. 1, January–February 1977, pp. 40–47.

30. David W. Belcher, *Compensation Administration*, Prentice–Hall, Englewood Cliffs, NJ, 1974, pp. 10–16, 58–68, 347–382.

31. Much of the discussion which follows is taken from Patten, "Intervening in Organizations Through Reward Systems," *op. cit.*, pp. 199–205, and Patten, *Pay: Employee Compensation and Incentive Plans, op. cit.*, pp. 568–572.

32. Frederick Herzberg, *Work and the Nature of Man*, World, Cleveland, OH, 1966, pp. 70–167.

33. Robert Dubin, *The World of Work*, Prentice–Hall, Englewood Cliffs, NJ, 1958, pp. 212–215.

34. For a recent discussion see Frederick S. Hills, "The Pay-for-Performance Dilemma," *Personnel*, Vol. 56, No. 5, September–October 1979, pp. 23–31.

35. William Foote Whyte *et al.*, *Money and Motivation*, Harper and Row, New York, 1955, provides an early summary of this research.

36. Belcher, *op. cit.*, pp. 448–457.

37. Sources include the following: Michael Beer and Edgar F. Huse, "A Systems Approach to Organization Development," *Journal of Applied Behavioral Science*, Vol. 8, No. 1, January–February 1972, pp. 93–96;

Donald L. Kirkpatrick, "MBO and Salary Administration," *Training and Development Journal*, Vol. 27, No. 9, September 1973, pp. 3–5; Dale D. McConkey, "The 'Jackass Effect' in Management Compensation," *Business Horizons*, Vol. 17, No. 3, June 1974, pp. 81–91; and Anthony P. Raia, *Managing by Objectives*, Scott, Foresman, Glenview, IL, 1974, pp. 53–56, 136–144, and 170.

38. Edward E. Lawler, *Pay and Organizational Effectiveness: A Psychological View*, McGraw–Hill, New York, 1971, pp. 1–7 and *passim*.

39. Fred E. Schuster and Alva F. Kindall, "Management by Objectives: Where We Stand—A Survey of the Fortune 500," *Human Resource Management*, Vol. 13, No. 1, Spring 1974, pp. 8–11.

40. William A. Dowling, "Conversation: An Interview with B. F. Skinner," *Organizational Dynamics*, Vol. 1, No. 3, Winter 1973, pp. 34–37.

41. Richard E. Farson, "Praise Reappraised," *Harvard Business Review*, Vol. 41, No. 5, September–October 1963, pp. 61–64.

42. Len Sperry and Lee R. Hess, *Contact Counseling*, Addison–Wesley, Reading, MA, 1974, pp. 138–140, 228–232.

43. Some of this work can be found in the following: portions of Rock, *op. cit.*; Fred E. Schuster, "History and Theory of Performance Appraisal," pp. 5-14–5-16; H. L. Judd, "Appraising Executive Performance," pp. 5-53–5-58; Ronald G. Foster, "Appraising Performance for Incentive Purposes," pp. 5-75–5-79; W. Earl Sasser and Samuel H. Pettway, "The Case of Big Mac's Pay Plans," *Harvard Business Review*, Vol. 52, No. 4, July–August 1974, pp. 31–44; F. Dean Hildebrandt, Jr., "Individual Performance in Incentive Compensation," *Compensation Review*, Vol. 10, No. 3, Third Quarter 1978, pp. 28–33; and Richard H. Allaway, Jr., "Incentives and Bonuses: Their Role in Compensating Executives," in *Compensating Executive Worth*, Russell F. Moore, Ed., American Management Association, New York, 1968, p. 125. Perhaps the most brilliant work is in Graef S. Crystal, *Executive Compensation: Money, Motivation, and Imagination*, AMACOM, New York, 1978, pp. 27–136. For a clear example of how MBO can be tied directly to base pay determination see Dale D. McConkey, *How to Manage by Results*, 3rd ed., AMACOM, New York, 1977, pp. 224–227.

44. Carl F. Frost *et al.*, *The Scanlon Plan for Organizational Development: Identity, Participation, and Equity*, Michigan State University Press, East Lansing, 1974, and Brian E. Moore and Timothy L. Ross, *The Scanlon Way to Improved Productivity*, Wiley, New York, 1978. Small group incentive plans could qualify as pay for teamwork also. However, they are only a minor factor in the payment of wages in the American economy covering relatively few firms.

45. Edward A. Robie, "Compensation Administration in the Coming Decade," *Compensation Review*, Vol. 2, No. 2, Second Quarter, 1970, p. 19.

46. Donald G. Winton and Charles R. Sutherland, "A Performance-Based Approach to Determining Executive Incentive Bonus Awards," *Compensation Review*, Vol. 8, No. 1, First Quarter 1976, pp. 14–26.

47. "How Companies Set the Base Salary and Incentive Bonus Opportunity for Chief Executive and Chief Operating Officers . . . *A Compensation Review* Symposium," *Compensation Review,* Vol. 8, No. 4, Quarter 1976, pp. 19–32; "How Companies Set Top- and Middle-Management Salaries . . . *A Compensation Review* Symposium," *Compensation Review*, Vol. 9, No. 1, First Quarter 1977, pp. 32–46; Ernest C. Miller, "Top- and Middle-Management Compensation—Part I: Determining Base Salary," *Compensation Review*, Vol. 8, No. 3, Third Quarter 1976, pp. 28–44, and "Top- and Middle-Management Compensation—Part 2: Incentive Bonus and Merit Increase Plans," *Compensation Review*, Vol. 8, No. 4, Fourth Quarter 1976, pp. 33–46.

48. Robert J. Greene, "Incentive Compensation for Staff Managers," *Compensation Review*, Vol. 10, No. 1, First Quarter 1978, pp. 20–24.

49. Robert E. Sibson, "New Practices and Ideas in Compensation Administration," *Compensation Review*, Vol. 6, No. 3, Third Quarter 1974, p. 47.

50. Lawrence M. Baytos, "Employee Participation in Compensation Planning," *Compensation Review*, Vol. 8, No. 2, Second Quarter 1976, pp. 25–38, and Bruce R. Ellig, "Employee Benefit Planning: Utilizing Employee Preferences," *Compensation Review*, Vol. 8, No. 2, Second Quarter 1976, pp. 39–50.

51. Edward E. Lawler, III and Raymond N. Olson, "Designing Reward Systems for New Organizations," *Personnel*, Vol. 54, No. 5, September–October 1977, pp. 48–60.

52. French and Hollmann, *op. cit.*, pp. 18–20.

53. Patten, *Pay: Employee Compensation and Incentive Plans, op. cit.*, pp. 572–586 covers much of the existing technology of this subject.

54. A modified version of this exercise was published in Thomas H. Patten, Jr., "MANDOERS: Organizational Clarification," in J. William Pfeiffer and John E. Jones, Eds., *The 1978 Annual Handbook for Group Facilitators*, University Associates, La Jolla, CA, 1978, pp. 71–76.

55. Thomas H. Patten, Jr. "Personnel Administration and the Will to Manage," *Human Resource Management*, Vol. 11, No. 3, Fall 1972, pp. 4–9.

chapter 9

TEAMBUILDING AND THE FUTURE OF OD

Throughout this book I have been emphasizing the need for flexible, open, authentic, and trusting behavior and goal-setting, problem-solving, decision-making, time-management, and reward-administering skills among managers who are, by virtue of their work, organizational linking pins. There is little more new material that can be added about these subjects, at least in the final chapter of a book such as this, but there is value in placing what has been said in a summarized overall perspective so that the reader is left with a feeling of closure and a frame of reference. In this final chapter I attempt to provide a perspective, reviewing some topics briefly touched upon in the book previously, such as power in OD, and then tie together some thinking about using technical personnel systems as interventions together with OD interventions. Lastly, I take out the crystal ball and discuss some ideas about the future use and changing nature of OD in the 1980s.

Teambuilding Perspective

Organizational development and improved management depend upon the growth of individuals who are in managerial positions and endeavor to build a work culture that is healthy in the ways described earlier in the book. I often find that growth as an executive begins with risk-taking. Risking to be open in encountering others can build trust. In turn, trust reduces defensiveness and makes teamwork possible.

The higher an executive's self-awareness and self-acceptance, the fewer the chances that he will be defensive. The lower the executive's defensiveness, the more open he will be to feedback. The more the executive learns to receive and give feedback, the more he will learn how to be an effective team member. Thus, to close the loop, from earlier chapters in which the Johari Window and FIRO-B were discussed it should be obvious that I have great confidence in openness in climate and interpersonal feedback as ingredients for organizational change and management improvement.

The design for change advocated in this book involves the Lewin hypothetical model of unfreezing, changing, and refreezing.[1] Unless individuals are open to change and are willing to give and receive feedback, change will come slowly and perhaps too late to help the organization progress or, indeed, survive. Organizations need to be open and to legitimize feedback so that their employees feel they are part of a team and will thus be willing to commit and dedicate themselves to organizational goal attainment.

Participation tends to increase the commitment of managers and employees. In fact, as Mahler has pointed out, commitment tends to heighten motivation. Motivation tends to make executives and all employees work more productively and conscientiously. More conscientious and productive work tends to result in personal and organizational goal attainment. Therefore, participation is desirable and needs to be built into organizational life.[2]

Another aspect of motivation is channeling it so that organizational goals are attained by means of individual human performance. In prior chapters, where I discussed performance review and the use of MBO in setting standards for performance, I remarked on the connection between participation, commitment, motivation and work results. I believe that managers and employees will improve their ability to obtain results on the job when they know the strengths and weaknesses in their current performance, know how they can improve it, have the delegated authority to make these changes themselves, and have the incentive to change. All of these are familiar ideas that were developed quite fully earlier in the book.

In examining performance itself and the incentive that a manager or an employee has to improve his performance, it is useful to consider some of the ideas of Lawler and the guidelines he advocates for utilizing pay as a performance lever.[3] First, employees must believe that good performance will lead to more pay. In order for employees to have this belief it would appear that there must be a foundation of trust so that the belief can be developed.

For pay to function as a performance lever employees must want more pay. In earlier chapters we considered to what extent employees' goals were financial as opposed to nonfinancial and whether they would be responsive to money as a motivator. Employees must not believe that good performance will lead to negative consequences. For example, they need to be assured that if their performance excels, the result will not be the imposition of a higher work standard upon them, which would have the obnoxious speedup effect of making them work harder in the same amount of time for the same level of compensation.

Also, employees must see that other desired rewards in addition to money result from good performance. Those employees who are strongly desirous of recognition, status symbols, power, authority, or other types of rewards need to see the connection between the granting of these and performance on the job.

Lastly, employees must believe that their efforts do lead to improved performance. The meaning of the word "effort" is not always clear in discussions of motivation, incentive, and performance. For the manual worker, the term probably has a basis in the amount of physical energy and effort it takes to accomplish work. For nonmanual workers, and particularly managers and executives, the word is not so easily defined. Thus, when I suggest that employees must believe that their efforts do lead to improved performance I am implying that employees must perceive that their inputs, contributions, and results in terms of attaining planned and agreed upon goals are fulfilled.

I believe that a review of some of the ideas that I have been discussing in this chapter will ordinarily be helpful toward the end of an intensive OD teambuilding effort. The review, to the extent it pulls together a number of complex ideas and restates them in a way that then makes final sense after an intensive learning experience, is likely to leave the team members with the feeling that they have learned something both cognitively and experientially.[4] Also at this time it is useful to remind managers and executives that one of their roles in an organization, particularly a healthy organization, is to extend themselves to one another and be helpful. Healthy organizations have highly developed methods of internal helping. Thus, it is valuable to discuss the helping relationship and then move into an exercise involving feedback. I discuss these learning loop closers next.

The Helping Relationship

I can readily identify a number of helping professions, but the profession of management is not ordinarily considered to be a helping profession. However, if we take an enlarged view of what is involved in helping, then it is quite clear that managers do have as one of their duties, as Mintzberg has pointed out, helping each other.[5]

Helping may be defined as a constructive process in which one person (a helper) assists another by affecting or influencing his thinking and/or behavior. The focus is upon improving a working relationship between the parties. Thus we can see that helping defined in this manner is implicit in counseling, teaching, training, and, clearly, in managing. All of these professional activities imply growth, learning, accepting responsibility, and developing personal autonomy. Yet these same activities downplay giving of advice, reprimanding, or punishing, all of which are more useful in implying a threat, wielding control, or taking actions that may cause surface change rather than genuine personal growth on the part of the person to whom the attention is directed.

The core of a helping relationship is an interpersonal process between at least two individuals. This process includes mutual acceptance, trust, valuing the other, and being genuinely concerned with his strengths and weaknesses. It also involves the content of problems and many feelings, attitudes, and understandings related to them. The process also requires joint exploration, that is, listening on both sides.

In the helping relationship that has been described, there are various goals and barriers. The goals of the helper are to be of assistance to the other party as the helper perceives it. The goals of the receiver of help are to use the assistance as he perceives it. It thus can be seen that the receiver has more power in the relationship than the helper because if help is going to be helpful it must be so perceived by the receiver.

Among the barriers to the helping relationship are those that affect the helper and those that affect the receiver. For example, the helper can be insensitive, concentrating more on his needs than on the receiver's needs; he can fail to confront; he can pressure the receiver; he can tell the receiver what he should do in a situation without really knowing the intricacies of the situation. In respect to the receiver, he can distrust or fear the help that is being offered; he can appear to be willing to accept sympathy but unwilling to search and cope for answers to his problem; he can take on the "uniqueness syndrome," thereby considering himself so different from anyone else and in such an entirely different situation from all others that he is truly unique; he can express a desire to be autonomous, if not totally counterdependent. The receiver of help can summon up many other types of defensive behavior. Bradford et al. have discussed these aspects of the helping relationship.[6]

There are various modes of helping that are available in the kinds of managerial interpersonal situations we have been discussing. One mode of helping is for the helper to show an understanding or demonstrate a response to the receiver that indicates that the helper knows and feels how the receiver is reacting to the situation or problem. Another mode of helping is probing or deliberate information-gathering, as in an interview, in order to delve more deeply into a point. Still another mode of helping is interpreting for someone what the helper thinks he might mean. The helper might suggest or impart meaning, or perhaps even try to persuade the person being helped as to what he ought to think!

Other modes include supporting, reassuring, pacifying, or suggesting that someone need not feel as he does. Lastly, evaluating or passing judgment on the rightness, effectiveness, or appropriateness of the receiver's behavior are also useful modes in the helping relationship.

All these modes can be used for the purposes of giving feedback to the receiver. The manner in which they can be used and the relative emphasis on each needs to be sensed by the helper so that he can make his help truly helpful. For example, there are times when probing is better than interpreting; there are occasions, of course, when evaluating or passing judgment is the only way to get feedback across. The important consideration in the helping relationship when it is explicitly singled out for use in a teambuilding effort is to direct it to the members of a team who have sufficiently exposed themselves to one another and worked toward the building of a team climate that they are receptive to feedback. Hopefully, they can then nondefensively examine it and determine whether they wish to utilize the feedback to begin individual behavior change.

Exercise on Feedback and Peer Evaluation

Figure 9.1 provides an example of a peer evaluation of team members who are participants in seminar/workshops on teambuilding. This format can be utilized at the end of a major segment of a teambuilding effort for the purpose of giving people undergoing the teambuilding experience a change to provide feedback to one another based upon the observation of behavior samples of one another that are sufficiently large to provide a meaningful bases for assessment. Normally, this should be attempted only after an interval of at least approximately five days of working and learning together so that the individual behavior sample provides sufficient data.

The exercise can be conducted in several ways but one useful way is for the OD team facilitator to require that the persons undergoing the team-building effort read the instructions for the evaluation and then simply go ahead and either write essays or complete sentences in relation to the eight points shown on the form. In this way, if there are five- or six-person teams, each member of the team obtains five unsigned evaluations from individuals who have worked with him in a teambuilding seminar/workshop for several days or a week. Those providing the feedback should also be made aware of

Figure 9.1   Peer Evaluation of Seminar/Workshop Participant

To: _____

Using the form below write a short statement pertaining to each point for each participant in your team. You will have a separate form for each team member. Give open, honest, authentic feedback to each person. He will be given your feedback and will not have a chance to discuss it with you or defend himself.

You will be giving each person in your team something that he will have to mull over and settle by himself. Thus, you should write only what you really want to say and communicate things that you think will help each person develop as an executive in the organization and function as a team member "back-home." In an important sense this is your performance appraisal of and for him; and it can be useful to him in seeking and obtaining rewards through changed executive behavior, both in his present job and perhaps in the long run for the duration of his career.

1. Interpersonal relations and openness

2. Skill in working in a team setting as a contributing team member

3. Willingness to confront and be confronted

4. Task-orientation vs. people-orientation

5. Problem-identification and problem-solving skills

6. Goal-setting skills

7. Strengths (overall)

8. Weaknesses (overall improvements desired)

Note: If you find the above format confining or inappropriate, write your comments as an essay.

the fact that they will be getting feedback from other members of their team.

All team members are encouraged to be candid in their feedback and not to pull punches; nevertheless, they should take a responsible attitude in writing the information that is included in the feedback format.

The instructions shown in Figure 9.1 encourage individuals to take time to formulate their feedback comments and emphasize that the recipient of the feedback will not have a chance to defend himself or rebut the comments that are given to him. The eight items should coincide with the goals of the teambuilding effort so that the individual is given feedback that is connected with behavior that was supposedly worked upon and is the primary subject of the teambuilding effort. In the event that some of the providers of feedback do not like a form such as that shown in Figure 9.1 they can be encouraged simply to write essays that incorporate the feedback which they wish to impart.

This exercise in providing feedback when sequenced after a theory input on the helping relationship and a more broad-gauged theory input that attempts to provide perspective on the overall goals of teambuilding normally has a very powerful effect on the persons who have undergone the teambuilding effort. There are several reasons for this. First, the individuals obtain feedback from people who have seen them at work in a number of exercises during a teambuilding effort and are in a position to have penetrated the Johari facade.[7] Second, the teambuilding effort has probably built a culture that encourages individuals to be much more open and to share their perceptions more fearlessly than they would in a nontrusting environment in a typical work situation. Third, individuals who have had a week or more of teambuilding have probably by this time acquired some skills in observing behavior, listening, and communicating with others in a way such that they are likely to be "heard." Fourth, individuals at this particular juncture in a teambuilding effort are probably eager for some kind of feedback and willing to provide feedback to others as well. In other words, there is a sense of closure developing at this point that sets up favorable circumstances for the giving and receiving of feedback.

Feedback obtained in this way permits the recipient to sort out what he wants to do with the help. He knows that as the receiver of feedback he is in the most powerful position from the standpoint of change. He can either uncritically reject all the help or choose from the feedback those items on which he desires to work. He can use the occasion to build an agenda on personal growth as a manager for himself, thus deciding which items he feels require his attention back on the job and in the remainder of his career as a manager. He can make these decisions free of duress and yet, unless he is such a closed person as to make the teambuilding effort entirely useless, he will know that the feedback he has been given cannot rightfully be ignored and dismissed.

In summary, at the end of a major phase it is valuable to review what has been learned from the teambuilding effort (such as five full days of seminar/workshops) so that the individual leaves the scene with a greater sense of self-awareness and group-awareness than he had before he came and a realization of having learned new skills that have "refrozen" his behavior into newer and more effective modes of coping in the managerial job. It is not necessary that the individual feel smugly satisfied at the end of the teambuilding program because, indeed, it may be of greatest help to him that he be jarred somewhat and forced to consider whether his behavior is as effective as it could be. Thus dissatisfactions that amount to dissonance and mild trouble or puzzlement to an individual may consist of social–emotional feedback that, in the long run, can be quite beneficial and encourage that individual to embark on a new and improved way of life, both as a manager and as a human being.

In this book I have been emphasizing that the OD facilitator role-model in his behavior what he believes about people and human nature in working with groups. His values should be reflected in his behavior. It is as valuable for him to get feedback from the individuals undergoing the teambuilding effort as it is for the team members to be appraised by one another. Also, any group facilitator who is professionally keen should desire feedback so that in his future career as an OD change agent he can enhance his skills. For all these reasons, it is useful for a group to feed back to the group facilitator their reactions to the teambuilding effort itself as well as the group facilitator's role in the effort. Figure 9.2 provides a useful format for this based upon the assumption that an initial thrust at teambuilding was the purpose of seminar/workshops.[8] This form is easily administered and analyzed and can indeed be scored immediately at the seminar site if that is desired.

The form contains several graphic scales ranging from poor to excellent, which can be scored from 1 to 5 then totaled and divided by the number of seminar participants in order to obtain an overall score. There is some opportunity for individuals in the program to fill in their reactions in their own words. Also, there is a projective question at the end that provides additional insight into whether the participants found the teambuilding effort sufficiently worthwhile to recommend it to others.

This testimonial-like instrument is merely a form of "reaction appraisal," but it does have value in communicating to the group facilitator (or the team of group facilitators if there are more than one) what the participants felt about the program design and his or their implementation of it.[9]

Unfortunately, at the present time in the literature of teambuilding there are very few long-range evaluations of teambuilding efforts. It has been found that longer-range data can be obtained by interviewing and observing team members two years or more after the teambuilding effort has been completed and the participants have returned to their normal organizational work roles. Such a study has recently been reported by Patten and Dorey and should be consulted for both methods and findings.[10]

Figure 9.2 Program and Seminar/Workshop Leader Evaluation

Executive Seminar on Organizational Development and Teambuilding

Thank you for participating in the seminar. We hope that you have enjoyed and benefited from the time spent here. In order that we may continually improve the quality of the program, we would like you to complete this evaluation and return it today before leaving. The evaluation will take only 5 minutes.

Please be frank. It is *not* necessary to identify yourself. Thank you in advance for your assistance.

1. Overall, I thought that the program was (Circle One):

    VERY

    POOR   FAIR   GOOD   GOOD   EXCELLENT

2. Considering the time and effort I put in, I thought that the program was (Circle One):

    OF NO   OF LITTLE   SOMEWHAT   EXTREMELY

    VALUE   VALUE   USEFUL   VALUABLE   VALUABLE

3. Considering the *contribution* of the seminar leader, please answer the following:

	POOR	FAIR	GOOD	VERY GOOD	EXCEL-LENT
a. Extent to which he held your attention during the presentations					
b. Degree of knowledge learned from him that can be applied directly or with minor "translation"					
c. The benefits of his part of the program in relation to your time and effort in the team exercises were					
d. How do you rate his overall effectiveness as a seminar leader?					

4. What is your opinion of the various teambuilding exercises? (Circle One):

    OF NO   OF LITTLE   SOMEWHAT   EXTREMELY

    VALUE   VALUE   USEFUL   VALUABLE   VALUABLE

5. In general, the program could have been improved by: _____

    _____

6. Would you recommend attending the seminar to other managers at your level who have executive development needs that are compatible with the goals of the seminar? (Circle One)

    YES   NO   NOT SURE

Changing Formal Organizational Structure

There are a number of other follow-up interventions that might be justified after the initial teambuilding effort has been completed and some employee behavioral change has been demonstrated. Naturally, I am assuming that either through external or internal change agents the change effort is being kept alive and the organization is becoming increasingly healthy.

The formal rearrangement of reporting relationships and the restructuring of the organizational blueprint structure itself may be desirable at this time. In fact, in many organizations the only known way of changing the organization is simply to rearrange reporting relationships and add position titles and other organizational elements to the organizational chart. In these instances, there is no real attempt to change the underlying dynamics of how people relate to one another and transforming a group of individuals who are relating poorly into a smooth-functioning team. This is not the place to discuss the mechanics of changing an organizational design to make it more purposive, but there are many books that can be consulted to obtain a better grasp of this topic.[11] In the OD field particularly, there is a great interest these days in such designs as matrix organization, project management, and other types of alterations that emphasize teamwork.[12] Probably the best recent writing on this topic has been done by Davis and Lawrence.[13] There is also an exhaustive literature on this same subject in the field of classical management.[14] OD specialists are likely to denigrate this literature and to suggest that formal structural interventions, although easy to make, are deceptive in their results because many undesirable patterns can be perpetuated in organizations that have changed only on the surface.

While recognizing the limitations of formal change, OD has to date concentrated less than it should on power and organizational politics as factors blocking and facilitating change.[15] In this book I have been assuming that the teambuilding effort has sufficiently high and widespread support to ultimately become a success. However, many organizations have never heard of OD or teambuilding and, even if they had, would probably never give either of them a chance as change technologies because the power structure of the organization is antithetical to change of any kind.

OD specialists have recently become more aware of the vacuum in respect to power in OD, but we find that the typical OD textbook makes only passing reference to power.[16] Zaleznik and Kets de Vries have provided us with the first OD-oriented book that attempts to evaluate power and discuss it in a way that has beneficial use to the OD facilitator.[17] Oshry has provided one of the few power exercises that can be consulted for possible application although it seems most useful in a laboratory situation emphasizing personal growth rather than teambuilding.[18] Starpower is yet another exercise that was given much attention several years ago.[19]

Byrd has provided a most interesting design that is useful in teambuilding; it causes individuals who are in a laboratory learning situation to produce and market a product using only their own resources and those they might by accident locate at the training site.[20] This particular design involves both organizing skills and practice in wielding power. His exercise reduces the number of participants to several companies who are units in a competitive market and are told to organize themselves, determine a product, and produce and sell their product to the OD facilitator or facilitators during the course of the teambuilding workshop. The facilitators must agree to purchase the product sold, actually pay for the products in cash; the team that attains the highest degree of profit is considered the winning team.

There is little more that has been reported in the literature about the use of power in teambuilding and in directing a teambuilding effort against a power structure or in concert with the power structure to attain organizational results. In many respects the connection between power and OD remains virgin territory that will undoubtedly be explored over the next decade. Certainly, the future of OD very much depends upon how OD can be facilitated in light of the fact that organizations are bound together by power (social cement as Bierstedt has put it[21]) and authority relations; these relations cannot be ignored.

Managerial Succession and Selection

Teambuilding ultimately provides individuals with skills; those who improve their ability to function as managers because of these skills may be the employees who are given greatest attention in future plans for managerial staffing. In this book much has been made of the connection between OD, MBO, and reward systems. However, other OD specialists, such as Kuriloff, believe that succession planning and MBO are technical systems that need to be well worked out as social technologies if an OD effort is to be successful.[22]

Until very recently the literature on personnel management and organizational behavior tended to treat planning and administering the managerial succession as topics of a technical nature quite unconnected with organizational development. As far back as the late 1940s the Standard Oil Company of New Jersey (now called Exxon) took a serious interest in identifying managerial talent and planning who would succeed whom in the managerial hierarchy so that, as positions were vacated in the future, replacements would be prepared.[23] In the last two decades many companies, and indeed many public agencies, have become interested in succession planning and have installed workable systems.[24] Mahler and Wrightnour have captured much of this experience and technology in their book.[25] Bright has reported on how he integrates succession planning with many computer applications in forecasting human resource requirements in the Union Oil Company.[26] Kuriloff has been perhaps the most insistent writer in arguing that succession planning be carefully integrated with organizational development.[27]

On the face of it, we develop organizations so that management is improved; however, we may not consciously be aware of the fact that succession planning should be administered in concert with OD. Yet, it seems obvious that the two should be connected; probably we will see more integration of the two in the future.

Equal Employment Opportunity

In the past 10 years private and public organizations have been under increasing legislative pressure and the surveillance of watchdog agencies to build equal employment opportunity into their work cultures. Organizations have also been directed to take affirmative action so that minorities and women are employed in a fairer manner than in the past and to develop affirmative action plans for the upward mobility of minorities and women.[28] Also, very recently there have been mandates to provide equal opportunity for older workers and for the handicapped. Thus, although I have focused upon teambuilding for the improvement of management by enabling managers to become more skillful in the conduct of their work, there is no reason why teambuilding could not also be used for integrating minorities and other excluded persons into the work force and taking action to enhance their careers.

The particular design advocated in this book has a different purpose. Yet the individuals who complete the type of teambuilding that has been discussed could then be exposed to modules in an OD mode that would focus upon increasing the awareness between males and females, blacks and whites, the handicapped and nonhandicapped, and younger and older workers, or any combination of these aforementioned groups. The OD facilitator needs simply to determine needs and proceed with the design of modules that are responsive to the needs uncovered in his own particular work organization.

There is an increasing literature on the use of laboratory learning for dealing with issues in race relations and intercultural awareness.[29] Patten and Dorey, for example, reported on the successful use of a design for an equal employment opportunity workshop that was intended to develop black and white change agents in a government organization.[30]

There is little doubt that in the future, teambuilding efforts will be directed toward other purposes than those that are the focus of this book. There is much room for ingenuity in designing such efforts.

Career Planning and Life Planning

Insofar as there is a connection between teambuilding, changing organizational structure, dealing with power, planning the managerial succession, and adapting teambuilding to EEO implementation, there is an equally apparent connection between teambuilding and the implementation of career planning and life planning systems. As I have pointed out previously, teambuilding became popular because organizations realized that members of its management needed to interface more effectively and collaborate in the conduct of their interdependent specialties. Career planning has been introduced in organizations today because the size of organizations tends to swallow up the individual; unless there is some way of identifying the individual and his career aspirations, well-performing individuals may leave the organization and seek employment elsewhere.[31] Similarly, without formal career planning programs, managerial vacancies when they occur cannot be filled by promotion from within because there is no real knowledge of the human resources employed in the organization and where they may be headed. Thus we are starting to find that discussions of career planning are becoming more refined and, in time, this subject will undoubtedly also be connected more closely with OD than in the past.

Perhaps the first book that combined a treatment of organization, manpower, compensation, and career planning, was written by McBeath.[32] He described many of the technical personnel systems that can be used to intervene in the organization and carry out various kinds of planning in an integrated way. Perhaps even more important has been Kellogg's recent work on career planning.[33] She indicates that career planning is not something carried out as a separate personnel system in a work organization, although there may be a monitoring of the progress of employees in the firm by some unit in the personnel staff. Kellogg's point is that career planning is instead an aspect of every personnel decision that is made, including decisions about selection, compensation, promotion, training program participation, and the like. Hence career planning needs to be viewed in the broadest possible terms so that when any major personnel decision is made some attention is given to the impact of that decision on the careers of specific employees. However, formal planning systems are probably necessary for the concrete management of careers; this recognized need (in addition to EEO pressures) explains why we are observing the creation of specific systems in large-scale organizations today.

Career planning may thus be viewed as a series of technical personnel interventions.[34] Life planning, on the other hand, which can be a catalyst in the individual's career choice processes, is carried out in a laboratory learning environment; however, it too can be integrated with teambuilding. Shepard,[35] Ford and Lippitt,[36] and others[37] have at various times described designs for life planning. The purpose of life planning is to encourage individuals to become aware of where they stand in the life cycle and determine if their present status is where they would like to be (or not). Another purpose is to help individuals determine where they would like to spend the remainder of their careers and what kinds of activities would be most satisfying to them over the duration of their employment.

There is considerable managerial mobility in the United States; there is little doubt that much of this is caused by individual dissatisfaction, owing in turn to people not being *what* they would like to be or not being *where* they would like to be occupationally. Individuals often feel that opportunities are closed to them—or they fear taking risks to change their line of work or to seek employment in an entirely new field of endeavor.[38] A life planning intervention can be useful for these people by providing an opportunity for self-examination and career-decision making. Thus, after there has been an initial teambuilding effort, the next behavioral intervention could very well be a life-planning intervention in which the members of the team share with one another their aspirations and senses of satisfaction and dissatisfaction with their careers and lives. The results of such a sharing could be installation of formal succession planning or the design of other interventions which would be responsive to helping individuals find greater satisfaction in the job, the company, or life itself. Thus, life planning is a very powerful intervention and one that probably has its greatest value only for people who are quite unfrozen from dysfunctional behaviors of the past and ready to look realistically and openly at the future with a sense of venturesomeness, risk, and renewed enthusiasm.

The Future of OD

To this point we have been discussing teambuilding, the addition of various modules to teambuilding, internal technical personnel systems, and the adaptation of organizations to change. OD is clearly a multipurpose behavioral technology and can be applied to many present and future situations. Ordinarily, we think of OD as applied to prosperity and not to times of economic depression or recession; we think of OD as applying mainly to employees rather than retirees and terminees. However, if OD is multipurposeful, its use in the future should reflect this versatility.[39] Let us examine the present trends and then turn to some of the future trends.

According to various experts, at the present time the following trends seem to be obvious in OD. OD is presently co-opting a sizeable portion of behavioral science and practitioner talent. It is quite obviously popular and unfortunately has many of the hallmarks of being a fad.[40]

OD is increasingly being chosen as an integrated change strategy rather than isolated techniques, such as T-group sessions, MBO, job enrichment, or any other single technical or nontechnical intervention. OD is no longer regarded as synonymous with the T-group or with any other single type of intervention but is instead regarded as a more inclusive term embracing combinations of different types of interventions that are tailored to meet the specific needs of clients.

OD teambuilding and consultation techniques are very well known at the present time among applied behavioral scientists in universities, consulting firms, and work organizations and do not seem to be declining in interest. The change model discussed earlier in the book involving the trinity of internal consultant or change agent, external consultant or change agent, and team at the top (or top management) seems to pinpoint the prime movers whose concerted energy brings about organizational change.[41] Additional models of change are increasingly being reported, as can be seen in the proliferation of articles in the *Journal of Applied Behavior Science* and *Group and Organization Studies,* but the trinity usually fits in somewhere.

Following from the above, I at present view OD as becoming an amalgam from the best thinking in the behavioral sciences. Although this is desirable from the standpoint of putting together the combination of techniques and designs which can be used for change, the amalgamation tends to make the field quite amorphous and difficult to learn for the uninitiated person. Also, it may give him the impression that OD is a hodgepodge consisting of a bag of tricks and gimmicks to be drawn from in almost any way desired by the OD facilitator.[42] Obviously, this is an erroneous assumption of the field, but the bewildering combination of techniques, research, and theory in OD puzzle many new initiates and observers.

The OD action research model continues to be the most useful one for tracking and staying on target in a change effort. The model involves people who are intimately connected with the change effort and who must personally accept or "own" its goals and outcomes if the change is to be durable. The action research model also provides the best known basis for focusing on the real problems and measuring progress against tangible or perceived changes.

OD has continued in recent years to emphasize changing the culture of a work organization, which seems to be the proper focus of attention and to have potentially the highest impact. Until recently a great deal of effort in OD has been built around working with the individual in the hope that institutional change will follow from change in the behavior of the individuals who participate in the institution.[43] This is the Gestalt view in the OD field of course, but it is one which has many adherents. In fact, many persons who may be unfamiliar with Gestalt views and may consider themselves primarily interested in organizations *per se* rather than people *per se* are likely to find that when they commence OD interventions they direct their change efforts essentially at the individual.[44] I have emphasized in this book that teambuilding efforts typically begin with the individual and that some of the other types of changes that *can* be introduced, such as specifically changing the formal organizational structure of a firm or agency, are likely to be less effective in changing human behavior than intervening to change human behavior directly. The state of intervention theory has been exhaustively discussed by Agyris,[45] but we still have much to learn about intervention and a great deal more thinking to do about why OD spends as much time with individual development and change as it does.

Lastly, my present view is that OD effort should be directed more toward working with the intact group in the work or other organization than with isolated people.[46] This is somewhat of a deviation from Gestalt views but is the essence of much basic thinking in teambuilding. However, there are many teambuilding efforts that work with cousins or semi-strangers rather than the intact group and appear to be successful. In fact, such arrangements may be the only manner in which to start teambuilding efforts in super-large organizations—those with 20,000 or more employees.

Turning to the future of OD there are a number of trends that deserve commentary. First, OD interventions at the interpersonal, structural, and goal-setting levels need to be linked to efforts to change technical systems in organizations. When we consider social change more broadly, we are apt to find that legal, political, and technological problems in society are vast and cause change in many spheres of life. Within work organizations we find that personnel management systems and reward systems have great effects on the lives of managers and other employees and that OD can and should be used, indeed, integrated with these in a planned way to bring about change. We are likely to see more of this integrated planning in the future and, in fact, will probably find that teams of change agents will be needed and must be properly managed if we are to bring about change in complex organizations.[47]

OD will be used more in the future if it can act in the present to surmount some of the possible causes of derailment of OD efforts. These problems would include avoiding premature formulation in concepts and social technology in OD. There seemed to be some stagnation setting in a few years ago in OD with the excessive interest in the T-group concept and technology despite the needs of an organization for other types of interventions. Similarly, OD needs to develop strategies for coping with immediate crises and for sustaining long-term efforts. This is important because OD probably has its greatest payoff in the longer period of time than in the shorter. However, organizations have immediate problems that often have to be dealt with before any attention can be given to the longer run.

OD will be used more in the future if it can avoid being co-opted by traditional organizational pressures and functional departments, thereby being absorbed into the organizational layer cake and eventually dying. I have seen organizations where different departments of the business, in seeking to expand their domains and build up empires, have sought to seize control over OD and use it as their tool for leverage in the battle for organizational power. Thus in some organizations the operations research people attempt to assert jurisdiction over OD, whereas in other organizations the training specialists attempt to seize OD and include it as a kind of management development program for the organization. Of course, the greatest potential of OD rests in its being used by top management and the internal and external change agent as a change strategy.[48]

OD also needs to refine its values and to continue this process of refinement so that it can be of greater assistance for renewing organizations and making them more human and effective, as Lippitt has pointed out.[49] In this connection it must be stated that OD is neither a value-free nor a neutral technology. OD is humanistic and scientific; so far it has had no room, for example, for fascists and charlatans who belittle action research and social facts.

In the future, OD needs to develop a greater variety of models. The T-group background has led to a stress on openness, trust, and collaborative models. Power issues need greater attention, as has been suggested, because action implementation in OD depends upon working within a power structure and not having OD efforts sidetracked because of miscalculations regarding the source and orientation of power blocs.[50]

Looking ahead, it is quite clear that we need to find more shortcuts in implementing OD efforts. We know that OD takes time and energy in order to get results and that certain types of interventions, such as MBO, may take 3 to 5 years before there has been a thorough application and the many technical problems of implementation have been eliminated. Yet there are often no apparent short cuts because the change process itself takes time. On the other hand, in the dynamic world in which we live, if change efforts are to be protracted, this means that many individuals who are involved in OD eventually retire, are promoted, are transferred, or quit the organization, before the full effects of OD have been felt. Yet we cannot always accelerate the installation of OD because human beings can apparently absorb change only at a certain tempo. If pushed beyond this, the change effort is likely to fail or stall. On the other hand, we are only deceiving ourselves about the real-world effectiveness of OD if OD interventions are strung out over an excessively long period of time and the turnover of personnel who have experienced OD efforts has served to cancel the cumulative buildup of imparted OD skills and knowledge.[51] Perhaps the prime problem of OD in the future is to find a way to accelerate the installation of OD in order to make certain that the implementation is effective! Three to five years may plainly be too long.

In the future, there must be ways found to relate changed organizations to hostile or incongruous external environments. Lippitt has pointed out that effective interfacing, searching, and confronting by individuals and teams may lead to environmental change.[52] There can be concert between internal and external change in organizations. However, if resource development is valued internally but resource exploitation is practiced externally, reconciliation is needed; and OD needs to find ways to achieve this.

The status of the economy in the future will also have an important bearing upon OD. Davis and Shepard have pointed out that OD will increasingly be used in good and bad times.[53] For example, in good times more stress might be placed on manpower planning, career planning, and life planning systems and interventions. Thus OD may help people confront the need to quit a job and embark on a new life. OD would be a true renewal stimulus in these situations. On the other hand, in bad times, more stress might be placed on coping with employee immobilization, paranoid behavior, energy withdrawal, survival depression, rumor production, reckless cost-cutting, deterioration in trouble-shooting skills, and the like. Here OD could be of help in assisting people confront layoffs and terminations in a more open and problem-solving mode.[54] Credibility and trust issues are preeminent in times of economic adversity, and OD should be helpful in layoffs and out-placements. At all times, OD should be proactive and reality-seeking in order to keep human energy strategically focused and to help people bring their values, needs, and objectives into focus. Put another way, if OD is a good thing in good times, it should also be a good thing in bad times.[55]

OD will continue in the future to affect notions of employee mental health and well-being and beliefs about a compatible managerial style. Now and continuing well into the future we should expect to see people rejecting work cultures that treat human resources as passive entities to select, direct, and evaluate. Individuals want more control over their destinies than did people of past generations and will withdraw from incompatible work cultures.

In the future we will see OD skills that are learned by managers and employees because of OD efforts in work organizations used outside the work setting to help these same people improve other organizations in their communities and even perhaps life in their families. Already many churches in the United States have undertaken OD efforts for not only the clergymen but also for the congregations and parishioners. OD skills can be used in a wide variety of functional associations in the community, which are the mechanisms through which individuals participate in the community, including not only churches but schools, fraternal organizations, social clubs, and the like.

In the future OD will be applied increasingly to labor relations issues, affirmative action programs, and safety and health programs in work organizations. There are many other areas in which OD could be applied, but the rapidity of increasing future applications will depend on the extent to which power models become available and well known. In respect to labor relations, OD has great potential for enabling the parties sitting across the bargaining table to reconsider whether they prefer adversary relationships or may be willing to engage in what Healy has called "creative collective bargaining."[56] Much traditional collective bargaining is a third-rate approach to problem-solving.[57] We are once again seeing through the Jamestown experience and in other localities across the country the reemergence of labor–management relations committees cooperating at the community level.[58] Unfortunately, countering this are individuals such as Myers[59] and Hughes[60] who have apparently been misapplying the term OD and suggesting that OD can be utilized either to keep out or destroy unions. If the full armamentarium of OD is used in labor relations, including the greater use of third-party interpersonal peace-making and process consultation, then we may have a chance to display that contemporary organizational development has a contribution to make to labor and industrial relations that is in no way sinister. I have already suggested how OD can be used for teambuilding in affirmative action and merely suggest here that OD has a place in surmounting the many occupational safety and health problems that must be addressed in order for organizations to be in compliance with the prevailing Federal and state occupational safety and health legislation.

In the future OD will be increasingly viewed as an "effort" and not a "program." It will be aimed at developing an organization's internal resources for effective change in the future. Its thrust will be to draw out and develop the resources of people to solve their own problems at work. It will do this by helping them perceive an increase in the range of behavioral options open to individuals and teams. It will be a truly collaborative process of managing the culture of an organization. It will not be something that is done *to* somebody but instead a transactional process of people working together to improve their mutual effectiveness in attaining their mutual objectives.[61]

Needless to say, as these future trends unfold we will find increasing professionalism in OD. Already there are three well-known organizations active in OD, and each of these is growing. I refer to the National Training Laboratory—Institute for Applied Behavioral Science OD Network, American Society for Training and Development—OD Division, and the Academy of Management—OD Division. As professionalization increases, research will also increase and confirm or refute much OD work that is presently underway. To date OD technology has tended to proliferate much more rapidly than the theory base and there is a lag that needs to be addressed through empirical research.

In order to obtain the kind of research needed to advance the field there is little doubt that new approaches and tools will be needed, as well as careful attention to the phenomena that are being included as "organizational development." Research sites need to be made available so that meaningful studies can be made. This is a particularly important problem in OD because the entity to be studied is not the individual outside of context but the organization in which the individual carries out his work. The *individual* has proven much more accessible for research purposes than the organization in the past; hopefully in the future OD researchers will be given an opportunity to conduct long- and short-range studies of *organizations* which have undertaken OD.

When Is the Team Built?

Teambuilding is broader than action research and inclusive of many widely disparate methods of OD diagnosis and types of intervention designs with which it can be integrated, such as seminar/workshops, the restructuring of organizations, and the like. Therefore, it is not mere rhetoric when closing this book to ask, how do we know when we have arrived at the stage of the built team?

Broadly, the team is always in the process of becoming something other

it is when viewed as a snapshot at one point in time. At our
.age of conceptualizing teambuilding in work organizations, it is
think of the built team as encompassing any group of individuals
social–emotional bonds have been tightened and whose technical or
skills have been sharpened in order to fulfill individual and organiza-
. purposes.[62] Yet there are some additional relevant criteria for a built
team that are more specific and closely intertwined.

One key criterion is the degree of the teambuilding group's process
awareness. A thorough understanding of this interpersonal problem-solving
process among team members is crucial to the building of a viable team.

Second are adequate communications because without them teambuilding could never begin. Although communication is sometimes used as a
broad vague term in applied behavioral science, it can be understood more
narrowly as the means (that is the verbal and nonverbal symbolism) whereby
one's beliefs and values can be meaningfully shared with other group members.[63] Communicative interaction between people permits the development
of group norms. These norms and the values associated with them will
influence how the group handles problems confronting it in the future.
Communication needs to be adequate for administration, in turn, to be
adequate.[64]

Third, group trust is built through the character of interpersonal communications. The more open the levels of communication are, the more trust
there will be among the members. Mistrust between individuals inhibits—
indeed destroys—team effort.

Fourth, the utilization of the resources of people within the group is
improved through both trust and communications. Obviously, if interpersonal communication channels are closed, resource knowledge is low and
inadequate. Constructive feedback will, as we have seen, aid in the clarification of intragroup communications. To be sure, the feedback can cause some
stress for participants, but if it is given in a caring mode it will ultimately be
of benefit to the group over time and improve its functioning.

Fifth, the member of the team with the highest organizational status (that
is, the formal leader) has an important part to play in a successful teambuilding effort.[65] He is responsible for modeling the behavior he wishes to
see displayed by the other team members. When the outside or inside consultant feels it is the appropriate time and situation, he should turn over the
full responsibility for the team's continuation to the leader. Then the leader
or top manager should be able to work with the team so that it can carry out
the problem-solving process on its own. The team under the leader's guidance will now move into a more mature stage in the life cycle and further the
dynamic emergent state of "becoming" discussed above.[66]

Finally, it can be said that a team is built when it can as a group analyze
and understand how it is currently functioning and—most importantly—
when it is willing to reevaluate continually those complex relationships
within the group so that the method will become a permanent process. Perhaps

the real proof of successful teambuilding is seen in how effectively and efficiently the group will handle its task problems. Through the improved teambuilding process, the members should have learned where various resources can be found. With this insight, expert authoritative knowledge can be tapped to analyze the problem or situation initially and give direction to its solution. When there is this type of group effort, there will be more commitment to group problem-solving, together with an obvious caring about the group's welfare, as well as extra effort demonstrated by the members to keep the group a productive and viable team.

Clearly, this examination of the concepts and criteria for teambuilding has shown that there is no one quick, pat characterization that will pinpoint exactly when a team has been built. The critical concerns are the team's development of an interpersonal process awareness and the team's ability to manage its own destiny within the larger organization. Put another way, the total team concept is based upon a continuous problem-solving effort. Therefore, the specific point in time that the team is built is not significant. Rather, what is important is how the group learns to work processually, thus determining how successfully the group will function as a cohesive team as long as it exists with a set of organizational tasks.

Organizational development holds great promise for improving life in work organizations. In turn, teambuilding seems to be the way that management and coordination within large-scale organizations can be improved while soliciting the collaborative efforts and providing the satisfactions human beings crave in committing their energies to cooperative enterprises. Organizational development through teambuilding deserves a fair trial and should be given it in the years ahead, beginning right now in the 1980s.

Notes

1. Warren G. Bennis and Edgar H. Schein, *Personal and Organizational Change Through Group Methods: The Laboratory Approach,* Wiley, New York, 1965, pp. 275–276.

2. Walter R. Mahler, *Diagnostic Studies,* Addison–Wesley, Reading, MA, 1974, pp. 1–15.

3. Edward E. Lawler, III, *Pay and Organizational Effectiveness: A Psychological View,* McGraw–Hill, New York, 1971.

4. The teambuilding seminar/workshop model discussed in this book has been evaluated numerous times. A retrospective experiential evaluation is provided in Thomas H. Patten, Jr. and Lester E. Dorey, "Long-Range Results of a Teambuilding Organizational Development Effort," *Personnel Management Review,* Vol. 6, No. 1, January–February 1977, pp. 31–50. The cognitive learning has been assessed in an imaginative study using metric multidimensional scaling by Gregory

Dela Cruz, *Organizational Socialization, Management Training and Development, and the Measurement of Change: An Inquiry* (Doctoral dissertation, Michigan State University, 1979).

5. Henry Mintzberg, *The Nature of Managerial Work,* Harper and Row, New York, 1973, pp. 177–186.

6. Leland P. Bradford et al., "Two Educational Innovations," in Leland P. Bradford et al., Eds., *T-Group Theory and Laboratory Method,* Wiley, New York, 1964, pp. 10–14. See also David A. Kolb and Richard E. Boyatzis, "On the Dynamics of the Helping Relationship," in David A. Kolb et al., Eds., *Organizational Psychology: A Book of Readings,* 3rd ed., Prentice–Hall, Englewood Cliffs, NJ, 1979, pp. 303–319.

7. Joseph Luft, *Group Processes, An Introduction to Group Dynamics,* 2nd ed., Mayfield, Palo Alto, CA, 1970, pp. 12–20.

8. Donald L. Kirkpatrick, "Evaluation of Training," in Robert L. Craig, Ed., *Training and Development Handbook,* 2nd ed., McGraw–Hill, New York, 1976, pp. 18-1–18-27, provides examples of testimonial-type evaluation formats.

9. *Ibid.,* pp. 18-5–18-12. Kirkpatrick discusses four types of appraisal—reaction, learning, behavior, and results, pp. 18-2–18-26.

10. Patten and Dorey, *op. cit.* 40–50.

11. Jay R. Galbraith, *Designing Complex Organizations,* Addison–Wesley, Reading, MA, 1973; Jay R. Galbraith, *Organization Design,* Addison–Wesley, Reading, MA, 1977; and William A. Pasmore and John J. Sherwood, Eds., *Sociotechnical Systems: A Sourcebook,* University Associates, La Jolla, CA, 1978.

12. Wendell L. French, *The Personnel Management Process: Human Resource Administration and Development,* 4th ed., Houghton Mifflin, Boston, 1978, pp. 58–64.

13. Stanley M. Davis and Paul R. Lawrence, *Matrix,* Addison–Wesley, Reading, MA, 1977.

14. Ernest Dale, *Planning and Developing the Company Organization Structure,* American Management Association, New York, 1952, sets forth traditional ideas about line and staff, centralization and decentralization, and the like.

15. Dennis C. King and John C. Glidewell, "Power," in J. William Pfeiffer and John E. Jones, *The 1976 Annual Handbook for Group Facilitators,* University Associates, La Jolla, CA, 1976, pp. 139–142.

16. Edgar F. Huse, *Organization Development and Change,* West, St.

Paul, 1975, pp. 68–76. See also the following: Mark A. Chesler et al., "Power Training: An Alternative Path to Conflict Management," *California Management Review*, Vol. 21, No. 2, Winter 1978, pp. 84–90; and William G. Dyer, "Caring and Power," *California Management Review*, Vol. 21, No. 4, Summer 1979, pp. 84–89.

17. Abraham Zaleznik and Manfred F. R. Kets de Vries, *Power and the Corporate Mind*, Houghton Mifflin, Cambridge, MA, 1975.

18. Barry Oshry, "Power and the Power Lab," in W. Warner Burke, Eds., *Contemporary Organization Development: Conceptual Orientations and Interventions*, NTL Institute for Applied Behavioral Science, 1972, pp. 242–254.

19. Star Power is an unpublished exercise attributed to R. Garry Shirts (c. 1972).

20. Richard E. Byrd created this exercise, which has not been published (c. 1967).

21. Robert Bierstedt, "An Analysis of Social Power," *American Sociological Review*, Vol. 15, No. 6, December 1950, pp. 730–736.

22. Arthur H. Kuriloff, *Organizational Development for Survival*, American Management Association, New York, 1972, pp. 153–267.

23. James W. Walker, Ed., *The Challenge of Human Resource Planning: Selected Readings*, Human Resource Planning Society, New York, 1979.

24. Richard B. Frantzreb, "Replacement Planning: Nuts and Bolts," in Walker, *op. cit.*, pp. 129–132.

25. Walter R. Mahler and William F. Wrightnour, *Executive Continuity: How to Build and Retain an Effective Team*, Dow-Jones Irwin, Homewood, IL, 1973.

26. William E. Bright, "How One Company Manages Its Human Resources," *Harvard Business Review*, Vol. 54, No. 1, January–February 1976, pp. 81–93.

27. Kuriloff, *op. cit.*, pp. 193–213.

28. William B. Chew and Richard L. Justice, "EEO Modeling for Large, Complex Organizations," *Human Resource Planning*, Vol. 2, No. 2, Spring 1979, pp. 57–70; and Lee Dyer and Elizabeth C. Wesman, "Affirmative Action Planning at AT & T: An Applied Model," *Human Resource Planning*, Vol. 2, No. 2, Spring 1979, pp. 81–90.

29. Howard L. Fromkin and John J. Sherwood, Eds., *Integrating the Organization: A Social Psychological Analysis*, Free Press, New York,

1974; and Howard L. Fromkin and John J. Sherwood, Eds., *Intergroup and Minority Relations: An Experiential Handbook,* University Associates, La Jolla, CA, 1976.

30. Thomas H. Patten, Jr., and Lester E. Dorey, "An Equal Employment Opportunity Sensitivity Workshop," *Training and Development Journal,* Vol. 26, No. 1, January 1972, pp. 42–53.

31. Edgar H. Schein, *Career Dynamics: Matching Individual and Organizational Needs,* Addison–Wesley, Reading, MA, 1978; and Douglas T. Hall, *Careers in Organizations,* Goodyear, Pacific Palisades, 1976. See also the following: Mariann Jelinek, Ed., *Career Management for the Individual and the Organization,* St. Clair Press, Chicago, 1979; and Marilyn A. Morgan, Ed., *Managing Career Development,* Van Nostrand, New York, 1980.

32. Gordon McBeath, *Organization and Manpower Planning,* 2nd ed., Business Books, London, 1969.

33. Marion S. Kellogg, *Career Management,* American Management Association, New York, 1972.

34. James W. Walker, "Personal and Career Development," in Dale Yoder and Herbert G. Heneman, Jr., *ASPA Handbook of Personnel and Industrial Relations, Training and Development,* Bureau of National Affairs, Washington, D.C., Vol. V, pp. 5-57–5-74.

35. Herbert A. Shepard, "Life Planning," in Kenneth D. Benne et al., Eds., *The Laboratory Method of Changing and Learning: Theory and Application,* Science and Behavior Books, Palo Alto, CA, 1975, pp. 240–251.

36. George A. Ford and Gordon L. Lippitt, *Planning Your Future: A Workbook for Personal Goal Setting,* University Associates, La Jolla, CA, 1972.

37. Richard H. Buskirk, *Your Career: How to Plan It, Manage It, Change It,* Cahners, Boston, MA, 1976; Richard N. Bolles, *What Color is Your Parachute?* rev. ed., Ten Speed Press, Berkeley, 1977; Nicholas W. Weiler, *Reality and Career Planning: A Guide for Personal Growth,* Addison–Wesley, Reading, MA, 1977; Janet Hagberg and Richard Leider, *The Inventurers: Excursions in Life and Career Renewal,* Addison–Wesley, Reading, MA, 1978; Arthur G. Kirn and Marie O'Donahue Kirn, *Life Work Planning,* McGraw–Hill, New York, 1978; and Richard N. Bolles, *The Three Boxes of Life and How to Get Out of Them,* Ten Speed Press, Berkeley, 1978.

38. W. Warner Burke, "The Demise of Organization Development,"

Journal of Contemporary Business, Vol. 1, No. 3, Summer 1972, pp. 59–61.

39. Herbert A. Shepard and Sheldon Davis, "Organization Development in Good Times and Bad," *Journal of Contemporary Business,* Vol. 1, No. 3, Summer 1972, pp. 65–78.

40. Wendell L. French and Cecil H. Bell, Jr., *Organization Development: Behavioral Science Interventions for Organization Improvement,* Prentice–Hall, Englewood Cliffs, NJ, 1973, pp. 198–199.

41. *Ibid.,* pp. 192–193.

42. An excellent up-to-date articulation of OD consultation methods and concepts can be found in Gordon L. Lippitt and Ronald Lippitt, *The Consulting Process in Action,* University Associates, La Jolla, CA, 1978.

43. French and Bell, *op. cit.,* pp. 193–194.

44. Gestalt views are explained in the following: H. B. Karp, "A Gestalt Approach to Collaboration in Organizations," in J. William Pfeiffer and John E. Jones, Eds., *The 1976 Annual Handbook for Group Facilitators,* University Associates, La Jolla, CA, 1976, pp. 203–210; Stanley M. Herman, "A Gestalt Orientation to Organization Development" in W. Warner Burke, Ed., *Contemporary Organization Development: Conceptual Orientations and Interventions,* NTL Institute, Arlington, VA, 1972, pp. 62–89; see also Herman's "The Shadow of Organization Development," in W. Warner Burke, Ed., *Current Issues and Strategies in Organization Development,* Human Sciences Press, New York, 1977, pp. 133–154.

45. Chris Argyris, *Intervention Theory and Method: A Behavioral Science View,* Addison–Wesley, Reading, MA, 1970.

46. French and Bell, *op. cit.,* pp. 112–120, 194.

47. *Ibid.,* pp. 194–195.

48. *Idem,* pp. 195–196.

49. Gordon L. Lippitt, *Organization Renewal,* Prentice–Hall, Englewood Cliffs, NJ, 1969, pp. 163–181.

50. Anthony P. Raia, "Organizational Development—Some Issues and Challenges," *California Management Review,* Vol. 14, No. 4, Summer 1972, pp. 17–18. See also Lyman K. Randall, "Common Questions and Tentative Answers Regarding Organization Development," *California Management Review,* Vol. 13, No. 3, Spring 1971, pp. 45–52.

51. Thomas H. Patten, Jr., "Time for Organizational Development?" *Personnel,* Vol. 54, No. 2, March–April, 1977, pp. 26–33.

52. Lippitt, *op. cit.,* pp. 123–141.

53. Shepard and Davis, *op. cit.,* pp. 66–69.

54. This should include retirement as well as human resource planning generally. See Leland P. Bradford, "Retirement and Organization Development," in W. Warner Burke, Ed., *The Cutting Edge: Current Theory and Practice in Organization Development,* University Associates, La Jolla, CA, 1978, pp. 278–292, and Thomas H. Patten, Jr., "Human Resource Planning and Organizational Development, *Human Resource Planning,* Vol. 1, No. 3, Summer 1978, pp. 179–184.

55. Shepard and Davis, *op. cit.,* pp. 69–73. See also George F. J. Lehner, "From Job Loss to Career Innovation," in W. Warner Burke, Ed., *Contemporary Organization Development: Conceptual Orientations and Interventions, op. cit.,* pp. 213–223.

56. James J. Healey, Ed., *Creative Collective Bargaining: Meeting Today's Challenges in Labor-Management Relations,* Prentice–Hall, Englewood Cliffs, NJ, 1965, pp. 106–288.

57. Thomas H. Patten, Jr., "Collective Bargaining and Consensus: The Potential of a Laboratory Training Input," *Management of Personnel Quarterly,* Vol. 16, No. 1, Spring 1970, pp. 29–37.

58. William L. Batt, Jr., and Edgar Weinberg, "Labor-Management Cooperation Today," *Harvard Business Review,* Vol. 56, No. 1, January–February, 1978, pp. 96–104, covers the Jamestown and other recent Quality of Working Life experiences and studies.

59. M. Scott Myers, "Overcoming Union Opposition to Job Enrichment," *Harvard Business Review,* Vol. 49, No. 3, May–June, 1971, pp. 37–49. See also Myers' two books: *Managing Without Unions,* Addison–Wesley, Reading, MA, 1976, pp. 23–144; and *Managing with Unions,* Addison–Wesley, Reading, MA, 1978, pp. 79–146.

60. Charles L. Hughes, *Making Unions Unnecessary,* Executive Enterprises, New York, 1976. The other side of union-busting is analyzed in William E. Fulmer, "When Employees Want to Oust Their Union," *Harvard Business Review,* Vol. 56, No. 2, March–April 1978, pp. 163–171.

61. French and Bell, *op. cit.,* p. 200.

62. Thomas H. Patten, Jr., "Team Building. Part 2. Conducting the Intervention," *Personnel,* Vol. 56, No. 2, March–April 1979, p. 68.

63. Jay Hall, "Communication Revisited," *California Management Review*, Vol. 15, No. 3, Spring 1973, pp. 56–67.

64. Elton Mayo, *The Human Problems of an Industrial Civilization*, Viking Press, New York, 1960, pp. 161–180.

65. William W. George, "Task Teams for Rapid Growth," *Harvard Business Review*, Vol. 55, No. 2, March–April 1977, pp. 71–80.

66. Paul Hersey and Kenneth H. Blanchard, *Management of Organizational Behavior: Utilizing Human Resources*, 3rd ed., Prentice–Hall, Englewood Cliffs, NJ, 1977, pp. 159–324, expound on group life-cycle theory.

BIBLIOGRAPHY

Books

Adams, John D., Ed., *Theory and Method in Organization Development: An Evolutionary Process*. Arlington: NTL Institute for Applied Behavioral Science, 1974. 391 pp.

Argyris, Chris, *Behind the Front Page: Organizational Self-Renewal in a Metropolitan Newspaper*. San Francisco: Jossey-Bass, 1974. 305 pp.

Argyris, Chris, *Intervention Theory and Method: A Behavioral Science View*. Reading: Addison–Wesley, 1970. 374 pp.

Argyris, Chris, *Management and Organizational Development: The Path from XA to YB*. New York: McGraw–Hill, 1971. 211 pp.

Argyris, Chris and Donald Schon, *Theory in Practice: Increasing Professional Effectiveness*. San Francisco: Jossey-Bass, 1975. 224 pp.

Bales, Robert Freed, *Interaction Process Analysis: A Method for the Study of Small Groups*. Cambridge: Addison-Wesley, 1950. 203 pp.

Bandura, Albert, *Principles of Behavior Modification*. New York: Holt, Rinehart and Winston, 1969. 677 pp.

Baritz, Loren, *The Servants of Power*. Middletown: Wesleyan University Press, 1960. 273 pp.

Barnes, Harry Elmer, ed., *An Introduction to the History of Sociology*. Chicago: University of Chicago Press, 1948. 960 pp.

Beck, Arthur C., Jr. and Ellis D. Hillmar, eds., *A Practical Approach to Organization Development Through MBO—Selected Readings*. Reading: Addison-Wesley, 1972. 256 pp.

Beck, Arthur C., Jr. and Ellis D. Hillmar, *Making MBO/R Work*. Reading: Addison-Wesley, 1976. 225 pp.

Beckhard, Richard, *Organization Development: Strategies and Models*. Reading: Addison-Wesley, 1969. 119 pp.

Beckhard, Richard and Reuben T. Harris, *Organizational Transition: Managing Complex Change*. Reading: Addison-Wesley, 1977, 110 pp.

Belcher, David W., *Compensation Administration*. Englewood Cliffs: Prentice-Hall, 1974. 606 pp.

Benne, Kenneth D., *et al.*, eds., *The Laboratory Method of Changing and Learning: Theory and Application*. Palo Alto: Science and Behavior Books, 1975. 589 pp.

Bennett, Dudley, *TA and the Manager*. New York: AMACOM, 1976. 243 pp.

Bennie, Warren G. and Edgar H. Schein, *Personal and Organizational Change Through Group Methods: The Laboratory Approach*. New York: Wiley, 1965. 376 pp.

Berg, J. Gary, *Managing Compensation*. New York: AMACOM, 1976. 250 pp.

Berne, Eric, *Games People Play*. New York: Ballantine Books, 1964. 192 pp.

Blake, Robert R. and Jane Srygley Mouton, *Corporate Excellence Through Grid Organization Development*. Houston: Gulf, 1968. 374 pp.

Blake, Robert R. and Jane Srygley Mouton, *Diary of an OD Man*, Houston: Gulf, 1976. 354 pp.

Blake, Robert R. and Jane Srygley Mouton, *The New Managerial Grid*, Houston: Gulf, 1979. 309 pp.

Bolles, Richard N., *The Three Boxes of Life and How to Get Out of Them*. Berkeley: Ten Speed Press, 1978. 466 pp.

Bolles, Richard N., *What Color is Your Parachute?* (rev. ed.), Berkeley: Ten Speed Press, 1977. 233 pp.

Bowers, David G., *Systems of Organization*. Ann Arbor: University of Michigan Press, 1976. 166 pp.

Bowers, David and Jerome L. Franklin, *Survey-Guided Development: Data Based Organizational Change*. Ann Arbor: Institute for Social Research, University of Michigan, 1976. 166 pp.

Bradford, Leland P. *et al.*, eds., *T-Group Theory and Laboratory Method*. New York: Wiley, 1964. 498 pp.

Bry, Adelaide, *60 Hours That Transform Your Life, EST, Erhard Seminar Training*. New York: Avon, 1976. 233 pp.

Burke, W. Warner, ed., *Contemporary Organization Development: Conceptual Orientations and Interventions*. Arlington: NTL Institute for Applied Behavioral Science, 1972. 276 pp.

Burke, W. Warner, ed., *The Cutting Edge: Current Theory and Practice in Organization Development*. La Jolla: University Associates, 1978. 302 pp.

Burke, W. Warner, ed., *Current Issues and Strategies in Organization Development*. New York: Human Sciences Press, 1977. 448 pp.

Buskirk, Richard H., *Your Career: How to Plan It, Manage It, Change It*. Boston: Cahners, 1976. 202 pp.

Byrd, Richard E., *A Guide To Personal Risk Taking*. New York: AMACOM, 1974. 248 pp.

Carroll, Stephen J., Jr. and Henry L. Tosi, Jr., *Management by Objectives: Applications and Research*. New York: Macmillan, 1973. 216 pp.

Cheek, Logan M., *Zero-Based Budgeting Comes of Age*. New York: AMACOM, 1978. 314 pp.

Cheeks, James E., *How To Compensate Executives*. Homewood: Dow Jones/Irwin, 1974. 288 pp.

Collins, Orvis F. *et al.*, *The Enterprising Man*. East Lansing: Michigan State University Press, 1964. 254 pp.

Cooper, C. L. and I. L. Mangham, *T-Groups: A Survey of Research*. New York: Wiley, 1971. 283 pp.

Cooper, Joseph D., *How to Get More Done in Less Time*. Garden City: Doubleday, 1962. 346 pp.

Craig, Robert L., ed., *Training and Development Handbook*. New York: McGraw-Hill, 1976. Various paging.

Crystal, Graef S., *Executive Compensation: Money, Motivation, Imagination*. AMACOM, 1978. 206 pp.

Cummings, Larry L. and Donald P. Schwab, *Performance in Organizations*. Glenview: Scott Foresman, 1973. 176 pp.

Cummings, Thomas G. and Edmond S. Molloy, *Improving Productivity and the Quality of Work Life*. New York: Praeger, 1977. 305 pp.

Dale, Ernest, *Planning and Developing the Company Organization Structure*. New York: American Management Association, 1952. 336 pp.

Davidson, James, *Effective Time Management: A Practical Workbook*. New York: Human Sciences Press, 1978. 104 pp.

Davis, Louis B. and Albert B. Chernes, eds., *The Quality of Work Life*. New York: Free Press, 1975. 2 vols.

Davis, Stanley M. and Paul R. Lawrence, *Matrix*. Reading: Addison-Wesley, 1977. 235 pp.

Deci, Edward L., *Intrinsic Motivation*. New York: Plenum, 1975. 324 pp.

Doyle, Michael and David Straus, *How to Make Meetings Work: The New Interaction Method*. Chicago: Playboy Press, 1977. 301 pp.

Drucker, Peter F., *Concept of the Corporation* (rev. ed.). New York: New American Library, 1972. 259 pp.

Drucker, Peter F., *Management: Tasks, Responsibilities, Duties*. New York: Harper and Row, 1973. 839 pp.

Drucker, Peter F., *The Effective Executive*. New York: Harper and Row, 1967. 178 pp.

Drucker, Peter F., *The Practice of Management*. New York: Harper, 1954. 404 pp.

Drucker, Peter F., *The Unseen Revolution*. New York: Harper and Row, 1976. 214 pp.

Dubin, Robert, ed., *Handbook of Work, Organization, and Society*. Chicago: Rand McNally, 1976. 1068 pp.

Dunlop, John T., *Industrial Relations Systems*. New York: Holt, 1958. 399 pp.

Dunnette, Marvin D., ed., *Handbook of Industrial and Organizational Psychology*. Chicago: Rand McNally, 1976. 1740 pp.

Dyer, William G., *Team Building: Issues and Alternatives*. Reading: Addison-Wesley, 1977. 139 pp.

Dyer, William G., ed., *Modern Theory and Method in Group Training*. New York: Van Nostrand Reinhold, 1972. 251 pp.

Eisenhower, Dwight D., *Crusade in Europe*. Garden City: Doubleday, 1949. 559 pp.

Ends, Earl J. and Curtis W. Page, *Organizational Team Building*. Cambridge: Winthrop, 1977. 206 pp.

Fagan, Joel and Irma Lee Shepherd, eds., *Gestalt Therapy Now*. New York: Harper Colophon Books, 1970. 328 pp.

Farace, Richard V. *et al., Communicating and Organizing*. Reading: Addison-Wesley, 1977. 281 pp.

Fensterheim, Herbert and Jean Baer, *Don't Say Yes When You Want To Say No*. New York: Dell, 1975. 304 pp.

Ferner, Jack D., *Successful Time Management*. New York: Wiley, 1980. 287 pp.

Filley, Alan C., *Interpersonal Conflict Resolution*. Glenview: Scott Foresman, 1975. 180 pp.

Ford, George A. and Gordon L. Lippitt, *Planning Your Future: A Workbook for Personal Goal Setting*. La Jolla, University Associates, 1972. 49 pp.

Fordyce, Jack K. and Raymond Weil, *Managing With People: A Manager's Handbook of Organization Development Methods*. Reading: Addison-Wesley, 1971. 187 pp.

Fox, Alan, *Beyond Contract: Work, Power, and Trust Relations*. London: Faber and Faber, 1974. 408 pp.

Francis, Dave and Mike Woodcock, *People at Work: A Practical Guide to Organizational Change*. La Jolla: University Associates, 1975. 198 pp.

French, Wendell L., *The Personnel Management Process: Human Resource Administration and Development*, 4th ed. Boston: Houghton Mifflin, 1978. 610 pp.

French, Wendell L. *et al.*, eds., *Organization Development: Theory, Practice, and Research*. Dallas: Business Publications, 1978. 526 pp.

French, Wendell L. and Cecil H. Bell, Jr., *Organization Development: Behavioral Science Interventions for Organization Improvement*. Englewood Cliffs: Prentice-Hall, 1973. 207 pp.

Friedman, Meyer and Ray H. Roseman, *Type A Behavior and Your Heart*. Greenwich: Fawcett, 1974. 319 pp.

Fromkin, Howard L. and John J. Sherwood, eds., *Integrating the Organization: A Social Psychological Analysis*. New York: Free Press, 1974. 370 pp.

Fromkin, Howard L. and John J. Sherwood, eds., *Intergroup and Minority Relations: An Experiential Handbook*. La Jolla: University Associates, 1976. 181 pp.

Frost, Carl F. *et al.*, *The Scanlon Plan for Organization Development: Identity, Participation, and Equity*. East Lansing: Michigan State University Press, 1974. 197 pp.

Galbraith, Jay R., *Organization Design*. Reading: Addison-Wesley, 1977. 426 pp.

Gellerman, Saul W., *Management by Motivation*. New York: American Management Association, 1968. 286 pp.

Gellerman, Saul W., *Motivation and Productivity*. New York: American Management Association, 1963. 304 pp.

Gibb, Jack R., ed., *Trust: A New View of Personal and Organizational Development*. Los Angeles: Guild of Tutors Press, 1978. 320 pp.

Glueck, William F., *Personnel: A Diagnostic Approach*. Dallas: Business Publications, 1974. 712 pp.

Gyllenhammar, Pehr G., *People At Work*. Reading: Addison-Wesley, 1977. 164 pp.

Hagberg, Janet and Richard Leider, *The Inventurers: Excursions in Life and Career Renewal*. Reading: Addison-Wesley, 1978. 178 pp.

Hall, Douglas T., *Careers in Organizations*. Pacific Palisades: Goodyear, 1976. 236 pp.

Harbison, Frederick H. and John R. Coleman, *Goals and Strategy in Collective Bargaining*. New York: Harper, 1951. 172 pp.

Harbison, Frederick H. and Robert Dubin, *Patterns of Union-Management Relations*. Chicago: Science Research Associates, 1947. 229 pp.

Harris, Thomas, *I'M OK—You're OK: A Practical Guide to Transactional Analysis*. New York: Harper and Row, 1967. 278 pp.

Harvey, Donald F. and Donald R. Brown, *An Experiential Approach to Organizational Development*. Englewood Cliffs: Prentice-Hall, 1976. 350 pp.

Hennig, Margaret and Anne Jardim, *The Managerial Woman*. Garden City: Doubleday, 1977. 221 pp.

Herbst, P. G., *Socio-Technical Design: Strategies in Multi-Disciplinary Research*. London: Tavistock, 1974. 242 pp.

Hersey, Paul and Kenneth J. Blanchard, *Management of Organizational Behavior: Utilizing Human Resources* (3rd ed.). Englewood Cliffs: Prentice-Hall, 1977. 360 pp.

Herzberg, Frederick, *Work and the Nature of Man*. Cleveland: World, 1966. 203 pp.

Heron, Alexander, *Why Men Work*. Stanford: Stanford University Press, 1948. 197 pp.

Hills, Christopher and Robert B. Stone, *Conduct Your Own Awareness Sessions*. New York: New American Library, 1970. 240 pp.

Howe, Roger J. and William I. Gordon, *Team Dynamics in Developing Organizations*. Dubuque: Kendall/Hunt, 1977. 205 pp.

Hughes, Charles L., *Making Unions Unnecessary*. New York: Executive Enterprises, 1976. 115 pp.

Humble, John W., ed., *Management by Objectives in Action*. New York: McGraw-Hill, 1970. 293 pp.

Huse, Edgar F., *Organizational Development and Change*. St. Paul: West, 1975. 448 pp.

James, Muriel, *The OK Boss*. Reading: Addison-Wesley, 1975. 153 pp.

Janov, Arthur, *The Primal Scream*. New York: Dell, 1970. 480 pp.

Jelinek, Marianne, ed., *Career Management for the Individual and the Organization*. Chicago: St. Clair Press, 1979. 393 pp.

Jenkins, David, *Job Power: Blue and White Collar Democracy*. Garden City: Doubleday, 1973. 375 pp.

Jongeward, Dorothy and Dru Scott, *Affirmative Action for Women: A Practical Guide*. Reading: Addison-Wesley, 1973. 334 pp.

Jongeward, Dorothy, *et al.*, *Everybody Wins: Transactional Analysis Applied to Organizations*. Reading: Addison-Wesley, 1973. 325 pp.

Juran, Joseph M., *Managerial Breakthrough*. New York: McGraw-Hill, 1964. 396 pp.

Kellogg, Marion S., *Career Management*. New York: American Management Association, 1972. 200 pp.

Kellogg, Marion S., *What To Do About Performance Appraisal* (rev. ed.). New York: AMACOM, 1975. 209 pp.

Kelly, G. A., *Theory of Personality: The Psychology of Personal Constructs*. New York: Norton, 1955. 2 vol., 1218 pp.

Kepner, Charles H. and Benjamin B. Tregoe, *The Rational Manager*. New York: McGraw-Hill, 1965. 275 pp.

Kirkpatrick, Donald L., *A Practical Guide for Supervisory Training and Development*. Reading: Addison-Wesley, 1971. 182 pp.

Kirn, Arthur G. and Marie O'Donahue Kirn, *Life Work Planning* (4th ed.). New York: McGraw-Hill, 1978. 205 pp.

Klein, Lisl, *New Forms of Work Organization*, Cambridge: Cambridge University Press, 1976. 106 pp.

Kobayashi, Shigeru, *Creative Management*. New York: American Management Association, 1971. 259 pp.

Kolb, David A. *et al.*, eds., *Organizational Psychology: A Book of Readings* (3rd ed.). Englewood Cliffs: Prentice-Hall, 1979. 563 pp.

Kolb, David A. *et al., Organizational Psychology: An Experiential Approach* (3rd ed.). Englewood Cliffs: Prentice-Hall, 1979. 496 pp.

Koontz, Harold, *Appraising Managers as Managers.* New York: McGraw-Hill, 1971. 239 pp.

Koontz, Harold and Cyril O'Donnell, *Principles of Management: An Analysis of Managerial Functions.* New York: McGraw-Hill, 1972. 748 pp.

Kornhauser, Arthur *et al.,* eds., *Industrial Conflict.* New York: McGraw-Hill, 1954. 551 pp.

Kuriloff, Arthur H., *Organizational Development for Survival.* New York: American Management Association, 1972. 275 pp.

Landsberger, Henry, *Hawthorne Revisited.* Ithaca: Cornell University Press, 1958. 119 pp.

Lawler, Edward E. III, *Motivation in Work Organizations.* Monterey: Brooks-Cole, 1973. 224 pp.

Lawler, Edward E. III, *Pay and Organizational Effectiveness: A Psychological View.* New York: McGraw-Hill, 1971. 318 pp.

Lawler, Edward E. III and John Grant Rhode, *Information and Control in Organizations.* Santa Monica: Goodyear, 1976. 217 pp.

Lawrence, Paul R. and Jay W. Lorsch, *Developing Organizations: Diagnosis and Action.* Reading: Addison-Wesley, 1969. 101 pp.

Levinson, Harry, *Organizational Diagnosis.* Cambridge: Harvard University Press, 1972. 557 pp.

Levinson, Harry, *Psychological Man.* Cambridge: Levinson Institute, 1976. 147 pp.

Levinson, Harry, *The Exceptional Executive: A Psychological Conception.* Cambridge: Harvard University Press, 1968. 297 pp.

Levinson, Harry, *The Great Jackass Fallacy.* Boston: Division of Research, Graduate School of Business Administration, Harvard University, 1973. 178 pp.

Levinson, Harry *et al., Men, Management and Mental Health,* Cambridge: Harvard University Press, 1963. 203 pp.

Lewin, Kurt, *Field Theory in Social Science.* New York: Harper and Row, 1951. 346 pp.

Lewin, Kurt, *Resolving Social Conflicts.* New York: Harper and Row, 1948. 230 pp.

Lewis, Howard R. and Harold S. Streitfeld, *Growth Games.* New York: Bantam Books, 1972. 301 pp.

Likert, Rensis, *New Patterns of Management.* New York: McGraw-Hill. 279 pp.

Likert, Rensis, *The Human Organization: Its Management and Value.* New York: McGraw-Hill, 1967. 258 pp.

Likert, Rensis and Jane Gibson Likert, *New Ways of Managing Conflict.* New York: McGraw-Hill, 1976. 375 pp.

Lippitt, Gordon L., *Organization Renewal.* Englewood Cliffs: Prentice-Hall, 1969. 321 pp.

Lippitt, Gordon L., *Visualizing Change: Model building and the Change Process.* La Jolla: University Associates, 1976. 370 pp.

Lippitt, Gordon L. *et al.,* eds., *Optimizing Human Resources: Readings in Individual and Organization Development.* Reading: Addison-Wesley, 1971. 425 pp.

Lippitt, Gordon L. and Ronald Lippitt, *The Consulting Process in Action.* La Jolla: University Associates, 1978. 130 pp.

Lippitt, Ronald *et al., The Dynamics of Planned Change.* New York: Harcourt, Brace, and World, 1958. 298 pp.

Livy, Bryan L., *Job Evaluation: A Critical Review*. New York: Wiley, 1975. 192 pp.

Lopez, Felix M., *Evaluating Employee Performance*. Chicago: Public Personnel Association, 1968. 306 pp.

Lorsch, Jay W. and John J. Morse, *Organizations and Their Members*. New York: Harper and Row, 1974. 177 pp.

Luft, Joseph, *Group Processes, An Introduction to Group Dynamics* (2nd ed.). Palo Alto: Mayfield, 1970. 122 pp.

MacKenzie, R. Alec, *The Time Trap: Managing Your Way Out*. New York: AMACOM, 1972. 195 pp.

McBeath, Gordon, *Organization and Manpower Planning* (2nd ed.). London: Business Books, 1969. 262 pp.

McCay, James T., *Management of Time*. Englewood Cliffs: Prentice-Hall, 1959. 178 pp.

McClelland, David C., *The Achieving Society*. Princeton: Van Nostrand, 1961. 512 pp.

McClelland, David C., *Power, The Inner Experience*. New York: Halstead, 1975. 427 pp.

McClelland, David C. and David G. Winter, *Motivating Economic Achievement*. New York: Free Press, 1969. 409 pp.

McConkey, Dale D., *How to Manage by Results* (3rd ed.). New York: AMACOM, 1976. 257 pp.

McConkey, Dale D., *MBO for Nonprofit Organizations*. New York: AMACOM, 1975. 223 pp.

McConkey, Dale D., *No-Nonsense Delegation*. New York: AMACOM, 1974. 228 pp.

McGregor, Douglas, *Leadership and Motivation*. Cambridge: MIT Press, 1966. 286 pp.

McGregor, Douglas, *The Human Side of Enterprise*. New York: McGraw-Hill, 1960. 246 pp.

McGregor, Douglas, *The Professional Manager*. New York: McGraw-Hill, 1967, 202 pp.

McGill, Michael E., *Organization Development for Operating Managers*. New York: AMACOM, 1977. 177 pp.

McLaughlin, David J., *The Executive Money Map*. New York: McGraw-Hill, 1975. 252 pp.

Mahler, Walter R., *Diagnostic Studies*. Reading: Addison-Wesley, 1974. 214 pp.

Mahler, Walter R. and William F. Wrightnour, *Executive Continuity: How to Build and Retain an Effective Team*. Homewood: Dow-Jones Irwin, 1973. 254 pp.

Mali, Paul, *Improving Total Productivity: MBO Strategies for Business, Government and Not-for-Profit Organizations*. New York: Wiley, 1978. 409 pp.

Mali, Paul, *Managing by Objectives*. New York: Wiley, 1972. 314 pp.

Maltz, Maxwell, *Psycho-Cybernetics*. New York: Pocket Books, 1960. 256 pp.

March, James G. and Herbert A. Simon, *Organizations*. New York: Wiley, 1959. 262 pp.

Margulies, Newton and John Wallace, *Organizational Change: Techniques and Applications*. Glenview: Scott, Foresman, 1973. 161 pp.

Marrow, Alfred J., *The Failure of Success*. New York: AMACOM, 1972. 339 pp.

Marrow, Alfred J., *Behind the Executive Mask*. New York: American Management Association, 1964. 143 pp.

Marrow, Alfred J., *The Practical Theorist: The Life and Work of Kurt Lewin*. New York: Columbia University Teachers College Press, 1969. 290 pp.

Marshall, Don R., *Successful Techniques for Solving Employee Compensation Problems*. New York: Wiley, 1978. 198 pp.

Maslow, Abraham H., *Eupsychian Management*. Homewood: Irwin/Dorsey, 1965. 277 pp.

Maslow, Abraham H., *Motivation and Personality*. New York: Harper, 1954, 411 pp.

Maslow, Abraham, H., *The Farther Reaches of Human Nature*. New York: 1971. 423 pp.

Maslow, Abraham H., *Toward a Psychology of Being*. New York: Van Nostrand Reinhold, 1968. 240 pp.

Mayo, Elton, *The Human Problems of an Industrial Civilization*. New York: Viking, 1960. 187 pp.

Merry, Uri, and Melvin E. Alleshand, *Developing Teams and Organizations, A Practical Handbook for Managers and Consultants*. Reading: Addison-Wesley, 1977. 422 pp.

Merton, Robert K. *et al.*, eds., *Reader in Bureaucracy*. Glencoe: Free Press, 1952. 464 pp.

Migliore, R. Henry, *MBO: Blue Collar to Executive*. Washington: Bureau of National Affairs, 1977. 178 pp.

Miles, Raymond E., *Theories of Management*. New York: McGraw-Hill, 1975. 240 pp.

Mintzberg, Henry, *The Nature of Managerial Work*. New York: Harper and Row, 1973. 298 pp.

Mirvis, Philip H. and David N. Berg, eds., *Failures in Organizational Development and Change*. New York: Wiley, 1977. 346 pp.

Moore, Brian E. and Timothy L. Ross, *The Scanlon Way to Improved Productivity*. New York: Wiley, 1978. 228 pp.

Morgan, Marilyn A., ed., *Managing Career Development*. New York: Van Nostrand, 1980. 285 pp.

Morris, William C. and Marshall Sashkin, *Organization Behavior in Action: Skill Building Experiences*. St. Paul: West, 1976. 292 pp.

Morrisey, George L., *Management by Objectives and Results*. Reading: Addison-Wesley, 1970. 164 pp.

Morrisey, George L., *Management by Objectives and Results in the Public Sector*. Reading: Addison-Wesley, 1976. 278 pp.

Myers, M. Scott, *Every Employee A Manager*. New York: McGraw-Hill, 1970. 233 pp.

Myers, M. Scott, *Managing With Unions*. Reading: Addison-Wesley, 1978. 168 pp.

Myers, M. Scott, *Managing Without Unions*. Reading: Addison-Wesley, 1976. 176 pp.

Nadler, David A., *Feedback and Organization Development: Using Data-Based Methods*. Reading: Addison-Wesley, 1977. 203 pp.

Nash, Allan N. and Stephen J. Carroll, Jr., *The Management of Compensation*. Monterey: Brooks/Cole, 1975. 304 pp.

Newburger, Howard M. and Marjorie Lee, *Winners and Losers*. New York: New American Library, 1974. 206 pp.

Oates, Wayne E., *Confessions of a Workaholic*. New York: World, 1971. 112 pp.

O'Banion, Terry and April O'Connell, *The Shared Journey: An Introduction to Encounter*. Englewood Cliffs: Prentice-Hall, 1970. 203 pp.

Odiorne, George, *MBO II: A System of Managerial Leadership for the 80s*. Belmont: Fearon Pitman, 1979. 360 pp.

Odiorne, George S., *Management by Objectives: A System of Managerial Leadership*. New York: Pitman, 1965. 204 pp.

Partin, J. Jennings, ed., *Current Perspectives in Organization Development*. Reading: Addison-Wesley, 1973. 279 pp.

Pasmore, William A. and John J. Sherwood, eds., *Sociotechnical Systems: A Sourcebook*. La Jolla: University Associates, 1978. 365 pp.

Patten, Thomas H., Jr., *Manpower Planning and the Development of Human Resources*. New York: Wiley, 1971. 737 pp.

Patten, Thomas H., Jr., *Pay: Employee Compensation and Incentive Plans*. New York: Free Press, 1977. 607 pp.

Patten, Thomas H., Jr., *The Foreman: Forgotten Man of Management*. New York: American Management Association, 1968. 191 pp.

Patten, Thomas H., Jr., ed., *OD: Emerging Dimensions and Concepts*. Madison: American Society for Training and Development, 1973. 112 pp.

Pearse, Robert F. and B. Purdy Pelzer, *Self-Directed Change for the Mid-Career Manager*. New York: AMACOM, 1975. 187 pp.

Peterson, Severin, *A Catalog of the Ways People Grow*. New York: Ballantine Books, 1971. 368 pp.

Plovnick, Mark S., *Task-Oriented Team Development*. New York: McGraw-Hill, 1978. 385 pp.

Poteet, James A., *Behavior Modification*. Minneapolis: Burgess, 1973. 104 pp.

Ramsden, Pamela, *Top Team Planning*. New York: Wiley, 1973. 262 pp.

Ray, George E. and William N. Bret, Jr., *Financial Incentives for Corporate Executives: Wealth-Building Programs and Techniques*. Englewood Cliffs: Prentice-Hall, 1976. 212 pp.

Reddin, W. J., *Effective Management by Objectives: The 3-D Method of MBO*. New York: McGraw-Hill, 1971. 224 pp.

Reddin, W. J., *Managerial Effectiveness*. New York: McGraw-Hill, 1970. 352 pp.

Richardson, Reed C., *Collective Bargaining by Objectives: A Positive Approach*. Englewood Cliffs: Prentice-Hall, 1977. 386 pp.

Robbins, Stephen P., *Managing Organizational Conflict*. Englewood Cliffs: Prentice-Hall, 1974. 156 pp.

Rock, Milton L., ed., *Handbook of Wage and Salary Administration*. New York: McGraw-Hill, 1972.

Sax, Saville and Sandra Hollander, *Reality Games*. New York: Popular Library, 1972. 352 pp.

Schachter, Stanley, *The Psychology of Affiliation: Experimental Studies of the Sources of Gregariousness*. Stanford: Stanford University Press, 1959. 141 pp.

Schein, Edgar H., *Career Dynamics: Matching Individual and Organizational Needs*. Reading: Addison-Wesley, 1978. 276 pp.

Schleh, Edward C., *Management by Results: The Dynamics of Profitable Management*. New York: McGraw-Hill, 1961. 266 pp.

Schleh, Edward C., *The Management Tactician: Executive Tactics for Getting Results*. New York: McGraw-Hill, 1974. 190 pp.

Schutz, William B., *Here Comes Everybody*. New York: Harper and Row, 1972. 362 pp.

Schutz, William B., *Profound Simplicity*. New York: Bantam Books, 1979. 218 pp.

Schutz, William C., *The Interpersonal Underworld*. Palo Alto: Consulting Psychologists Press, 1966. 242 pp.

Selekman, B. M. *et al.*, *Problems in Labor Relations* (3rd ed.). New York: McGraw-Hill, 1964. 754 pp.

Selye, Hans, *Stress Without Distress*. New York: New American Library, 1975. 193 pp.

Serrin, William, *The Company and The Union: The "Civilized Relationship: of the General Motors Corporation and the United Automobile Workers."* New York: Knopf, 1973. 308 pp.

Sheehy, Gail, *Passages: Predictable Crises of Adult Life.* New York: Bantam Books, 1976. 560 pp.

Sibson, Robert E., *Compensation.* New York: AMACOM, 1974. 239 pp.

Sibson, Robert E., *Increasing Employee Productivity.* New York: AMACOM, 1976. 210 pp.

Smith, Manuel J., *When I Say No I Feel Guilty.* New York: Bantam Books, 1975. 324 pp.

Sperry, Len and Lee R. Hess, *Contact Counseling: Techniques for Developing People in Organizations.* Reading: Addison-Wesley, 1974. 281 pp.

Stagner, Ross, *The Psychology of Industrial Conflict.* New York: Wiley, 1956. 550 pp.

Steele, Fritz, *Consulting For Organizational Change.* Amherst: University of Massachusetts Press, 1975. 202 pp.

Steele, Fritz, *The Open Organization: The Impact of Secrecy and Disclosure on People.* Reading: Addison-Wesley, 1975. 204 pp.

Stein, Mark L., *The T Factor.* Chicago: Playboy Press, 1976. 184 pp.

Steinmetz, Lawrence L., *Managing the Marginal and Unsatisfactory Performer.* Reading: Addison-Wesley, 1969. 213 pp.

Steinmetz, Lawrence L., *The Art and Skill of Delegation.* Reading: Addison-Wesley, 1976. 204 pp.

Stevens, John O., *Awareness: Exploring, Experimenting, Experiencing.* New York: Bantam Books, 1973. 309 pp.

Strauss, George *et al.,* eds., *Organizational Behavior, Research and Issues.* Madison: Industrial Relations Research Association, 1974. 236 pp.

Tannenbaum, Robert *et al.,* eds., *Leadership and Organization: A Behavioral Science Approach.* New York: McGraw-Hill, 1961. 456 pp.

Tarrant, John J., *Drucker: The Man Who Invented the Corporate Society.* Boston: Cahners, 1976. 300 pp.

Terry, George R., *Principles of Management* (4th ed.). Homewood: Irwin, 1964. 822 pp.

Townsend, Robert, *Up the Organization: How to Stop the Corporation From Stifling People and Strangling Profits.* Greenwich: Fawcett, 1970. 220 pp.

Varney, Glenn H., *An Organization Development Approach to Management Development.* Reading: Addison-Wesley, 1976. 176 pp.

Vaughan, James A. and Samuel D. Deep, *Program of Exercises for Management and Organization Development.* Beverly Hills: Glencoe Press, 1975. 204 pp.

Vroom, Victor H. and Philip W. Yetton, *Leadership and Decision-Making.* Pittsburgh: University of Pittsburgh Press, 1973. 233 pp.

Walker, James W., ed., *The Challenge of Human Resource Planning: Selected Readings.* New York: Human Resource Planning Society, 1979. 220 pp.

Walters, Roy W., *Job Enrichment for Results: Strategies for Successful Implementation.* Reading: Addison-Wesley, 1975. 307 pp.

Walton, Richard E. and Robert B. McKersie, *A Behavioral Theory of Labor Negotiations.* New York: McGraw-Hill, 1965. 437 pp.

Webber, Ross A., *Time and Management.* New York: Van Nostrand and Reinhold, 1972. 167 pp.

Weber, Max, *The Theory of Economic and Social Organization* (translated by A. M. Henderson and Talcott Parsons). New York: Oxford University Press, 1947. 436 pp.

Weiler, Nicholas W., *Reality and Career Planning: A Guide for Personal Growth.* Reading: Addison-Wesley, 1977. 247 pp.

Weisbord, Marvin R., *Organizational Diagnosis: A Workbook of Theory and Practice.* Reading: Addison-Wesley, 1977. 180 pp.

Whistler, Thomas L. and Shirley F. Harper, *Performance Appraisal: Research and Practice.* New York: Holt, Rinehart and Winston, 1962. 593 pp.

Whyte, William Foote and Edith Lentz Hamilton, *Action Research for Management.* Homewood: Irwin, 1964. 282 pp.

Wild, Ray, *Work Organization.* New York: Wiley, 1975. 226 pp.

Wofford, Jerry C. *et al., Organizational Communication: The Keystone to Managerial Effectiveness.* New York: McGraw-Hill, 1977. 477 pp.

Yaney, Joseph P., *Personnel Management: Reaching Organizational and Human Goals.* Columbus: Merrill, 1975. 428 pp.

Zaleznik, Abraham and Manfred F. R. Kets de Vries, *Power and the Corporate Mind.* Cambridge: Houghton Mifflin, 1975. 288 pp.

Zaltman, Gerald and Robert Duncan, *Strategies for Planned Change.* New York: Wiley, 1977. 404 pp.

Articles

Adams, Jerome and John J. Sherwood, "An Evaluation of Organizational Effectiveness: An Appraisal of How Army Internal Consultants Use Survey Feedback in a Military Setting," *Group and Organization Studies,* Vol. 4, No. 2, June 1979, pp. 170–188.

Adcock, Robert L. and John W. Lee, "Time, One More Time," *California Management Review,* Vol. 14, No. 2, Winter 1971, pp. 28–33.

Armenakis, Achilles A. *et al.,* "Evaluation Guidelines for the OD Practitioner," *Personnel Journal,* Vol. 54, No. 2, February 1975, pp. 99–103, 106.

Baker, H. Kent, "The Hows and Whys of Team Building," *Personnel Journal,* Vol. 58, No. 8, June 1979, pp. 367–370.

Batt, William L., Jr. and Edgar Weinberg, "Labor-Management Cooperation Today," *Harvard Business Review,* Vol. 56, No. 1, January–February 1978, pp. 96–104.

Baytos, Lawrence M., "Employee Participation in Compensation Planning," *Compensation Review,* Vol. 8, No. 2, Second Quarter 1976, pp. 25–38.

Beck, Arthur C., Jr. and Ellis D. Hillmar, "OD to MBO or MBO to OD: Does It Make A Difference?," *Personnel Journal,* Vol. 51, No. 11, November 1972, pp. 827–834.

Beckhard, Richard, "Optimizing Team-Building Efforts," *Journal of Contemporary Business,* Vol. 1, No. 3, Summer 1972, pp. 23–32.

Beckhard, Richard, "The Confrontation Meeting," *Harvard Business Review,* Vol. 45, No. 2, March–April 1967, pp.149–155.

Beer, Michael, "On Gaining Influence and Power for OD," *Journal of Applied Behavioral Science,* Vol. 12, No. 1, January-February-March 1976, pp. 44–50.

Bierstedt, Robert, "An Analysis of Social Power," *American Sociological Review,* Vol. 15, No. 6, December 1950, pp. 730–736.

Blake, Robert R. and Jane Srygley Mouton, "Behavioral Science Theories Underlying Organization Development," *Journal of Contemporary Business,* Vol. 1, No. 3, Summer 1972, pp. 9–22.

Blake, Robert R. and Jane Srygley Mouton, "Some Effects of Managerial Grid Seminar Training on Union and Management Attitudes Toward Supervision," *Journal of Applied Behavioral Science,* Vol. 2, No. 4, October-November-December 1966, pp. 387–400.

Blake, Robert R. *et al.,* "The Union-Management Intergroup Laboratory," *Journal of Applied Behavioral Science,* Vol. 1, No. 1, January-February-March 1965, pp. 25–57.

Bordonaro, Frank P., "The Dilemma Created by Praise," *Business Horizons,* Vol. 19, No. 5, October 1976, pp. 76–81.

Bowers, David G. and Jerome L. Franklin, "Survey-Guided Development: Using Human Resources Measurement in Organizational Change," *Journal of Contemporary Business,* Vol. 1, No. 3, Summer 1972, pp. 43–55.

Brady, Rodney L., "MBO Goes to Work in the Public Sector," *Harvard Business Review,* Vol. 51, No. 2, March-April 1973, pp. 65–74.

Bright, William E., "How One Company Manages Its Human Resources," *Harvard Business Review,* Vol. 54, No. 1, January-February 1976, pp. 81–93.

Browning, Larry D., "Diagnosing Teams in Organizational Settings," *Group and Organization Studies,* Vol. 2, No. 2, June 1977, pp. 187–197.

Bucalo, Jack, "Personnel Directors . . . What You Should Know Before Recommending MBO," *Personnel Journal,* Vol. 56, No. 4, April 1977, pp. 176–178, 202.

Buchanan, Paul C., "An OD Strategy at the IRS," *Personnel,* Vol. 56, No. 2, March-April 1979, pp. 44–61.

Burke, W. Warner, "Organization Development in Transition," *Journal of Applied Behavioral Science,* Vol. 12, No. 1, January-February-March 1976, pp. 22–43.

Burke, W. Warner, "The Demise of Organization Development," *Journal of Contemporary Business,* Vol. 1, No. 3, Summer 1972, pp. 57–63.

Byrd, Richard E. and John Cowan, "MBO: A Behavioral Science Approach," *Personnel,* Vol. 51, No. 2, March-April 1974, pp. 42–50.

Cahn, Meyer Michael and William J. Crockett, "Organization Development at Saga: An Interview with William J. Crockett," *Journal of Applied Behavioral Science,* Vol. 14, No. 2, April-May-June 1978, pp. 223–235.

Carlisle, Arthur Elliott, "MacGregor," *Organizational Dynamics,* Vol. 5, No. 1, Summer 1976, pp. 50–62.

Chesler, Mark A. *et al.,* "Power Training: An Alternative Path to Conflict Management," *California Management Review,* Vol. 21, No. 2, Winter 1978, pp. 84–90.

Chew, William B. and Richard L. Justice, "EEO Modeling for Large, Complex Organizations," *Human Resource Planning,* Vol. 2, No. 2, Spring 1979, pp. 57–70.

Colossi, Thomas R., "The Use of Modified NASA in Dispute Resolution," *Personnel Journal,* Vol. 53, No. 10, October 1974, pp. 761–766.

Conley, W. D. and F. W. Miller, "MBO, Pay, and Productivity," *Personnel,* Vol. 50, No. 1, January-February 1973, pp. 21–25.

Cooper, Cary L., "How Psychologically Dangerous are T Groups?," *Human Relations,* Vol. 28, No. 3, April 1975, pp. 239–260.

Cummings, Thomas G. *et al.,* "Intervention Strategies for Improving Productivity and the Quality of Work Life," *Organizational Dynamics,* Vol. 4, No. 1, Summer 1975, pp. 52–67.

Daniel, D. Ronald, "Team at the Top," *Harvard Business Review,* Vol. 43, No. 2, March-April 1965, pp. 74–82.

DeLaPorte, P. C. Andre, "Group Norms: Key to Building A Winning Team," *Personnel,* Vol. 51, No. 5, September-October 1974, pp. 60–67.

Derr, C. Brooklyn, "Managing Organizational Conflict: Collaboration, Bargaining, and Power Approaches," *California Management Review,* Vol. 21, No. 2, Winter 1978, pp. 76–83.

Diamond, Daniel E. and Hrach Bedrosian, "Job Performance and the New Credentialism," *California Management Review,* Vol. 14, No. 4, Summer 1972, pp. 21–28.

Digman, Lester A., "How Well-Managed Organizations Develop Their Executives," *Organizational Dynamics,* Vol. 7, No. 2, Autumn 1978, pp. 63–80.

Dowling, William F., "At Emery Air Freight: Positive Reinforcement Boosts Performance," *Organizational Dynamics,* Vol. 1, No. 3, Winter, 1973, pp. 41–68.

Dowling, William F., "At General Motors: System 4 Builds Performance and Profits," *Organizational Dynamics,* Vol. 3, No. 3, Winter 1975, pp. 23–38.

Dowling, William F., "At Lever Brothers—Sales Moves Toward System 4," *Organizational Dynamics,* Vol. 2, No. 1, Summer 1973, pp. 50–66.

Dowling, William F., "Consensus Management at Graphic Controls," *Organizational Dynamics,* Vol. 5, No. 3, Winter 1977, pp. 22–47.

Dowling, William F., "Conversation: An Interview with Rensis Likert," *Organizational Dynamics,* Vol. 2, No. 1, Summer 1973, pp. 32–49.

Dowling, William F., "Conversation: An Interview with B. F. Skinner," *Organizational Dynamics,* Vol. 1, No. 3, Winter 1973, pp. 31–40.

Dowling, William F., "Job Redesign on the Assembly Line: Farewell to Blue-Collar Blues," *Organizational Dynamics,* Vol. 2, No. 2, Autumn 1973, pp. 51–67.

Dowling, William F., "To Move an Organization: The Corning Approach to Organization Development," *Organizational Dynamics,* Vol. 3, No. 4, Spring 1975, pp. 16–35.

Dowling, William F., "Using the Managerial Grid to Ensure MBO," *Organizational Dynamics,* Vol. 2, No. 4, Spring 1974, pp. 54–65.

Driscoll, James W., "Working Creatively With a Union: Lessons from the Scanlon Plan," *Organizational Dynamics,* Vol. 8, No. 1, Summer 1979, pp. 61–80.

Dubin, Robert, "Industrial Workers' Worlds: A Study of the 'Central Life Interests' of Industrial Workers," *Social Problems,* Vol. 3, No. 3, January 1956, pp. 131–142.

Dyer, Lee and Elizabeth C. Wesman, "Affirmative Action Planning at AT & T: An Applied Model," *Human Resource Planning,* Vol. 2, No. 2, Spring 1979, pp. 81–90.

Dyer, William G., "Caring and Power," *California Management Review,* Vol. 21, No. 4, Summer 1979, pp. 84–89.

Edmonds, Charles P. III and John H. Hand, "What Are the Real Long-Run Objectives of Business?", *Business Horizons,* Vol. 19, No. 6, December 1976, pp. 75–81.

Ellig, Bruce R., "Employee Benefit Planning: Utilizing Employee Preferences," *Compensation Review,* Vol. 8, No. 2, Second Quarter, 1976, pp. 39–50.

Farson, Richard E., "Praise Reappraised," *Harvard Business Review,* Vol. 41, No. 1, January-February 1963, pp. 61–66.

Filley, Alan C., "Some Normative Issues in Conflict Management," *California Management Review,* Vol. 21, No. 2, Winter 1978, pp. 61–66.

Fitzgerald, Thomas H., "Why Motivation Theory Doesn't Work," *Harvard Business Review,* Vol. 49, No. 4, July-August 1971, pp. 37–44.

Ford, Charles H., "MBO: An Idea Whose Time Has Gone?," *Business Horizons,* Vol. 22, No. 6, December 1979, pp. 48–57.

Ford, Charles H., "Manage by Decisions, Not by Objectives," *Business Horizons,* Vol. 23, No. 1, February 1980, pp. 7–18.

Franklin, Jerome L., "Characteristics of Successful and Unsuccessful Organization Development," *Journal of Applied Behavioral Science,* Vol. 12, No. 4, October-November-December 1976, pp. 471–492.

French, Wendell, "Extending Directions and Family for OD," *Journal of Applied Behavioral Science,* Vol. 12, No. 1, January-February-March 1976, pp. 51–58.

French, Wendell L. and Cecil H. Bell, Jr., "A Brief History of Organization Development," *Journal of Contemporary Business,* Vol. 1, No. 3, Summer 1972, pp. 1–8.

French, Wendell L. and Robert W. Hollmann, "Management By Objectives: The Team Approach," *California Management Review,* Vol. 17, No. 3, Spring 1975, pp. 13–22.

Fri, Robert W., "How to Manage the Government for Results—The Rise of MBO," *Organizational Dynamics,* Vol. 2, No. 4, Spring 1974, pp. 18–53.

Friedlander, Frank, "OD Reaches Adolescence: An Exploration of Its Underlying Values," *Journal of Applied Behavioral Science,* Vol. 12, No. 1, January-February-March 1976, pp. 7–21.

Fulmer, William E., "When Employees Want to Oust Their Union," *Harvard Business Review,* Vol. 56, No. 2, March-April 1978, pp. 163–171.

George, William W., "Task Teams for Rapid Growth," *Harvard Business Review,* Vol. 55, No. 2, March-April 1977, pp. 71–80.

Gibb, Jack R., "TORI Theory: Consultantless Team-Building," *Journal of Contemporary Business,* Vol. 1, No. 3, Summer 1972, pp. 33–41.

Giegold, William C., "Just Managing: MBO After All These Years," *Conference Board Record,* Vol. 12, No. 7, July 1975, pp. 49–52.

Golde, Roger A., "Are Your Meetings Like This One?," *Harvard Business Review,* Vol. 50, No. 1, January-February 1972, pp. 68–77.

Gomersall, Earl R. and M. Scott Myers, "Breakthrough in On-the-Job Training," *Harvard Business Review,* Vol. 44, No. 4, July-August 1966, pp. 62–72.

Greene, Robert J., "Incentive Compensation for Staff Managers," *Compensation Review,* Vol. 10, No. 1, First Quarter 1978, pp. 20–24.

Gyllenhammar, Pehr G., "How Volvo Adapts Work to People," *Harvard Business Review,* Vol. 55, No. 4, July-August 1977, pp. 102–113.

Hackman, J. Richard, "The Design of Work in the 1980s," *Organizational Dynamics,* Vol. 7, No. 1, Summer 1978, pp. 2–17.

Halal, William E., "Organization Development in the Future," *California Management Review,* Vol. 16, No. 3, Spring 1974, pp. 35–41.

Hall, Jay, "Communication Revisited," *California Management Review,* Vol. 15, No. 3, Spring 1973, pp. 56–67.

Hall, Jay, "Observations on the Invalid Scoring Algorithm of 'NASA' and Similar Consensus Tasks: A Response," *Group and Organization Studies,* Vol. 4, No. 1, March 1979, pp. 116–118.

Hall, Jay, "To Achieve or Not: The Manager's Choice," *California Management Review,* Vol. 18, No. 4, Summer 1976, pp. 5–18.

Hall, Jay and Martha S. Williams, "Group Dynamics Training and Improved Decision-Making," *Journal of Applied Behavioral Science,* Vol. 6, No. 1, January-February-March 1970, pp. 39–68.

Hamner, W. Clay and Ellen P. Hamner, "Behavior Modification on the Bottom Line," *Organizational Dynamics,* Vol. 4, No. 4, Spring 1976, pp. 2–21.

Hand, Herbert H. and A. Thomas Hollingsworth, "Tailoring MBO to Hospitals," *Business Horizons,* Vol. 18, No. 1, February 1975, pp. 45–56.

Hart, Howard A., "The Grid Appraised—Phases 1 and 2," *Personnel,* Vol. 51, No. 5, September-October 1974, pp. 44–59.

Harvey, Jerry B., "Organizations as Phrog Farms," *Organizational Dynamics,* Vol. 5, No. 4, Spring 1977, pp. 15–43.

Harvey, Jerry B., "The Abilene Paradox: The Management of Agreement," *Organizational Dynamics,* Vol. 3, No. 1, Summer 1974, pp. 63–80.

Heisler, W. J., "Patterns of OD in Practice," *Business Horizons,* Vol. 18, No. 1, February 1975, pp. 77–84.

Hersey, Paul *et al.*, "Situational Leadership, Perception, and the Impact of Power," *Group and Organizational Studies,* Vol. 4, No. 4, December 1979, pp. 418–428.

Herzberg, Frederick, "One More Time: How Do You Motivate Employees?," *Harvard Business Review,* Vol. 46, No. 1, January-February 1968, pp. 53–62.

Herzberg, Frederick, "The Wise Old Turk," *Harvard Business Review,* Vol. 52, No. 5, September-October 1974, pp. 70–80.

Herzberg, Frederick and Edmund A. Rafalko, "Efficiency in the Military: Cutting Costs With Orthodox Job Enrichment," *Personnel,* Vol. 52, No. 6, November-December 1975, pp. 38–48.

Herzberg, Frederick *et al.*, "Job Enrichment Pays Off," *Harvard Business Review,* Vol. 47, No. 2, March-April 1969, pp. 61–67.

Hildebrandt, F. Dean, Jr., "Individual Performance in Incentive Compensation," *Compensation Review,* Vol. 10, No. 3, Third Quarter 1978, pp. 28–33.

Hill, Raymond E., "Interpersonal Compatibility and Workgroup Performance," *Journal of Applied Behavioral Science,* Vol. 11, No. 2, April-May-June 1975, pp. 210–219.

Hills, Frederick S., "The Pay-for-Performance Dilemma," *Personnel,* Vol. 56, No. 5, September-October 1979, pp. 23–31.

Hinrichs, John R., "Where Has All the Time Gone?," *Personnel,* Vol. 53, No. 4, July-August 1976, pp. 44–49.

"How Companies Set the Base Salary and Incentive Bonus Opportunity for Chief Executive and Chief Operating Officers . . . A *Compensation Review* Symposium," *Compensation Review,* Vol. 8, No. 4, Fourth Quarter 1976, pp. 19–32.

"How Companies Set Top- and Middle-Management Salaries . . . A *Compensation Review* Symposium," *Compensation Review,* Vol. 9, No. 1, First Quarter 1977, pp. 32–46.

Howe, Roger J., "Building Teams for Increased Productivity," *Personnel Journal,* Vol. 56, No. 1, January 1977, pp. 16–22.

Hunady, Ronald J. and Glenn H. Varney, "Salary Administration: A Reason for MBO!," *Training and Development Journal,* Vol. 28, No. 9, September 1974, pp. 24–28.

Jaques, Elliott, "Social-Analysis and the Glacier Project," *Human Relations,* Vol. 17, No. 4, November 1964, pp. 361–375.

Jones, Curtis H., "The Money Value of Time," *Harvard Business Review,* Vol. 46, No. 4, July-August 1968, pp. 94–100.

Juran, Joseph M., "Universals in Management Planning and Controlling," *Management Review,* Vol. 43, No. 11, November 1954, pp. 748–761.

Katzell, Raymond A. and Daniel Yankelovich, "Improving Productivity and Job Satisfaction," *Organizational Dynamics,* Vol. 4, No. 1, Summer 1975, pp. 69–80.

Keller, Robert R., "A Longitudinal Assessment of A Managerial Grid Seminar Training Program," *Group and Organization Studies*, Vol. 3, No. 3, September 1978, pp. 343–355.

Kelly, Joe, "Make Conflict Work for You," *Harvard Business Review,* Vol. 48, No. 4, July-August 1970, pp. 103–113.

Kelley, Robert E., "Should You Have An Internal Consultant?," *Harvard Business Review,* Vol. 57, No. 6, November-December 1979, pp. 110–120.

King, Dennis C., "Packages for Progress: Team Goal-Setting Techniques," *Personnel Journal,* Vol. 54, No. 12, December 1975, pp. 606–608.

Kirkpatrick, Donald L., "MBO and Salary Administration," *Training and Development Journal,* Vol. 27, No. 9, September 1973, pp. 3–5.

Kleber, Thomas. "Forty Common Goal-Setting Errors," *Human Resource Management*, Vol. 11, No. 3, Fall 1972, pp. 10–13.

Kleber, Thomas P., "The Six Hardest Areas To Manage by Objectives," *Personnel Journal,* Vol. 51, No. 8, August 1972, pp. 571–575.

Kochan, Thomas A. and Lee Dyer, "A Model of Organizational Change in the Context of Union-Management Relationships," *Journal of Applied Behavioral Science,* Vol. 12, No. 1, January-February-March 1976, pp. 59–78.

Koontz, Harold, "Making MBO Effective," *California Management Review,* Vol. 20, No. 1, Fall 1977, pp. 5–13.

Kotter, John Paul, "The Psychological Contract: Managing the Joining-Up Process," *California Management Review,* Vol. 15, No. 3, Spring 1973, pp. 91–99.

Kyser, Robert C., Jr., "Applying IE and Behavioral Science," *Industrial Engineering*, Vol. 7, No. 4, April 1975, pp. 36–41.

Lasagna, John B., "Make Your MBO Pragmatic," *Harvard Business Review,* Vol. 49, No. 6, November-December 1971, pp. 64–69.

Lawler, Edward E. III, "The New Plant Revolution," *Organizational Dynamics*, Vol. 6, No. 3, Winter 1978, pp. 2–12.

Lawler, Edward E. III and Raymond N. Olson, "Designing Reward Systems for New Organizations," *Personnel,* Vol. 54, No. 5, September-October 1977, pp. 48–60.

Lazer, Robert I., "The 'Discrimination Danger' in Performance Appraisal," *Conference Board Record,* Vol. 13, No. 3, March 1976, pp. 60–64.

LeBoeuf, Michael, "Managing Time Means Managing Yourself," *Business Horizons,* Vol. 23, No. 1, February 1980, pp. 41–46.

Lee, M. Blaine and William L. Zwerman, "Designing a Motivating and Team Building Employee Appraisal System," *Personnel Journal,* Vol. 55, No. 7, July 1976, pp. 354–357.

Lehner, George F. J., "How to Manage the Victims of a Cutback," *Innovation,* No. 21, May 1971, pp. 42–47.

Levinson, Harry, "Appraisal of *What* Performance?," *Harvard Business Review,* Vol. 54, No. 4, July-August 1976, pp. 30–48.

Levinson, Harry, "Asinine Attitudes Toward Motivation," *Harvard Business Review,* Vol. 51, No. 1, January-February 1983, pp. 70–76.

Levinson, Harry, "Management by Whose Objectives?," *Harvard Business Review,* Vol. 48, No. 4, July-August 1970, pp. 125–134.

Lewicki, Roy J. and Clayton P. Alderfer, "The Tensions Between Research and Intervention in Intergroup Conflict," *Journal of Applied Behavioral Science,* Vol. 9, No. 4, July-August 1973, pp. 424–449.

Likert, Rensis and M. Scott Fisher, "MBGO: Putting Some Team Spirit into MBO," *Personnel,* Vol. 54, No. 1, January-February 1977, pp. 40–47.

Loomis, Carol J., "The Leaning Tower of Sears," *Fortune,* Vol. 99, No. 13, July 2, 1979, pp. 78–85.

Louis, Arthur M., "They're Striking Some Strange Bargains at Diamond Shamrock," *Fortune,* Vol. 93, No. 1, January 1976, pp. 142–153.

Luthans, Fred and William E. Reif, "Job Enrichment: Long on Theory, Short on Practice," *Organizational Dynamics,* Vol. 2, No. 3, Winter 1974, pp. 30–49.

McClelland, David C., "Achievement Motivation Can Be Developed," *Harvard Business Review,* Vol. 43, No. 6, November-December 1965, pp. 6–24, 178.

McClelland, David C., "Business Drive and National Achievement," *Harvard Business Review,* Vol. 40, No. 4, July-August 1962, pp. 99–112.

McClelland, David C. and David H. Burnham, "Power is the Great Motivator," *Harvard Business Review,* Vol. 54, No. 2, March-April 1976, pp. 100–110.

McConkey, Dale D., "The 'Jackass Effect' in Management Compensation," *Business Horizons,* Vol. 17, No. 3, June 1974, pp. 81–91.

McConkie, Mark L., "Classifying and Reviewing the Empirical Work on MBO: Some Implications," *Group and Organization Studies,* Vol. 4, No. 4, December 1979, pp. 461–475.

McGregor, Douglas, "An Uneasy Look at Performance Appraisal," *Harvard Business Review,* Vol. 35, No. 3, May-June 1957, pp. 89–94.

Miewald, Robert D., "The Greatly Exaggerated Death of Bureaucracy," *California Management Review,* Vol. 13, No. 2, Winter 1970, pp. 65–69.

Miles, Raymond E., "Human Relations or Human Resources?," *Harvard Business Review,* Vol. 43, No. 4, July-August 1965, pp. 148–155.

Miles, Raymond E. and J. B. Ritchie, "Participative Management: Quality vs. Quantity," *California Management Review,* Vol. 13, No. 4, Summer 1971, pp. 48–56.

Miller, Ernest C., "Top- and Middle-Management Compensation Part 1: Determining Base Salary," *Compensation Review,* Vol. 8, No. 3, Third Quarter 1976, pp. 28–44.

Miller, Ernest C., "Top- and Middle-Management Compensation Part 2: Incentive Bonus and Merit Increase Plans," *Compensation Review,* Vol. 8, No. 4, Fourth Quarter 1976, pp. 33–46.

Mills, D. Quinn, "Managing Human Relationships Among Organizations: Theory and Practice," *Organizational Dynamics,* Vol. 3, No. 4, Spring 1975, pp. 35–50.

Miron, David and David C. McClelland, "The Impact of Achievement Motivation Training on Small Businesses," *California Management Review,* Vol. 21, No. 4, Spring 1979, pp. 13–28.

Mobley, William H., "The Link Between MBO and Merit Compensation," *Personnel Journal,* Vol. 53, No. 6, June 1974, pp. 423–427.

Moore, Leo B., "Managerial Time," *Industrial Management Review,* Vol. 9, No. 3, Spring 1968, pp. 77–85.

Moravec, Milan, "Is HRD Enough?," *Personnel,* Vol. 56, No. 1, January-February 1979, pp. 53–57.

Muench, G. A., "A Clinical Psychologist's Treatment of Labor–Management Conflicts," *Personnel Psychology,* Vol. 13, No. 2, Summer 1960, pp. 165–172.

Muench, G. A., "A Clinical Psychologist's Treatment of Labor–Management Conflicts: A Four-Year Study," *Journal of Humanistic Psychology*, Vol. 3, No. 1, Spring 1963, pp. 92–97.

Myers, M. Scott, "Overcoming Union Opposition to Job Enrichment," *Harvard Business Review*, Vol. 49, No. 3, May-June 1971, pp. 37–49.

Nord, Walter R., "The Failure of Current Applied Behavioral Science: A Marxian Perspective," *Journal of Applied Behavioral Science*, Vol. 10, No. 4, October-November-December 1974, pp. 557–578.

Nord, Walter R. and Douglas E. Durand, "What's Wrong With the Human Resources Approach to Management?," *Organizational Dynamics*, Vol. 6, No. 3, Winter 1978, pp. 13–25.

Nystrom, Paul C., "Save MBO by Disowning It!," *Personnel Journal*, Vol. 56, No. 8, August 1977, pp. 391–393.

Oncken, William, Jr. and Donald L. Wass, "Management Time: Who's Got the Monkey?," *Harvard Business Review*, Vol. 52, No. 6, November-December 1974, pp. 75–80.

Ouchi, William G. and Raymond L. Price, "Hierarchies, Clans, and Theory Z: A New Perspective on Organization Development," *Organizational Dynamics*, Vol. 6, No. 2, Autumn 1978, pp. 25–44.

Patten, Thomas H., Jr., "Collective Bargaining and Consensus: The Potential of a Laboratory Training Input," *Management of Personnel Quarterly*, Vol. 16, No. 1, Spring 1970, pp. 29–37.

Patten, Thomas H., Jr., "Human Resource Planning and Organizational Development," *Human Resource Planning*, Vol. 1, No. 3, Summer 1978, pp. 179–184.

Patten, Thomas H., Jr., "Intervening in Organizations Through Reward Systems," in John E. Jones and J. William Pfeiffer, eds., *The 1977 Annual Handbook for Group Facilitators*, La Jolla: University Associates, 1977. pp. 175–207.

Patten, Thomas H., Jr., "Personnel Administration and the Will to Manage," *Human Resource Management*, Vol. 11, No. 3, Fall 1972, pp. 4–9.

Patten, Thomas H., Jr., "Team Building. Part 1. Designing the Intervention," *Personnel*, Vol. 56, No. 1, January-February 1979, pp. 11–21.

Patten, Thomas H., Jr., "Team Building. Part 2. Conducting the Intervention," *Personnel*, Vol. 56, No. 2, March-April 1979, pp. 62–68.

Patten, Thomas H., Jr., "The Behavioral Science Roots of Organizational Development: An Integrated and Overall Perspective," in John E. Jones and J. William Pfeiffer, eds., *The 1979 Annual Handbook for Group Facilitators*, La Jolla: University Associates, 1979, pp. 194–206.

Patten, Thomas H., Jr., "Time for Organizational Development?," *Personnel*, Vol. 54, No. 2, March-April 1977, pp. 26–33.

Patten, Thomas H., Jr. and Karen L. Fraser, "Using the Organizational Rewards System as an OD Lever: A Case Study of a Data-Based Intervention," *Journal of Applied Behavioral Science*, Vol. 11, No. 4, October-November-December 1975, pp. 457–474.

Patten, Thomas H, Jr. and Lester E. Dorey, "An Equal Employment Opportunity Sensitivity Workshop," *Training and Development Journal*, Vol. 26, No. 1, January 1972, pp. 42–53.

Patten, Thomas H, Jr. and Lester E. Dorey, "Long Range Results of a Teambuilding Organizational Development Effort," *Personnel Management Review*, Vol. 6, No. 1, January-February 1977, pp. 31–50.

Perrow, Charles, "The Short and Glorious History of Organizational Theory," *Organizational Dynamics*, Vol. 2, No. 1, Summer 1973, pp. 2–15.

Pfeiffer, J. William and John E. Jones, "A Current Assessment of OD: What It Is and Why It Often Fails," in J. William Pfeiffer and John E. Jones, eds., *The 1976 Annual Handbook for Group Facilitators*, La Jolla: University Associates, 1976, pp. 225–232.

Popular, John J., "U.S. Mediators Try to Build Common Objectives," *World of Work Report,* Vol. 1, No. 7, September 1976, pp. 1–3.

Powell, Reed M. and John E. Stinson, "The Worth of Laboratory Training: Impact on Leadership and Productivity," *Business Horizons,* Vol. 14, No. 4, August 1971, pp. 87–95.

Prince, George M., "Creative Meetings Through Power Sharing," *Harvard Business Review,* Vol. 50, No. 4, July-August 1972, pp. 47–54.

Prince, George M., "How to be A Better Meeting Chairman," *Harvard Business Review,* Vol. 47, No. 1, January-February 1969, pp. 98–108.

Psathas, George and Ronald Hardert, "Trainer Interventions and Normative Patterns in the T Group," *Journal of Applied Behavioral Science,* Vol. 2, No. 2, April-May-June 1966, pp. 149–169.

Purcell, Theodore V., "How GE Measures Managers in Fair Employment," *Harvard Business Review*, Vol. 52, No. 6, November-December 1974, pp. 99–104.

Raia, Anthony P., "Organizational Development—Some Issues and Challenges," *California Management Review,* Vol. 14, No. 4, Summer 1972, pp. 13–20.

Randall, Lyman K., "Common Questions and Tentative Answers Regarding Organization Development," *California Management Review,* Vol. 13, No. 3, Spring 1971, pp. 45–52.

Reddin, W. J., "The Tri-Dimensional Grid," *Training and Development Journal*, Vol. 18, No. 7, July 1964, pp. 9–18.

Rice, Paul L., "Making Minutes Count," *Business Horizons,* Vol. 6, No. 3, December 1973, pp. 15–22.

Robbins, Stephen P., " 'Conflict Management' and 'Conflict Resolution' are not Synonymous Terms," *California Management Review,* Vol. 21, No. 2, Winter 1978, pp. 67–75.

Robie, Edward A., "Compensation Administration in the Coming Decade," *Compensation Review,* Vol. 2, No. 2, Second Quarter 1970, pp. 15–20.

Rowan, Roger, "Keeping the Clock from Running Out," *Fortune*, Vol. 89, No. 9, November 6, 1978, pp. 76–82.

Schein, Edgar H., "How to Break in the College Graduate," *Harvard Business Review,* Vol. 42, No. 6, November-December 1964, pp. 68–76.

Schein, Edgar H., "In Defense of Theory Y," *Organizational Dynamics,* Vol. 4, No. 1, Summer 1975, pp. 17–30.

Schein, Virginia E. and Larry E. Greiner, "Can Organization Development Be Fine Tuned to Bureaucracies?," *Organizational Dynamics,* Vol. 5, No. 3, Winter 1977, pp. 48–61.

Scherer, John J., "Can Team Building Increase Productivity? or How Can Something that Feels So Good Not Be Worthwhile?," *Group and Organization Studies,* Vol. 4, No. 3, September 1979, pp. 335–351.

Schon, Donald A., "Deutero-Learning in Organizations: Learning for Increased Effectiveness," *Organizational Dynamics,* Vol. 4, No. 1, Summer 1975, pp. 2–16.

Schuster, Fred E. and Alva F. Kindall, "Management By Objectives: Where We Stand—A Survey of the Fortune 500," *Human Resource Management,* Vol. 13, No. 1, Spring 1974, pp. 8–11.

Schutz, William C., "The Interpersonal Underworld," *Harvard Business Review,* Vol. 36, No. 4, July-August 1958, pp. 123–135.

Shepard, Herbert A. and Sheldon Davis, "Organization Development in Good Times and Bad," *Journal of Contemporary Business,* Vol. 1, No. 3, Summer 1972, pp. 65–74.

Sherwin, Douglas S., "Management *of* Objectives," *Harvard Business Review,* Vol. 54, No. 3, May-June 1976, pp. 149–160.

Shetty, Y. K., "New Look at Corporate Goals," *California Management Review,* Vol. 22, No. 2, Winter 1979, pp. 71–79.

Sibson, Robert L., "New Practices and Ideas in Compensation Administration," *Compensation Review,* Vol. 6, No. 3, Third Quarter, pp. 40–50.

Slevin, Dennis P., "Observations on the Invalid Scoring Algorithm of 'NASA' and Similar Consensus Tasks," *Group and Organization Studies,* Vol. 3, No. 4, December 1978, pp. 497–507.

Slusher, E. Allen and Henry P. Sims, Jr., "The Practice of Business Commitment Through MBO Interviews," *Business Horizons,* Vol. 18, No. 2, April 1975, pp. 5–12.

Soat, Douglas M., "An OD Strategy at Parker Pen," *Personnel,* Vol. 56, No. 2, March-April 1979, pp. 39–43.

Stein, Carroll I., "Objective Management Systems: Two to Five Years After Implementation," *Personnel Journal,* Vol. 54, No. 10, October 1975, pp. 525–528, 548.

Stern, Irving and Robert F. Pearse, "Collective Bargaining: A Union's Program for Reducing Conflict," *Personnel,* Vol. 45, No. 3, July-August 1968, pp. 61–72.

Strauss, George, "Organizational Development: Credits and Debits," *Organizational Dynamics,* Vol. 1, No. 3, Winter 1973, pp. 2–19.

Stumpf, Stephen A. *et al.,* "Equal Employment Opportunity and Change in Compensation Practices," *Journal of Applied Behavioral Science,* Vol. 16, No. 1, January-February-March 1980, pp. 29–40.

Tannenbaum, Robert and Warren H. Schmidt, "How to Choose A Leadership Pattern," *Harvard Business Review,* Vol. 51, No. 3, May-June 1973, pp. 162–172.

Tichy, Noel M. and Jay N. Nisberg, "When Does Job Restructuring Work? Organizational Interventions at Volvo and GM," *Organizational Dynamics,* Vol. 5, No. 1, Summer 1976, pp. 63–80.

Todd, John, "Management Control Systems: A Key Link Between Strategy, Structure, and Employee Performance," *Organizational Dynamics,* Vol. 5, No. 4, Spring 1977, pp. 65–78.

Trickett, Joseph M., "A More Effective Use of Time," *California Management Review,* Vol. 4, No. 4, Summer 1962, pp. 4–15.

Underwood, William J. and Larry J. Krafft, "Interpersonal Compatibility and Managerial Work Effectiveness: A Test of the Fundamental Inter-Personal Relations Orientation Theory," *Journal of Applied Psychology,* Vol. 58, No. 1, August 1973, pp. 89–94.

Vance, Stanley C., "Toward A Collegial Office of the President," *California Management Review,* Vol. 15, No. 1, Fall 1972, pp. 106–116.

Varney, Glenn H. and Ronald J. Hunady, "Energizing Commitment to Change in A Team-Building Intervention: A FIRO-B Approach," *Group and Organization Studies,* Vol. 3, No. 4, December 1978, pp. 435–446.

Walker, James W. and Robert Armes, "Implementing Management Succession Planning in Diversified Companies," *Human Resource Planning,* Vol. 2, No. 3, Summer 1979, pp. 123–133.

Walton, Richard E., "The Diffusion of New Work Structures: Explaining Why Success Didn't Take," *Organizational Dynamics,* Vol. 3, No. 3, Winter 1975, pp. 2–21.

Werther, William B., Jr., and Heinz Weihrich, "Refining MBO Through Negotiations," *MSU Business Topics,* Vol. 23, No. 3, Summer 1975, pp. 53–59.

Wessman, Fred, "The Group Construct: A Model for OD Interventions," *Personnel,* Vol. 50, No. 5, September-October 1973, pp. 19–29.

Whyte, William Foote, "Interviewing for Organizational Research," *Human Organization,* Vol. 12, No. 2, Summer 1953, pp. 15–22.

Winton, Donald G. and Charles R. Sutherland, "A Performance-Based Approach to Determining Executive Incentive Bonus Awards," *Compensation Review,* Vol. 8, No. 1, First Quarter 1976, pp. 14–26.

Wood, Jeanne D., "The Dog and Pony Show," *Personnel Journal,* Vol. 52, No. 1, January 1973, pp. 57–59.

Zenger, John H. and Dale E. Miller, "Building Effective Teams," *Personnel,* Vol. 51, No. 2, March-April 1974, pp. 20–29.

Other Resources

The Annual Handbook for Group Facilitators, 1972–1980, published variously at Iowa City, La Jolla, and San Diego and Co-edited by J. William Pfeiffer and John E. Jones, was used extensively in the preparation of this book (and contributed to by the author on numerous occasions). The handbook is undoubtedly the best source of current material on intellectual developments in OD today. A set of other handbooks on structured experiences also edited by Pfeiffer and Jones is an invaluable resource of experiential learning exercises.

Pfeiffer, J. William and John E. Jones, *The Annual Handbook for Group Facilitators.* San Diego and elsewhere: University Associates, 1972–80. 9 Volumes.

Pfeiffer, J. William and John E. Jones, *A Handbook of Structured Experiences for Human Relations Training.* La Jolla and elsewhere: University Associates, 1969–79. 7 Volumes.

Lieberman, Harvey R. and Erwin Rausch. *Managing and Allocating Time, A Didactic Simulation Exercise.* Cranford: Didactic Systems, 1976. 38 pp. (spiral-bound).

Rausch, Erwin and Wallach Wohlking, *Handling Conflict in Management: III.* Cranford: Didactic Game Co., 1969. 35 pp.

Ryan, Leo Robert, *Clinical Interpretation of the FIRO-B* (1977 ed.). Palo Alto: Consulting Psychologists Press, 1977. 39 pp.

Schutz, William C., *The FIRO-B Scales Manual.* Palo Alto: Consulting Psychologists Press, 1967. 19 pp.

Vaill, Peter B., *The Practice of Organization Development.* Madison: American Society for Training and Development, 1971. 53 pp.

Wikstrom, Walter S., *Managing By—and With—Objectives* (Studies in Personnel Policy No. 212). New York: National Industrial Conference Board, 1968. 77 pp.

INDEX